SCREAMS
OF REASON

SCREAMS

OF REASON

MAD SCIENCE AND MODERN CULTURE

DAVID J. SKAL

W. W. NORTON & COMPANY

NEW YORK • LONDON

For information about permission to reproduce selections from this book, write to
Permissions, W. W. Norton & Company, Inc., 500 Fifth Avenue, New York, NY 10110.

The text of this book is composed in Garamond 3
with the display set in Corvinus Skyline.
Composition by ComCom
Page make-up by BTD
Manufacturing by the Courier Companies, Inc.
Book design by BTD/Beth Tondreau

LIBRARY OF CONGRESS CATALOGING-IN-PUBLICATION DATA
Skal, David J.
Screams of reason : mad science and modern culture / by David J. Skal.
p. cm.
Includes bibliographical references and index.
ISBN 0-393-04582-X
1. Horror films—History and criticism. I. Title.
PN1995.9.H6S58   1998   97-52594
791.43'6164—dc21   CIP

W. W. Norton & Company, Inc., 500 Fifth Avenue, New York, N.Y. 10110
http:www.wwnorton.com

W. W. Norton & Company Ltd., 10 Coptic Street, London WC1A 1PU
1 2 3 4 5 6 7 8 9 0

FOR
Scott MacQueen

Contents

Science! true daughter of Old Time thou art!
Who alterest all things with thy peering eyes.
Why preyest thou thus upon the poet's heart,
Vulture, whose wings are dull realities?
EDGAR ALLAN POE

The Industrial Revolution and its consequences
have been a disaster for the human race.
THE UNABOMBER

An actual letter, written in 1976, from the mayor of Cambridge, Massachusetts, to the president of the National Academy of Sciences, arising from concerns about genetic engineering research at Harvard University.

Dear Mr. Handler,

As Mayor of the City of Cambridge, I would like to respectfully make a request of you. In today's edition of the Boston Herald American, a Hearst Publication, there are two reports which concern me greatly. In Dover, Massachusetts, a "strange, orange-eyed creature" was sighted, and in Hollis, New Hampshire, a man and his two sons were confronted by a "hairy nine foot creature." I would respectfully ask that your prestigious institution investigate these findings. I would hope as well that you might check to see whether or not these "strange creatures," should they in fact exist, are in any way connected to recombinant DNA experiments taking place in the New England area. Thanking you in advance for your cooperation in this matter, I remain

Very truly yours,
Alfred E. Vellucci

Laughing Sal and the Science of Screams

Outwardly, the gleaming dome at Epcot Center, crowning symbol of the futuristic Disney theme park in Orlando, Florida, presents a quintessentially modern image of high-tech rationality. But inside the dome a different mood dominates. The history of science and technology is presented not in terms of illumination but rather as a curious ascent into murk;

Laughing Sal, mechanical mistress of the "Funscience House," at Euclid Beach Park, Cleveland, Ohio. *Author's collection.*

the visitor rides up a corkscrewing track past dimly lit tableaux presented less as a science museum than as an old-fashioned spookhouse, populated by crepuscular, rubber-skinned automatons. Leonardo da Vinci in his under-lighted workshop resembles a shadowy, glowering ayatollah; other major figures in history of progress and invention emerge similarly as disquiet-ing technozombies, robotic denizens of a futuristic necropolis. As Italo Calvino once noted, "The more enlightened our houses are, the more their walls ooze ghosts."

When I was growing up, in the fifties and sixties, near Cleveland, Ohio, there was no Epcot Center. But there was Euclid Beach Park, a venerable amusement center on Lake Erie. In addition to the park's stupendous col-lection of vintage wooden roller coasters (which I loved, for a time, more than anything in the universe), there was an attraction that never failed to arrest my attention, the Surprise House. Built in 1935 and originally called, as I later learned, the Funscience House, the building presented a hard-edged art deco facade, the kind of design ordinarily associated with long-faded world's fairs. Outside the Surprise House was a mechanical fat woman with a dis-embodied laugh. She was the come-on to passersby, and her name was Laugh-ing Sal.

Inside her house the logical lines and planes of the building's exterior were revealed for the jokes they were. Einstein's theories of relativity, so ab-struse yet so disturbing in the popular press of the 1930s, here were made cartoonily concrete in distorted chambers where ordinary perceptions of scale could not be trusted. Mirrors stretched and squeezed the human image like taffy. Rooms and stairways were built at crazy angles, rather like the German expressionist film *The Cabinet of Dr. Caligari.* Jets of air lifted women's skirts and elicited screams in an odd demonstration of technological harassment. Gravity was undependable. Illusions and tricks were the specialty of the house. Outside, audible even within, was Laughing Sal, fat and crazy on the inflated promises of modernism, a coarsened counterpart to the female robot in Fritz Lang's *Metropolis,* pumped up to *Hindenburg* proportions. Laughing Sal had, in fact, been introduced to Cleveland the same summer that another constructed woman, the *Bride of Frankenstein,* had been unleashed upon the nation's movie screens. Sal, a coarse techno-bumpkin, was what Frankenstein's mate would have looked like had she been played by Marie Dressler instead of Elsa Lanchester. "Ho-ho-ho," she seemed to say, "come see what the modern world has to offer you! Come in, and get it out of your system! There's nothing inside me—ho-ho-ho—and there's nothing inside you. We're all just clockworks and cams! *And since there's nothing you can do about it, you might as well laugh!*"

I didn't find Laughing Sal very funny. I turned away when my grandmother first stood me before the Surprise House and introduced me to her. There was something scary and obscene about the bloated mechanical form, the painted clownlike face, the disembodied voice. Laughing Sal was an automated freak show, the traditional circus fat lady gone berserkly android. Likewise, I didn't like another nearby attraction, the Laff in the Dark, a classic ghost train I rode at least a dozen times before I was brave enough to open my eyes. In the world outside, deep in the century of Henry Ford, people drove cars. Here the cars drove you, through the frightening flip side of the automotive dream.

The old amusement parks and dark rides have gradually been replaced by more sophisticated technological analogs. The humble roller coaster has given way to Walt Disney World's Space Mountain—a kind of Laff in the Dark on atomic steroids—juxtaposing the expansive promises of the space age with a visceral evocation of a screaming abyss.

The master of ceremonies of this sophisticated scream circus goes by many names: Victor Frankenstein, Henry Jekyll, the doctors Moreau, Phibes, Mirakle, and Strangelove. The mere mention of the words "mad scientist" conjures a vivid array of imagery: incensed villagers rising up with pitchforks and torches, ready to storm the fortress laboratory; inside the lab, whether in a converted medieval castle or on a uncharted jungle island, the scientist amid the bubbling test tubes and crackling electrical equipment. The mad scientist wears many faces. At his most malignant he looks like Boris Karloff, Bela Lugosi, or Vincent Price; in a less intimidating guise he is the bumbling, buck-toothed Jerry Lewis (or, later, Eddie Murphy) in *The Nutty Professor;* at his most ambiguous he looks like Albert Einstein, simultaneously childlike and ancient, his unruly shock of hair hinting at a possibly corresponding disorder within the skull itself, the braincase from which every mushroom cloud has risen and threatens to rise from again. (For sheer icono-graphic staying power, Einstein's hair has influenced more images of de-mented doctors than any other visual cue.)

A prototype outsider, shunted to the sidelines of serious discourse, to the no-man's-land of B movies, pulp novels, and comic books, the mad sci-entist has served as a lightning rod for otherwise unbearable anxieties about the meaning of scientific thinking and the uses and consequences of modern technology. The mad scientist seems anarchic but often serves to support the status quo; instead of pressing us to confront the serious questions of ethics, power, and the social impact of technological advances, he too often allows us to laugh off notions that science might occasionally be the handmaiden of megalomania, greed, and sadism. And while he is often written off as the product of knee-jerk anti-intellectualism, upon closer examination, he reveals himself (mad scientists are almost always men) to be a far more complicated symbol of civilization and its split-level discontents.

This scary game of paradoxical peekaboo with mad science and mad sci-entists forms the core of *Screams of Reason.* It has been frequently asserted that the characteristic alienation and anomie of modern life have their roots in the mind-body schism formalized by philosopher René Descartes. The resulting cul-de-sac of split-brain thinking has dug what might be termed a Cartesian well of loneliness, in which the consciousness is held to be separate from, or irrelevant to, the body and the world. In other words, a classic feature of clin-ical schizophrenia may have become an accepted way to conceptualize reality.

The controversial psychotherapist R. D. Laing (1927–1989), whom many clinical colleagues considered a species of mad doctor, turned psychi-atry topsy-turvy with his heretical theories about the nature of schizophre-nia, which he viewed as a retreat from an unbearable false self imposed by society and the family into a true self, unfettered in madness. In a similar vein, psychologist Louis Sass, in his provocative study *Madness and Mod-ernism* (1992), observes that the schizophrenic, rather than represent a descent into "wild" irrationality—the classical view of insanity—may in fact display a highly exaggerated rationality. Sass notes the striking similarities between schizophrenic symptoms and the excessive self-consciousness of much mod-ern art and literature. His thesis is an impressive one, and while Sass doesn't begin to examine popular culture, it becomes immediately clear that a relationship between madness and hyperintellectualism is also an overwhelming preoccupation of mass media science fiction. Even "serious" science fiction, closely examined, reveals itself to be frequently and deeply hostile to ideas. The s-f writer and critic Barry N. Malzberg makes the point in his book *The Engines of the Night* (1982): "Science fiction, for all its trappings, its talk of 'new horizons' and 'new approaches' and 'thinking things through from the beginning' and 'new literary excitement' is a very conservative form of literature. It is probably more conservative than westerns, mysteries or gothics, let alone that most reactionary of all literatures, pornography. Most of its writers and editors are genuinely troubled by innovative styles or concepts . . . they have a deep stake by the time they have achieved any position in the field in *not appearing crazy.*"

As an occasional writer of unapologetically "crazy" science fiction myself, I would argue (and cite Malzberg's work itself as evidence) that the genre excels at its thematic and stylistic extremes. *Screams of Reason* makes no pretense of providing an evenhanded survey of literary science fiction, a vast and unruly realm. The mad scientist was an important preoccupation of the genre during its formative century—Shelley's Frankenstein, Stevenson's Jekyll, and Wells's Moreau remain towering, glowering icons to the present day—but much of modern *literary* science fiction, with its relentlessly upbeat attitude toward almost anything technological, has looked upon the mad scientist as an antediluvian embarrassment.

The critic Lionel Trilling once went so far as to declare (quite prematurely, of course) the mad scientist dead. In *The Liberal Imagination* (1950) Trilling says that the "social position of science requires that it should cease," noting that any exploration of the dark, unconscious side of science and scientists is generally taboo. "But no one who has ever lived observantly among scientists will claim that they are without an unconscious or even that they are free from neurosis," Trilling writes. "How often, indeed, it is apparent that the devotion to science, if it cannot be called a neurotic manifestation, at least can be understood as going very cozily with neurotic elements in the temperament. . . ." Since science fiction literature has itself remained cozy with the scientific establishment, it has been left to mass media science fiction to keep alive the essential mythology of the mad scientist in all his overreaching, exultant, tragic glory.

As a precocious midwestern grade schooler I was attracted to science fiction stories and films specifically because of their surreality, their nuttiness, their cracked-mirror reflections of a frightening cold war decade when everything seemed on the verge of explosion and extinction. I didn't make a meaningful distinction between science fiction and horror; after all, weren't they always shelved next to each other at the library and the bookstore? The uncanny, otherworldly images of Ray Bradbury, Bram Stoker, H. G. Wells, and Edgar Allan Poe all merged together for me in a single escapist continuum.

My first clear memory of watching a motion picture of any genre was at the age of six in late 1958, when *Frankenstein Meets the Wolf Man* was first broadcast on Cleveland television. As on cable television today, the films were shown repeatedly throughout the week of their premieres; I encountered the momentous doubleheader monster bill one Saturday afternoon on our hefty Magnavox console.

Frankenstein Meets the Wolf Man, despite its absurd plot, still contains a cartoonish distillation of the classic Apollonian-Dionysian struggle, acted out by a pair of superhuman beings, one a monster of science, one a monster of superstition. High art it ain't, but it's a clear example of how pop culture manages to deliver mighty themes to vast audiences of ordinary people indifferent to the higher realms of literature, music and art. In the blue-collar suburb I grew up in, people who didn't have much use for *Don Giovanni* responded to *Dracula,* and *Frankenstein* proved a serviceable substitute for *Faust.* For me, the archetypal passion of the mad scientist provided a useful construct on which to hang my own emerging creative aspirations, my adolescent emotional turmoil, and my precocious intellectual curiosity, which frequently left me feeling alienated and misunderstood.

In the backyard and basement I conducted my own experiments in monster making, building *my* creations not with dead tissue but with tissue paper, painstakingly applied to the faces and hands of willing or perhaps simply bored neighborhood children, who might emerge from my subterranean workshop as desiccated mummies, fantastic space aliens, brides of Frankenstein, or simply spectacularly blistered and maimed. Using well-thumbed

Faces of mad science. Clockwise from top left: Charles Laughton in *The Island of Lost Souls* (1933); *courtesy of David Del Valle/The Del Valle Archive*. Ernest Thesiger in *Bride of Frankenstein* (1935). Humphrey Bogart in *The Return of Dr. X* (1939). Peter Sellers in *Dr. Strangelove or How I Learned to Stop Worrying and Love the Bomb* (1964).

copies of *Famous Monsters of Filmland* as my guides, with Charmin, Elmer's glue, and gooey red tempera paint as my primary tools, I brought forth countless monstrosities, applying neck bolts, third-degree burns, dangling eyeballs, and wavering antennae to the faces of wide-eyed innocents. Often I recorded the fruits of my toil on eight-millimeter movie film, or sometimes I just sent my compliant creations staggering through the wooded field that separated our neighborhood from the next, the better to startle and annoy an unsuspecting populace.

Needless to say, a lot of people thought I was nuts. Certainly I identified with mad scientists and monsters. Why not? In the overheated cold war days of the early 1960s, an age of duck-and-cover drills and the omnipresent threat of nuclear annihilation, why not get on the good side of the guys who controlled the bombs and radiation and superhuman creations that nothing could kill? (In retrospect, those Hiroshima-style burn makeups I applied to my friends seem especially unsettling.) It's no wonder that a certain stripe of hard-core sci-fi fan often displays all the signs associated with the classic mad scientist: a profound social alienation counterbalanced by a grandiose power fantasy; the dream of "scientific mastery" barely covering a sense of vulnerability and inadequacy; the fear of being "out of control" or crazy. My personal annihilation anxieties during the Cuban missile crisis may have been particularly acute, but a fantasy identification with overreaching science can appeal to a much wider range of quieter desperations.

In a pointed essay called "The Embarrassments of Science Fiction," Thomas M. Disch notes the perennial popularity of s-f for blue-collar audiences. Tracing the social origins of the genre, Disch observes that the "pulp magazines that arose at the turn of the century, had, as a matter of survival, to cater to the needs of the newly literate working classes. SF is rife with fantasies of powerless individuals, of ambiguous antecedents, rising to positions of commanding importance. Often they become world saviors. The appeal of such fantasies is doubtless greater to one whose prevailing sense of himself is of being undervalued and meanly employed; who believes his essential worth is hidden under the bushel of a life that somehow hasn't worked out as planned; whose most rooted conviction is that he is capable of *more,* though as to the nature of this unrealized potential he may not be too precise."

The crazed villains of pulp s-f are paradoxically driven by the same dreams and frustrations as the fictional heroes and their real-life readers. Like Dracula, another penny dreadful power icon for the powerless, the mad scientist is a working-class hero, something to be.

Other aspects of mad science transcend class issues and go straight for the metaphysical jugular. The problem of infusing dead matter with life, a central concern of mad scientists everywhere, is also a pointed allegory of the modern world's difficulties in reconciling the seeming contradictions of matter and mind, science and superstition. In the mechanistic modern universe, consciousness is taboo, an embarrassing wild card inexplicable in Newtonian terms, even though it should be self-evident that the universe reveals itself only through the medium of consciousness. We know that we are not dead, that we possess subjectivity and volition, but respectable, reductionistic science tends to tell us otherwise.

The mad scientist, on the other hand, is a restless synthesizer, scuttling around his laboratory, stitching together our central schisms, digging into graves while pulling down the energy of the sky. In addition to bringing dead things to life, the mad scientist reconciles evolved consciousness with lower life-forms, another perennial preoccupation of the crazed clinicians in literature and popular culture.

Collective reveries about mad science often interact with the real world in forms beyond escape and entertainment. Take, for example, the case of a New Mexico doctor, Jean B. Rosenbaum, who, while a freshman medical student, witnessed the untimely death of a woman from heart disease. Rosenbaum wrote in 1967:

> I despaired at the loss of life in such a young person and was irritated at the useless procedures applied in the effort to restore her heartbeat. After brooding over her death for several weeks I decided to take an active approach—to consider the possibility of more effective ways to reactivate the stilled heart.
>
> No sooner had the problem presented itself than *Frankenstein* came to mind. I had not thought of the film for many years, having been rather frightened as well as excited by it as a child. Nonetheless, there was the scene before me: the grotesque and lifeless monster high on a platform in that creepy

The mad doctor as modern priest. Top: Vincent Price in *The Abominable Dr. Phibes* (1972).
Bottom: Gene Wilder with Peter Boyle in *Young Frankenstein* (1974).

old castle; vivid ominous lightning crackling; threatening thunder rumbling; awesome devices gathering energy and spitting electrical bolts. At last the energy made its potent way to the monster. Electricity stimulated his body and he came to life. Absurd as this drama may be to the sophisticated audiences of today, I was fascinated.

Just as Rosenbaum was about to let go of the memory, an inspiration flashed: *Frankenstein* showed how a stopped human heart could be forced to beat again. The result was Rosenbaum's invention of the first cardiac pacemaker in 1951.

Other concrete manifestations of mad science are far less salutary. The twenty-five-billion-dollar boondoggle of Ronald Reagan's Strategic Defense Initiative, popularly known as Star Wars,* was driven by the fantastic premise of a nuclear X-ray laser, which did not exist in fact and existed only very shakily in theory. The main proponent of this dubious death ray was Dr. Edward Teller, popularly known as the father of the H-bomb. Teller detested the mad scientist colorations attending his reputation and, according to some observers, saw the peacemaking potential of a nuclear umbrella in space as a way to salvage his good name, which was on shaky ground in the age of the growing antinuclear movement, Three Mile Island, and Chernobyl. But the public and its legislative representatives, conditioned by decades of science fiction imagery and increasingly compelling special effects technology, were willing to accept the premise. Why not? We had already seen it a thousand times before.

Our relationship to science and technology is complex and increasingly embattled. A puritanical suspicion of the intellect is still deeply ingrained in the American character; ideas, like sex (not to mention ideas about sex), are still regarded in many quarters as a slippery slope to hell. Science and technology bashing has been increasingly the subject of popular books, with authors taking both the offense and the defense. Although our cultural and economic futures are highly dependent on scientific training and techno-

---

*Much to the chagrin of George Lucas, director of the movie *Star Wars,* who tried unsuccessfully to enjoin the use of his film title by organizations lobbying for and against SDI.

logical innovation, we maintain a maddening Jekyll and Hyde hypocrisy in the basic areas of educational funding, teachers' salaries, etc. Specialized knowledge, scientific and otherwise, is routinely stifled and belittled, sometimes—as even scientists will occasionally admit—with a certain amount of justification.

In a 1993 essay Princeton University scientist Freeman J. Dyson candidly discusses the popular backlash against science, which he predicts will become increasingly bitter as long as economic inequities persist. While refusing to blame science alone for the fraying of the social and economic fabric, Dyson holds that scientists are "more responsible than most of us are willing to admit."

> We are responsible for the heavy preponderance of toys for the rich over necessities for the poor in the output of our laboratories. We have allowed government and university laboratories to become a welfare program for the middle class while the technical products of our discoveries take away jobs from the poor. We have helped to bring about a widening split between the technically-competent and computer-owning rich and the computerless and technically illiterate poor. . . . I recently listened to a distinguished academic computer scientist who told us joyfully how electronic data bases piped into homes through fiber-optic cables are about to put newspapers out of business. He did not care what this triumph of technological progress would do to the poor citizen who cannot afford fiber optics and would still like to read a newspaper.

It has become something of an argumentative cliché (and a winning one, as the steamrollering progress of the genetic engineering industry demonstrates) for scientists to insist on a clear line of demarcation between pure science and its technological applications. This strikes me as a bit disingenuous and immediately calls to mind the old Tom Lehrer song: "Once the rockets go up / Who cares where they come down? / That's not my department / Says Wernher von Braun." Few, if any, modern scientists work in a technological vaccuum; even "pure research" in educational settings is funded by somebody, and that somebody is likely to be industry or the military. I will therefore avoid clumsy constructions like "mad science and/or technology" (the term "mad technologist," after all, has never exactly taken hold). Despite a regrettable tendency for many science professionals to affect the attitudes of a privileged, priestly caste, scientists inhabit the same society as the rest of us and are motivated by the same range of drives, ambitions, and weaknesses as other people. Our prevalent, hyperbolic images of the madly overreaching scientist may be a half-conscious balloon-popping response to the perception—correct or not—that too much of modern life is controlled by arrogant and irresponsible science-related structures and systems.

This book is not a critique of science per se, although I am disturbed by scientism, or science transmuted into a self-congratulatory, quasi-religious belief system from its more proper role as a systematic means of understanding the physical world. Some of the recent claims made about the nature of artificial intelligence and virtual reality and cyborgs strike me as almost mad, truly crackpot and delusional. (I deal with them at some length

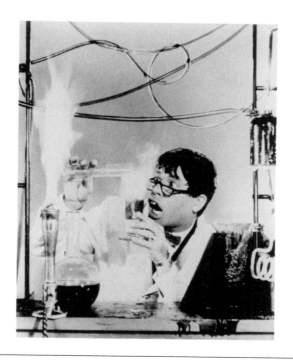

Mad science played for laughs: Jerry Lewis in *The Nutty Professor* (1964).

in my last chapter, "Vile Bodies.") But my primary interest here is not the machinations of science itself but the fascinating life and times of its dark doppelgänger, the mad scientist, in all his overreaching glory. *Screams of Reason* itself may be a slightly crazed experiment, but what better way to explore our multilevel cultural waltz with the maniac in the lab coat: where he's been leading us, what he's trying to tell us, and why he never really goes away.

SCREAMS
OF REASON

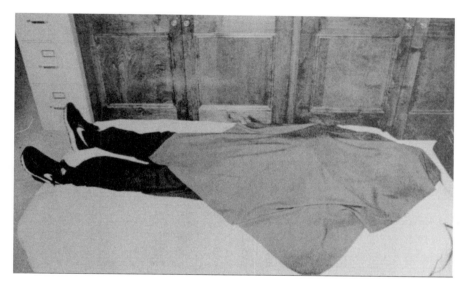

CHAPTER ONE

Frankenstein's Gate

"He's not dead, only resting—waiting for a new life to come."

A creaky line from an ancient B movie, not much invoked outside the world of genre film aficionados, was given an eerie jolt of up-to-date energy during the last week of March 1997 as an image of a lifeless, draped human form laid out on a cot flashed around the world, in print, on the airwaves, and, perhaps most significantly, via the World Wide Web. The body was one of thirty-nine, all similarly draped, all blankly surveyed

Mad science casualty: Rancho Santa Fe, California, March 1997.

by the square-headed computer terminals that provided the group with a simulacrum of human companionship. The thing on the cot wore black, thick-soled shoes, oddly reminiscent of a movie monster's clodhoppers. It faced heavenward, as if anticipating the cosmic energy that would renew the spark of life.

The thing's creator was named Marshall Herff Applewhite, and like the Hollywood's Frankenstein monster, its head contained a stolen brain—at least if one considers brainwashing and mind control a calculated form of thievery. Applewhite was the leader of a technological religious cult called Heaven's Gate, whose members lived in a virtual world of computer simulations and television sci-fi. Based in a rented mansion in the affluent enclave of Rancho Santa Fe, California, the Heaven's Gate commune shared the larger culture's fascination with computers and the Internet and supported itself by designing state-of-the-art Web sites for a variety of clients, many in the entertainment industry. Male or female, the members cropped their hair closely and wore unisex attire. Their appearance strikingly recalled that of the artificial workers in Karl Čapek's allegorical drama *R. U. R.,* which introduced the word "robot" into the English language.

Like many mad scientists, Applewhite had considerable difficulties integrating sexuality into his life and had sublimated his conflicted carnality (a secret gay life, it turned out) into a mad scheme to liberate himself and thirty-eight followers from their bodies completely. Unorthodox surgeries performed by clandestine personnel in secret locations rendered Applewhite and several of his followers eunuchs; they looked forward to a techno-transfiguration in a place where sex wouldn't matter anymore. Their final escape would be achieved through a low-tech combination of barbiturates, vodka, and asphyxiating plastic bags. Once free of their detested "containers," Applewhite and his guinea pigs looked forward to a close encounter with fantastic technologies that blurred with the supernatural. Transported to a spaceship they believed to be hiding behind a comet, piloted by sexless aliens who were also the very model of death and rebirth—embryos morphed with cadavers—the Heaven's Gate cultists would conquer death and rise again as superior, perfected beings.

Like Dr. Frankenstein, locked away in a secluded laboratory/mansion,

Marshall Applewhite created monsters and was destroyed with them. While he encouraged his flock to gorge themselves on television fare like *The X-Files* and *Millennium,* in which science provides a portal into weird new dimensions, he forbade them from watching a video of the latest version of H. G. Wells's *The Island of Dr. Moreau,* in which a mad scientist's creations rise in bloody mutiny. And while he didn't actually stitch together his monsters, he certainly pieced them together, in a manner of speaking, from odd scraps of the zeitgeist. In time-honored fashion, Applewhite animated his flock with energy from the heavens—not the traditional lightning bolts but the more rarefied emanations of comets and UFOs. The big brow of the Frankenstein monster was effectively replaced by the bulging braincase of the species of "alien abductor" known as the "small gray."

The Frankenstein myth had its origins in the nineteenth-century Romantic rebellion against scientific rationalism, reintegrating notions of science with the mystery and emotion of alchemy. The Heaven's Gate spectacle might be viewed, in its tawdry way, as an emblematic late-twentieth-century attempt to reconcile science and soul, which have been traveling on rival tracks since the Age of Reason divided spirit and matter into separate realms. The sense that there is "something missing" in the modern, materialist worldview underlies much of the recent reaction against scientific rationality, including everything from the occult revival to UFO abductions to the ongoing demands of Christian fundamentalists for "creation science" textbooks in the public schools. But the recent controversies over creationism versus evolution overlook the central point: that the most potent creation myth of modern times is not Genesis or Darwin but *Frankenstein.* As we shall see, the Frankenstein tradition took shape in the nineteenth-century struggle between Scripture and science, romanticism and rationality. Along the way the story inspired many sideline experiments: the mad scientific dabbling of Drs. Jekyll and Moreau, for instance, not to mention the surprisingly science-obsessed legend of Dracula. These narratives in turn have fed and reenergized the original myth.

Today Frankenstein energy has become so ambient, so much part of the air that we breathe that we barely blink when the media dub an irradiated tomato Frankenfood, when laboratory-created life-forms are the stuff of ordinary commerce, subject to patent protection, or when images of Boris Karloff in full monster drag are used to illustrate newspaper feature stories on Dolly, the cloned sheep. The traditional Frankenstein mythos, with its dire warnings against divine presumption, seems almost quaint in a world where science no longer presumes but presides.

The modern myth of the mad scientist took shape over the course of the nineteenth century, formed primarily by fiction and the theater. At its origins the mad scientist icon had surprisingly little to do with science per se, drawing energy instead from unorthodox experiments with sex roles, marriage, and the family. The story of *Frankenstein*'s creation and cultural evolution is worth revisiting, if only to remind us that the most enduring monsters lurk not in secluded castles but in the laboratory of the self.

"THE FOULEST TOADSTOOL that has yet sprung up from the reeking dunghill of the present times," wrote one disgusted literary figure on the flyleaf of his copy of the book. But another luminary of letters, Sir Walter Scott, came away from the tale most favorably impressed with "the author's original genius and happy power of expression," commending to his readers an innovative work "which excites new reflections and untried sources of emotion."

The event that elicited such diverse and emotional appraisals was *Frankenstein, or the Modern Prometheus,* published anonymously in 1818. The absence of authorial credit was particularly ironic, given the book's extraordinary theme of superhuman creativity. *Frankenstein* told the story of a brilliant student of the sciences who creates a hideous artificial man. Spurned by its maker, the monster escapes from its laboratory/womb a vindictive Caliban, relentlessly setting in motion its creator's destruction.

As the book was dedicated to William Godwin, novelist and notorious philosophical leftist, it was assumed by nearly everybody that *Frankenstein* was the handiwork of his equally notorious son-in-law, the poet Percy Bysshe Shelley, whose revolutionary fantasy *Queen Mab* (1813) railed against religion and other forms of institutionalized authority. Shelley had already developed a scandalous reputation when he abandoned his young wife, Harriet, and eloped to the Continent with his mentor's seventeen-year-old daughter, Mary Godwin. That the couple had been welcomed into the circle of Europe's

Mary Wollstonecraft Shelley, circa 1840; oil portrait by Richard Rothwell.

most celebrated and reviled libertine—the poet George Gordon, Lord Byron—did little to elevate the public's estimation. And Harriet Westbrook Shelley's watery suicide in 1816 provided a lurid capper to the general atmosphere of scandal, sexual license, and irresponsibility that surrounded the Shelley entourage. It was hardly surprising that Percy Shelley would compose a sensational fiction centering on the blasphemous ambitions of a renegade intellectual at the cutting edge of science.

What the public didn't know, and would not know until *Frankenstein* appeared in a second edition several years later, was that the author was not Shelley but his teenaged bride Mary. Mary Wollstonecraft Shelley, whose name eventually became synonymous with improved, technologically augmented forms of human reproduction, was born on August 30, 1797, killing her own mother in the process. Mary Wollstonecraft Godwin, the pioneering feminist and author of *A Vindication of the Rights of Woman* (published posthumously in 1798), contracted a fatal infection of the uterus when her daughter's placenta failed to expel. The attending doctor, who tried picking out pieces of afterbirth with his unwashed hands, no doubt hastened the disease process. Mary's mother died after ten agonizing days of puerperal fever, barely recognizing her daughter.

Issues of parenthood and parent-child relations were colored by tragedy and estrangement through Mary's early adulthood. Mary's father encouraged his daughter's intellectual pursuits from an early age, although he remained emotionally distant. When the rising poet Percy Shelley came into the Godwin household, first as her father's admirer, then as his benefactor, Mary quickly fell in love—though to scandalized onlookers, it seemed that Shelley, a married man, had simply bought himself a pliable concubine from a financially desperate father. Shelley had determined that the intellectual gulf between himself and his wife was insurmountable and likened their marriage to "a dead & living body . . . linked together in some loathsome and horrible communion." Despite the necrophile overtones, Shelley nonetheless wooed Mary at the Wollstonecraft gravesite at St. Pancras Cemetery, where she often retreated to read the writings of the mother she never knew. In 1814 Mary fled to the Continent with Shelley and was quickly impregnated, only in February 1815 to deliver prematurely a daughter who died a few weeks later.

But there came over Mary a fantasy of revivification, which she recorded in her journal: "Dream that my little baby came to life again; that it had only been cold, and that we rubbed it before the fire, and it lived. Awake and find no baby." William Godwin, despite his philosophical advocacy of free love—Mary herself had been conceived out of wedlock—found sexual and reproductive experimentation somewhat less acceptable in his family than in his writings. But even in the face of his ostracism, Mary bore another illegitimate child, William, who accompanied his parents on another sojourn to the Continent, once more in the company of Mary's half sister Claire Clairmont. Claire was a dark-haired, emotionally volatile beauty who had already been Lord Byron's mistress in London and now, pregnant with his child, was eager to rekindle the flame in Switzerland, where the brooding twenty-eight-year-old bard dwelled in a self-imposed exile.

The entourage arrived in Geneva during what proved to be one of the most inclement summers on record. Byron was immediately taken with Shelley, less so with Mary, who found him intimidating. The Shelleys and Claire rented the Villa Chapuis in the village of Cologny, just outside the city limits of Geneva. Byron leased the nearby Villa Diodati with its commanding view of Lake Leman and the mountains—not to mention the spectacular thunderstorms that persisted throughout the summer. The group was completed by Byron's high-strung traveling companion and physician, John Polidori, contracted by a London publisher to keep a diary of the sojourn.

By the middle of June the group's evening discussions had turned to fantastic and speculative themes. The constant display of lightning prompted discussion of electricity as the basis of life. Galvanism was a hot topic of scientific debate at the time, and Shelley considered the work of Benjamin Franklin in harnessing natural electricity positively "Promethean." Shelley himself had once performed a youthful electrical experiment on a dead cat, possibly in imitation of European scientists who had carried out experiments in which batteries were applied to dead animals and human cadavers, creating muscular contractions. Mary recalled that Erasmus Darwin, the grandfather of Charles, was alleged to have created a living organism out of a piece of vermicelli. Although that particular story wasn't true, it fitted neatly into the vision of a humanistic universe that had been on the ascendancy since the Renaissance. In an age of rational enlightenment scientists could espouse godlike ambitions without the swift censure of the church; ideas so blasphemous they would once have brought death at the stake could now be casually discussed, at least in Shelley's atheistic circle. "Perhaps a corpse would be reanimated," Mary later recalled of the thoughts that seized her as she listened to Shelley's and Byron's discussion, noting that "galvanism had given token of such things: perhaps the component parts of a creature might be manufactured, brought together, and endued with vital warmth." Talk of wild science segued easily into outright fantasy, and the party took turns reading aloud from the *Fantasmagoriana,* a collection of German ghost stories translated into the French, in which themes of early death and fateful retribution figured prominently. Literary gothicism was in its full flower; thousands of ghostly, ghastly novels had been published in Europe and America in the wake of such seminal works as Horace Walpole's *The Castle of Otranto* (1764) and Ann Radcliffe's *The Mysteries of Udolpho* (1794).

The gothic movement, in its reaction against the purely rational and its celebration of intense, uncanny emotions, anticipated the Romantic rebellion against the tyranny of narrow reason; it might be said that gothic novels were culturally and intellectually incorrect, thus providing a natural point of gravitation for revolutionaries and iconoclasts.

Fired by the creepy, metaphysically expansive visions of the *Fantasmagoriana,* Byron proposed a literary contest. "We will each write a ghost story," he said. Mary found the challenge intimidating, as did Polidori, whose writing had already been cruelly ridiculed by Byron. As Mary recalled in 1831, "I thought and pondered—vainly. I felt that blank incapacity of invention which is the greatest misery of authorship, when dull Nothing replies to our anxious invocations. 'Have you thought of a story?' I was asked each morning, and each morning I was forced to reply with a mortifying negative."

It must be said that the two star writers of the group were not exactly inspired by the contest, either. Byron started, and lost interest in, the tale of a dying man who makes a pact with a friend, promising that he will return from the grave. Only an introductory fragment of the story survives and is likely all that was ever written. Byron had better projects to attend to that summer; he was busily completing the third canto of *Childe Harold.* Shelley also produced a fragment, about a grandmother and a ghost composed of ashes, but likewise abandoned the task for far more memorable endeavors, including the "Hymn to Intellectual Beauty." Polidori later surprised everyone when his reworking of Byron's fragmentary story was published as "The Vampyre" in 1819. At first taken as the work of Byron himself—even by Goethe—"The Vampyre" inspired a veritable cottage industry of dramatic and operatic adaptations and generated the prototype of the Romantic male vampire that has continued to inspire writers, dramatists, and filmmakers to the present day.

Mary, of course, hardly suspected that she would write a tale to trump the efforts of the others, ultimately reaching an audience larger than Shelley's and Byron's combined. For the moment she didn't even have a story. Exhausted by her efforts to force an idea, she fell into bed long after midnight, only to have a trancelike vision: "When I placed my head on my pillow I did not sleep, nor could I be said to think. My imagination, unbidden, possessed and guided me, gifting the successive images that arose in my mind with a vividness far beyond the usual bounds of reverie. I saw—with shut eyes, but acute mental vision—I saw the pale student of unhallowed arts kneeling beside the thing he had put together. I saw the hideous phantasm of a man stretched out, and then, on the working of some powerful engine, show signs of life and stir with an uneasy, half-vital motion."

Terrified, she opened her eyes, only to realize that she had found her story. "Swift as light and as cheering was the idea that broke in upon me, she wrote. " 'What terrified me will terrify others; and I need only to describe the spectre which had haunted my midnight pillow.' "

The following morning she announced to the others that she at last would begin her tale and immediately began setting down her impressions of the creation scene, not yet knowing the specifics of the plot: "It was a dreary night in November, that I beheld the accomplishment of my toils. With an anxiety that almost amounted to agony, I collected the instruments of life around me, that I might infuse a spark of being into the lifeless thing that lay at my feet. It was already one in the morning; the rain pattered dismally against the panes, and my candle was almost burnt out, when, by the glimmer of the half-extinguished light, I saw the dull yellow eye of the creature open; it breathed hard, and a convulsive motion agitated its limbs."

These initial passages, appearing in Chapter 4 of the 1818 edition and Chapter 5 of the revised version, have a dreamlike urgency, and the paradoxical appearance of the monster effectively conveys the characteristic reversals of dream logic: "His limbs were in proportion, and I had selected his features as beautiful. Beautiful!—Great God! His yellow skin scarcely covered the work of muscles and arteries beneath; his hair was of a lustrous black, and flowing; his teeth of a pearly whiteness; but these luxuriances only formed a more horrid contrast with his watery eyes, that seemed almost of the same colour as the dun white sockets in which they were set, his shrivelled complexion, and straight black lips."

The monster's creator seeks escape in real sleep, but to no avail; he dreams of an encounter with his fiancée, "in the bloom of health": "Delighted and surprised, I embraced her; but as I imprinted the first kiss on her lips, they became livid with the hue of death; her features began to change, and I thought that I held the corpse of my dead mother in my arms; a shroud enveloped her form, and I saw the grave-worms crawling in the folds of the flannel."

Working outward from this riveting passage, which draws its primal energy from a density of paradoxical images—parenthood and creation superimposed over visions of death, beauty juxtaposed with deformity, science equated with darkness and gloom instead of light—Mary began plotting and writing her story. The novel opens with a series of introductory letters, written by an Arctic explorer named Robert Walton, describing events that leave his ship stranded in ice. Since they are hundreds of miles from land, the crew is surprised to sight a man of apparently gigantic stature in the distance, being pulled on a sled by a team of dogs. The next day they rescue a second, near-frozen man from the ice and offer him haven. With Walton's help he regains some strength, and the men establish a rapport. Fearing he may die, the stranger asks Walton to hear and record the story of the circumstances that have driven him to this polar wasteland and the nature of the mysterious man on the sled. Walton agrees, and the novel continues in the first-person narrative he dutifully transcribes.

Mary Shelley (Elsa Lanchester) and Lord Byron (Gavin Gordon) in the prologue to James Whale's *Bride of Frankenstein* (1935). *Courtesy of Ronald V. Borst/Hollywood Movie Posters.*

The rescued man's name is Victor Frankenstein, a Genevese by birth and the son of a distinguished family. As a child Victor becomes fascinated with the writings of men whose alchemical theories were exploded by the advances of rationalist thought. Later, at the University of Ingolstadt, he combines his studies in the natural sciences with his earlier obsession with discovering "the elixir of life." He sets about a monumental task: the animation of lifeless matter. "I collected bones from charnel houses; and disturbed, with profane fingers, the tremendous secrets of the human frame," Frankenstein recalls. "In a solitary chamber, or rather a cell, at the top of the house, and separated from all other apartments by a gallery and a staircase, I kept my workshop of filthy creation. . . . The dissecting room and the slaughter-house furnished many of my materials; and often did my human nature turn with loathing from my occupation. . . ."

Frankenstein succeeds in bringing the patchwork corpse to life but is horrified by the thing he has created. He flees, abandoning the hideous being. He tries to dismiss the whole business as a kind of nightmare but nearly two years later receives word of the murder of his seven-year-old brother, William. A young girl, Justine Moritz, has been accused of the crime. Frankenstein intuits the truth—that the artificial man he created is somehow responsible—but he obviously has no proof and realizes that any statement he might make would brand him as a madman. Justine is hanged, and now there are two deaths on Frankenstein's conscience.

Seeking refuge and isolation, Frankenstein climbs high into the Alps, only to be confronted by his creation, which recounts the story of its two years: Deserted by its maker, the creature learns to survive in the woods, eventually finding a secure hiding place next to a cottage inhabited by a blind old man and his family. Observing them through crevices in the walls, the monster becomes acquainted with ordinary forms of human interaction. Secretly borrowing books from the cottage, it teaches itself to read and soon is deeply immersed in such works as Milton's *Paradise Lost* and Goethe's *The Sorrows of Young Werther* as well as papers of Victor Frankenstein it has carried in its clothes, which reveal the story of its own creation. The creature finally dares to introduce itself to the blind man, who, unaffected by its appearance, is sympathetic to the monster's plight. But when the returning family members encounter their father's new friend, they react with horror, and the monster flees.

Declaring itself an enemy of humankind, the monster travels to Geneva, where it encounters and kills Victor's young brother, murderously incensed when the boy identifies himself as a Frankenstein. The creature takes a locket from the child's corpse and places it in the pocket of a young girl he finds sleeping in a barn. The girl is Justine Moritz, who is summarily tried and executed for murder.

The monster then reaches the real purpose of its rendezvous with Victor. It wishes to have a female companion as hideously misshapen as itself, a being that Frankenstein must create. Victor at first refuses but then takes pity on the monster, which pledges to quit civilization with its mate and live for the rest of their days in a South American jungle. Upon the monster's oath to leave Europe forever, Victor agrees to the terrible request.

The third volume of the novel finds Frankenstein avoiding the task to which he has committed himself. His father urges him to marry his childhood sweetheart, Elizabeth, and he agrees. But first he travels to London, there to conduct additional studies, and then to the remotest part of Scotland, where he establishes a workshop in an isolated hut. All the while he feels the presence of the monster, which has warned him that his every move would be watched until the promise of a mate was fulfilled. Finally the implications of his work become clear: He fears that the monster and its mate will not go quietly into exile but instead propagate a race of fiends. In a rage he tears to pieces the half-constructed creature on his table, and the monster, which has witnessed the act, promises that "I will be with you on your wedding-night."

First, the monster kills Victor's friend Henry Clerval, and then, despite all precautions, it strangles Elizabeth on the night of her wedding, tossing her body like a broken doll across the marriage bed. Possessed by rage and a blinding desire to destroy the monster once and for all, Frankenstein picks up the trail and follows the creature progressively northward; the monster wants to lure him to "the everlasting ices of the north, where you will feel the misery of cold and frost, to which I am impassive." When at last his sled dogs are dying and he is near death from cold and exposure, Frankenstein is rescued by Walton's ship. After telling his story, he dies, and Walton shortly thereafter encounters the towering figure of the monster in the dead man's cabin, grieving its creator. It confesses to Walton its guilty self-hatred and promises to "quit your vessel on the ice-raft which brought me hither, and shall seek the most northern extremity of the globe; I shall collect my funeral pile, and consume to ashes this miserable frame, that its remains may afford no light to any curious and unhallowed wretch, who would create such another as I. . . ." The monster then springs from the cabin onto an ice floe, to be "borne away by the waves, and lost in darkness and distance."

Documents concerning the actual composition of *Frankenstein* are sparse; even the manuscript has not survived in its entirety. There is no conclusive proof, for instance, of the source of the name Frankenstein. Radu Florescu, in his *In Search of Frankenstein* (1975), makes a persuasive, though speculative, argument that the Shelley entourage visited the actual town of Frankenstein with its imposing castle and gothic legends during their initial trip to the Continent in 1814.

Other commentators have pointed out the similarity between the names of the fictional *Frank*enstein and the real-life Benjamin *Frank*lin, both contemporaneous seekers of electrical mysteries. Some influences are less obscure: The shadow of *Paradise Lost* falls heavily across the narrative, with a quote from Milton used as an epigraph: "Did I request thee, Maker, from my clay/To mould me man? Did I solicit thee/From Darkness to promote me?—" *Frankenstein* ambiguously conflates the archetypal characters of God, Adam, and Satan. Frankenstein himself combines aspects of all three as cre-

Overleaf: The changing face of the Frankenstein monster. 1826: Thomas Potter Cooke in *Le Monstre et le magicien;* 1910: Charles Ogle in *Frankenstein;* 1930: Hamilton Deane in *Frankenstein: An Adventure in the Macabre.* 1931: Boris Karloff in *Frankenstein;* 1935: Boris Karloff in *Bride of Frankenstein.* 1939: Boris Karloff in *Son of Frankenstein;* 1941: Lon Chaney, Jr., in *Ghost of Frankenstein.* 1943; Bela Lugosi in *Frankenstein Meets the Wolf Man;* 1945: Glenn Strange in *House of Frankenstein;* 1957: Primo Carnera in *Frankenstein* (television); 1957: Christopher Lee in *The Curse of Frankenstein;* 1957: Gary Conway in *I Was a Teenage Frankenstein;* 1964: Kiwi Kingston in *The Evil of Frankenstein;* 1973: Michael Sarazin in *Frankenstein: The True Story;* 1974: Bo Svenson in *Frankenstein;* 1974: Peter Boyle in *Young Frankenstein;* 1990: Nick Brimble in *Frankenstein Unbound;* 1994: Robert De Niro in *Mary Shelley's Frankenstein. Courtesy of Ronald V. Borst/Hollywood Movie Posters.*

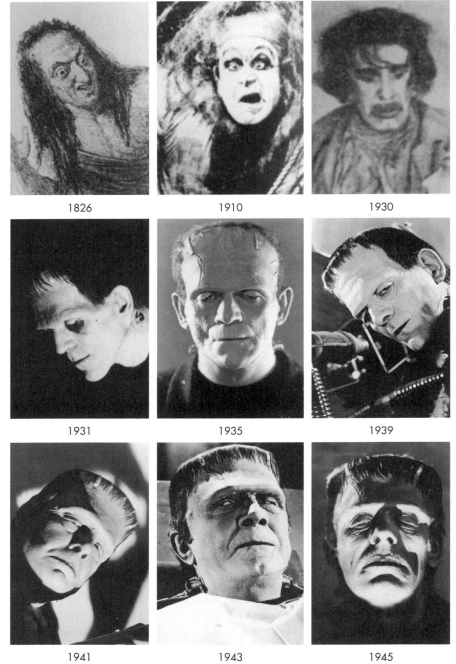

1826   1910   1930

1931   1935   1939

1941   1943   1945

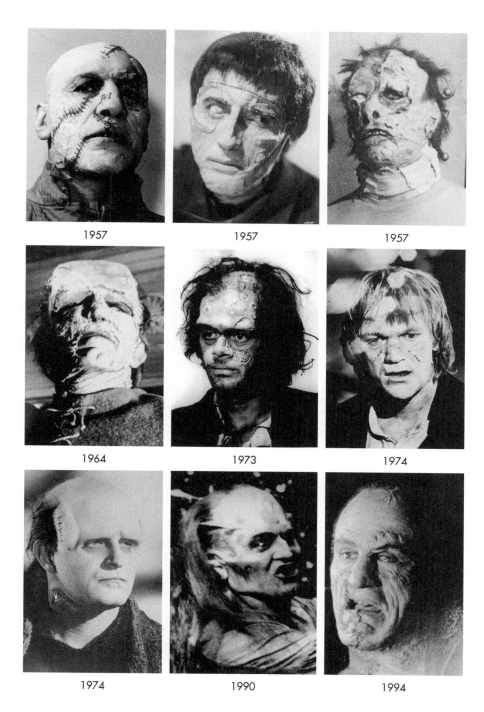

1957   1957   1957

1964   1973   1974

1974   1990   1994

ator, as romantic and rebellious angel, and as mortal man destroyed by presumptive knowledge. The monster, of course, simultaneously evokes the image of the fallen angel as well as Adam after his expulsion from Eden. The related figure of Prometheus, a major Romantic icon, is evoked not just in the familiar sense of the metaphysical fire stealer punished for his presumption but also in the older, lesser-known Prometheus of Ovid's *Metamorphoses,* who created man from clay.

Frankenstein had any number of literary and historical precursors, if not direct influences. In Western civilization, ancient proscriptions against forbidden knowledge are most powerfully crystallized in Genesis. Beyond Prometheus, classical mythology offers many examples of human beings who seek superhuman powers: Daedalus and his son, Icarus, escape from a labyrinth prison on man-made wings, but the boy, giddy with his new freedom and power, flies too close to the sun (i.e., enlightenment), melts his wings, and plummets to his death in the sea. Pygmalion, who created an idealized statue of a woman and fell so in love with it that the gods took pity and allowed Galatea to come to life, is an exception to the usual pattern of divine impatience with mortals who seek godlike powers.

Much nearer the time of *Frankenstein,* in the late eighteenth and early nineteenth centuries, there was a European vogue for clockwork automatons, eerily realistic human mannequins that could mimic all manner of advanced human activities: handwriting, chess playing, or proficiency with musical instruments. E. T. A. Hoffmann's famous story "The Sandman" (1814), certainly within Mary's purview, included the story of a automaton maker named Coppelius, who creates a beautiful dancing doll named Olympia, with whom a flesh-and-blood young man falls rapturously in love, with the expected unhappy results. The story was the inspiration for the ballet *Coppelia* as well as the opera *Tales of Hoffmann.*

Another influential tale of an artificial being, almost universally invoked in discussions of *Frankenstein,* is the legend of the Jewish golem. The word "golem" appears in the Old Testament and the Talmud, signifying a yet unformed, potential human form. The esoteric Ashkenazi Hasidim of eleventh- and twelfth-century Germany first formalized the techniques of golem creation, drawing inspiration from a seminal Jewish text, the Sefer Yezirah, or Book of Creation. The golem was molded by kneading dust and water while writing or reciting combinations of letters from the Hebrew alphabet. In the most famous telling of the tale, the creature was brought to life in the sixteenth century by Rabbi Judah Loew ben Bezalel of Prague, to protect the inhabitants of the ghetto against the blood libel—the accusation that Jews utilized the blood of Christian children in Passover rites. Loew's golem efficiently patrolled the ghetto streets, preventing false evidence from being planted by Gentile conspirators.

The golem tradition is exceedingly complex and in many ways analogous to the contemporaneous search by medieval and Renaissance alchemists for the elusive philosopher stone that would transmute base metals into gold. Some variations of the story, in which the golem runs amok and must be destroyed by its maker, are cautionary in the Frankenstein manner. One version of the golem story, in which the mindless creature empties endless buckets of water into the rabbi's house, is the obvious inspiration for "The Sorcerer's Apprentice."

But the precise relationship, if any, between the golem legend and *Frankenstein* is far from clear. William Godwin had written a book called *The Lives of the Necromancers,* which Mary finally had published in 1854, despite public objection to its irreligious tone. The father of the author of *Frankenstein* was fascinated by legendary occultists and alchemists, whose increasingly systematic explorations in the Renaissance laid the foundation for the modern scientific method. Godwin chronicled several of the of the inventor-alchemists whom Victor Frankenstein cites by name: Albertus Magnus (c.1206–1280), reputed to have created a talkative artificial man entirely from brass, only to smash it with a hammer when its conversation became vexatious; Paracelsus (1493–1541), who sought to create a miniature human being, or homunculus, from a mixture of "magnetized" human sperm and horse manure; and Cornelius Agrippa (c.1486–1535), another quester of the homunculus, who employed mandrake root instead of manure to fertilize his mad dream. Agrippa, it is known, was intrigued by the legend of the golem, so a very tenuous case might be made for an indirect influence upon Mary Shelley.

While Paracelsus and Agrippa today are relatively obscure figures, another alchemist chronicled by Godwin has entered the currency of common language. The ancient legend of the alchemist Johannes (or Georg) Faust, and

Woodcut illustration for Christopher Marlowe's *Doctor Faustus*.

his devil's bargain for esoteric power and knowledge, pulses beneath the surface of *Frankenstein*, though Mary Shelley never mentions him by name. The real Faust, to the extent that he can be identified, seems to have been born in Germany in the late fifteenth century and may have received a divinity degree at Heidelberg in 1509. Nineteen years later he was drummed out of another college town, Ingolstadt, the very site of Victor Frankenstein's notorious studies.

Faust was an alchemical charlatan adept at a variety of scams; he was reputed to use an early magic lantern to conjure up the "apparitions" of historical heroes, practiced quack medicine (his prescription of a chemical depilatory to remove the beard from the face of a prison chaplain was said to have removed flesh as well as hair), and lived a life of general disrepute. According to Faust scholar H. G. Haile, ". . . Faust was a man of known moral laxity, given to drink and sexual perversions—undoubtably to a risky personal existence in general—so that vague reports of his spectacular, violent death around 1540 are entirely credible." Faust's earthly end came in the town of Staufen, where preparing a batch of dubious potions in a local inn, the mountebank blew himself to pieces. The lingering chemical reek was widely taken as the smell of brimstone itself, and so the story began that Faust had been spirited off by the devil.

By 1587 Faust's reputation had been elaborated into popular myth, and the stories of his exploits were published anonymously in Germany as the *Historia von D. Iohan Fausten* and translated into English five years later as *The History of the Damnable Life and Deserved Death of Doctor John Faustus.*

The popularity of these pamphlets suggests that legendary Faust had coalesced around a deep-seated mythic structure. In *The Myth of the Magus* E. M. Butler traces the origins of the Faust persona in ritual magic, wizardry, and shamanism, noting the protean character of the myth: ". . . all Faust's predecessors and successors as well as Faust himself [are] essentially one and the same person under many different guises. . . . Founders and teachers of religion; sacrificed saviour-gods; rebels and martyrs; sinners and saints; mystery-men and occultists; conjurers, charlatans and quacks; they all behaved in a similar manner and their lives went according to the same plan. . . ." In its most evolved form the plan usually involved the ritual steps of occult or diabolic initiation, wandering or exile, magical contests and displays, persecution, and a violent, unnatural death. Faust's original comeuppance was particularly disgusting, even by today's splatterpunk standards: ". . . when it was day, the students that had taken no rest that night arose and went into the hall in which they had left Dr. Faustus . . . they found no Faustus, but all the hall lay besprinkled with blood, his brains cleaving to the wall. For the devil had beaten him from one wall against another: in one corner lay his eyes, in another his teeth . . . they came into the yard, where they found his body lying on the horse dung, most monstrously torn and fearful to behold, for his head and all his joints were dashed in pieces."

Almost immediately after the Faust book's English publication, playwright Christopher Marlowe began work on a dramatic adaptation, *The Tragical History of the Life and Death of Doctor Faustus.* Marlowe discarded the original's crude and often farcical episodes for a lyrical allegory of his own era's central schism: Renaissance pride and presumption versus medieval faith and humility. Marlowe's final speech, delivered by the chorus after Mephistophilis has dragged Faustus down to hell, has been imitated and echoed in the denouements of countless B movie morality plays in our own time:

> Faustus is gone: regard his hellish fall,
> Whose fiendish fortune may exhort the wise
> Only to wonder at unlawful things
> Whose deepness doth entice such forward wits
> To practice more than heavenly power permits.

If Mary Shelley didn't know the Faust story through her father's study of it, or through Marlowe's play, she was almost certainly familiar with the first part of Goethe's masterpiece *Faust,* published in 1773. (Goethe had first encountered the story in a puppet show version he saw as a boy in Frankfurt.) After all, even her own monster was well acquainted with *Werther.*

Around the time of *Frankenstein*'s publication, Percy Shelley began work on his own masterwork *Prometheus Unbound* (1820), an elaboration on Aeschylus. Shelley himself may have provided Mary with a model for Victor Frankenstein, at least according to his close friend and biographer Thomas Jefferson Hogg, who wrote a vivid portrait of the poet during his time of scientific studies at Oxford: Shelley's cluttered quarters seemed "as if the young chemist, in order to analyse the mystery of creation, had endeavored first to reconstruct the primeval chaos. . . . An electrical machine, an air-pump, the galvanic trough, a solar microscope, and large glass jars and receivers, were conspicuous amidst the mass of matter."

> Then he proceeded, with much eagerness and enthusiasm, to show me the various instruments, especially the electrical apparatus; turning round the handle very rapidly, so that the fierce, crackling sparks flew forth . . . his long, wild locks bristled and stood on end. Afterwards he charged a powerful battery of several jars; labouring with vast energy, and discoursing with increasing vehemence of the marvellous powers of electricity, of thunder and lightning, describing an electrical kite that he had made at home, and projecting . . . a combination of many kites, that would draw down from the sky an immense

volume of electricity, the whole ammunition of a mighty thunderstorm; and this being directed to some point would there produce the most stupendous results.

Mary finished *Frankenstein* in the spring of 1817, its composition overlapping with more family tragedy: the suicide of Fanny Godwin, Mary's half sister, by an overdose of laudanum, and the aforementioned suicide of Harriet Shelley—the walking corpse of Shelley's estimation now made an actual, swimming one. Harriet's death made possible Percy's and Mary's legal marriage less than two weeks later, on December 20, 1816.

Shelley assisted in the editing of *Frankenstein,* though hardly to the extent that Mary's later detractors would like to believe. He did, however, assume his wife's literary voice in order to compose the original introduction to the novel, including the first public mention of the writing contest of that "haunted" summer of 1816, and a flattering nod to himself and Byron ("a tale from the pen of one of whom would be far more acceptable to the public than any thing I can ever hope to produce"). In the summer of 1817 both Byron's publisher, John Murray, and Shelley's, Charles Ollier, rejected *Frankenstein,* but in late August, Lackington, Hughes, Harding, Mavor & Jones, publishers of popular novels in cheap editions, agreed to take on the book, which they published anonymously.

The initial response to the book was mixed and often divided along political lines. Tory-leaning journals that suspected Shelley's involvement (they already had the radically tainted evidence of the book's dedication to William Godwin for ammunition) condemned the novel. The *Quarterly Review,* after presenting a synopsis, opined: "Our readers will guess from this summary, what a tissue of horrible and disgusting absurdity this work presents.—It is piously dedicated to Mr. Godwin, and written in the spirit of his school. The dreams of insanity are embodied in the strong and striking language of the insane, and the author, notwithstanding the rationality of his preface, often leaves us in doubt whether he is not as mad as his hero." The reviewer allowed that the book possessed a "vigor of fancy and language," but, that said:

. . . when we have thus admitted that Frankenstein has passages which appal the mind and make the flesh creep, we have given it all the praise (if praise it

can be called) which we dare to bestow. Our taste and our judgement alike revolt at this kind of writing, and the greater the ability with which it may be
executed the worse it is—it inculcates no lesson of conduct, manners, or
morality; it cannot mend, and will not even amuse its readers, unless their
taste have been deplorably vitiated—it fatigues the feelings without interesting the understanding; it gratuitously harasses the heart, and wantonly
adds to the store, already too great, of painful sensations.

The reviewer concluded that the unnamed author had "powers, both of
conception and language, which employed in a happier direction might,
perhaps (we speak dubiously), give him a name among those whose writings
amuse or amend their fellow creatures," but expressed doubts that the author
of *Frankenstein* "really had any other object in view than that of leaving the
wearied reader, after a struggle between laughter and loathing, in doubt
whether the head or the heart of the author be the most diseased."

The *British Critic,* also Tory, confessed to be "in doubt to what class we
shall refer writings of this extravagant character; that they bear marks of considerable power, it is impossible to deny; but this power is so abused and perverted, that we should almost prefer imbecility . . . we feel ourselves as
much harassed, after rising from the perusal of these three spirit-wearing volumes, as if we had been over-dosed with laudanum, or hag-ridden by the
night-mare."

The identity of the author was not apparently quite the secret described
by most of Mary Shelley's biographers; the *Critic*'s reviewer noted that "the
writer of [*Frankenstein*] is, we understand, a female . . . if the authoress can
forget the gentleness of her sex, it is no reason why we should; and we shall
therefore dismiss the novel without further comment." The *Literary
Panorama and National Register* noted that it had "heard that this work is
written by Mr. Shelley; but should be disposed to attribute it to even a less
experienced writer than he is. In fact we have some idea that it is the production of the daughter of a celebrated living novelist."

Percy Shelley responded to *Frankenstein*'s detractors with his own,
highly partisan review, which remained unpublished until a decade after his
death. He called the book "one of the most original and complete produc-

tions of the day," and while admitting that there were perhaps "some points of subordinate importance, which prove that it is the author's first attempt," he nevertheless maintained that *Frankenstein* was "conducted throughout with a firm and steady hand."

Shelley went on to reiterate the Godwinian premise, by way of Rousseau, of the inherent goodness of natural man and the perverse effects of civilization, as demonstrated by the treatment of the monster. ("Treat a person ill, and he will become wicked . . . too often in society, those who are best qualified to be its benefactors and it ornaments, are branded by some accident with scorn, and changed, by neglect and solitude of heart, into a scourge and a curse.")

Mary's authorship finally became general knowledge with the publication of a one-volume edition in 1823. *Blackwood's Edinburgh Magazine,* in its March issue of that year, observed, with backhanded praise, "For a man it was excellent, but for a woman it was wonderful." By this time Mary's life had darkened considerably. Her second daughter, Clara Everina, born during the writing of *Frankenstein,* died of a fever at the age of nineteen months; not long after, in June 1819, her son, William, was claimed by malaria. In November of the same year she gave birth to a son, Percy Florence, the only Shelley offspring to survive childhood. A fifth pregnancy ended in a near-fatal miscarriage in June 1822, followed by the drowning of Percy Shelley three weeks later. By the mid-1820s the original Diodati group had been decimated by tragedy. John Polidori, who gave up medicine for the life of a recluse, seems to have killed himself with prussic acid in 1821. The daughter of Byron and Claire Clairmont succumbed to typhus the same year. Byron died in 1824 of a malady contracted while fighting in the Greek War of Independence from the Turks. Of the entire group, only Claire Clairmont lived into old age.

Mary sank into near poverty after Shelley's death and supported herself with whatever literary work she could find: articles, reviews, and fiction, including the novels *Valperga* (1823) and *The Last Man* (1826), an apocalyptic plague fantasy that underscored the degree to which she had drifted from the utopian precepts of her upbringing. She directed much of her energy in the 1820s and 1830s to keeping alive the flame of Shelley's reputation and extensively edited and annotated his works for publication. Her critics and biographers alike have noted the degree to which she strove to project the image of a respectable lady of letters, evidence of which can be found in the revised text and new introduction for *Frankenstein* she prepared in 1831. Until very recently this text was the only one readily available to the general reader.

Recent commentators, such as Anne K. Mellor, interpret the revisions as signs of a growing conservatism, if not an outright rejection of her radical roots. As Mellor points out in *Mary Shelley: Her Life, Her Fiction, Her Monsters,* the book's original, underlying themes of Romantic idealism—for instance, the monster's plight as an object lesson for social reform—were consistently sabotaged by the author upon revision. "In 1818," writes Mellor, "Victor Frankenstein possessed free will or the capacity for meaningful moral choice—he could have abandoned his quest for the 'principle of life,' he could have cared for his creature, he could have protected Elizabeth." But in the revised text, "He is the pawn of forces beyond his knowledge or control. Again and again Mary Shelley reassigns human actions to chance or fate."

The accumulation of arbitrary tragedy in the author's life since the first publication of *Frankenstein* could understandably turn anyone fatalistic. But the new introduction, with its famous story of Mary's midnight vision, altered more than just the text. It substantially changed the perception of the book as the work of a renegade female literary prodigy to something else entirely: a freak example of automatic writing, its author's contributions more hysterical and mediumistic than intellectual. It was, in short, the account of a writer who seemed unwilling to take full responsibility for what she had written.

Among the revisions, for example, was the changing of Elizabeth from an adopted cousin to a foundling with no family connection to Frankenstein, apparently to quell any hint of incest, along with generous dollops of bourgeois sentimentality. But in the long run the book's "respectability" was severely hampered by the author's new introduction, which gave generations of critics ample ammunition for not taking the book seriously. Their contemptuous attitude was perhaps best summed up by Mario Praz, author of the influential study *The Romantic Agony* (1933), who declares, "All Mrs.

Shelley did was to provide a passive reflection for some of the wild fantasies which, as it were, hung in the air around her."

Mary Shelley indeed set herself up as a kind of blank canvas for the wild fantasies of critics—but only as a result of her revisions and revisionist commentary, which we might now regard as misguided. Christopher Frayling, in an insightful essay on the genesis of Polidori's "Vampyre," argues convincingly that Mary's account of the genesis of *Frankenstein* was not only inaccurate in many respects but contrived for commercial ends. At this point in her life she may have been concerned, understandably, more with profitable mythmaking than with issues of strict historical accuracy. But it is a shame that she chose to disown *Frankenstein*'s considerable intellectual and philosophical enterprise—however unruly—for the more socially palatable image of a passive, semi-mediumistic young woman who stumbles across her story in sleep, as if not to challenge the literary primacy of the men in her life. The book wasn't really written, in other words; it mystically possessed the writer and forced her to the act of composition.

With Mary Shelley, sex role ambivalences and mad science fantasies became formally, and permanently, entangled. *Frankenstein*'s fevered dream of asexual, asocial human reproduction and its disastrous consequences is on one level a cautionary cartoon of everything that can go wrong when prevailing paradigms of sexuality, marriage, and society are overturned.

Frankenstein, as Mary Shelley wrote it, constitutes a personal meditation on the moral responsibilities of parenthood and the disaster of unconventional procreation. Mary Shelley is less of a modern feminist than recent commentary would suggest; her work is riddled with the guilt and confusion of an illegitimate, inadvertent matricide (and, like Frankenstein, an illicit procreator), who finally rejected the radicalism of her upbringing for a strained semblance of middle-class respectability.

Depictions of Mary Shelley in twentieth-century popular culture have never known quite what to make of the writer sexually. In some, like the arch, "literary" prologue to James Whale's *Bride of Frankenstein* (1935)—in which the Diodati group reassembles to discuss a sequel to Mary's yet unpublished novel—she is a prim but provocative enigma. As played by Elsa Lanchester, the world's most celebrated horror writer is demurely deferential to Byron and Shelley and swoons at the sight of a pinprick of blood suffered in the course of her needlepoint. Yet there are signs of an aggressive sexuality; the dress she chooses for fireside ghost story telling is cut so low that the Hollywood censors demanded all close-ups be eliminated. In Roger Corman's *Frankenstein Unbound* (1990), Mary (Bridget Fonda) is not presented as a dream-struck novelist but is creatively downgraded even further as a sort of lady journalist who records the Frankenstein story as it unfolds in real life around her. A time-traveling scientist (John Hurt) helps her crib by having his car's computer print her a copy of the finished book she has only begun to write. She thanks him with enthusiastic sex play. "Percy and Byron preach free love," she tells the scientist. "I practice it."

The purported sexual license of the Diodati group has repeatedly been dramatized as being germane to the genesis of *Frankenstein:* In Ivan Passer's film *Haunted Summer* (1988) Byron (Philip Anglim) treats Polidori (Alex Winter) as less a traveling companion than as outright boy toy ("Pollydolly"), and Ken Russell's hyperbolic *Gothic* (1986) reached some kind of visual benchmark with a group sex scene in the Diodati parlor, wherein Claire Clairmont (Miriam Cyr) bestows a languorous, moonlit blow job on Lord Byron (Gabriel Byrne).

Mary's character in these last two films emerged as a muddle, but the overriding implication is clear: Drawing on a hothouse atmosphere of unbridled sex, Mary Shelley wrote the supreme story of unbridled science. Themes of sexual boundaries and sexual ambivalence have haunted the literature, theater, and cinema of mad science ever since; homosexuality in particular emerged as a subtext of science-horror movies of the 1930s, as we shall see. If horror films are often considered campy, it is with good reason.

The genius and longevity of *Frankenstein* lie in its capacity to tap into ambient cultural themes, be they those of the Industrial Revolution, the Sexual Revolution, or the advent of designer DNA. Mary Shelley's essential ambivalence, unsettled even by her revisions, has probably served to keep the myth ambiguous and therefore adaptable, subject to legitimate analyses from a variety of perspectives. George Levine and U. C. Knoepflmacher, in their introduction to *The Endurance of Frankenstein* (1979), a provocative anthology of essays, put it aptly: "*Frankenstein* invites, even requires, alterna-

tive readings because its mythic core is so flexible, polymorphous, and dependent on antithetical possibilities."

The most fashionable critical model of *Frankenstein* in the politically
sensitized, reproductively polarized present is that of a visionary shriek from
the politicized womb—as if Mary Shelley had somehow intuited in 1816 the
startling reproductive technologies and battles of the late twentieth century. (After all, doesn't the monster refer to itself at one point as an "abortion"?) In an oft-cited 1974 essay, "Female Gothic," Ellen Moers reinterpreted
the novel not merely as a creation myth but as a birth myth, a dark allegory
of gestation and postpartum depression. Not all critics are taken with such
trends; Joyce Carol Oates called "Female Gothic" "virtually a parody of feminist mythmaking," reducing *Frankenstein* to "scarcely a *literary* work at all.
Did Mary Shelley's womb, or her brain, write *Frankenstein?*"

Nevertheless, disturbing images of human reproduction continue to
haunt our response to *Frankenstein,* which, through its countless incarna-
tions, has become the dominant, if despairing, creation myth of modern
times. The image of the dead or abused or abandoned child is a powerful archetype, a cultural dream link between a nineteenth-century writer's grief for
a miscarried child and the failed, metaphorical brainchildren of dysfunc-
tional technology today. In very modern terms, *Frankenstein* might even be
read, only half-facetiously, as an abortion rights debate, pitting Frankenstein's quest to destroy his ill-conceived and unwanted progeny against the
monster's right to life. In Ken Russell's *Gothic,* there is a remarkable coda
image of a dead baby floating beneath the surface of Lake Geneva as a tour
boat guide tells the story of Villa Diodati and the genesis of *Frankenstein;* the
camera moves in on the baby, the frame freezing as a ripple subtly distorts
the face into an angular evocation of the square-headed monster we know all
too well.

Mary Shelley did not become rich on *Frankenstein,* though she was able
to see the beginnings of the book's remarkable afterlife in other media. Several adaptations—none of which accrued royalties for the original author,
owing to the copyright vagaries of the time—were mounted in London beginning in 1823, but the only documentation of her reaction to any of these
is a letter of September 9, 1823, to Leigh Hunt, after she saw the very first

adaptation, entitled *Presumption; or, The Fate of Frankenstein* by Richard Brinsley Peake at the English Opera House (later known as the Lyceum). Frankenstein was played by James Wallack, and the monster by Thomas Potter
Cooke, who had already scored a success in the title role of a related melodrama, *The Vampyre,* based on Polidori's story. Cooke seems to have been the
world's first genuine horror star in his popular impersonations of both the romantic vampire Lord Ruthven and the Frankenstein monster, both in England and on the Continent. Mary Shelley was enthusiastic:

> But lo and behold! I found myself famous. "Frankenstein" had prodigious
> success as a drama, and was about to be repeated, for the twenty-third night,
> at the English Opera House. The play-bill amused me extremely, for, in the
> list of *dramatis personae,* came "————, by Mr. T. Cooke"; this nameless mode
> of naming the unnameable is rather good. . . . Wallack looked very well as
> Frankenstein. He is at the beginning full of hope and expectation. At the end
> of the first act the stage represents a room with a staircase leading to Franken-
> stein's workshop; he goes to it, and you see his light at a small window
> through which a frightened servant peeps, who runs off in terror when
> Frankenstein exclaims, "It lives." Presently Frankenstein himself rushes in
> horror and trepidation from the room, and, while still expressing his agony
> and terror, ["————"] throws down the door of the laboratory, leaps the stair-
> case, and presents his unearthly and monstrous person upon the stage.

Mary was not impressed by the adaptation overall ("The story is not
well managed . . .")* but thought that Cooke played his part "extremely well;
his seeking, as it were, for support; his trying to grasp at the sounds he
heard . . . appeared to create a breathless excitement in the audience." So
much, in fact, that another adaptation, *Frankenstein; or, The Demon of Switzerland,* by Henry Milner, was mounted the same year at the Coburg Theatre,

---

*The published reviews of *Presumption* amplified Mary Shelley's reservations about the piece.
As the *Examiner* noted, "Now a monster's birth being granted, we think a few passable
human beings might have been supplied for its play-fellows, instead of which 'dishes of skim
milk' (as *Hotspur* put it) were served up, which no talent upon earth could move into 'hon-
orable action.' "

The monster mourns its maker. Illustration by Nino Carbe (1932).

Courtesy of Ronald V. Borst/Hollywood Movie Posters

along with three burlesques of the book (or the melodramas) at the Adelphi—this one was written by Peake himself—, the Surrey, and Davis's Royal Amphitheatre. The original Peake melodrama had the greatest success and was revived the following year at the English Opera House and at Covent Garden.

Peake's physical conception of the monster has a certain historical interest, especially because it differs so radically from the withered, walking corpse of Mary Shelley's description. According to Peake, the monster has "Dark black flowing hair—*a la Octavian*—his face, hands, arms and legs all bare, being one colour, the same as his body, which is a light blue or French gray cotton dress, fitting quite close, as if it were his flesh, with a slate colour scarf round his middle, passing over one shoulder." Despite this rather mild, neoclassical description, Peake included in his text a speech taken almost verbatim from the novel describing the "dull yellow eye," the "cadaverous skin [that] scarcely covers the work of muscles and arteries beneath . . . a mummy embued with animation," etc.

No fewer than fifteen stage adaptations of *Frankenstein,* melodramatic and burlesque, appeared between between 1823 and 1826. French audiences quickly seized upon the story as a political allegory, associating the monster with the threat of mob violence. In England dramatizations of the book irritated conservatives, who, as Steven Earl Forry has noted, ever since the French Revolution "linked social reform with mob rule. The times themselves proved ripe for such a symbol. . . . Frankenstein immediately became associated with unbridled revolution, atheism, and blind progress in science and technology."

There is no evidence that Mary Shelley followed the progress of the myth she set in motion, though it is difficult to believe she was unaware of the many adaptations and the controversies they raised. But since she tried to dissociate herself from radical themes generally, perhaps it is not surprising that she did not comment on the burgeoning Frankenstein industry and the passions it aroused. She died in February 1851 at the age of fifty-four, following a series of increasingly debilitating strokes. She was buried in Bournemouth, along with Percy Shelley's heart; it had failed to burn at his cremation, and Mary had carefully preserved the relic in linen for more than a quarter of a century. She never dreamed of the extent to which her "hideous progeny," as she called her most famous book, would demonstrate a similar, eerie resiliency.

MARY SHELLEY'S MONSTER was much more than a collage of human corpses; most commentators overlook the revealing detail that Victor Frankenstein scavenged for his working materials in the abattoir as well as the charnel house. The creature's superhuman size was presumably the result of animal bones macabrely draped with human tissue. While *Frankenstein* does not dwell on the implications of a being combining human and animal components, Shelley nonetheless introduced a dominant mad science motif for the remainder of the nineteenth century and much of the twentieth.

Evolution per se was not on Mary Shelley's mind. Charles Darwin's theories were still decades from being formalized, though his grandfather Erasmus Darwin (cited by name in the novel's 1818 and 1831 introductions) had laid the conceptual groundwork for the work that was to be finished by Charles. To the Romantics, man's relationship to the natural world hardly provoked horror; Erasmus Darwin, a scientist as well as a poet, espoused a belief in humanity's essential unity with nature, a view that helped endear him to the Romantic sensibility.

Likewise, there is little to suggest that Mary Shelley intended *Frankenstein* as a comment on the disruptions and dislocations caused by the Industrial Revolution. Her letters and diaries make no mention, for instance, of the Luddite rebellion of 1811–1816, an organized workers' movement (named after its founder, Ned Ludd) that advocated the destruction of manufacturing machinery (on the ground that mechanized factories caused widespread unemployment), and it is quite a stretch to read a specifically technological critique in her tale. Although there was much talk of galvanic batteries and the like swirling around her at the time of *Frankenstein*'s composition, it is only in the introduction to the revised version of the novel that she even recalls the dream of a "powerful engine" as instrumental to the monster's creation.

Long before Darwin's publication of his theories there were many signs in art and literature of a swelling unease at the prospect of a blurred boundary between human beings and lower life-forms. Classical mythology had presented images of sphinxes, satyrs, and chimeras; these hybrid visions were also favorite subjects of nineteenth-century academic painters, and today they survive primarily as special effects creations in horror and science fiction movies. Werewolves and other were-creatures were staples of world folklore, forging a constant reminder of humankind's animal shadow. The plot and impact of Edgar Allan Poe's short story "The Murders in the Rue Morgue" (1843), often cited as the world's first detective story—a new, "scientific" literary form—turned on the reader's naive assumption that the killer's persona was human, only to be revealed as malevolently simian. "The Murders in the Rue Morgue," in its later cinematic distortions, would prove a major inspiration for Hollywood horrors revolving around ape-obsessed scientists. But aside from Poe himself, with his quasi-scientific approach of literary "ratiocination," there were no scientists described in or associated with the original story.

The fossil record, of course, preceded Darwin's observations, but naturalists tended to view such evidence through the biblical doctrine of a Noachian deluge: Animals that didn't accompany Noah on the dark did not survive; Noah's flood was considered the most recent catastrophe of its kind. The Bible wasn't strictly contradicted, just recontextualized. Science could continue to coexist with theology, however uneasily. But Darwin's ideas would leave no room for biblical literalism; the rise of all life on earth was the result of brutal competition and blind adaptation.

Darwin's theories were delivered to the public in two waves. In *The Origin of Species* (1859) he introduced the concept of natural selection among lower animals without explicitly applying his ideas to humans, though the implication was unmistakable and no doubt magnified the outrage of conservative critics. He let the other shoe drop with *The Descent of Man* (1871), making his point brutally clear: "Man is descended from a hairy quadruped, furnished with a tail and pointed ears, probably arboreal in its habits . . . all the higher animals are probably derived from an ancient marsupial animal, and this through a long line of diversified forms, either from some reptile-like, or some amphibian-like creature, and this again from some fishlike animal."

Decadent Darwinism: illustration by Aubrey Beardsley for Edgar Allan Poe's "Murders in the Rue Morgue"

The rapid acceptance of Darwin's theories in the nineteenth century marked one of the most monumental paradigm shifts since Copernicus knocked the earth from the center of the universe. Religion, which had been losing its grip on human affairs since the Renaissance and Enlightenment, took another major hit with Darwin and responded in various ways. Mainstream theologians tried to accommodate the new science by reinterpreting the seven-day Creation in Genesis as a metaphor, though fundamentalists clung stubbornly—and continue to cling—to a literal reading of Scripture.

To secular society, scriptural literalism was beside the point. Darwinism offered seductive metaphors—all of them completely unsupported by the substance of Darwin's science—to justify existing social, political, and economic trends. "Social Darwinism" neatly rationalized nearly everything excessive, unbalanced, or cruel in nineteenth-century life. According to the ascendant doctrine of the survival of the fittest, the weak and disenfranchised deserved their lot, just as the rich and powerful had earned theirs, ipso facto. It was nature, after all, that selected the winners. Darwin had simplified everything; any moral compass could now be set on ideological autopilot. Britain's imperial expansionism was justified on quasi-evolutionary grounds; British control of heathens was in the final analysis for their own good: to encourage their own evolution and progress. Darwin, of course, never equated evolution and progress; the process of selective adaptation he described had only survival as a goal, and as the fossils of countless extinct species demonstrated, survival was never guaranteed.

The Victorian era was developing a pronounced taste for the fantastic and bizarre, and on one level Darwin's theories certainly fitted the bill. Richard Jefferies's novel *After London* (1855) imagines a cataclysmic cultural meltdown in which London reverts to environmental and social wildness, strikingly anticipating the similarly decadent futures envisioned by J. G. Ballard a century later. Gillian Beer notes that "Jefferies' work condenses fears which in the 1870s and 1880s intensified in the wake of Darwinian controversy: fears that decadence may be an energy as strong as development, and extinction a fate more probable than progress."

Charles Darwin. Nineteenth-century caricature; artist unknown.

Grotesque images often appeal to cultures under stress, and the nineteenth century had no shortage of social stressors—especially in crowded centers of literary and artistic production. Part of evolutionary theory's fascination for the public may have been its bizarre novelty, the sense of catching a glimpse of oneself in a distorted mirror. With its inequities, squalor, and trapped lives, Dickensian London was in many sad ways a true human zoo, and a sense of mordant recognition may have accompanied the reception of Darwin's strange, unsettling news.

Freak shows and dime museums in England and America almost immediately began to capitalize on the notoriety and controversy of Darwin's theories. The very year following the publication of *The Origin of Species,* P. T. Barnum's American Museum in New York displayed a "What Is It? or The Man-Monkey!" The person in question was really one William Henry

Johnson, a black man afflicted with microcephaly, or an abnormally small cranium. (Johnson was better known throughout his long career—he kept working until his death in 1926—as Zip, the pinhead.) Barnum's museum described its star attraction in a ballyhoo pamphlet as "a most singular animal, which though it has many of the features and characteristics of both the human and the brute, is not, apparently, either, but, in appearance, a mixture of both—the connecting link between humanity and brute creation." Johnson typically wore a fur-covered "monkey suit" while performing, and he shaved his head save for a small topknot that exaggerated its "pointedness." "Wild Men of Borneo," "Ancient Aztec Children," and other ersatz atavisms became sideshow staples; one of the most cruelly deformed carnival freaks of all time, England's Joseph Merrick, became immortalized as the Elephant Man, a variety of missing link that had never even occurred to Darwin. Victorian missing links were usually presented with great "scientific" ceremony and trappings, although the most advanced science involved was that of bilking the public.

Since scientific and technological progress were associated with numerous destabilizing developments in the nineteenth century—industrial dislocations, evolutionary reductionism, laissez-faire excesses of all kinds— it is not surprising that the scientist was a frequently problematic literary figure. In America Nathaniel Hawthorne's fiction often hinged on the theme of overreaching intellectual pride and its unpleasant consequences, and many of his stories amount to proto-science fiction, of the cautionary type. In "The Artist of the Beautiful" (1844) an obsessive craftsman pours his life energy into building a perfect clockwork simulacrum of a living butterfly, only to have an excited child snatch it from the air, destroying it instantly. "Dr. Heiddegger's Experiment" (1837) concerns an eccentric physician's failed search for an elixir of rejuvenation.

"Rappaccini's Daughter" (1844) is the best known of Hawthorne's allegories, recounting the experiment of a Paduan doctor who believes that all medicinal virtue finally derives from botanical poisons. Like other Hawthorne characters, he cares "infinitely more for science than mankind." He has cultivated a beautiful and utterly toxic garden, the centerpiece of which is not a plant but his own daughter. Raised on fatal fragrances from birth, Beatrice Rappaccini is beautiful but physically poisonous, cloistered in the garden of her father's obsession. In order to give his daughter companionship and to continue his experiment, he encourages a young student, Giovanni, to visit her. As Giovanni's infatuation grows, so does the poison he absorbs from being in Beatrice's company. When he finally realizes that his own breath has the power to kill insects, he seeks an antidote from one of Rappaccini's rivals. But since poison is Beatrice's life, the cure can only be death. She perishes at the feet of her father and Giovanni, "the poor victim of man's ingenuity and thwarted nature, and of the fatality that attends all such efforts of perverted wisdom." "Rappaccini's Daughter" remains a key work in the evolution of the modern mad scientist icon, its evocation of scientific perversity and environmental poison having a particular resonance for the late twentieth century.

Hawthorne's final, unpublished work, labored over from 1860 until his death in 1864, was a novel to be called *Dr. Grimshawe's Secret.* Although he was never able to give the story a coherent shape in a finished book, the manuscript contains some striking images of scientific obsession, centered on the title character. Dr. Grimshawe has fixed all his intellectual energies on the activities of spiders, to the point that his cobweb-festooned workroom resembles a vampire's crypt. Grimshawe has discovered certain valuable medicinal applications deriving from spider silk and perceived much larger revelations in the exquisite geometry of arachnid industry: ". . . all science was to be received and established on a sure ground by no other means than this. The cobweb was the magic clue by which mankind was to be rescued from all its errors, and guided safely back to the right. And so he cherished spiders above all things. . . ."

The higher activities of the scientific mind are thus neatly associated with gothic decay. Hawthorne, writing in the years immediately following the publication of *The Origin of Species,* implies a dehumanizing link between narrow scientific thinking and submammalian life; the intellectually "advanced" Grimshawe is as single-minded as the lowly spiders he studies. Like Frankenstein, Grimshawe eschews feminine companionship: ". . . it was the general opinion that the Doctor's celibacy was in great measure due to the impossibility of finding a woman who would pledge herself to cooperate with him in this great ambition of his life—that of reducing the world to a cobweb factory." He had had prior bad luck with women and spiderwebs, and "the destruction . . . wrought upon this precious fabric by the house-maid's broom, and insisted upon by foolish women who claimed to be good housewives."

Grimshawe has grandiose plans for his brave new paradigm of spider-think: ". . . he had projects for the cultivation of cobwebs, to which end, in the good Doctor's opinion, it seemed desirable to devote a certain part of the national income; and, not content with this, all public spirited citizens would probably be induced to devote as much of their times and means as they could, to the same end." In Hawthorne's second draft, the Faustian overtones are relentlessly underscored: The doctor now possesses a monstrous, fascinating, jewel-colored tarantula, "the pride of the grim Doctor's heart, his treasure, his glory, the pearl of his soul, and, as many people said, the demon to whom he had sold his salvation, on condition of possessing the web of the foul creature for a certain number of years."

In Edgar Allan Poe's sensational short story "The Facts in the Case of M. Valdemar" (1845), the attempt of a mesmerist to hold a patient in a state of suspended animation at the moment of death proves to be a particularly ill-advised bit of hubris; released from his trance after months of living death, Valdemar immediately makes up for lost time in achieving the real thing: "As I rapidly made the mesmeric passes, amid ejaculations of 'dead! dead!' absolutely *bursting* from the tongue and not from the lips of the sufferer, his whole frame at once—within the space of a single minute, or even less, shrunk, crumbled—absolutely *rotted* away beneath my hands. Upon the bed, before that whole company, there lay a nearly liquid mass of loathsome—of detestable putridity." Poe doesn't spell out a moral, but in attempting to assume control of life and death, his mesmerist has obviously wandered onto a theological minefield and receives a most unpleasant rebuke for his presumption.

In France Honoré de Balzac's 1834 novel *La Recherche de l'absolu (The Quest of the Absolute,* originally translated in 1844 as *The Philosopher's Stone)* was the first full-length study of scientific obsession and its destructive impact on a bourgeois family. The physicist Balthazar Claes ruins his family and finances in a mad fixation on discovering an ever-elusive "compelling force" in nature. Balzac presents science as an addiction to which Claes will sacrifice anything in the search for a modern equivalent of the alchemist's philosopher's stone. His brokenhearted wife on her deathbed articulates a theme that still reverberated in pulp science fiction novels and B movies more than a century later—namely, that the pursuit of science is antithetical to a happy family life and corrosive to harmonious relationships between the sexes:

> "This illness began long ago, Balthazar, from the day when you first made it clear to me, here in this room where I am about to die, that the claims of science were stronger than family ties.
>
> "You will discover nothing but shame for yourself and misery for your children," continued the dying woman. "Already they call you 'Claes the Alchemist;' a little later, and it will be 'Claes the Madman!' As for me, I believe in you; I know how great and learned you are; I know that you have genius, but ordinary minds draw no distinction between genius and madness. Glory is the sun of the dead; yours will be the fate of all greatness here on earth; you will know no happiness as long as you live. . . ."

Balzac arguably contributed more to the mad scientist persona than did another celebrated French author whose work is immediately associated with flamboyant, very nearly mad images of science and technology. The enormously popular novels of Jules Verne didn't feature mad scientists as such, but they often presented eccentric, alienated inventor-explorers like the Byronic Captain Nemo of *Twenty Thousand Leagues under the Sea* (1870), who added coloration to an archetype under construction.

Despite these Continental influences, in Britain, the most compelling mad scientists drew their energy from Darwin. In 1886, one of literature's most enduring mad scientists, second only to Frankenstein, was created by Robert Louis Stevenson in his novella *The Strange Case of Dr. Jekyll and Mr. Hyde.* Loosely inspired by the real-life story of Edinburgh's notorious Deacon Brodie (a respectable prelate by day and a vicious criminal by night), *Dr. Jekyll and Mr. Hyde* obliquely reflects the Victorian era's dilemma vis-à-vis evolutionary theory: how to reconcile the human personality's higher and lower natures. Although Stevenson sets this struggle in terms of good and evil, befitting his own Calvinist upbringing, the evolutionary tensions are unmistakable: Dr. Henry Jekyll's chemically induced alter ego, Edward Hyde, is described as "hardly human," "troglodytic," his fury while committing a murder "ape-like." Hyde is also of significantly smaller stature than Jekyll, a rung down the evolutionary ladder. Even the name Hyde is a homophone for animal skin. But Stevenson wisely refrains from close detail in depicting Edward Hyde, recounting instead the vague but visceral feelings of disgust he elicits in Henry Jekyll's friends (". . . he gave an impression of deformity without any namable malformation." And: "He is not easy to describe. There is something wrong with his appearance; something displeasing, something downright detestable. I never saw a man I so dislike, and yet I scarce know why").

Such deliberate ambiguity on Stevenson's part has, no doubt, given the story much of its staying power; each generation of readers is in effect invited to put its own face on the moving target of Mr. Hyde, personalizing him with all the power of current cultural anxiety. Mr. Hyde is often effectively portrayed without the use of monster makeup, as in Spencer Tracy's celebrated 1940 characterization; the evil is recognized by cultural consensus.

In 1886 the cultural anxieties were largely Darwinian, with evolutionary metaphor coloring a wide range of social issues. Today, the Jekyll and Hyde archetype underlies the public fascination with events like the O. J. Simpson trial, in which a respected public figure is superimposed with the image of a bestial madman; with the claims of celebrities (like television's Roseanne) to affliction by multiple personality disorder; and, on a much wider scale, with the whole American obsession with pharmaceutical personality alteration and self-transformation generally.

Like Victor Frankenstein, in frantic flight from his wedding night, Henry Jekyll pursues his life and experiments without female companionship. All the principal characters of *Jekyll and Hyde* are male; Stevenson sets up the story as a thinly disguised mystery about a homosexual blackmail. Hyde, a younger, thuggish man, seems to wield a terrible power over the doctor, extracting money and protection, and even has himself named heir to Jekyll's entire estate. In collated fragments of Stevenson's manuscript drafts, we find some fascinating deleted material in Jekyll's first-person nar-

Richard Mansfield as Dr. Jekyll and Mr. Hyde (1887–1888). *The Library of Congress.*

rative: "From an early age . . . I became in secret the slave of certain appetites," plunged into a "mire of vices" that "were at once criminal in the sight of the law and abhorrent in themselves."

Elaine Showalter, author of *Sexual Anarchy,* notes that "Jekyll's apparent infatuation with Hyde reflects the late-nineteenth-century's upper-middle-class eroticization of working-class men as the ideal homosexual objects." She also finds some striking symbols, no doubt unconscious on Stevenson's part, that inform a reading of the story as a homosexual allegory: "The male homosexual body is also represented in the narrative in a series of images suggestive of anality and anal intercourse. Hyde travels in the 'chocolate-brown fog' that beats about the 'back-end of the evening'; while the streets he traverses are invariably 'muddy' and 'dark,' Jekyll's house, with its two entrances, is the most vivid representation of the male body. Hyde always enters it through the blistered back door, which, in Stevenson's words, is 'equipped with neither bell nor knocker' and which bears the 'marks of prolonged and sordid negligence."

Homosexuality was criminalized in Britain the same year *Dr. Jekyll and Mr. Hyde* was published, and while Stevenson's story elicited no sexual analysis—on the surface it seems like a celibate narrative—five years later, a related text, Oscar Wilde's *The Picture of Dorian Gray* created a firestorm with its story of an effete Victorian shadowed not by a chemically created doppelgänger but by a portrait that grows increasingly repulsive as its decadent young subject remains supernaturally youthful.

The American novelist Gertrude Atherton, in London during the years preceding Wilde's 1895 trial, turned down the chance to meet him on the

basis of her visceral reaction to a
photographic portrait shown to
her by the writer's mother—a virtual daguerreotype of Dorian Gray,
in Atherton's description: "His
mouth covered half his face, the
most lascivious coarse repulsive
mouth I have ever seen. I might
stand it in a large crowded drawing room, but not in a parlor
eight-by-eight lit by three tallow
candles. I should feel as if I were
under the sea pursued by some
bloated monster of the deep, and
have nightmares for a week thereafter."

Illustration by H. Pyle for *Dr. Jekyll and Mr. Hyde,* 1895.

Oscar Wilde, for all his intellectual brilliance, often set off Dar-
winish anxieties in his detractors and sometimes even in his partisans. Again
and again he was described as pale and bloodless, a fleshy engulfing amoeba.
His admirer Richard Le Gallienne admitted to a "queer feeling of distaste,
as my hand seemed literally to sink into his, which were soft and plushy."
"The face was clean shaven, and almost leaden-coloured," recalled Horace
Wyndam in *The Nineteen Hundreds,* "with heavy pouches under the eyes, and
thick blubbery lips. Indeed, he rather resembled a fat white slug, and even
to my untutored eye, there was something curiously repulsive and unhealthy
in his whole appearance." Alice Kipling, Rudyard's sister, also detected signs
of invertebrate life: "He is like a bad copy of a bust of a very decadent Roman
Emperor, roughly modeled in suet pudding. I sat opposite him and could not
make out what his lips reminded me of—they are exactly like the big brown
slugs we used to hate so in the garden. . . ." Whistler once caricatured Wilde
as a pig. During his 1882 American tour, the *Washington Post* depicted him
outright as an evolutionary throwback, "The Wild[e] Man of Borneo." An
anonymous postcard mailed to Wilde in prison banished him even deeper

HOW FAR IS IT FROM

THIS

TO

THIS?

Oscar Wilde as the missing link. An 1888 cartoon from the *Washington Post.*

down the evolutionary rabbit hole, equating him with the lumbering, claw-thumbed dinosaur *Iguanodon.* And capitalizing on the author's fondness for the sunflower as an "aesthetic" prop, many graphic satirists of the 1880s chose to go even further, casting Wilde even lower than the animal realm as a droopy, half-vegetable monstrosity.

Dorian Gray was Wilde's *Frankenstein.* As in Shelley, a narcissistic quest for beauty produces a monster instead; Dorian's increasingly corrupted portrait reflects the Victorian age's progressive confrontation with its own underlying animalism. Dorian's doppelgänger is repeatedly described by Wilde as a leering, ancient satyr, the satyr being a favorite Victorian artistic motif, bridging the human and animal worlds. Without the ascendancy of Darwinian science, it is hard to imagine the goat god Pan achieving the cultural prominence it did achieve during the latter half of the nineteenth century, especially in academic painting.

As a Faustian horror story, *Dorian Gray* eclipsed *Dr. Jekyll and Mr. Hyde;* twentieth-century dramatic adaptations, beginning with glimpses of John Barrymore ogling women in lower-class dives, instinctively merged the two narratives in a lucrative hybrid formula, cemented in Rouben Mamoulian's 1931 film. Wilde's work of course had sex interest, a quality lacking (at least on the surface) in Stevenson's. Dorian Gray's ruination of the actress Sybil Vane would be transmuted into the now–time-honored convention of a scientifically sublimated Victorian protagonist with a shadow appetite for showgirls and prostitutes.

The concept of degeneracy (fueled by the notion that humanity had, almost by a force of will, climbed a shaky, always-ready-to-collapse evolutionary ladder) was a hot-button Victorian issue, given a tremendous amount of publicity at the time of Oscar Wilde's trial by the appearance of the English translation of Max Nordau's *Degeneration* (1895). Nordau, a Budapest-born Austrian physician and novelist (1849–1926), wrote what is possibly one of the crankiest works of cultural criticism ever published. His goal was nothing short of the medicalizing of literature and art. "Degenerates are not always criminals . . . they are often authors and artists. These, however, manifest the same mental characteristics, and for the most part the same somatic features as assassins and anarchists." It is almost incomprehensible that Nordau, an active Zionist, would spout the kind of physiognomist claptrap that was most frequently used against Jews in the 1890s and supremely ironic to see his theories eerily echoed by the eugenics movement of the early twentieth century and finally by the Nazis in their quest to stamp out *entarte Kunst,* or "degenerate art."*

Nordau excoriated Wilde, Rossetti, Zola, Whitman, and countless others for their perceived crimes against humanity, and his book was one of the most discussed and debated of its time. The *Outlook,* a British publication, dismissed the "fanciful analogy which he puts forth with so grave and scientific an air" but was taken by Nordau's "industry in amassing material, the

---

*The Nazis, however, had little sympathy with Nordau's estimation of Richard Wagner and Friedrich Nietzsche, both of whom he also considered degenerates.

pitiless ferocity with which he pursues his victims to their last hiding place, his energy and earnestness [which] necessarily excite a certain admiration and prevent one from yielding to the temptation to take the whole performance as a stupendous joke." *The Critic* noted Nordau's contention that the ambiguous Victorian medical conditions of neurasthenia and hysteria, which, with a slight assist from accelerated technology, were "instrumental in developing the degenerate tastes and tendencies of the *fin-de-siècle* mind. During the past two generations, they have greatly increased; the cause of the increase may be attributed to the restless, feverish activities of the age; railway travel has given rise to a new class of nervous disorders from the constant jarring of the spine. . . ."

Other critics, such as Hugh E. M. Stutfield in *Blackwood's Edinburgh Magazine,* used Nordau's ideas as a launching pad for tirades of their own.

Max Nordau, author of *Degeneration.*

"Hysteria," Stutfield writes, "whether in politics or art, has the same in-evitable effect of sapping manliness and making people flabby. . . . The sturdy Radical of former years, whose ideal was independence and a disdain of Governmental petting, is being superseded by the political 'degenerate,' who preaches the doctrine that all men are equal, when experience proves precisely the opposite, and dislikes the notion of the best man winning in the struggle to live."

Phrases like "sapping manliness" and the frequently invoked epithet "effeminate" are rampant throughout the literature of degeneracy and reflect a persistent antifemale bias. Bram Dijkstra's exhaustively documented *Idols of Perversity* (1986) catalogs the multitude of late-Victorian slurs directed against women in art and literature: "In the fantasy world of turn-of-the-century painters women could be found whiling away their hours staring at a variety of bowls and cages containing a remarkable selection of flowers and lowly creatures from the animal world, in whose captive state they were supposed to find significant analogies to their own predestined fate. . . ."

On the scale of social Darwinism, women didn't fare well. Nordau's protégé Cesare Lombroso, to whom *Degeneration* was dedicated, believed that women have a congenital tendency toward criminality and chaos. Woman's evolutionary "progress," to the degree it could be achieved at all, was mea-sured by the degree to which she became increasingly "feminine"—accord-ing to the prevailing cultural standards of the time, of course. But even if women accepted their evolutionary fate, that didn't mean feminine qualities were necessarily good. Whole cultures, it was written with scholarly solem-nity, could rise and fall owing to the degree of "effeminacy" in a population. Burgeoning feminism bore the brunt of male hysteria: If the "new women" could mutate into quasi-males, then what was the corollary prospect for men? It was better to excoriate a "new woman" than linger too long on the humiliating details of what being a "new man" might entail.

Antipathy toward homosexuals was also couched in Darwinian terms of the degenerate feminine. Oscar Wilde's downfall in 1895 influenced an im-portant writer then revising a novel featuring not only satyr-like beings but also pig-people, ape-men, and assorted multitudes of "Beast Folk." "There was a scandalous trial about that time," wrote H. G. Wells almost thirty

H. G. Wells in the early 1890s.

years later, "the graceless and pitiful downfall of a man of genius, and the story was the response of an imaginative mind to the reminder that humanity is but animal rough-hewn to a reasonable shape and in perpetual internal conflict between instinct and injunction." Wells, who ten years earlier had studied Darwinian biology with T. H. Huxley (one of Darwin's chief proponents), had already created a sensation with *The Time Machine* (1895) with its bleak evolutionary future in which the forces of natural selection have stratified the world into two races, the docile Eloi and the brutal, predatory Morlocks.

Two years earlier Wells had presented the readers of the *Pall Mall Gazette* with an even more startling image of man's evolutionary future. Just as the bird was the creature of the wing, so man was the creature of the brain and hand; therefore, Wells argued, only half-facetiously, evolution would slowly but inexorably whittle away everything nonessential on the human form. The head and face would become a minimalist bulb: "Eyes large, lustrous, beautiful, soulful; above them, no longer separated by rugged brow ridges, is the top of the head, a glistening, hairless dome, terete* and

*Smooth, rounded, slightly tapered.

beautiful; no craggy nose rises to disturb by its unmeaning shadows the symmetry of that calm face; no vestigial ears project; the mouth is a small, perfectly round aperture, toothless and gumless, jawless, unanimal, no futile emotions disturbing its roundness as it lies, like the harvest moon or the evening star, in the wide firmament of face." Hardly anything more than enormous heads hopping on oversized hands, the successors to humanity in the Year Million will nourish themselves elegantly by immersion in tubs of nutritive fluids; their "whole muscular system, their legs, their abdomens . . . are shrivelled to nothing, a dangling, degraded pendant to their minds." At the end stage of their development, Wells's pale tadpole people seem paradoxically devolved—soft, big-headed, more fetal than futuristic. There is, perhaps, more than a glimmer of a Wells self-portrait to be discerned in this strange cartoon; sickly and tubercular, Wells was haunted by the fear of early death, his own body no doubt often seeming like a "degraded pendant" to his intellect.

Wells ascribed his essential interest in evolutionary themes not to scientific schooling but to his own difficult struggle to transcend working-class roots. He once called himself, in the third person, "a child of change . . . still enormously aware of and eager to understand and express, the process of adaptation. . . ." His next novel, *The Island of Dr. Moreau* (1896), is a brutal fable of that process, centering on an exiled vivisectionist who rules over a remote South Pacific outpost. A shipwrecked sailor, Edward Prendick, arrives at Moreau's island and is startled by the appearance of the natives, who seem as much animal as human. They are, in fact, the creations of Moreau, who employs advanced techniques of vivisection to mold quasi-humans from apes, wolves, pumas, and pigs. The Beast Folk have their own primitive social structure and language; in addition to surgery in his "House of Pain," Moreau uses hypnosis to expand their mental capabilities, replacing instinct with an overlay of education.

But the doctor is troubled by one problem: Even in his most successful experiments, "the stubborn beast flesh" grows relentlessly back, his grand plans to direct evolution thwarted by a Darwinian drift toward reversion. A turning point is reached when the Beast Folk, taught by Moreau not to drink blood—one of several ritualized injunctions, enforced with the threat

Original frontispiece for *The Island of Dr. Moreau* (1896).

of torture in the House of Pain—begin to hunt again. An insurrection en-
sues, and Moreau is savagely killed by his half-human puma. Prendick remains on the island for several months, watching the Beast Folk revert to
their natural state. When he finally returns to London, he too has been transformed. In an eerie epilogue, emblemizing the nineteenth century's traumatic assimilation of Darwin and anticipating the looming twentieth
century's further dehumanizing developments, he can no longer accept the
human as necessarily human. Even in public libraries, "intent faces over the
books seemed but patient creatures waiting for prey. Particularly nauseous
were the blank expressionless faces of people in trains and omnibuses; they
seemed no more my fellow-creatures than dead bodies would be, so that I did
not dare to travel unless I was assured of being alone. And even it seemed that
I, too, was not a reasonable creature, but only an animal tormented with
some strange disorder in its brain, that sent it to wander alone. . . ."

The critical reaction to *Moreau* was swift and caustic. "The horrors described by Mr. Wells in his latest book," wrote the *Athenaeum*'s reviewer,
"very pertinently raise the question how far it is legitimate to create feelings of disgust in a work of art." The *Speaker* complained that Wells "has
achieved originality at the expense of decency" and compared *Moreau* to the
detestable work of degenerate "new woman" novelists. "We should have
thought it impossible for any work of fiction to surpass in gruesome horror some of the problem-novels relating to the great sexual question which
have been recently published, if we had not read the 'Island of Dr. Moreau'
by H. G. Wells. Having read it, we are bound to admit that there are still
lower depths of nastiness, and still cruder manifestations of fantastic imbecility than any attained by the ladies who have been so much with us in recent years."

The *Saturday Review* speculated that Wells, "during the inception of his
story, like his own creatures, has tasted blood. . . . [T]he author, not content
with the horror inevitable in his idea . . . sought out revolting details with
the zeal of a sanitary inspector probing out a crowded graveyard." In a review
headed bluntly "A Loathsome and Repulsive Book," the *Times* of London admitted that it had hesitated "as to whether we ought to notice *The Island of
Dr. Moreau* by H. G. Wells at all. We know that sending a book to the *Index*

Expurgatorious is a sure means of giving it a certain advertisement. Yet we feel bound to expostulate against a new departure which may lead us we know not wither [*sic*] and to give a word of warning to the unsuspecting. . . ."

Although later in life Wells told his son that he had intended *Moreau* to be a tribute to Jonathan Swift (whose *Gulliver's Travels* had satirically depicted a race of voluble horses, the Houyhnyms, as well as the devolved society of Yahoos), the *New York Times* could discern no secondary meanings: "His biological nightmare may be intended as a sort of allegory, but . . . if that is the case the allegory is very cleverly veiled. . . ."

Some of the hostility may have come from Wells's evoking the specter of a real-world mad scientist of Victorian times, the vivisectionist. (As the *Saturday Review* commented, "Dr. Moreau himself is a *cliché* from the pages of an anti-vivisection pamphlet. . . . [Y]ou can hear the shuddering ladies handing over the guineas. . . ." Aside from legitimate moral issues surrounding surgical experiments performed on living animals, the rise of antivivisection campaigns also drew energy from the flip side of evolution anxiety, the sentimentalization of animals. Evolutionary science, and attendant horrors like vivisection, had made the Fall almost literal, as an unbridled quest for knowledge cast the human race from its protected garden into a tooth-and-claw jungle. Biologist Midas Dekkers notes one strategy employed by middle-class Victorians to maintain a sense of propriety in the face of the steamrollering new paradigms of scientific reductionism: "To prevent human beings, already fallen angels, [from] descending to the level of animals, the animal was raised to the human level." In many zoological gardens, apes, "which up till then had been stamped as hairy brutes were hurriedly given coats, caps, pipes and teacups. . . ."

Wells was stung by the negative reception to *Moreau,* reacted defensively to press attacks, and may not have been completely sure of his own purposes at the time he wrote the book. Like Mary Shelley, who spin-doctored her own account of *Frankenstein*'s inception, Wells later grasped for proper explanations: a Wildean parable, a Swiftian satire, a youthful blasphemy. His son, Anthony West, in *H. G. Wells: Aspects of a Life* (1984) maintains that *Moreau* was originally driven by images, not a preconceived theme. "He had been meaning to do something in the manner of Conrad, and had 'seen' the open boat with a lost man . . . he had become aware soon after the story had started to move that it was being fed with details that came unbidden from the darker corners of his mind and owed nothing to the requirements of a coherent scheme."

In a recent introduction to the novel, British science fiction writer Brian W. Aldiss, his own work much influenced by the Wellsian legacy, notes the duality of Wells's attraction to Darwin. The acuity of Darwin's argument impressed him mightily, but "It appealed also to his darker side. Humankind was no great distance from the brutes—as he himself had yet to put distance between himself and his working class origins. . . . Wells pitches his dark fable right in the middle of his own struggles as well as the philosophical struggles of his day." Moreau is finally a symbol for "God the cruel experimental scientist," the Deity in essence regressed to an Old Testament form, with newfangled laboratory trappings.

Bram Stoker's perennial best seller *Dracula* (1897) flourished in the overlapping shadows of *Dorian Gray* and *Dr. Moreau.* Stoker, by day the business manager for the Victorian actor and impresario Sir Henry Irving (from whom he learned a few things about melodrama) had an amateur interest in phrenology and evidently accepted many of the precepts of Nordau's pseudoscience. Darwin and Moreau lurk in the margins of almost every page in *Dracula,* along with Nordau and Lombroso, who are actually cited in the text to give credence to a diagnosis of the master vampire's clinical degeneracy. In *Dracula,* Stoker achieved a zeitgeist evocation of atavistic debasement that nonetheless proffered a kind of human immortality, however compromised and hellish—Darwin dancing with Dante, as it were.

Count Dracula, the five-hundred-year-old Transylvanian vampire, invades England obscured in a cloud of strange scientific images and metaphors. At the close of Darwin's century he is the unliving embodiment of everything disturbing about evolutionary doctrine. Clive Leatherdale, in his detailed study of Stoker's novel, makes the point succinctly: "The Count is nature personified—red in tooth and claw." Like Dorian Gray's portrait at its nadir, Dracula is the very image of an ancient, leering satyr—exactly the kind of grotesque superman that might result from Moreau's experiments carried on to an uninhibited climax. Stoker directly appropriates Lombroso's "scientific" description of the "typical" criminal degenerate from his book in his portrait of the count: "a protuberance" on the upper part of the ear, "a relic of the pointed ear characteristic of apes"; "strongly developed" canine teeth; "the nose . . . often aquiline like the beak of a bird of prey"; and bushy eyebrows that "tend to meet across the nose." Following is Stoker's description of the count: "His face was a strong—a very strong—aquiline, with high bridge of the thin nose and peculiarly arched nostrils; with lofty domed forehead, and hair growing scantily round the temples, but profusely elsewhere. His eyebrows were very massive, almost meeting over the nose, and with bushy hair that seemed to curl in its own profusion. The mouth, so far as I could see it under the heavy moustache, was fixed and rather cruel-looking, with peculiarly sharp white teeth; these protruded over the lips . . . his ears were pale and at the tops extremely pointed. . . ."

Lombroso also maintained that powerfully developed prehensile toes were another mark of criminal degeneracy; one of Stoker's most memorable images in *Dracula* is the moment when the real estate solicitor Jonathan Harker, imprisoned in the count's castle, peers out a window to witness the vampire crawling down a wall like a strange amalgam of bat and reptile: "I saw the fingers and toes grasp the corners of the stones, worn clear of the mortar by the stress of years, and thus by using every projection and inequality move downwards with considerable speed, just as a lizard moves. . . ." And Dracula's domestic arrangement with three devolved, but voluptuous, vampire wives instantly brings to mind any number of Victorian paintings depicting pointy-eared satyrs frolicking ferally with bevies of bacchantes. Dijkstra and other commentators have also pointed out the relationship between the physiognomy of satyrs and the stereotypes of anti-Semitism as promulgated by pseudoscientists like Nordau and Lombroso. Dracula, in Stoker's description, is very much a Transylvanian Shylock or Fagin.

Stoker was not the first writer to associate animal transmutations with vampires; legends of the undead had long been entwined with werewolfery, and in some traditions the monsters are indistinguishable. Stoker does seem to have introduced the bat as a favored vampire disguise. (J. Sheridan Le Fanu, whose vampire novel *Carmilla* [1872] had greatly influenced Stoker, introduced a lesbian vampire whose sexual proclivities set her back evolutionarily: In her bedside manner, Carmilla takes the form of "a sooty black animal that resembled a monstrous cat . . . I felt it spring lightly on the bed. The two broad eyes approached my face, and suddenly I felt a stinging pain as if two large needles darted, an inch or two apart, deep into my breast.")

Once Dracula relocates to England, the story's primary setting is a true bastion of "mad" science: a lunatic asylum near Purlfleet. *Dracula*'s late-Victorian scientists are Dr. John Seward, proprietor of the madhouse, and Professor Abraham Van Helsing, an eccentric Dutch alienist. The men wrestle desperately to reconcile science and metaphysics in much the same way the spiritualist movement used the quasi-scientific theatrics of séances and table rapping to bargain with the prospect of a meaningless "new death" (to coin a phrase) as promulgated by modern physics. Without concern for an afterlife comeuppance, the new death let out the animal, justifying social, sexual, economic, and political predation in the here and now. If we were animals, then so be it—after all, it was only nature's way. The blind, material forces of nature, as described by Darwin, seemed to make a mockery of traditional human values (no wonder the popular Victorian fetish for living room terraria: nature, contained and controlled.)

Leatherdale notes that "Dracula, of course, is an active materialist, for whom all phenomena are simply examples of matter in motion. Like all vampires, the Count is shorn of a soul, physical existence being all that concerns him. Stoker self-evidently does believe in souls, and his novel takes the appearance of a protest—however veiled—against the blasphemies of Darwin and Huxley." Under Dracula's Darwinian spell, the sanitarium patient Renfield, obsessed with absorbing the life force of progressively larger animals he devours—first flies and spiders, next mice, then a whole bird, including its feathers—eats his way up the evolutionary ladder, while metaphorically chewing the scenery (in the best Henry Irving manner) of the greatest intellectual drama of his time. His systematic abuse of animals neatly evokes the mad methodology of the vivisectionist. Relentless materialism lands Renfield—and, by extension, all of us—in a padded cell. "I want no souls. Life is all I want," says Renfield to Dr. Seward. Souls "would be no manner of use to me. I couldn't eat them or—" Renfield leaves the essential act of vampirism unspoken, but it is clear that Dracula's soulless physical survivalism captures his imagination more than the promise of a Christian afterlife.

The nineteenth-century struggle between science and religion is one of the most powerful subtexts of *Dracula* but oddly one of the least explored in the twentieth century. Owing, perhaps, to fashions in academic publishing, the dominant interpretations of Stoker's novel today are psychosexual, political, postmodernist. The rise of gender and gay studies in recent years has, however, elucidated the anxious undercurrents of misogyny and homoeroticism that, in Stoker's time, were clearly linked to then-respectable theories of evolutionary regression. Once vampirized by Dracula, Lucy Westenra becomes a gross caricature of the "new woman" with her frightening, liberated sexuality.

On another level, *Dracula* can be read as an all-male fantasy in which the women are merely a conduit for displaced homoerotic impulses. A minor cottage industry of speculation about Stoker's own sexual psychology has been recently flourishing, to the point that novelist Fay Weldon, in a recent introduction to a Stoker omnibus, accepts Stoker's homosexuality as almost a matter of proved fact. "Few 'came out' in those days," she writes, and "fewer still were aware of how writing could betray the sexual orientation of the writer; who'd ever heard of a sub-text then?" Unlike many commentators, Weldon also acknowledges that "it is the fashion of the times for biographers and critics to be lavish in their suggestion of sexual deviance and scandalous habits and why should I strain against the current?"

Stoker was writing *Dracula* the year Oscar Wilde (a longtime Stoker acquaintance who had once courted Stoker's wife, Florence) was tried and convicted for sodomy. Talia Schaffer, in a provocative essay entitled "A Wild[e] Desire Took Me," is particularly resourceful in her efforts to pry open Stoker's closet, exploring the multiplicity of tensions between the two men in their twenty-year relationship, their mutual adoration of Walt Whitman (to whom Stoker, as a student, wrote passionate letters expressing his desire for an ecstatic, androgynous fusion), Stoker's slavish professional "marriage" to the Victorian actor Sir Henry Irving, whose affairs he managed, the sense of revulsion attending expressions of female sexuality in *Dracula,* and so on. In one of the novel's most memorable scenes, Jonathan Harker must open Drac-

The vampire as troglodyte: cover illustration for an early edition of *Dracula* by Bram Stoker. *Courtesy of Ronald V. Borst/Hollywood Movie Posters.*

ula's coffin-bed to search for an elusive key; the count, torpid after feeding, has become the very image of the "degenerate" Oscar Wilde as previously described by his many detractors: "The cheeks were fuller. . . . [T]he deep burning eyes seemed set amongst swollen flesh, for the lids and pouches underneath were bloated. . . . [H]e lay like a filthy leech, exhausted with his repletion. I shuddered as I bent over to touch him, and every sense in me revolted at the contact. . . . The coming night might see my own body a banquet. . . ." Without any knowledge of the mechanisms of vampire contagion, Harker suddenly intuits that Dracula will "satiate his lust . . . and create a new and ever-widening circle of semi-demons." A judge at Wilde's trial had similarly described the accused as "the center of a hideous circle of corruption." Schaffer goes Elaine Showalter's examination of Dr. Jekyll's "rear entrance" one better by likening Dracula's bed box of dirt to the evidence of fecal-stained bed linen presented at Wilde's trial. And so on.

Because he left no narrative account of *Dracula*'s composition, we will never know with certainty Stoker's state of mind when he wrote the book; *Dracula* is a virtual maelstrom of late-Victorian anxieties, some of which may have bedeviled Stoker more than others. It is undeniable, however, that he wrote at the close of a century that had witnessed a wrenching struggle between materialistic science and religious faith and in a decade suffused with pseudoscience verging on the occult. Almost any Sunday newspaper at the turn of the century in Britain or America reveals an endless parade of advertisements offering magical remedies for a range of blood contaminations and insufficiencies ("Pink Pills for Pale People") that overlap strikingly with Stoker's conception of vampirism. In reality, the obsession with "bad blood" reflected the justified fear of syphilis, then incurable and epidemic. The infected joined the ranks of degenerate pariahs, including the "parasitic" poor, the insane, the feebleminded, feminists, homosexuals, Jews, and foreigners. (AIDS, the syphilis of our own time, also set off a Darwinish panic in the early 1980s with feverish, inconclusive speculation that the disease might have bubbled up from the simian world, the result perhaps of bestial sex practices between humans and monkeys.)

Bram Stoker was well acquainted with pseudoscience; once, during a transatlantic crossing with Henry Irving's company, he went so far as to concoct a lecture on the secrets of mesmerism, colluding with a company actor for a convincing demonstration of the same. Mesmeric trance was a favorite "scientific" route to evidence of personal survival after death; an article from the *Westminster Gazette,* appearing a few weeks before the publication of *Dracula,* reveals the ritual form the popular obsession had achieved on both sides of the Atlantic:

A most unexpected development of a hypnotic performance is reported to have occurred at Simcoe, Ontario. In accordance with an announcement a man was hypnotised, placed in a coffin, and duly buried on Tuesday. The disinterment took place yesterday [Friday] and the coffin with its occupant was carried to the local theatre, which was packed with spectators as tightly as it would hold. The lid was taken off the coffin and the man was lifted out and laid upon the stage, and the hypnotiser removed the hypnotic influence. The subject of the experiment sprang to his feet in wild delirium. He smashed the coffin, demolished various chairs and tables, and broke the windows with the fragments. Then he turned his attention to a group of men who were near him, and injured eight of them seriously. Apparently possessed of inhuman strength, he tore up some of the boards of the stage, plunged into the orchestra, and then among the spectators, who fled panic-stricken. Finally, after a struggle, five men threw him to the floor and held him down until his fit of delirium had passed.

As in *Dracula,* death had been held uneasily at bay in a weird collusion with "mad" science. Like Stoker's vampire, the hypnotic Canadian had triumphed over the grave ("smashed the coffin"), displayed superhuman strength, and, like Dracula's victim Renfield, was subdued by force according to the rules of a Victorian asylum. Above all, the spectacle was orchestrated by an authoritarian, pseudoscientific mesmerist, who, for an entertaining moment, seemed to reconcile the materialist reductionism of nineteenth-century science with the stubborn craving for spiritual transcendence. New hybrids of science and superstition proliferated. H. G. Wells's *The Invisible Man* (1897) is on one level the story of a single-minded scientist whose excessive rationality turns him into a vengeful ghost. In *The War of the Worlds* (1898), published the year after *Dracula,* Wells's race of invading Martians combined aspects of the hypercerebral "Man of the Year Million" with the atavism of a vampire: "They were heads—merely heads. Entrails they had none. They did not eat, much less digest. Instead, they took the fresh, living blood of other creatures, and *injected* it into their own veins."

As a new century dawned, it was not completely clear where biological evolution was leading. But the machine age had its own burgeoning evolutionary myths, and with the aid of new techno-magi, the world began to flock to science for salvation, wonders, and wizards.

CHAPTER TWO

Miracles for the Masses

W ithout a cloud in the sky, lightning flashed, and the fifteen miles of the firmament between Colorado Springs and Cripple Creek cracked and shuddered with deafening peals of thunder. The year was 1899, and the lightning was man-made. Arcs measuring millions of volts and up to 135 feet in length—a feat never again humanly duplicated—erupted from a copper globe perched twenty stories above the laboratory of their

The wizard of Colorado Springs: Nikola Tesla and a million-volt energy field.

creator, an eccentric inventor who worked in brooding seclusion with a trusted male assistant, who shunned the company of women, and who could recite the whole of Goethe's *Faust* by heart.

Nikola Tesla (1856–1943) was an undisputed genius of American engineering who trumped Edison with his intuitive grasp of the practical advantages of alternating, rather than direct, electrical current. In 1888, inspired by a sudden vision of rotating electrical fields, the Austro-Hungarian immigrant patented a complete system of polyphase transformers, motors, and dynamos that laid the groundwork of the electric power industry as we know it today. His scientific contribution is therefore almost immeasurable in its impact; Tesla provided the practical basis for mass production and robotics, gave the world radar, radio, and remote control.

But Tesla, perhaps more than any other scientific thinker of modern times, also embodied a stunning number of traits that still inform the idea of the mad scientist in the machine age. Tesla's famous coil—an air-core transformer generating showy, writhing electrical arcs and sparks—eventually became Hollywood shorthand, immediately understandable to audiences around the world, for the very idea of science run wild. Tesla himself was a flamboyant showman and gave spectacular demonstrations at venues ranging from world's fairs to society salons. Chauncey McGovern, a writer for *Pearson's Magazine,* the British journal that had first serialized Wells's *The Invisible Man,* described a visit to Tesla's laboratory in lower Manhattan: "Fancy yourself seated in a large, well-lighted room, with mountains of curious-looking machinery on all sides. A tall, thin young man walks up to you, and by merely snapping his fingers creates instantaneously a ball of leaping red flame, and holds it calmly in his hands. As you gaze you are surprised to see it does not burn his fingers. He lets it fall upon his clothing, on his hair, into your lap, and finally, puts the ball of flame into a wooden box. You are amazed to see that nowhere does the flame leave the slightest trace, and you rub your eyes to make sure you are not asleep."

Tesla's Promethean feats with plasmas at the turn of the century continue to defy explanation, but there is little doubt that they occurred. Celebrities like Mark Twain paid visits to his workshop and came away dumbstruck after experiencing spectacles more in keeping with the

Mad scientist prototype: Nikola Tesla near the end of his life.

repertoire of the Théâtre Robert-Houdin (the nineteenth-century master magician, from whom Houdini took his name) than with the principles of modern physics. But Tesla's basic ideas *were* theatrically grandiose and suffused with the inventor's superman obsessions. Even his most practical inventions seemed to have drawn inspiration from nearly megalomaniacal fever dreams: the total conquest of nature; communication with other worlds; the transformation of the earth's atmosphere into a glowing electrical lamp, banishing darkness forever. In an essay entitled "Man's Greatest Achievement," Tesla envisioned human powers "almost unlimited and supernatural." "At his command, with but a slight effort on his part, old worlds would disappear and new ones of his planning would spring into being. He could fix, solidify and preserve the ethereal shapes of his imagining, the fleeting visions of his dreams. He could express all the creations of his mind on any scale, in forms concrete and imperishable. He could alter the size of this planet, control its seasons, guide it along any path he might choose through the depths of the Universe. He could cause planets to collide and produce his suns and stars, his heat and light. He could originate and develop life in all its infinite forms."

A 1902 *Nation* editorial cited the persistence of magical thinking in popular scientific discourse. "Something of the mediaeval notion of science as a variation of the black art seems to survive . . ." the publication noted. "Marconi is a 'magician.' Edison, a 'wizard.' " These words, the *Nation* editor wrote, "well express the real mental attitude of millions of honest folk toward science. To them it remains a region of wonder and mystery. Any miracle may come out of it any day. Tesla's fevered dreams are as credible as Marconi's sober and guarded forecasts. To one in this state of mind the scientist necessarily appears akin to the medicine-man. He is the thaumaturge [miracle worker] of to-day. . . . There is in all this little resemblance to [Thomas] Huxley's definition of science as simply 'organized and trained common sense.' "

Although it took the mechanized cataclysm of World War I to foster a widespread cultural ambivalence toward the fruits of science and technology, the potential dark side of modern inventiveness was well perceived by certain popular writers at the dawn of the twentieth century. Playwright André de Lorde, later the *chef d'horreur* of the Parisian Grand Guignol, wrote an especially prescient one-act chiller with Charles Foley called *At the Telephone* (1902). Anticipating the basic stratagem of much dystopian science fiction, Lorde and Foley spun a nasty little melodrama concocting the deepest imaginable downside to what was generally regarded modern communications

At the Telephone: early communications age jitters.

convenience. André Marex, a French bourgeois, installs a telephone in his country house to keep in better touch with his business and his family. But the dream of long-distance communication becomes a nightmare when, in his absence, an intruder breaks into the house and kills his wife and child. Forced to listen to the murders in progress helplessly over the telephone, Marex goes mad.

While *At the Telephone* has no overt purpose beyond creating a sense of horrifying suspense, it makes a clear, if unintentional, statement about dislocated consciousness in the age of the machine. Even today, on the streets of Manhattan, it is sometimes unclear whether the person walking next to you, talking into the air, is an excited schizophrenic or simply using a cell phone. Like the motion picture, the telephone separated perception from the body in a way that could inspire amazement as well as dread. The Italian playwright Luigi Pirandello, who lived through the period of cinema's infancy, found it a dehumanizing invention. "The film actor," he wrote, "feels as if in exile—exiled not only from the stage but also from himself. With a vague sense of discomfort he feels inexplicable emptiness: his body loses its corporeality, it evaporates. . . ."

Up-to-date scientific and technological marvels like the motion picture and telephonic communication were, paradoxically, analogues of ancient mystical and occult concepts like clairvoyance, remote viewing, and astral projection. The telephone and motion picture took the user and viewer out of his or her body for an effect simultaneously exhilarating and depressing; a thrilling sense of omniscience countervailed, as in *At the Telephone* by an ultimate feeling of infantile helplessness. Lorde and Foley intuitively anticipated a media culture that would present distant, uncontrollable images of crime, war, atrocity, and famine as an all-purpose stimulant/narcotic, leading inexorably to personal and social insanity. Marex's madness at the climax of *At the Telephone* is a good analog for our present-day response to ghastly cataclysms like Bosnia, nightmares we seem to have no possibility of influencing, much less resolving, served up as technologically mediated, luridly voyeuristic infotainment.

The twentieth century has often been described as an age of alienation, the pervading sense of dislocation deriving from the displacement of direct

Information overload: illustration by Georges Méliès for his trick film *The Man with the Rubber Head* (1902).

human experience with media analogs. It is no wonder, for instance, that the popular fascination with out-of-body experiences in the 1980s and 1990s has coincided with the explosive growth of extended-consciousness media, like computers in the office and home, cable and satellite television, virtual reality games, etc. For ever-increasing numbers of people, both work and relaxation—almost the totality of waking life—are consumed by indirect perceptions of the world through a variety of glowing view screens. The overkill use of "experience" as an advertising buzzword during the same period certainly speaks to a broad popular craving for tangible, not virtual, realities.

Significantly, the technology of motion pictures was first introduced to the public in the familiar trappings of magic. The French film pioneer Georges Méliès (1861–1938) began his career as a stage illusionist, integrating short films into his variety programs at the Théâtre Robert-Houdin beginning in 1896. Within a few years he was turning out scores of droll featurettes, intuitively mixing the techniques of stage magic with new forms of sleight of hand achievable only through the camera. Méliès's films anticipated a new century of technological marvels and in the process created and refined the basic vocabulary of camera tricks—double exposure, stop motion, miniatures—that were utilized until the advent of computer animation. Méliès often depicted fantastic inventor-artists in outlandish laboratory-studios; both scientific and artistic creation was depicted in the zaniest terms possible. His most famous film, *A Trip to the Moon* (1902), ridiculed ideas of space travel as proposed by the likes of Jules Verne. In the film's most celebrated image, the bulletlike spaceship, fired from an earthbound cannon, lands squarely in the eye of an anthropomorphic man in the moon, who is something less than pleased.

Today, some of Méliès's efforts seem startlingly perceptive. What greater evocation of the mind and body dilemma could there be than his 1902 film of a scientist using an air pump to inflate a disembodied head (Méliès's own) to the point of explosion? Bulging, overloaded braincases proved a favorite image of science fiction films in the decades to come, from the cubistic cranium of Hollywood's Frankenstein monster to the big-brained atomic mutations of the fifties.

While modern technological know-how has not yet actually created life (hysterical recent claims for the sentience of the computer notwithstanding), it has given rise to the specter of the moving image, which, to an alarming extent, is increasingly accepted as a pretty good substitute for vitality or perhaps even something better. As the filmmaker Francis Ford Coppola, the very latest producer of a *Frankenstein* film, commented on the medium, "Basically, it's about creating life."

It is perhaps fitting that Thomas Alva Edison, the great technological magus of the late nineteenth and early twentieth centuries, having already astounded the world with the mechanical golem he first called the kinetoscope, lent his name to the first motion-picture version of *Frankenstein*. Produced in early 1910 under the direction of J. Searle Dawley and filmed at the Edison Manufacturing Company studio at Bedford Park, the Bronx, the world's first horror movie ran sixteen and a half minutes, was color-tinted to create daylight and night effects, with accompanying dramatic music cues drawing especially from Carl Maria von Weber's 1821 opera *Der Freischutz,* providing at least a tenuous connection to German Romanticism. "Trick" films of various kinds, taking inspiration from Méliès, were much in vogue in America in the years preceding World War I, and *Frankenstein* contained numerous examples of optical illusions beyond the reach of proscenium-bound stagecraft.

The *Film Index* offered a synopsis of the Edison film a week before it was unleashed on an unsuspecting world:

Frankenstein, which will be released March 18, is a liberal adaptation of Mrs. Shelley's famous story. . . . As told in the film, the story shows Frankenstein, a young student of the sciences, leaving his father and sweetheart to pursue his studies at college. In the course of his researches he discovers the awful mystery of life and death and immediately determines to realize his one consuming ambition—to create the most perfect human being that the world has ever seen. Alone in his room he conducts the experiment and after an almost breathless suspense is rewarded by seeing an object forming and rising from the blazing cauldron in which he has poured his ingredients,—a vague, shapeless thing at first but which gradually assumes a human form and exhibits signs of animation. His joy at the success of his experiment is quickly turned to horror and dismay, however, when he finally beholds the fruition of his labor; for the evil thoughts that swayed his mind before and during the experiment have so influenced his handwork that, instead of a human being endowed with beauty of face and form, he has created a hideous monster of colossal, unshapely proportions and most frightful mien.

The monster, as portrayed by Charles Ogle, was a Kabuki-like apparition in whiteface with a flyaway fright wig. The creature was dressed in rags, ropes, and bandages and possessed hands so deformed they seemed more like vegetation than flesh. Because the Edison company was eager "to eliminate all the actually repulsive situations" and concentrate on the story's "mystic and psychological problems," any suggestion that the monster might be composed of pieced-together cadavers was discarded, the creature now being the result of purely chemical combustion. The creation, accomplished in a contraption resembling an oversize magician's box, seems to have been achieved by burning a dummy of the monster and photographing it in reverse, thus giving a convincing impression of pyrotechnic "birth."

Frankenstein (Augustus Phillips) flees the workshop for his bedroom, only to have the monster peer at him through the bed curtains. Frankenstein faints, and the monster vanishes. When Frankenstein returns to his fiancée (Mary Fuller), the nightmare seems to have been dispelled, but then the monster's reflection appears in a mirror and steps into the room. According to the Edison company's original synopsis:

> All the terror of the past comes over him and fearing lest his sweetheart should learn the truth, he bids the monster conceal himself behind the curtain, while he hurriedly gets his sweetheart, who then comes in, to stay only a moment. There follows a strong, dramatic scene. The monster who is following his creator with the devotion of a dog, is insanely jealous of anyone else. He snatches the rose from Frankenstein's coat, which his sweetheart has given him and in the struggle throws Frankenstein to the floor. Here he looks up and for the first time confronts his own reflection in the mirror. Appalled and horrified at his own image he flees in terror from the room.

Unable to remain separated from his creator, the monster returns on Frankenstein's wedding night, this time to seek out the cause of his jealousy. Hearing his bride's scream, Frankenstein interrupts the monster's attack. Once more the creature flees. In a final scene, the Edison notes explain, "comes the point which we have endeavored to bring out": ". . . with the strength of Frankenstein's love for his bride and the effect of this upon his own mind, the monster cannot exist. Therefore, from this comes the reason for the next and closing scene which has probably never been surpassed in anything shown on the moving picture screen. The monster broken down by his unsuccessful attempts to be with his creator enters the room, stands before a large mirror holding out his arms entreatingly, but gradually the real monster fades away, leaving only the image in the mirror."

Frankenstein himself then enters the room and stands before the mirror, the monster's image reflected instead of his own. Gradually, however (the Edison company took pains to make clear), "under the effect of love and his better nature, the monster's image fades and Frankenstein sees himself in his young manhood in the mirror. His bride joins him, and the film ends with their embrace, Frankenstein's mind now being clear of the awful horror and weight it has been laboring under for so long." The metaphysics of the picture may well have proved murky and confusing to audiences of 1910; *Frankenstein* historian Steven Earl Forry states: "In reaction to adverse reviews of the film, of which perhaps no more than one hundred copies were struck, Edison removed it from Nickelodeons soon after its release." All currently accessible evaluations of the picture, however, are uniformly positive. The *Moving Picture World* assessed the film a few weeks after its release, calling it "vividly and sympathetically acted," and was especially taken with the special effects: "The formation of the monster in that cauldron of blazing chemicals is a piece of photographic work which will rank with the best of its kind. . . . The entire film is one that will create a new impression of the pos-

Augustus Phillips in the Edison company's *Frankenstein* (1910). *Courtesy of George Turner.*

sibilities of the motion picture as a means of expressing dramatic scenes. Sometimes the value of the motion picture in reproducing these stories is scarcely realized, yet they do much for literature. . . . [M]any, for example, will see this picture who have never read the story, and will acquire a lasting impression of its power."

"Lasting impressions" in the cinema of course require a stable photographic medium and careful conservation efforts, neither of which existed in the earliest days of motion-picture technology and its volatile nitrate film stocks. Film archives were nonexistent; following their short commercial lives, early motion pictures—purchased from manufacturers outright, rather like yard goods—were likely sold to junk dealers for their silver content, often for as little as twenty-five cents a reel. Although the Edison company donated hundreds of its negatives to the Museum of Modern Art in 1936, the Edison *Frankenstein* was not among them.

Alois Dettlaff was one of the few people who were intrigued enough by film to consider motion pictures worth saving and collecting. His collection today is recognized as a significant one, if maddeningly inaccessible from the standpoint of professional preservation standards and scholarly research. While private and amateur archives are an important source of cinematic rarities, their owners often have an emotional stake in their collections at odds with the viewpoints and values of institutional preservationists.

During the 1930s Dettlaff acquired many of his films from the owner of the White House Theater in his hometown of Cudahy, Wisconsin. "At that time they were like yesterday's newspaper," Dettlaff told a Milwaukee reporter in 1976. During the Depression and war years he held screenings for local children in the basement of his father's drugstore, using a Prohibition era vault for prescription liquor as a projection booth. He cranked the films by hand while the kids sat on benches and empty liquor crates.

In the late 1950s, Dettlaff acquired an assortment of old films from his wife's grandmother. Among them was a thirty-five-millimeter toned and tinted print of the Edison *Frankenstein* in an excellent state of preservation. At first he didn't know the film's significance. "I realized then that I had something unusual, but I didn't know how unusual," he told an interviewer in 1985.

Word of the rediscovery of Edison's film began leaking out in newspaper articles and film journals in the 1970s, and Dettlaff allowed a three-minute clip to be incorporated into a British television documentary for a one-time payment of two thousand dollars. Dettlaff stirred considerable interest in film circles when he traveled to Los Angeles with his dormant celluloid monster in its canister. He managed to arrange a meeting with the veteran film director Robert Wise, then president of the Academy of Motion Picture Arts and Sciences, to discuss the possibility of a seventy-fifth anniversary screening during the 1985 Oscar ceremonies, with some sort of special citation given to Dettlaff for his preservation efforts. The discussions broke down, however, over such matters as the amount of the film that could rationally be shown during a national telecast.

Dettlaff told a Milwaukee newspaper that he had turned down offers to purchase the film from the Museum of Science and Industry in Chicago, the Museum of Modern Art, and the Ford Foundation. According to the *Milwaukee Sentinel,* Dettlaff "feels a museum should place the same value on such films as it does original paintings, and expect to pay a sizable amount in acquiring them." Dettlaff said: "I'm not in this for glory or aggrandizement, a pat on the back," adding bluntly, "Let's have some American cash."

Who would control the resurrection of the Edison *Frankenstein?* Did the monster belong to the populace, to excitable fans and hobbyists—or to the anointed priests of preservation, performing techno-rituals in dignified institutional cloisters? The mystique of the Edison *Frankenstein,* with its central theme of a dead thing technologically revived, presents an irresistible metaphor for film preservation, not to mention the godlike aims of modern science. One must wonder whether major institutions and preservations would have been quite so interested in a lost film version, say, of *Rumplestiltskin* instead of the zeitgeist-redolent *Frankenstein.**

In 1915 a second American *Frankenstein* was filmed under the title *Life*

---

*By 1997 Dettlaff had still not relinquished control of his monster. He did, however, release a "copy-protected" videotape (i.e., a tape disfigured from beginning to end with a rolling supertitle, PROPERTY OF AL DETTLAFF). Although his intention was to stir commercial interest in the film, the move probably served only to kill the curiosity factor that had made the film valuable in the first place.

without Soul, directed by Joseph W. Smiley and released by the Ocean Film Corporation. It was Ocean's first feature-length (five-reel) effort, and it nearly bankrupted the company, which was forced to sell the film to another distributor shortly after release. The name Frankenstein was inexplicably changed to Frawley (some anti-German sentiment may well have been at work here, though America had not yet entered the European conflict). The story was both modernized and Americanized. The overreaching scientist, Victor Frawley, was played by William W. Cohill, and his monster by the British actor Percy Darrell Standing. No print of the film is known to survive.

During the years of the Great War science themes in American films revolved primarily around munitions and militarism. *The Flying Torpedo* (1916), *The Greatest Power* (1917), starring Ethel Barrymore, and *Swat the Spy* (1918) were examples of pictures whose plots involved war-related super-weapons. After the war the European imagination was captured by themes of scientific authoritarianism and somnabulism while the concurrent rise of bolshevism in Russia gave rise to politically revolutionary themes in the arts. Czech playwright Karel Čapek's 1921 allegorical melodrama *R. U. R. (Rossum's Universal Robots)* dealt ironically with the relationship between capital and labor as soulless automatons, created for industrial efficiency, gradually displace their human masters.

With *R. U. R.,* Čapek introduced the word "robot"—a Czech word for "worker"—to the international vocabulary. In fact, Čapek's robots are androids, cultivated organically in chemical vats, somehow (and however illogically) recycled via stamping mills. Čapek's initial difficulty defining his artificial beings is perhaps less a failure of dramaturgy than a reflection of the protean potency of the robot as a cultural symbol—even at the moment of its birth a shape-shifting archetype transcending easy categorization.

R. U. R. is set sometime in the future on a remote allegorical island, rather in the manner of Prospero or Moreau. The island is home to the factories of Rossum's Universal Robots, which have radically transformed the world by providing limitless cheap labor, freeing human beings from soulless drudgery. To the island comes Helena Glory, the vapid emissary of a do-good organization, the League of Humanity, objecting to the inhumane treatment of beings that aren't human to begin with. Her revolutionary rhetoric falls upon deaf ears. The robots—which, in the Theatre Guild's 1922 costumes and makeup, strikingly anticipated the appearance of *Star Trek*'s Mr. Spock four decades later—experience no discomfort, no matter how hard they work. This leads to expensive accidents and repairs. One of Rossum's research scientists begins introducing improved models with the

The revolt of the robots: the first American production of Karel Čapek's *R. U. R.* (1922).

capacity to feel pain, in the hope that they will take better care of themselves, extending their useful lives and improving Rossum's profits. Instead they begin to develop grudges and rise up collectively to destroy the entire human race. In a seemingly paradoxical epilogue a robot and robotress—now mortal since Helena Glory has destroyed the secret of their manufacture—discover love, transcending both the mechanical and human orders.

Čapek's half-chilling, half-satirical story generated tremendous press

John Barrymore in and out of character in *Dr. Jekyll and Mr. Hyde* (1920).

discussion in Europe and America. John Corbin, commenting in the *New York Times* on the Theatre Guild's 1922 production, understood the play's metaphorical conception of the robot. "The true enemy of civilization is not the machine, but the mechanized human being—dwarfed in intelligence, stunted in sympathy, swayed by the only idea one can ever derive from the seamy side of the industrial fabric, the idea of soulless mastery, sheer physical power." Writing in *Life,* Robert C. Benchley notes: "The scene in which the last half-dozen humans are waiting in the house surrounded by thousands of quietly approaching robots, is terrific. And when one of the scientists, peering out through the barricade, says with a shudder: 'We shouldn't have made their faces all alike,' the effect is hardly to be borne." Benchley was fully aware of the play's political allegory. "The symbolism of the story is obvious, and, in the present depleted condition of the world, accepted by practically everyone as true," he writes. "Five years ago the Vigilantes would have run the play out of town, and, when next we want to go to war, the members of the Theatre Guild will probably be watched by Military Intelligence officers for having produced anti-war propaganda in 1922."

The years preceding, during, and following the trauma of World War I saw a surge of diabolical authority figures in popular culture. *The Cabinet of Dr. Caligari* provided an influential cinematic prototype of the megalomaniacal pseudoscientist who controls a soulless monster. *Caligari*'s story of a sideshow mesmerist (Werner Krauss) and his murderous sleepwalker (Conrad Veidt) was originally intended as an allegory of the Great War, the somnabulist representing an Everyman soldier-slave, sent out to kill and be killed by a crazy master. *The Golem,* with its *Frankenstein*-like story of an artificially created man, was filmed twice in Germany by Paul Wegener, in 1914 and 1920 (the first version set in modern times, the second, in medieval). Otto Rippert's *Homunculus* (1916) was a six-part six-hour serial about an artificially created superman that, learning of his unnatural origins, becomes a destructive monster. *Dr. Jekyll and Mr. Hyde* had been filmed six times before the war, but John Barrymore's 1920 screen performance was the

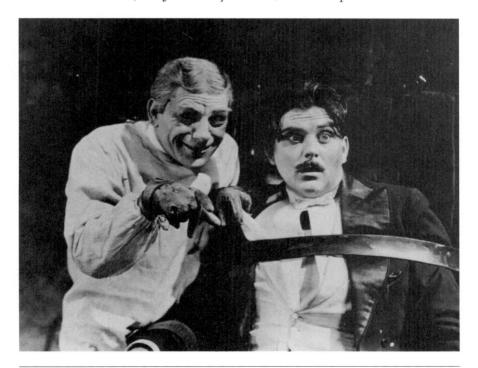

Lon Chaney and Hallam Cooley in *The Monster* (1925).

first internationally successful screen interpretation. Arguably, postwar audiences were more receptive to the startling idea that a "good doctor" (traditionally one of the most familiar embodiments of benign authority and scientific progress) might have a darker, destructive side.

The mad scientist received an especially rococo theatrical treatment in Crane Wilbur's flamboyant melodrama *The Monster,* which, despite poor reviews, entertained Broadway audiences for several months in 1922. Wilbur's "monster" was Dr. Ziska, an obsessed surgeon who traps motorists near his isolated Long Island estate, equipped with sliding panels, a hulking servant, an operating table, and even an electric chair. Upon the release of Goldwyn's mad science melodrama *A Blind Bargain* (1922), *Variety* noted "the 'horror' situation so prevalent in fiction, theatre and on the screen for the past year." *A Blind Bargain* starred Lon Chaney in the dual role of a crazed surgeon and the hunchbacked ape-man he has created, and was one of the first Hollywood films to deal with evolutionary science in a sensational way.

In 1925 MGM adapted Wilbur's *The Monster* as a screen vehicle for Lon Chaney, who played the evil Dr. Ziska. While a truly ridiculous film, *The Monster* is significant for formalizing certain mad science plot conventions (e.g., the scientist leering at the helpless heroine, strapped to his laboratory table; the laboratory located in the basement of an isolated mansion, etc.) that were recycled in B movies for decades.

Actor-director James Cruze, who had starred in one of the early screen versions of *Dr. Jekyll and Mr. Hyde,* had been eager to film *R.U.R.* for Paramount, but his plans were derailed when the studio became involved in the bailout financing of an ambitious German film called *Metropolis* (1927), a futuristic story that also turned on the theme of robots. Directed by Fritz Lang, who had previously mounted the epic *Die Nibelungen* (1924) for UFA, *Metropolis* took two years to produce and was at the time the most expensive German film ever attempted.

The story of *Metropolis,* based on a novel by Lang's then wife, Thea von Harbou, and coscripted (uncredited) by Lang himself, is set a hundred years into an expressionist future where a 1920s and leftist perspective on the relationship between capital and labor is deliriously literalized as a stratified

Metropolis (1927). Top: The mad exultation of Rotwang (Rudolf Klein-Rogge) upon the birth of his female robot (Brigitte Helm). Bottom: The techno-maw of modernism. *Courtesy of Ronald V. Borst/Hollywood Movie Posters.*

world of soaring, pleasure dome–topped skyscrapers sustained by a subterranean army of oppressed workers. What exactly the grim machinery of their
factories produces to enrich the overworld is never made clear, but tending
the menacingly oversize flashing dials is a backbreaking, purgatorial endeavor. When Freder (Gustav Frohlich), the son of Metropolis's industrial
overlord, Fredersen (Alfred Abel), wanders down to the workers' level, he is
overcome by a fevered vision of the downtrodden laborers marching re-
signedly into the devouring mouth of a machine god—still one of the great
antitechnological images in popular culture. When Freder falls in love with
a reform-minded worker, Maria (Brigitte Helm), his father has her kidnapped by a half-crazy inventor, Rotwang (Rudolf Klein-Rogge) who repli-
cates her outward appearance as a kind of fleshy costume for a female robot
he has manufactured in his gothic, pentagram-adorned spookhouse in the
middle of the otherwise gleaming city. The doppelgänger has political
charisma and harangues the workers toward a self-defeating revolt. But the
false Maria's efforts go much farther than anticipated, resulting in an uncontrollable uprising that nearly destroys all of Metropolis. After the robot
is found out and burned at the stake—another indelible image—the real
Maria steps forward to reconcile father and son, admonishing them that "the
heart must mediate between the head and the hand."

It is a mawkish moment, but no more excessive and naive than almost
everything about *Metropolis*. At the time of its release, however, the sheer
scale of the enterprise blinded many commentators to the inherent absurdi-
ties. The *New York Times* gave prominent display to its coverage of the Berlin
premiere and found significant (if completely unintentional) symbolism in
a perceived resemblance between Henry Ford and the actor who played Metropolis's overlord.

The character of Rotwang provides an important cinematic bridge between Dr. Caligari and Dr. Frankenstein, his medieval workshop magically
alive with Tesla-style pyrotechnics. He was the first of a long line of mad scientists (or their creations) to possess a withered, deformed, transplanted, or
mechanical hand. In his 1919 essay "The Uncanny," Sigmund Freud first
identified the image of the disembodied hand as a persistent motif in fantastic literature, a potent symbol of disrupted identity. The central schisms

of modern consciousness are often represented in a dreamlike manner in horror and science fiction films and stories, where the single-minded pursuit of a scientific obsession can result in a "lost grip" of reality. Damaged, missing, or replaced hands figured prominently in the Hollywood Frankenstein films, in the silent *Hands of Orlac* (1924) and its quasi-remake *Mad Love* (1935), and most famously, in Stanley Kubrick's *Dr. Strangelove* (1963).

Its design coinciding with the peak of the machine age aesthetic in the mid-1920s, *Metropolis*'s female robot (played by actress Helm in a skintight costume that had been laboriously crafted over a full-body plaster cast of her body) remains a stunning piece of sculpture, an elegantly constructed metaphor of mechanistic reductionism—not to mention its perennial, seductive appeal—that has never really been equaled. But not everyone was impressed by the robot or the film.

H. G. Wells, for instance, hated *Metropolis*. He found the creation of the false Maria "the crowning imbecility of the film," which "gives in one eddying concentration almost every possible foolishness, cliché, platitude and muddlement about mechanical progress and progress in general, served up with a sauce of sentimentality that is all its own." He went on to attack *Metropolis*, a supremely expressionistic effort, for failing to be a rigorously logical one. Wells's hostility, recorded at length in an April 1927 *New York Times* appraisal, derived from his belief that the scenario was unduly influenced by his own work: "Possibly I dislike this soupy whirlpool none the less because I find decaying fragments of my own juvenile work of thirty years ago, 'The Sleeper Awakes,' floating about in it." (Later in the piece Wells goes so far as to use the word "plagiarized.")

Apparently unaware of the gothic underpinnings of scientific romances (he refers to "that soulless mechanical monster of Mary Shelley's," a rather extraordinary statement, suggesting that Wells had never read *Frankenstein* or hadn't understand what he read), Wells attacked the expressionist film for being insufficiently logical. "By some no doubt abominable means Rotwang has squeezed a vast and well-equipped modern laboratory into this little house. It is ever so much bigger than the house, but no doubt he has fallen back on Einstein and other modern bewilderment." Paradox, in science and in art, was apparently not a subject to which Wells warmed easily. He was appalled by the antiscience, antiprogress tone of Lang's film, which heretically challenged the technological assumption—which Wells accepted as fact—that mechanization had essentially solved the problem of oppressive, soul-killing labor. "[M]echanical civilization has no use for mere drudges. The more efficient the machinery the less need there is for the quasi-mechanical minder. . . . The hopeless drudge stage of human labor lies behind us," Wells declared. "With a sort of malignant stupidity this film contradicts these facts."

How dare *Metropolis* make a political-metaphorical, emotional-artistic statement rather than a rational one! "[I]t would have been almost as easy, and no more costly and far more interesting to . . . gather opinions of a few bright young research students and ambitious modernizing architects and engineers about the trend of modern invention and develop these artistically." Suggesting that "any technical school would have been delighted to supply sketches and suggestions for the aviation and transport of 2027 A.D.," Wells pragmatically cited the "masses of literature upon the organization of labor for efficiency that could have been boiled down at very small cost. The question of development of industrial control, the relation of industrial to political direction, the way all that is going, is of the liveliest current interest. Apparently the Ufa people did not know of these things and did not want to know of them. . . . After the worst traditions of the cinema world, monstrously self-satisfied and self-sufficient, convinced of the power of loud advertisement . . . they set to work in their huge studio to produce furlong after furlong of this ignorant old-fashioned balderdash and ruin the market for any better film along these lines."

In fact, Lang and UFA had done exactly what Wells wished they would have done: No less a publication than *Scientific American* commended Lang for having "consulted with prominent German industrialists and scientists" before creating his vision of the future, with which it recorded no quibbles. The evidently authoritarian editors of *Scientific American* especially appreciated Lang's touch of loudspeakers "constantly giving orders" to Metropolis's regimented work force. Wells, of course, confused a metaphorical conception of the present as future with a considered prediction of things to come. Despite his appreciation for scientific satire—amply demonstrated in *The Island of Dr. Moreau*—Wells by 1927 was showing little tolerance for anything other than utopian representations of science and technology. He summed up his distaste for German Romanticism—the wellspring of his own favored genre—succinctly: "Walpurgis Night is the name day of the German poetic imagination, and the national fantasy capers securely forever with a broomstick between its legs."

IN 1920S AMERICA national fantasies were considerably more streamlined and up-to-date. "The prestige of science was colossal," wrote historian Frederick Lewis Allen. "The man in the street and the woman in the kitchen, confronted on every hand with new machines and devices which they owed to the laboratory, were ready to believe that science could accomplish almost anything." The public was bombarded by scientific information, and misinformation, as if by cosmic rays. Science was everywhere.

> . . . a new dictum from Albert Einstein was now front page stuff though practically nobody could understand it. Outlines of knowledge poured from the presses to tell people about the planetismal hypothesis and the constitution of the atom, to describe for them in unwarranted detail the daily life of the caveman, and to acquaint them with electrons, endocrines, hormones, vitamins, and psychoses. . . . The word science had become a shibboleth. To preface a statement with "Science teaches us" was enough to silence argument. If a sales manager wanted to put over a promotional scheme or a clergyman to recommend a charity, they both hastened to say that it was scientific.

According to science historian Peter J. Kuznick, "Science's new prestige accrued largely from [the] close identification in the public mind with the prosperity of the 1920s, an identification scientists took pains to cultivate." The number of industrial research laboratories more than quadrupled in the 1920s, and while corporate and philanthropic grants for pure research also grew, the most important development was the employment surge of scientists into the private sector. By the mid-twenties, Kuznick notes, fully 70 percent of all chemists were employed by industry. Scientists, it seemed, wanted it both ways now: the mystique of the ivory tower and the perks of the corporate suite.

For the most part the commercialization of science was taken in stride, but there was the occasional cranky dissenter. In late 1927 the *New York Times* ran an article headlined WANTS 10-YEAR PAUSE IN SCIENTIST'S EFFORTS. In Leeds, England, the bishop of Ripon conducted a service attended largely by members of the British Association for the Advancement of Science. "With all his new mastery over nature," the bishop opined, "man has not seemed really to be advancing his own cause. . . . We could get on very much more happily if aviation, wireless, television and the like were advanced no further than at the present. "Dare I even suggest, at the risk of being lynched by some of my hearers, that the sum of human happiness, outside of scientific circles, would not necessarily be reduced if, for, say ten years, every physical and chemical laboratory were closed, and the patient and resourceful energy displayed in them transferred to finding a formula for making the ends meet in the scale of human life?"

Joseph Wood Krutch, in his 1929 book *The Modern Temper,* took a more measured approach to the same territory. In a chapter essay entitled "The Disillusion with the Laboratory," Krutch maintains that scientists, "impatient and a little scornful of the speculations, dreams, and fancies which have occupied the man ignorant of the laboratory and its marvels," labor under a delusion that they are dealing in the realm of truth and reality. But what is reality? In Krutch's observation, "the contact of the human mind with reality is so slight that two thousand years of epistemology have not been able to decide exactly what the nexus is, and it is easier to argue that our consciousness exists in utter isolation than to prove it is actually aware of the external phenomena by which it is surrounded." The most important aspect of our lives—"sensations, emotions, desires and aspirations—takes place in a universe of illusions which science can attenuate or destroy, but which it is powerless to enrich."

Science, to be sure, has sometimes imagined a wholly scientific man of the future, and the more thoroughgoing sort of scientist has sometimes predicted that the time would come when the world of the human mind would be precisely the world of the laboratory and nothing more. Conceiving a daily life far more thoroughly mechanized than that of today—of a society that sped through the air at incredible speed, that took its nourishment in the form of concentrated pellets and generated its children from selected seeds in an annealed glass womb—he has imagined a man possessed of a soul fit for such surroundings . . . the happy being to whom the roar of wheels will be the sweets melody and a laboratory the only tabernacle. . . .

By the late 1920s the American public had become familiar with flamboyant, if not slightly mad, visions of technologically transformed worlds in tabernacular periodicals like *Science and Invention* (fiction and nonfiction, founded in 1920) and *Amazing Stories* (fiction, founded in 1926), both edited by Hugo Gernsback (1884–1967), a Luxembourg-born devotee of Nikola Tesla (who privately commissioned a death mask of the inventor in 1944). Gernsback was an unabashed technophile, and his magazines, unlike the media of film and theater, put the most positive spin possible on all aspects of science and progress. But Gernsback's worldview remained distinctly out of step with the marching orders of popular culture. With the onset of the Great Depression, much pulp science fiction took a disturbing dystopian turn. In the meantime, it was left to the stage and screen to provide showcases for some of Tesla's most theatrical inventions.

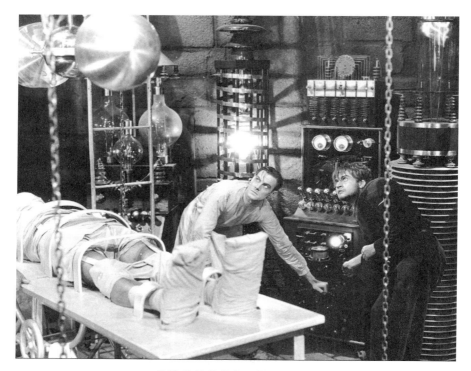

CHAPTER THREE

Snap, Crackle, Scream

Mary Shelley described, in the introduction to her revised edition of *Frankenstein,* a vision of "the working of some powerful engine" attending the birth of her monster. She couldn't have imagined Tesla's air coils and fire rings, nor could she have imagined the powerful cultural engine that came to be known as Hollywood. But Shelley had once seen her monster brought to life in the theater, and after nearly a half century of dor-

Colin Clive and Dwight Frye prepare to make a star of Boris Karloff in *Frankenstein* (1931).

mancy, the stage was about to rediscover her original melodrama and in the process give it the shock of its unnatural life.

Peggy Webling's *Frankenstein: An Adventure in the Macabre* was commissioned in 1928 by the British-Irish actor-manager Hamilton Deane as a repertory companion piece to his extraordinarily successful adaptation of *Dracula,* which had toured the provinces for three seasons before opening at London's Little Theatre in February 1927. *Frankenstein* took the same circuitous route to the West End, opening in early 1930, with Deane himself in the role of the monster.

Webling, a former child actress, novelist, and biographer of the saints, was the first *Frankenstein* dramatist to portray the monster as an aspect of its maker's personality. Indeed, she went to far as to name the *monster* Frankenstein, choosing the name Henry (rather than Shelley's Victor) for the scientist. (It is possible that Webling was influenced by the 1910 Thomas Edison film version of *Frankenstein,* in which the monster was similarly presented as a kind of psychological doppelgänger.) Webling deliberately plays with the confusion of names in the script:

EMILIE [Frankenstein's fiancé]: Who is the man concealed in that room? Henry, *who* is it?

HENRY: Stand back—I will make him be quiet—farther away—(he pushes her across the room, then unlocks and opens door left) Frankenstein!

EMILIE: *(in amazement)* Frankenstein? *(Frankenstein bursts into the room with Henry. They stand facing the girl in exactly the same attitude. She screams.)* Henry, who is this? You are both alike! I am afraid—let me go—let me go—! *(she rushes out. Henry follows her to the door.)*

Deane's performance was the most praised feature of the production, with a makeup that emphasized the monster's devolved simian characteristics. As Henry's friend Victor describes the creature's countenance, "It is the death mask of a strange, inhuman being. Look, doctor! Look at the great lips and the brow." Deane used heavy greasepaint in colors of blue, green, and red—the last intended to exaggerate the size of his lips and mouth. His monster generated considerably more pathos than any previous characterization. The following scene from Webling's 1928 script will be immediately identifiable as the source of a famous scene in the classic 1931 film. The monster is having a conversation with Henry Frankenstein's mentor, Dr. Waldman, about the disappearance of Henry's crippled younger sister, Katrina.

FRANKENSTEIN: *(bewildered)* She took me—*(points to door R.)* down to the boat. I—I—pushed it away from land. On the water. The leaves floated—like the bird—on the water—

WALDMAN: Go on! Go on! What then?

FRANKENSTEIN: *(with expressive gestures)* I took her—her hands. I—lifted her and laid her down—on the water *(looks at them vaguely)*

WALDMAN: Go on, Frankenstein.

FRANKENSTEIN: She held my hands—but I—shook her off. I—wanted to see her—like the bird—on the water. "Oh! Oh!" she cried. Then—I pressed her down—under the water. Beauty—beauty—her hair—her face—under the water.

WALDMAN: You held her under the water—ah!—

FRANKENSTEIN: Down—down—I held her a long time. A long time. Then—then—I took her out. She was still—still—like that!

When Henry refuses to provide him with a bride, the monster kills his maker, and delivers a final speech:

FRANKENSTEIN: *(gasping)* Shall each man have his wife—each beast his mate—and I be alone. I killed him—because he robbed me—of all *she* would have given me. All men hate me—and now—I hate myself. *(looks down at Henry)* He is dead who brought me to life, and I—shall be dead soon—and find—God. Rest! Rest! Dead—very soon—soon—rest—rest—*(he groans and moves blindly toward the centre doors. There is a vivid flash of lightning that strikes him and he falls, instantly, shattered. A terrific roll of thunder. Waldman stands immovable, gazing at Henry's dead body.)*

Although the play did not match the commercial success of *Dracula,* it immediately attracted the attention of the flamboyant American publisher-producer Horace Liveright and playwright John L. Balderston, who had previously joined forces to adapt Deane's *Dracula* for Broadway. Plans were announced, with fanfare, for Deane to repeat his performance in New York in early 1931.

At the height of Deane's euphoria over the prospect of a transatlantic transfiguration of his star vehicle, he gave a fascinating interview on "The Technique of Terror" to the the British theatrical trade publication the *Era*.

The interviewer asked Deane where he had learned the technique of the thriller. "What first got me interested in the manufacture of stage shockers was the Grand Guignol in New York.* When I was over there I was a constant visitor at the theatre where it was given. They put over some of the most amazing thrills I have ever seen. . . . The subtler points of a thriller may not always be appreciated by professional critics, but, believe me, the general public responds to them extraordinarily quickly."

According to Deane, the best way to get the "leaven of terror" working in an audience "is through a process of suggestion. In *Dracula* we did nothing actually scarifying on the stage; we merely suggested something horrible, and that suggestion, once it had soaked into the minds of the audience, caused a bigger reaction than the placing of a mechanical thrill before them could have done."

In Deane's production of *Frankenstein* "the preparation of the audience for the shock we wish to give . . . has to be effected gradually. If the inert figure of the monster came to life a few moments after the rise of the curtain, the proper 'punch' would be lacking. But by using a few of the legitimate tricks of the theatre, of which the chief one is suspense, we manage, I think, to build up that atmosphere in which it is possible to create the maximum sensation."

Deane predicted that the "thriller of the future will be entirely on the

---

*The world-famous Théâtre du Grand Guignol of Paris had a New York season in 1923, to which Deane is probably referring here. In addition, English-language adaptations of the Grand Guignol repertory were presented by Sybil Thorndike at London's Little Theatre in 1920, which no doubt also came to Deane's attention. He borrowed Thorndike's promotional gimmick of stationing a nurse in the lobby for his own staging of *Dracula,* beginning in 1924.

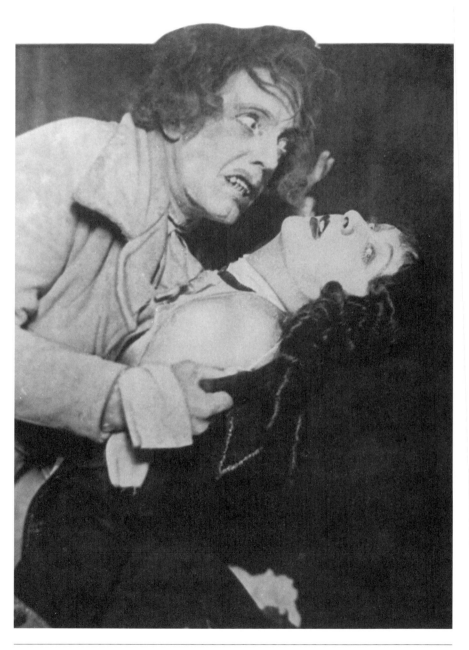

Hamilton Deane and Kathleen Grace in Peggy Webling's *Frankenstein: An Adventure in the Macabre* (1930). *Free Library of Philadelphia Theatre Collection.*

mental plane. . . . The public taste is for subtler methods. In the best Grand Guignol, the horror always comes from the minds of the audience, and very seldom from actual happenings on the stage. Scenes of torture, imitation blood, and other clap-trap of the Parisian Grand Guignol don't thrill the average playgoer; they are more inclined to make him laugh. But get at his imagination, set it working along certain lines, and you stand a better chance of awakening terror. . . ."

Unfortunately, Deane clashed repeatedly with producer Liveright over script and directorial matters and withdrew from the project. Liveright replaced Deane with the noted character actor Lyn Harding (who had just appeared with Raymond Massey in the 1930 British film version of A. Conan Doyle's Sherlock Holmes story "The Speckled Band"), but the entire project fell through when Liveright—who also became convinced that he could persuade Universal to let him personally direct a film version—was unable to raise production funds. Webling and Balderston sold the screen rights directly to Universal Pictures, which had just scored a major hit with *Dracula* and was eager to film *Frankenstein* without the intervening delay of a stage production. Through their agent, Harold Freedman, the two sold *Frankenstein* for a purchase price of twenty thousand dollars plus 1 percent of the world receipts. Without his option, Horace Liveright was left begging for crumbs. As with *Dracula,* Liveright and his theatrical manager, Louis Cline,

Peggy Webling, author of *Frankenstein: An Adventure in the Macabre.*

finally signed a quitclaim relinquishing all rights to their contributions to the script for a flat 1 percent of Balderston's and Webling's advance—one thousand dollars apiece. The ultimate irony was that the final screenplay would make at least as much use of Liveright's and Cline's material as of Balderston's and Webling's.

Having secured the film rights, however, the studio promptly lost interest in the stage play. While perverse and not a little wasteful, this was not an unusual move; it was necessary for legal reasons for Universal to have free title to the property, but once it had been won, the realpolitik of the studio system took over.

Richard Schayer, head of Universal's scenario department, had the first crack at a script but had completed only half a screenplay by May 1931. The ball then landed with Garrett Fort, a chubby, bespectacled screenwriter who had scored a hit with his shooting script for *Dracula* and so was considered a natural for the assignment. Fort worked with the input of a young director new at Universal, the thirty-year-old Robert Florey, a transplanted Frenchman who had received positive attention for his codirection of the Marx Brothers' classic *The Cocoanuts* at Paramount in 1929 and who was being considered for the directorial slot on *Frankenstein.*

Florey was deeply interested in the techniques of European expressionism and fantasy; as a boy in Paris he had visited the workshop of the legendary Georges Méliès as he developed the cinema's basic vocabulary of special effects, and he was well acquainted with moody aesthetic of silent era classics like *The Cabinet of Dr. Caligari* (1920), *The Golem* (1920), and *Nosferatu* (1922). Richard Schayer had approached Florey to submit some ideas for *Frankenstein,* which was then conceived as a vehicle for Bela Lugosi, to follow his international success in *Dracula.* The world was still waiting for a "new Lon Chaney," and Lugosi was the leading contender, at least for the moment.

Florey assumed that Lugosi would play the role of Henry Frankenstein and submitted a five-page synopsis from which Garrett Fort developed a complete screenplay. The full extent of Florey's collaboration with Fort cannot be ascertained; in his later years Florey contended it was substantial, but Fort received sole billing on the script. (A copy of the script that Florey circulated to fan-collectors in the 1970s contains a bogus title page, giving Florey a grandiose credit.)

Whatever the contributions of either man, the Fort-Florey script for *Frankenstein* provided a nearly finished structure for the produced film, as well as much of the now-familiar dialogue. The story opens with Frankenstein (here named Henry, as in the Webling-Balderston versions) and his dwarf assistant, Fritz (after Liveright-Cline; the character here is still mute), robbing graves and scavenging from gallows to assemble the raw materials for Frankenstein's great experiment. Fritz steals a brain from the medical school of Frankenstein's former teacher, Dr. Waldman, unaware that the brain is that of a violent criminal. During a raging thunderstorm a concerned Waldman and Victor Moritz (Frankenstein's friend and rival for the attention of his fiancée, Elizabeth) interrupt Frankenstein in the old windmill he has outfitted as a laboratory, just as he is about to animate the patchwork corpse he has assembled. The experiment is a success. "It's alive!" Henry cries giddily. "Now I know how it feels to be God!"

His creation, however, is a vicious brute that must be kept in chains like a wild animal. The monster kills Fritz and is sedated by Frankenstein and Waldman. Waldman is killed when the monster wakes unexpectedly as he prepares to dissect it. The creature goes on a cold-blooded rampage, slaughtering a peasant couple after watching them make love and killing a small girl who innocently offers him a flower. Henry and Elizabeth's wedding day is interrupted by news of the murders; Frankenstein guiltily joins the manhunt, during which he is attacked by the monster himself and dragged back to the old windmill. The posse surrounds the mill, and the father of the murdered girl fatally shoots Frankenstein as he tries to leap to safety. The monster hurls its maker's body down at the mob, who torch the mill and bring the creature's reign of terror to a fiery conclusion.

In its attempt to create a "star" part for Bela Lugosi, the Fort-Florey script subverted the intentions of the stage play, in which the monster was the key role. But Fort and Florey jettisoned any sense of pathos, reducing the monster to a grunting beast in order to save prime screen time for the real star—Henry Frankenstein. Therefore, it must have come as shock to all concerned that the front office decided that Bela Lugosi should play the *monster,* not the scientist.

In retrospect, one can half understand the studio's strategy. Universal was eager to groom a successor to Lon Chaney, and Chaney mystique was dependent on grotesque and elaborate makeup effects. In addition, Lugosi was a year short of fifty years old (and touchy about it—he was known to have misrepresented his age while working on the New York stage), with a cumbersome Hungarian accent that made him distinctly a character type, not a leading man. The actor was less than pleased with the decision and fumed at the prospect of a mute role (in the days of early talkies this must have seemed especially insulting) with his features obliterated by putty and paint.

Florey was asked to shoot some test footage with Lugosi as the monster and the actors Edward Van Sloan (Lugosi's nemesis Van Helsing in *Dracula*) and Dwight Frye (*Dracula*'s fly-eating Renfield) as Waldman and Fritz, with the roles of Henry and Victor taken by unrecorded contract players. The test for *Frankenstein* has apparently been lost forever, but it continues to generate speculation and debate in film circles, especially because of the maddeningly contradictory recollections of the people directly involved (all now dead). The point that stirs the most curiosity and impassioned opinion: Exactly what did Bela Lugosi look like in his test makeup for the monster?

The man most directly responsible for the monster's appearance was a diminutive forty-two-year-old former jockey and semiprofessional shortstop from Chicago named Jack Piccolo Pierce, who had drifted into film work in 1910, when his dreams of playing ball in the Coast League were dashed because of his smallness. First a nickelodeon projectionist, then a theater manager, Pierce moved to the production side of the business in 1914 as an actor and assistant cameraman. He had a distinct talent for making up and lighting performers, a skill spectacularly showcased in an ape-man disguise for Fox Films' *The Monkey Talks* in 1926. The following year he was appointed chief of makeup for Universal, where he devised a death's-head grin for Conrad Veidt in the studio's lavish adaptation of Victor Hugo's *The Man Who Laughs* (1928). The *New York Times* described Veidt as "a gnarled little Nibelung gnome of a fellow . . . a perfect bit of type casting" for his role of monster-midwife.

During the filming of *Dracula* Pierce had relented to a stubborn Bela Lugosi's insistence on applying his own makeup, as he had done onstage; this time, however, the task was so complex that Lugosi had no choice other than submit to Pierce's will, at least theoretically. But "Lugosi had too many ideas of his own, which didn't coincide with those of the producer," Pierce said in a 1966 fan magazine interview. "Lugosi thought his ideas were better than better than anybody's." One must wonder if Lugosi's headstrong "ideas" weren't calculated from the outset to get him out of the assignment. As his widow, Lillian Lugosi Donleavy, told film historian Gregory William Mank in 1976, "Bela wanted out! He said, 'I'll get a doctor's excuse.' . . . [H]e couldn't see himself moaning and grunting."

But Lugosi had no difficulty moaning about the indignity of the test and makeup, and he did so endlessly. Florey recalled: "As I was working with the other actors, during a time when the monster had not yet 'come to life,' Lugosi kept exclaiming, 'Enough is enough;' that he was not going to be a grunting, babbling idiot for anybody and that any tall extra could be the monster. 'I was a star in my country and I will not be a scarecrow over here,' he said repeatedly."

The script described the "scarecrow's" features as "chalkily white and expressionless—moulded so as to be just a trifle out of proportion, something just this side of human—but that narrow margin is sufficient to make it insidiously horrible." But what actually found its way into the lost screen test—and onto Lugosi's face—remains tantalizingly elusive. Cameraman Paul Ivano, who photographed the test reel, wrote a partial description in a letter published in 1970: "[Pierce's] makeup included not only the face, but also a false cranium that flattened the top of the head," which was held together by "hinges" and a "screw projecting from each side of the neck." According to Ivano, Lugosi's costume included heavy elevated shoes. "After several weeks of corrections, changes, and modifications, such as new makeup for the hands, Laemmle and Florey found agreement," Ivano says. The script had called for the monster to possess hands without fingernails that shed the blackness of death as the creature came to life. This effect, if filmed, would have been achieved through the use of blue to red color filters, undetectable on black-and-white film.

Boris Karloff, the actor who ultimately inherited the role, told interviewers in 1966 that he had not personally seen the Lugosi test footage, "but I was once told that he insisted on doing his makeup himself—and did this awful hairy creature, not at all like our Monster." The *Los Angeles Record* ran a humorous item in reporting that Lugosi's monster makeup—utilizing multicolored greasepaint in "stripes, streaks, and striations"—kept melting

I MADE HIM! . . . I MADE HIM WITH MY OWN HANDS !!

. . . and I gave him everything a man could have
. . . except a soul !

. . . the wild, weird wonderful tale of the man
who made a monster
and was consumed by
his own creation . . .

. . . a creature doomed
to aimless havoc . . .
without conscience . . .
without pity . . . with-
out remorse . . .
without love !

You hate it . . . fear it
. . . yet it wrings your
heart with pity !

CARL LAEMMLE
presents

FRANKENSTEIN

-- THE MAN WHO MADE A MONSTER

A FRIENDLY WARNING

If you have a weak heart and cannot stand intense excite-
ment or even shock, we advise you NOT to see this production.
If, on the contrary, you like an unusual thrill, you will find it in
''FRANKENSTEIN''

**COLIN CLIVE • MAE CLARKE • JOHN BOLES
BORIS KARLOFF • Dwight Frye • Edward Van
Sloan • Frederic Kerr. Directed by JAMES WHALE**
Produced by Carl Laemmle, Jr. From the story by Mary Wollstonecraft
Shelley. Adapted by John L. Balderston from the play by Peggy Webling.

A UNIVERSAL SUPER ATTRACTION

Advertisement for *Frankenstein* (1931). *Courtesy of Scott MacQueen.*

under the hot sun during the journey between makeup chair and sound stage, leaving the actor looking more clownish than corpselike. Edward Van Sloan, who acted in the test, stated in 1964 that Lugosi wore a broad wig that dramatically exaggerated the size of his head ("four times normal size") and "polished, clay-like skin." Partial descriptions of Lugosi's makeup suggest an eclectic blending of earlier film and stage monsters: the Edison version ("awful, hairy"), the golem ("clay-like skin" and a "broad wig"), and Hamilton Deane's theatrical approach (greasepaint and "striations")

Nevertheless, Florey maintained until the end of his life that Lugosi, Karloff, and several other actors all tested in "identical" or "similar" Pierce makeups (he stopped short, however, of stating that any of these test makeups actually matched the one that finally appeared in the film). Florey himself took credit for suggesting the electrode bolts in the creature's neck, details now so famous that they alone can conjure the monster in the absence of any other makeup or costuming. But Florey's claims seem to be contradicted by producer Carl Laemmle, Jr. (then the studio's twenty-one-year-old heir apparent), who stated that he "laughed like a hyena" upon seeing the Lugosi test makeup—hardly a credible response to the stark, subtle, unforgettable makeup actually used.

Almost every published account of Lugosi's refusal to play the part of the monster interprets his decision as evidence of fatal vanity coupled with a spectacularly bad business sense. Somehow "he should have known" what a hit the film would be, what a cultural icon the monster would become. But this argument overlooks the fact that the role as originally written was a lousy part for an actor and indeed could have been played by an extra. The monster had been given a kind of half-life on the page but not yet a soul. And even if the subtlety had been present in the screenplay, it is an open question whether Lugosi's broadly operatic acting style would have been appropriate.

"I made up for the role and had tests taken, which were pronounced O.K.," Lugosi told a press interviewer in 1935. "Then I read the script, which I didn't like. So I asked to be withdrawn from the picture. Carl Laemmle [Jr.] said he'd permit it, if I'd furnish an actor to play the part." While Universal had a legendary reputation for informality in business matters, the idea that it would entrust a major casting assignment to a temperamental contract player stretches credulity. Nonetheless, Lugosi claimed that he "scouted the agencies—and came upon Boris Karloff. I recommended him. He took tests. And that's how he happened to become a famous star of horror pictures—my rival, in fact."

Whether or not Lugosi "discovered" Karloff—another dubious proposition—the forty-three-year-old English character actor came into the project shortly after Laemmle decided that *Frankenstein* would be better entrusted to other hands than Robert Florey's. He offered any script under development to James Whale, a celebrated British stage director who had come to Hollywood's attention for his staging of *Journey's End,* which he also directed as a film for Tiffany Studios in 1930. The success of *Journey's End* led to a five-year contract with Universal, beginning with *Waterloo Bridge* (1931), based on the play by Robert E. Sherwood. Again, the theme was the Great War, during which a wounded American soldier falls impossibly in love with a London prostitute.

Whale was not particularly excited about directing *Frankenstein* but considered the assignment, in part, because it wasn't another war picture. His only previous sojourns into the macabre had been not as a director but as an actor at London's Little Theatre, where both *Dracula* and *Frankenstein* had been produced by Hamilton Deane; Whale had parts in the chilling melodrama *A Man with Red Hair* (1928), which established Charles Laughton as a leading character actor, and the following year in an evening of Grand Guignol plays. Whale had taken the singular role of an unjustly executed man whose head is kept alive by a laboratory machine long enough to confront his executioners with their miscarriage of justice.

Whale didn't know what to think of *Frankenstein.* "At first I thought it was a gag," he later told the *New York Herald Tribune.* He took a copy of the Shelley novel home to his lover, David Lewis (with whom he lived openly), to get an opinion. Lewis, then a story reader and later a producer, found the novel interesting but "weird." But under Junior Laemmle's persistent prodding, Whale took the assignment. Robert Florey and his intended cameraman, Karl Freund (who had shot *Dracula* and *Metropolis*), were quickly assigned to commit *Murders in the Rue Morgue* to the screen as a starring—and very talkative—vehicle for Bela Lugosi.

Several actors were tested for the part, though no official record was made of their names. John Carradine, then working in Hollywood under the name of John Peter Richmond, claimed in his later years (without evidence) to have been one of those tested and that he turned down the part for much the same reason as Lugosi. Sensing that director Whale was at sea with the casting, David Lewis asked if he had considered Boris Karloff, whose performance as a convict in the gangster melodrama *The Criminal Code* at Columbia had struck Lewis as a powerful piece of work.

Born William Henry Pratt in Camberwell, England, the actor had made nearly eighty films since his screen debut as an extra in *The Dumb Girl of Portici* in 1916 but was still essentially unknown in the public mind. Karloff (the origin of the name is obscure; the actor claimed it was a family name on his mother's side, but no biographer has discovered evidence of this) was the youngest of eight children in a family of career diplomats and something of the black sheep of the lot. Billy, as he was called, first acted at the age of nine, in a school production of *Cinderella.* Karloff said he decided to be an actor at that moment, and the role he played—the Demon King— foreshadowed the ultimate course of his career.

Karloff emigrated in 1909 to Canada, where he lived hand to mouth, working as both a laborer and actor. He applied for permanent American residence in 1913 (he never became an U.S. citizen, however). By 1930 Karloff was being cast regularly in small parts, often as heavies "outside the law"; his role as a convict in *The Criminal Code,* which had so impressed David Lewis, was followed by the part of a murderer in *Graft* at Universal. Whale introduced himself to Karloff in the studio commissary. Over the years Karloff (and others) recounted the encounter with many variations of details; following is Cynthia Lindsay's version from her anecdotal biography *Dear Boris.* Whale, said Karloff, asked me to sit down. I did, holding my breath, and then he said: 'Your face has startling possibilities. . . .' I cast my eyes down modestly, and then he said, 'I'd like you to test for the monster in *Frankenstein.'* It was shattering—for the first time in my life I had been gainfully employed long enough to buy myself some new clothes and spruce up a bit—actually, I rather fancied myself! Now, to hide all this newfound beauty under monster makeup?"

Whale knew that he had his man, though Karloff's "physique was weaker than I could wish, but that queer, penetrating personality of his, I felt, was more important than his shape, which could easily be altered." Karloff, who was thin and bow-legged—he had suffered from rickets as a child—indeed required some padding; in classical stage roles he always wore "symmetricals," or padded undertights, to fill out his legs. Refinements of the test makeup continued; Whale said he found Karloff's face fascinating and made sketches of his own.

Although Jack Pierce has been given the lion's share of credit for the monster's appearance, there are indications that Whale himself was largely responsible. For one thing, the makeup (like that of the monster's bride four years later, another Whale/Pierce collaboration) is obviously influenced by modernist trends in the theater and visual arts—notably expressionism, constructivism, and the machine aesthetic generally. Though he was indisputably a gifted technician, there is no record that Pierce was influenced by or had any particular interest in modern art; none of his other celebrated monster creations—the Mummy, the Wolf Man, etc.—display even a glimmer of cultural metaphor. Whale, however, was himself an amateur painter, and was fully steeped in the professional theater. His late 1920s companion and lifelong friend Doris Zinkeisen was both a set designer (Čapek's *The Insect Play* [1924]) and, in collaboration with her sister, a graphic artist responsible for innumerable machine-age murals and advertisements featuring theatrically stylized human forms. In Los Angeles, the summer he was assigned to *Frankenstein,* Whale could have easily seen Adolph Bolm's constructivist *The Spirit of the Factory* at the Hollywood Bowl, with its starkly angular costumes and choreography.

Since the advent of modern latex prosthetics was still decades away, the rectangular brow of the monster had to be painstakingly built up each day with layers of cheesecloth and collodion. To increase the cadaverous appearance, Karloff removed some bridgework from the right side of his mouth, creating an additional hollow. One photograph of near-final makeup survives, featuring tapering, almost machine-tooled protuberances embedded with a pair of decorative metal rings. Karloff claimed that the heavy-lidded eyes (built up by layers of wax) were his own invention, suggested as a way of

Science versus domesticity: Boris Karloff disrupts Mae Clarke's wedding plans in *Frankenstein* (1931).

keeping the creature from looking too wide-awake. Invisible wire clamps widened and pulled down the corners of his mouth. Karloff's makeup, costume, padding, back brace, and weighted boots weighed nearly fifty pounds.

"Removing the make-up was not much easier than putting it on," wrote British film journalist Helen Weigel Brown. "First the eyelids came off—most painful, to say the least, and enough to inspire any quantity of questionable language. The deep scar in the monster's forehead was then pried into as a good starting point, and from then it was just one pry and push and acid soaking after another until Boris was himself again."

With Whale's probable input, the *Frankenstein* script was delivered into its nearly finished form by screenwriter John Russell, who added the plot twist of Frankenstein's assistant's accidentally dropping a normal brain and substituting a criminal one. (This of course amounted to a major subversion of Shelley's intended moral; it is not Henry's divine presumption that sets in motion the catastrophe, but a deception and cover-up by a handicapped employee.) Veteran scenarist Francis Edwards Faragoh contributed the most important finishing touches, significantly tightening the dialogue (as well as creating dialogue for the hitherto speechless Fritz), and, most important, going back to the Balderston-Webling play and Shelley novel to reinstate the crucial element of pity for the monster. The previous script treated the monster's encounter with a little girl as virtually a cutaway rape; the final screenplay combined the scene with the stage play's accidental drowning of Katrina, who the monster believes will float like leaves on the surface of the lake. Although the creature remained mute in the shooting script, the pathos was made all the more acute and utterly transformed the character.

Whale made several modifications to the approved shooting script. The creation scene originally featured a gleamingly modern operating table, surrounded by vacuum tubing, that rose to a height of fifteen feet on telescoping hydraulic legs. In the finished film the table is hoisted on ropes through the ceiling, rather like a piece of "flown" stage scenery—perhaps another directorial homage to the theater. And one of the picture's most memorable speeches, Henry Frankenstein's wistful musing about the mystery of what turns night into day, or life into death, does not appear in the script and was presumably added during production.

Mae Clarke, cast as Frankenstein's fiancée, Elizabeth, remembered

Karloff "towering over the tall Mr. Whale, listening meekly as an obedient child, both so softly spoken I couldn't hear a word—then he'd nod his head and Whale would give him an affectionate push at his enormous hanging arms and call out, 'Ready for camera.' "

Karloff recalled in 1965 that "Whale and I both saw the creature as an innocent one. Within the heavy restrictions of my make-up, I tried to play it that way." Karloff considered the monster "a pathetic creature who, like us all, had neither wish nor say in his creation and certainly did not wish upon itself the hideous image which automatically terrified humans whom it tried to befriend." What astonished both Karloff and the director were "the fantastic numbers of ordinary people that got this general air of sympathy. I found all my letters heavy with it. Many also wanted to offer help and friendship. It was one of the most moving experiences of my life."

In the role of Henry Frankenstein, Whale cast Colin Clive, an edgy but brilliant English actor who had been unforgettable in the stage and film versions of *Journey's End* as a tortured, alcoholic World War I captain. The pain and turmoil of Clive's characterization may have had some basis in his own unhappy life: R. C. Sherriff, the playwright, recalled how during tense London rehearsals for *Journey's End* he had suggested the actor try taking a couple of stiff drinks before the run-through. The results pleased everyone, but Sherriff may have unwittingly handed Clive a crutch he should have avoided; within a few years, like Horace Liveright, he was on a fatal collision course with alcohol.

The "powerful engine" to which Mary Shelley had alluded in 1830 found a spectacular realization in 1931 through the Tesla-inspired constructions of Hollywood technician Kenneth Strickfaden. For *Frankenstein,* Strickfaden concocted a snap, crackle, scream display of writhing electrical arcs along with inoperative yet convincing pops fashioned from industrial salvage. Strickfaden kept all the equipment in his garage in Santa Monica and profitably leased it back to Universal for its sequel *Frankenstein* films.*

Frankenstein's method of imbuing his creation with life had been con-

---

*The buzzing gadgets made their final screen appearance in Mel Brooks's 1974 comedy *Young Frankenstein.*

siderably modernized from the alchemical elixir employed in Peggy Webling's dramatization. Cosmic rays were a hot topic in popular science during the late 1920s and early 1930s, the subject of countless magazine and newspaper articles. Accordingly, in the film Colin Clive announces to his mentor, Dr. Waldman (Edward Van Sloan), "I learned a great deal from you at the university—about the violet ray, the *ultra*violet ray, which you said was the highest color in the spectrum. You were wrong. Here in this machinery, I have gone beyond that. I have discovered the great ray that first brought life into the world!" In the wake of the film, commercial bunko involving "cosmic rays" reached its own critical mass; one 1932 product, the Bioray, was hawked as a kind of radioactive air freshener, promising to bathe the user in a constant stream of benevolent, health-restorative gamma radiation.

Frankenstein began shooting at Universal City on August 24 and wrapped on October 3, 1931. (Curiously, the filming coincided with the long deathwatch for electrical wizard and onetime *Frankenstein* producer Thomas Edison. In late summer Edison's doctors announced that he had only days to live, but he stubbornly clung to life for weeks, as if in a miraculous demonstration of Lazarus-like powers.) At a final cost of $291,000, the picture ran about $30,000 over budget. But any studio displeasure that may have arisen over the cost was dispelled the following month, when late-November screenings of the film made it clear that Universal had a major hit on its hands. Like *Dracula* earlier in the year, *Frankenstein* seemed to tap the public's need to confront images of dread during what turned out to be the most dreadful year of the Great Depression. A general anxiety about the prospects of resurrecting a dead economy was curiously refracted in the back-from-the-grave themes of both films.

The *New York Times'* Mordaunt Hall called the film "stirring" and "artistically conceived," reporting that it "aroused so much excitement at the Mayfair yesterday that many in the audience laughed to cover their true feelings." *Frankenstein* became a major holiday attraction around the country, opening for Thanksgiving in many cities and closer to Christmas elsewhere. Universal spared no promotional effort to drum up audiences. Andrew J. Sharick, who oversaw the campaign, recalled the Chicago engagement, where "[w]e invited people to sit through the film at midnight.

We got a boy and a girl student from the University of Chicago in there before breakfast and hitched up their pulses to a lie detector. It made the front page on the Chicago Daily News. We paid a babe to sit all night in a cemetery after seeing the picture, and then recount her experiences."

The reviews across the country were almost uniformly raves. Objections of state censor boards—primarily to Frankenstein's exultant "Now I know what it feels like to be God!" and the killing of the little girl—only fueled press coverage and public interest. But the box-office success of the picture obscured a number of legitimate problems with the film, which even today is regarded with perhaps excessive critical reverence. While Universal's *Frankenstein* undeniably gave birth to an indelible cultural icon in the form of Karloff's monster—an image as instantly recognizable around the world as Lugosi's Dracula, Chaplin's tramp, Santa Claus, or Mickey Mouse—the film itself has often been carelessly overpraised in the intervening six decades. But a close examination of newspaper morgues and microfilm vaults reveal many examples of clearheaded and skeptical appraisals of Whale's film at the time of its first release. The *Cleveland Plain Dealer* expressed surprise at being able to "count the wrinkles on the cyclorama" (a backdrop meant to represent the sky and clouds) during the climactic chase scenes. In truth, one can only wonder at the inattention, cynicism, or budget pressures that allowed the sky not only to lower but actually to sag. Reviewer Rob Wagner noted: "After seeing *London* [*sic*] *Bridge* I expected great things of James Whale, but his direction of *Frankenstein* is ridiculously old-fashioned. His crowd scenes look as artificial as grand opera, especially when the villagers set out with torches and clubs to hunt the monster amid the papier-mache mountains." Wagner noted the improbability of a windmill on the top of a mountain—windmills, for reasons of practical necessity, are always built in valleys—and decried the "Mack Sennett scare-sequence gags." In Britain the *Era* critic G. A. Atkinson commented on the film's racial overtones: "The narrative degenerates through rapid stages into a brutal and debasing man-hunt, ending with the incineration of the monster in a windmill, almost as if it were a Georgia lynching, which, in fact, the chase strongly resembles. The parallel may be unkind, but it is irresistible." Atkinson also commented acerbically on Whale's new career track: " 'Frankenstein' seriously imperils the artistic

The London premiere of *Frankenstein* (1931).

reputation which Mr. Whale has built up in Hollywood. It has been assumed, a little rashly, that he had conquered the Hollywood 'Frankenstein monster' of machine-made conventions, but his latest effort is as Hollywooden in conception as anything we have seen . . . a catalogue of crude horrors, without a single spiritual idea, and as destitute of imaginative insight as a brick."

The rarefied opinions of the *Era* carried little weight in Hollywood, of course, and Carl Laemmle, Sr., was far more interested in the public response than to even his own original reaction. Despite his initial opposition to his son's interest in horror movies, Laemmle, Sr. (or, more likely, one of his publicists), called *Frankenstein* "the best thing that happened to the trade" in 1931:

In the first place, it was the outstanding money maker of the year. That certainly is important. In the second place, it was that distinctly "something different" which the industry is always looking for and which does so much to stimulate interest. "Frankenstein" enlisted the interest of many persons whose attention in the cinema was flagging and caught the interest of many new patrons. Third, it successfully demonstrated the feasibility of the return of action photography as contrasted with dialogue. It has been hailed everywhere as the most effective combination of the two and a model for the future.

Even before *Frankenstein* had been finished, Universal started to develop more mad science properties. On September 17, 1931, Francis Edward Faragoh submitted a complete script for *Murders in the Rue Morgue* that wildly expanded on Poe's detective story of a brutal Paris murder that is finally discovered to be the work of an ape. Poe, of course, had neglected to include a mad doctor in his story, but Faragoh happily made up for the Hollywood deficiency. In a part tailored from the start for Lugosi, Faragoh named his caped madman Dr. Ramey and had him operate a traveling wax museum and freak show as a front for his evolutionary experiments. "My fame is great," he tells a visitor to his tent. "I am the creator of the bird-boy, of the two-headed dog, of a thousand and one amazing, stupendous monsters. . . . But my new handiwork will be greater than any of them! That's why I needed these women . . . that's why they've had to die . . . for science . . . for my secret . . . to produce a new freak . . . the crowning glory of my career!" The precise nature of this freak is not revealed until the end. It is a new female being, carrying within her human and simian blood: "A freak greater than any ever created! Ape-woman! Ape-girl!"

Bela Lugosi in *Murders in the Rue Morgue* (1932). *Courtesy of Ronald V. Borst/Hollywood Movie Posters.*

Faragoh's concepts were toned down considerably, and while many of his atmospheric concepts were used in *Rue Morgue*, he did not receive screen billing. The screenplay was credited to Tom Reed and Dale Van Every, with additional dialogue by Hollywood newcomer John Huston. Lugosi's character was renamed Dr. Mirakle (perhaps as a nod to Dr. Miracle in *The Tales of Hoffmann*), and his traveling chamber of horrors was streamlined to a single exhibit: Erik, the ape, displayed in a Caligari-style tent to anxious Parisians at the dawn of Darwinism. Because the specific goals of Mirakle's blood experiments are not revealed, the audience is free to imagine a good deal more than mere transfusions. As *Variety* noted, "it can be easily assumed by any auditor that the doc's idea is to mate the women with the ape. But nobody can prove it, or bluntly declare that to be the purpose." Florey's direction provides intriguing clues to the high-expressionist sensibility and visuals he would have brought to *Frankenstein*. In particular, Karl Freund's camerawork in *Rue Morgue* (which utilizes some of the sets from *Frankenstein*) is far more evocative, ambitious, and theatrical than Arthur Edeson's very competent, but extremely conventional, photography of *Frankenstein*.

By 1932, when *Rue Morgue* was released, Depression era pop culture was awash with atavistic themes often paradoxically connected to advanced "science." Audiences may well have responded to such stories as fractured reflections of a devolving economy, in which quasi-Darwinian economic forces were brutally unleashed on large segments of the population.

A few weeks after the release of *Frankenstein,* Rouben Mamoulian's *Dr. Jekyll and Mr. Hyde* hit the theaters with an Academy Award–winning performance by Fredric March. For the first time Mr. Hyde was presented as an outright Neanderthal who becomes even more apelike as the film unreels. Standard readings of the film pick up the visceral evolutionary jitters, shrewdly juxtaposed against uncommonly elegant production values. But in retrospect the film also hints, semiconsciously, at the bitter, widening socioeconomic divisions of the early Depression. In a provocative contemporary assessment of Mamoulian's film, Annalee Newitz views Jekyll and Hyde's bifurcation as "a nightmare of [the] class consciousness" constructed by the Depression and emerging New Deal policies of 1932 presidential candidate Franklin Roosevelt. The prospect of reconciliation between haves and have-nots becomes problematic and scary as Dr. Jekyll's initially philanthropic contact with the lower classes (represented by the dance hall prostitute Ivy,

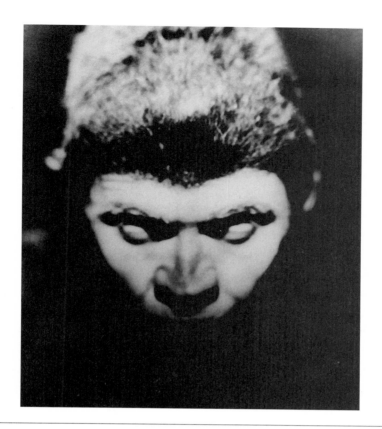

The dark side of Fredric March, in *Dr. Jekyll and Mr. Hyde* (1931). *Courtesy of David De Valle/The Del Valle Archive.*

played by Miriam Hopkins) only manages to bring out the beast. "Hyde arouses the liberal audience's worst fears about class consciousness," Newitz writes. "Rather than allowing Jekyll to experience a new sense of community and social awareness, Hyde forces Jekyll to perform criminal, even primitive, acts already associated with proletarian culture."

Though not connected explicitly to evolutionary science, the moral degeneracy of the villainess in Tod Browning's *Freaks* (1932) culminates in her brutal transformation into a legless "duck woman" by a band of sideshow freaks who also wear feathers, scamper near the ground, and wriggle in the mud. In *Chandu the Magician* (1932), the mad genius Roxor (Bela Lugosi, after *Dracula* forever an avatar of the civilized facade that covers the basest of instincts), intent on world domination with a death ray machine, is bestial and predatory in direct relationship to his access to advanced technology.

"At last, I am king of them all!" Roxor exults. "That lever [of the death ray] is my scepter. London, New York, Imperial Rome—I can blast them all into a heap of smoking ruins! Cities of the world shall perish. All that lives shall know me as master, and tremble at my word!" Boris Karloff's portrayal of the mad mandarin in *The Mask of Fu Manchu* also employs gleaming scientific marvels (including some of Kenneth Strickfaden's electrical gadgetry from *Frankenstein*) to advance his most brutish impulses.

The third annual meeting of the International Congress of Eugenics, held at the American Museum of Natural History in New York City in late August 1932, demonstrated that fears about devolutionary brutishness were hardly the province of Hollywood. Charles Darwin's son, Major Leonard Darwin, sent a message to the conferees apologizing for the fact that at the age of eighty-two, he was too biologically infirm to attend. But he vigorously put forth his "firm conviction" that "if widespread eugenic reforms are not adopted during the next hundred years or so, our Western civilization is inevitably destined to such a slow and gradual decay as that which has been experienced in the past by every great ancient civilization. The size and importance of the United States throws [*sic*] on you a special responsibility in your endeavors to safeguard the future of our race." On the same page of the *New York Times,* a doctor in attendance at the same Atlantic City convention urged "biological investigation" on an international level of all immigrants for "recessive characteristics."

Film critic Robert Sherwood, writing in early 1932, reflected a general exasperation with incomprehensible scientific pronouncements and technological displays. He told his newspaper column readers: "It will be quite satisfactory with me if I don't see another chemical laboratory on screen during the next decade." Sherwood went on to explain:

For several weeks now my dreams have been disturbed by boiling retorts, smoking test tubes and Leyden jars from which emerge bolts of lightning and monsters. "Frankenstein," "Arrowsmith," "Dr. Jekyll and Mr. Hyde," and "The Murders in the Rue Morgue"—each one of these has centered on a laboratory which contains enough equipment to overstock the Rockefeller and Pasteur Institutes combined. . . . And by the way—I have been meaning for some time to complain about the elaborate mixture of chemicals that enables Dr. Jekyll to convert himself into Mr. Hyde and return. The mixture is obviously a very delicate one, necessitating great care in the measuring of each drop, but Dr. Jekyll does it differently each time. Sometime smoke results, and sometimes it turns out flat. Occasionally, the doctor is as careless and sloppy about it as is a too-generous host mixing the fourth round of cocktails.

"If we must have so much diabolic science in our screen entertainment," Sherwood concluded, "let it at least have the appearance of being scientific." Sherwood was wrong about this, of course; diabolic science was compelling to the extent that it resembled black magic, promising esoteric revelations and transformation.

Albert Einstein, visiting Hollywood for the first time in the early 1930s, wasn't perceived as exactly diabolic, but he was considered odd; the press regularly paid more notice to his unruly hair and purported eccentricities than to his scientific ideas. Einstein himself may have abetted such coverage when he gave a public endorsement to a theatrical psychic named Anna Eva Fay. Hollywood publisher Rob Wagner noted the particulars in an item subtitled "Genius Ballyhoos for Sideshow" in his magazine *Script* on February 20, 1932:

> Strange as it may seem, scientists are peculiarly susceptible to psychic bunk. The reason is because they live in a bunkless world. Nature may withhold her secrets but she never deliberately cheats. . . . That is why we regret to see Doctor Einstein degraded by being made a party to a clairvoyant attraction employed to buck-up sagging box office returns. We do not know what the young lady now appearing at Warner's Theatre told the dear doctor, but apparently he went gaga and permitted a cinematic interview to be made of himself and the young seeress, which is being shown at the theatre so as to add authenticity to her stage performance.

The film studios didn't need a seeress to understand the public's willingness to view just about everyone and everything connected with scientific progress as a little spooky. For many people, the expansive promises of the machine age seemed to have gone smash, with frightening implications for the future. The exploits of mad scientists and inventors, so rampant in the 1930s, may have put a face on otherwise ill-defined concerns about technologically mediated progress, prosperity, and longevity.

Even Disney shorts of the 1930s picked up on mad science mania; with the aid of animators, Fredric March's Dr. Jekyll transmuted into Mr. Hyde en route to his Academy Award in *Mickey's Gala Premiere* (1932). In *The Mad Doctor* (1932), Disney pulled out all the stops as a lab-coated fiend attempted to "graft a chicken's gizzard onto the wishbone of a dog"—in this case, Mickey's faithful mutt Pluto. By 1936 Mickey himself acted the part of a benignly nutty experimenter in *The Worm Turns,* with a sunny California bungalow replacing the spooky laboratory/castle of *The Mad Doctor.* But it was to take Disney sixty years more to make literal film critic Parker Tyler's celebrated metaphorical linkage of animated cartoons and movie monsters; in *Runaway Brain* (1996) Mickey himself is transformed into a hulking, neck-bolted monstrosity, domiciled at 1313 Lobotomy Lane.

In 1932 the master fantasist Ray Bradbury was a twelve-year-old fan of Disney, Dracula, and every other imaginative Hollywood concoction; he later recalled his encounter with a Tesla-style "electrical man" the summer after *Frankenstein* had taken the country by storm, and its relationship to a burgeoning awareness of his own mortality:

> He arrived with a seedy two-bit carnival, The Dill Brothers Combined Shows, during Labor Day weekend. . . . Every night for three nights, Mr. Electrico sat in his electric chair, being fired with ten billion volts of pure blue sizzling power. Reaching out to the audience, his eyes flaming, his white hair standing on end, sparks leaping between his smiling teeth, he brushed an Excalibur sword over the heads of the children, knighting them with fire. When he came to me, he tapped me on both shoulders and then the tip of my nose. The lightning jumped into me. Mr. Electrico cried: *"Live forever!"*

"I decided that was the greatest idea I had ever heard," Bradbury wrote.

But other observers took less inspiration from the more outlandish promises of science, especially as the Great Depression tightened its stranglehold. Specialists of all kinds were viewed suspiciously; hadn't the whole scientific, technological, economic overreaching of the 1920s created the current mess and its attendant misery?

Medical docudramas—a species of entertainment founded on the spectacle of human misery—traded in many of the stock situations established by horror movies. In *Arrowsmith* (1931) the research scientist title character (Ronald Colman) drives his young wife (Helen Hayes) to tears when he sets a laboratory percolating in their kitchen, making it impossible for her to cook. (Boris Karloff treading on Mae Clarke's bridal gown is only a slightly more melodramatic statement of the same science-versus-spouse apprehension.) Like Frankenstein, Arrowsmith is perceived as playing God when he insists on a controlled experiment to test a bubonic plague vaccine. Obviously the patients who receive the placebo will die, but the advancement of science requires a certain amount of divine presumption. In *The Story of Louis Pasteur* (1934), Pasteur (Paul Muni) is at first considered a madman for challenging accepted science with his theory of microbial pathogens but finally achieves his own victory over death (or at least death by anthrax). Along the way his wife and betrothed daughter learn a basic fact of marriage already well known to fans of the *Frankenstein* pictures: When push comes to shove, science comes first.

Mainstream Hollywood rebukes to science were mild in comparison to those mounted by left-leaning publications. One of the shrillest attacks on science came from the journal *Social Forces,* which in March 1933 printed an inspired piece of red-meat rhetoric titled "Scientists as Citizen" by Read Bain of Miami University, who held that "Scientists, with a few notable exceptions, are the worst citizens of the Republic; they, more than any other single factor, threaten the persistence of Western culture. They are wholesale, though unconscious traitors to the civilization they have created." But Bain was only beginning. "Racketeers are running sores on the social body, but unsocialized scientists are a foul corruption in the very heart's blood of society. They are not prophets of light and leading but workers of Black Magic, workers of weird spells, progenitors of destruction. Their calling has become a cult, a dark mystery cult. They have opened Pandora's box. They have released mighty forces that are pulverizing ancient social structures, producing personal and social disorganization; but they refuse to accept any responsibility in the creation of new modes of social control to counteract the devastation produced by machine technique."

With considerable gusto, Bain laid in to the scientific pretension of dispassionate objectivity. "They sell their services to the exploiters of human life. They make a fetish of 'research' and 'scientific method.' They produce powerful mechanisms and proudly proclaim that they 'do not care how they are used—leave that to the moralists.' They are blatantly a-moral, un-moral or non-moral. . . . They are parasites upon the body politic but they refuse to accept any political responsibility." Ridiculing artists, laughing at the civic-minded, scientists are content to "let things in general run merrily to the devil. Practical things do not concern the 'pure' scientists. The 'pure' scientist has to be a moral eunuch or a civil hermit."

In fairness, it must be said that all scientists of the Depression era were not lacking in social convictions. In fact, scientists as a group were badly hit by the economic downturn as academic and corporate research money dwindled. With their own self-interest on the line, many scientists became vocally reform-minded. As historian Peter J. Kuznick notes, "Although worlds apart in terms of means, even at the start of the 1930s, scientists shared a striking kinship with many radical reformers in terms of their view of a sane future society. At its best, the scientific worldview embraced meliorism, internationalism, creativity, reason, planning, cooperative effort, enlightenment, peace and prosperity." In Great Britain particularly, the scientific mainstream moved politically to the left, espousing a mistrust of capitalism and denouncing the exploitation of scientists by industry and the military. British physicist J. D. Bernal, in his book *The Social Uses of Science,* went so far as to say, ". . . science is communism. In science men have learned consciously to subordinate themselves to a common purpose without losing the individuality of their achievements." And following Hitler's acendancy in 1933, the scientific community embraced antifascism in worldwide efforts to assist expatriate German scientists.

But the public remained skeptical that the scientific engineers of the failed socioeconomic experiment of the postwar era had really had a change of heart. This skepticism was nowhere better crystallized than in Aldous Huxley's futuristic satire *Brave New World,* published in the immediate wake of the science-anxious films *Frankenstein* and *Dr. Jekyll and Mr. Hyde.* In

Huxley's novel all the utopian promises of advanced technology mass production are carried to their logical, and simultaneously nutty, conclusions. The word "Ford" has replaced "God," and the Model T is an object of materialist devotion. Human beings are no longer born but "decanted" in eugenic hatcheries, which provide a rigid caste system (labeled "Alpha" to "Epsilon") with exactly the proportions of brain or muscle power the supremely efficient economy requires. The standardized textures of society are made tolerable in large part by a narcotic called soma, a "perfect" drug combining "[a]ll the advantages of Christianity and alcohol; none of their defects." In part, Huxley was taking a jab at H. G. Wells's ever more pronounced utopianism; *Brave New World* might be considered a dystopian version of Wells's *Men like Gods* (1923), debunking Wells's sunny prediction of a society whose every ill has been technologized away. (Ironically, Huxley's grandfather T. H. Huxley had been one of Wells's scientific mentors) "In theory, I am for man living scientifically, creating his own destiny and so forth," Huxley wrote in 1929. "But in practice I doubt whether he can." In a BBC broadcast a few weeks before the publication of *Brave New World,* Huxley employed a Frankenstein metaphor to explain his guarded attitudes. "The very arts and sciences which we have used to conquer Nature have turned on their creators and are now conquering us." (James Whale's *Frankenstein* had just opened in London, and it is not unlikely that Huxley had just seen it.) "Science is the organised search for truth and, as such, must be looked on as an end in itself. . . . But truth about the nature of things gives us, when discovered, a certain control over those things. Science is power as well as truth. Besides being an end in itself, it is a means to other ends."

Despite *Brave New World*'s present status as a modern classic, it received mixed notices. The review *Books* called it "a lugubrious and heavy-handed piece of propaganda." "The trouble with Mr. Huxley's satire," according to the *Springfield* (Massachusetts) *Republican,* "is that it is not easy to become interested in the scientifically imagined details of life in this mechanical utopia. Nor is there compensation for the amount of attention that he gives to the abundant sex life of these denatured human beings. The narrative . . . moved rather laboriously. . . ." The *Spectator* also had difficulty. "This novel will shock some people and shake a good many more. It is an astonishing feat of sheer intellect: but disgust, its driving force . . . needs to be couple with exceptional *human* imagination, as in Swift, and of human imagination Mr. Huxley has little."

Hollywood, perhaps, also found Huxley's book too removed from proved box-office formulas and didn't get around to a screen adaptation of *Brave New World* until 1980, when it was produced as a disappointing television film. But the 1930s studios, however indirectly and unconsciously, understood perfectly the gist of Huxley's dystopian view of science, and rapidly transformed it into ever more lucrative forms of popular entertainment. H. G. Wells had long eschewed attempts to expand the life of his scientific romances via the stage or screen—in particular he had refused in no uncertain terms a proposed French theatrical adaptation of *The Island of Dr. Moreau* in 1919—but in the early thirties he finally gave in to Hollywood's specific interest in his two novels dealing with mad scientists—*Moreau* and *The Invisible Man.* Paramount acquired the rights to the former, and Universal sewed up the latter.

The Island of Dr. Moreau went through numerous treatments and drafts, beginning with an unproduced 1931 stage play called *His Creatures* by Frank Vreeland, only "suggested" by the Wells book and in fact changing the names of all characters: Dr. Moreau became Dr. Cushing, his man-beast

Examples of Beast-Folk makeup from *Island of Lost Souls* (1933). *Courtesy of David Del Valle/ The Del Valle Archive.*

servant Caliban, and so on. From the start, all the adaptors ignored Wells's satirical intentions, setting sail instead for grimmest melodrama. Cyril Hume's treatment followed the action of the Wells book closely, jettisoning all irony. Garrett Fort, who had worked on the scripts of both *Dracula* and *Frankenstein,* was then teamed with Philip Wylie to produce two more treatments, both pushing the sensation quotient considerably. In a treatment retitled *Island of Lost Souls,* a furious Moreau is depicted "beating the daylights" out of a snarling, half-nude cat-woman. The pantherette has spoiled an experimental attempt to mate her with a young boy, whom she has instead torn to pieces. In an especially perverse climax, Moreau is not destroyed but instead reveals to Prendick his most horrifying creation of all: a shackled male monstrosity lacking a face, human or otherwise. Prendick's own visage is the intended, finishing touch.

Fort and Wylie finally settled on a far more conventional finish, in which Moreau is destroyed in a Beast-Folk uprising, Prendick escaping with a thoroughly human love interest. Finally, Wylie would share screen credit with Waldemar Young, who polished the script, presumably on the basis of the expert assistance he had given Tod Browning in the silent era to create lurid screen melodramas starring Lon Chaney portraying dehumanized protagonists in exotic locales. Charles Laughton portrayed Moreau with remarkable understatement as an androgynous gentleman monster in a tropical suit, and Bela Lugosi (unrecognizable under a bristling face wig of yak hair) played the Sayer of the Law, leader of Moreau's half-human dominion. The film was directed by Erle C. Kenton, and reportedly featured—unbilled—several "evolving" Hollywood stars, including Randolph Scott, Alan Ladd, and Buster Crabbe, all buried unrecognizable beneath mountains of putty and fuzz. Ironically, Scott had once been announced by the studio, prematurely, as the second male lead.

On some level, obviously, the racist concerns of the Third International Congress of Eugenics, however inadvertently, found a far wider audience through *The Island of Lost Souls* than through the *New York Times* or any scientific journal. America apparently was going to hell in a handbasket, and just as in the mid-1990s controversy over *The Bell Curve,* the fantasy of genetic backsliding provided an easy scapegoat for a cultural morass essentially

Newspaper caricature of Charles Laughton in *Island of Lost Souls* (1933).

economic and political in origin. It was comforting to believe that socially and (supposedly) biologically inferior people were somehow—magically!—to blame for the excesses of privileged capitalists of the 1920s who had brought about an international monetary collapse and thereby the economically debased, "animalized" millions thrown out of work in the early 1930s. A publicity stunt for the film involved tracking down an ideal working-class animal, an ordinary young woman from the American heartland who would play Moreau's ultimate creation—the sinuous Panther Woman, Lota. Veteran publicist Arthur Mayer, who helped mastermind the competition, recalled the hoopla:

> All over the country, attractive lassies, regardless of rosy cheeks and dovelike features, flooded the offices of the newspapers with whom we were cooperating, to make their bid for this feline short cut to fame and fortune. Local winners, the Panther Woman of Dixie, New England, Rocky Mountains and the like, were transported to Hollywood for the final eliminations. Strangely enough, those who came accompanied by mothers did not last as long as the unchaperoned ones. Among these, the final victor [Kathleen Burke] was a charming though scarcely talented young woman from Chicago, where, by a peculiar coincidence, Paramount happened to operate more theatres than in any other city.

James Whale, who had been in transition between English and American culture during the years immediately preceding and following the stock market crash, had not been particularly enthusiastic to direct the original *Frankenstein* and was eager to move on to other projects. He began developing a distinctive, humorously idiosyncratic voice in films like *The Old Dark House* (1932), in which Karloff played a hulking, subhuman, and (of course) disfigured butler, along with a small repertory company of Whale's West End cronies, including Charles Laughton and the eccentrically epicene Ernest Thesiger. *The Invisible Man* (1933), first intended as a starring vehicle for Karloff but filmed with Claude Rains, further established Whale's talent for mixing thrills and chills with ironic chuckles and helped him delay his inevitable reunion with *Frankenstein.* Whale was overjoyed with R. C. Sherriff's extremely screenworthy script for *The Invisible Man,* which Universal had been on the verge of scrapping after a string of rejected treatments by a slew of house writers, including one by Preston Sturges. Sturges had inexplicably transplanted Wells's story from England to Russia and split the main character into two, a scientist (a part intended for Paul Lukas) and a mentally deficient guinea pig (a role conceived for Boris Karloff and advertised as such in trade publications). But Universal's scenario head, Richard Schayer, had extreme reservations about its new superstar, Karloff, enacting yet another imbecile role. Schayer tried, unsuccessfully, to revise the script, and the project ended up being temporarily shelved. One treatment, Whale is said to have complained, "changed the character of the Invisible Man into a giant octopus which captured the heroine in its writhing tentacles."

The studio had encouraged Whale to forget about H. G. Wells and return to Mary Shelley and *Frankenstein.* "They've had a script made for a sequel," Whale told Sherriff, "and it stinks to heaven. In any case I've squeezed the idea dry on the original picture, and never want to work on it again."

"They were pressing him for a decision," Sherriff recalled, "and he was facing up to the miserable ordeal of the *Frankenstein* sequel when my script came to him like a gift from heaven."

Sherriff wowed the Universal brass through a bit of scenarial subterfuge: Knowing that they were unlikely to find a copy of—much less actually read—Wells's novel, he located one himself in a secondhand bookstore and submitted a treatment based largely on Wells. In true Hollywood fashion, Sherriff was praised roundly for his originality.

The Invisible Man was released in November 1933, receiving immediate acclaim for its taut, entertaining rendition of Wells's story and its innovative use of optical effects. The spectacle (or, perhaps more accurately, unspectacle) of Claude Rains peeling away his head bandages to reveal a seeming nothingness was yet another reminder to the public that there might not be so much after all to the promises of science-driven modernism. In a sense, scientific reductionism had never been given such a concise visual depiction as in *The Invisible Man.* Advanced knowledge itself, in the form of the invisiblity elixir, was presented as a mental poison producing the unfortunate side effects of grandiosity and paranoia. H. G. Wells was mildly critical of the addition of insanity: "If the man had remained sane, we should have had the inherent monstrosity of an ordinary man in this extraordinary position. But instead of an Invisible Man, we now have an Invisible Lunatic!" Whale had a ready retort, which caused Wells himself to chuckle: "If a man said to you that he was about to make himself invisible, would you think he was crazy already?" Whale's wit was also well reflected on-screen, and he truly came into his own with the film, which fully displayed a sardonic sensibility almost invisible in the original *Frankenstein.*

In addition to *The Invisible Man,* 1933 produced such films as *The Vampire Bat* (with Lionel Atwill as a crazed scientist who hides his morbid evolutionary experiments under the cover of a "vampire" scam to distract the villagers), *King Kong* (with its distorted, though recognizably Darwinian, fixation on a curiously human superape—another Scopes era relic), and the American release of *The Testament of Dr. Mabuse,* Fritz Lang's talking sequel to his 1922 silent classic *Dr. Mabuse the Gambler,* about a master scientist-criminal (Rudolf Klein-Rogge, *Metropolis's* evil genius) who directs his gang from the confines of an insane asylum. The Nazis banned *Dr. Mabuse,* with its implicit critique of mad authoritarianism, but Hitler himself was so impressed with the rousing spectacle of *Metropolis* that he ordered Joseph Goebbels to offer Lang the position of chief film propangandist. Lang, whose mother was Jewish, was properly horrified, and he fled Germany. He also left his wife and collaborator, Thea von Harbou, who had outgrown the schmaltzy sentimentality of the *Metropolis* days and was now eager to embrace the Nazi cause and its ugly eugenic underpinnings.

The reanimation of a belligerent Germany provoked fearful fantasies of militarism in the thirties, not only in pulp science fiction magazines but in the mainstream media as well. Nikola Tesla, though becoming a bit dotty in his old age, still had even his most flamboyant visions treated with respect by the press. On the occasion of his seventy-eighth birthday in 1934, the *New York Times* unskeptically reported that Tesla had invented a powerful "death-beam" capable of downing ten thousand enemy planes at a distance of hundreds of miles or causing an army of a million soldiers to drop dead in its tracks. Such a device was not at all dissimilar to the superweapons popularized in *Chandu the Magician,* the science fiction pulps, the new comic strip by Alex Raymond called *Flash Gordon,* and any number of serials to come.

Science under surveillance: The villagers have their doubts about *The Invisible Man* (1933). *Courtesy of David Del Valle/The Del Valle Archive.*

Anticipating Ronald Reagan's Strategic Defense Initiative by decades, Tesla's invention would make war obsolete, surrounding each country "like an invisible Chinese wall, only a million times more impenetrable," the *Times* told its readers. Tesla claimed his invention would be used only for defensive purposes but somehow never got around to filing patents or producing prototypes.

The public's appetite for mad science—in films, radio serials, pulp magazines, and comic books—had never been stronger. While James Whale was finishing *The Invisible Man,* Carl Laemmle, Jr., turned over the languishing *Frankenstein* sequel to director Kurt Neumann, who planned to pair Boris Karloff and Bela Lugosi for the first time, with Lugosi as the doctor and Karloff as the monster. The treatments, however, proved unsatisfactory. Robert Florey, shortly before his death in 1979, recounted to a French film magazine that he had been asked by Universal, as early as 1931, to submit some ideas for a sequel to *Frankenstein.* Florey wrote a seven-page treatment, "The New Adventures of Frankenstein: The Monster Lives," that drew heavily on the Shelley novel, including a now-talkative monster's demand for a mate and a melancholy climax in Arctic seas, where, following Frankenstein's death, the monster marches into a pyre it has constructed on the ice. The treatment was summarily rejected, an experience that only fueled Florey's lifelong bitterness at having been denied the chance to direct the horror classic.

The shadow of *Frankenstein*'s success as a film loomed over Whale's future, a career monster that demanded a sequel for a mate. Carl Laemmle, Jr., finally convinced Whale to reconsider the follow-up to *Frankenstein,* possibly with assurances that he could approach the project with a large budget and an unusually free directorial hand.

Whale, who had at first thought the original *Frankenstein* to be a joke, soon decided that the sequel would be most viable if approached with humor from the outset. He discarded the grimly melodramatic tone that John L. Balderston had been developing, retaining Balderston's structure, especially a prologue set piece featuring Mary Shelley, her husband, and Lord Byron. The last collaborator was William J. Hurlbut, who had just completed Universal's *Imitation of Life* and was considered a specialist in "women's" pictures. A "confirmed bachelor," according to press interviews, Hurlbut often took a distinctly supercilious view of marriage and religion; his 1926 drama *The Bride of the Lamb* told the lurid tale of an unhappily married woman who develops a passion for an Elmer Gantry–style preacher. Her love unrequited, she cracks, kills her alcoholic husband by feeding him shoe polish, then triumphantly introduces all assembled to her new husband, Jesus Christ, whom she escorts unseen onto the stage like Harvey, the invisible rabbit.

Hurlbut's sensibility was well suited to Whale's new conception of the film but would be the source of endless tussling with the censors. The Hays Office had already voiced problems with John Balderston's scrapped screenplay: a scene in which the monster watches a couple make love, the use of the word "mate" for the monster's intended bride, and, as in 1931, references that "compare [Frankenstein] to God and his creation of the monster to God's creation of man. All such references should be deleted. . . ."

A lengthy opinion piece that ran in *Film Weekly* during the thick of Whale's wrangling with the Hays Office (and almost a half year before filming began) reads suspiciously like a clever studio plant, foreshadowing and preparing the professional purifiers for the black comedy already being planned. The writer argued that the screen, an "objective" medium, was ill suited to convey the internalized, psychological component of classic horror stories:

> There is a purity campaign against undesirable pictures at present . . . adult entertainment of a type no child could understand. If there is a film to which we can object, it is the horror film. Such macabre products should never be made. The cinema cannot treat them in the way they deserve. But wait . . . ! We have a medium for the horror man. The cartoon is his ideal realm. He can swallow fellow beings, distort himself, and do almost anything a horror man should do. His object would be to amuse, not thrill, and that is the true function of a Frankenstein. Make him a comedian and all his faults disappear. *The Invisible Man* was made that way. It was a good, novel entertainment. *The Bride of Frankenstein* should be similarly treated. Humour is the only salvation of the macabre on the screen.

Hurlbut's script (with additional dialogue by R. C. Sherriff, despite his later claims to have not worked on the film) was a real corker, flawlessly

Strange bedfellows: Dr. Pretorius (Ernest Thesiger) and Henry Frankenstein (Colin Clive) concoct an all-male reproductive paradigm in *Bride of Frankenstein* (1935).

walking the thin line between horror and hilarity. As if to emphasize the Faustian undercurrents of the story, Frankenstein was given a Mephistophelian mentor, Dr. Pretorius, a role first planned for Claude Rains but then assigned to the waspish British character actor Ernest Thesiger. Pretorius is more a medieval alchemist than a modern scientist, equally adept at creating life as Frankenstein, except that he grows his fantastic miniature people "as nature does, from seeds." He befriends the monster, which has crawled out of the burned wreckage of the old windmill hungry for companionship, and uses it to blackmail Frankenstein into creating the monster's mate. Legend has it that at one point in the script's development, the brain of Frankenstein's fiancée, Elizabeth, was installed in the body of the bride, but the macabre gambit was dropped for the shooting script, in which she is simply held hostage. The bride is brought to life in a crackling follow-up to the original creation sequence,* only to reject the lumbering monster with a catlike shriek of revulsion. The monster, heartbroken and enraged, allows Henry to escape the laboratory, then throws a lever that triggers a cataclysmic explosion, destroying Pretorius, monster, and the unwed bride.

Hurlbut was no stranger to the dramatic uses of Freudian insight and seems to have instinctively grasped the psychosexual implications of Henry Frankenstein's failure to consummate his marriage and his mad dream of creating life without heterosexual contact. Homosexuality is never men-

Newspaper caricature of Elsa Lanchester in *Bride of Frankenstein* (1935).

tioned explicitly in the script, but it remains a powerful subtext. As critic Monika Morgan has commented, "While hindsight is rightly suspect as a critical tool, particularly when it's a cover for revisionist views that expect an earlier era to reflect the mores of today, it does provide a key to Whale's achievement and what lies behind his film. [*Bride of Frankenstein*] can be read from a modern perspective as a homosexual joke on the heterosexual communities Whale—a gay man—served: his 'masters' at Universal and the mass audience to whom he could present unconventional images and ideas and see them unknowingly endorsed and approved in the most direct way possible—by ticket sales."

Morgan notes that *Bride of Frankenstein* "teems with homosexual presences behind and before the camera, and within the narrative itself," and

---

*This time incorporating the electrical kites that had fascinated Percy Shelley, if not his wife.

amounts to a subversive "camp assault" on conventional society. A peasant couple are killed by the monster in the opening scenes, as if to clear the decks for brave new forms of domestic partnership. Pretorius seduces Frankenstein into a male-only reproductive dyad, their relationship shadowed by the pair of male graverobbers who act as midwives. The monster, spurned and hated by the small-minded villagers, finds momentary respite in a "marriage" with a blind hermit. And so on.

But the most outrageous visual evocation of the all-male reproductive paradigm was to be found in the sudden evolution of the monster's forehead scar from a superficial gash to an astonishingly blatant vulval fissure, with clearly defined inner and outer lips; what better birth canal for the ultimate "brainchild" of male science? Whether this was one of Whale's private jokes or the cosmetic equivalent of a Freudian slip on the part of Jack Pierce cannot be determined. But whatever its immediate inspiration, the scar reminds us of that ancient, archetypal myth of male self-replication: the Greek god Zeus and his prodigiously fecund brow.

The bride herself, brilliantly conceived by Whale himself as an art deco Nefertiti, anticipates the highly stylized women—fashion models, pop divas, disco queens—who would so often become cultural icons for gay men. With her exaggerated head, the bride is superior to the body and its emotions, utterly uninterested in the clumsy sentimentalism and crude sexuality of the heterosexual monster. The evocation of Nefertiti is especially telling. As Camille Paglia has noted, Nefertiti "is the triumph of Apollonian image over the humpiness and horror of mother earth. Everything fat, slack, and sleepy is gone. The western eye is open and alert. . . . But the liberation of the eye has its price. Taut, still, and truncated, Nefertiti is western ego under glass. The radiant glamour of this supreme sexual persona comes to us from a palace-prison, the overdeveloped brain."

Whale's choice of Elsa Lanchester to portray the female monster (as well as Mary Shelley in the prologue) suggests a half-intended synergy between the actress's private life and the curious role of the bride. In his inventive 1995 novel *Father of Frankenstein,* based on the life of James Whale, Christopher Bram invents a dishy line of dialogue for Ernest Thesiger upon first gazing upon Lanchester in full regalia as the monster's mate: "Is the audience to presume that Colin and I have done her hair? I thought we were mad scientists. Not hairdressers."

Lanchester was no stranger to homosexuality; two years after she married the actor Charles Laughton, she learned that his real interest was in young men. Even *Time* magazine, in a sidebar to its review of *Bride of Frankenstein,* saw fit to allude to a certain unconventionality in their marriage (". . . he is known for his plump effeminacy, she is mannish in dress"). Laughton was tormented by his sexual orientation and unsuccessfully sought a cure from Dr. Ernest Jones, the psychoanalyst (and biographer of Freud) who first applied Freudian analysis to monsters and vampires in his influential book *On the Nightmare* (1931).

The subversive sexuality of *Bride of Frankenstein* is, of course, largely between the lines, and while it may have caused the censors discomfort, they were more easily able to voice their concerns about more tangible issues. Joseph Breen of the Hays Office complained about "ten separate scenes in which the monster either strangles or tramples people to death—this in addition to some other murders by subsidiary characters. . . . Your studio is, of course, too well aware of the difficulty which attended the release of the first *Frankenstein* picture . . . based principally on the two elements of undue gruesomeness and an alleged irreverent attitude. . . ." Specific objections to the script included dialogue of the Shelley and Byron entourage, including the line "We are all three infidels, scoffers at marriage ties . . . , which was cut, along with attendant boasts of infidelity and adultery.

The brow of Zeus? Boris Karloff and his evocative forehead scar in *Bride of Frankenstein* (1935). *Courtesy of Ronald V. Borst/Hollywood Movie Posters.*

Even within its Hays-approved form, *Bride of Frankenstein* had extreme problems with state, local, and foreign censor boards. Critics and audiences, however, were highly enthusiastic, at least in the United States. *Time* noted that *Bride* contained "none of the hang-dog air that one expects in sequels" and that the producers "have given it the macabre intensity proper to all good horror pieces, but have substituted a queer kind of mechanistic pathos for the sheer evil that was *Frankenstein.*" Many of the American reviewers picked up on the film's humor in the tone of their reviews. Commenting on the the faux finality of the picture's climax, one critic speculated that the laboratory wreckage would probably "hold the monster until next year when he crawls out of the debris for the premiere of *Frankenstein's Baby,* featuring some Shirley Temple with a couple of rivets in her neck."

As with *Frankenstein,* the *Times* of London remained cool toward James Whale's accomplishments in Hollywood.

It is fortunate that this film has its moments of unconscious humour, for otherwise it would be an intolerably morbid affair with its preoccupation with murder, the coffin and the grave. As it is, in the intervals of watching the Monster—he deserves a capital letter—stalking about the countryside seeking someone he may love, or alternatively, devour and Mr. Ernest Thesiger, disguised as a professor with a dubious reputation, prowling drunkenly about deserted churchyards, there is time for reflection.

What period, for instance, does the director imagine he is in? As Frankenstein, the creator of the Monster, Mr. Colin Clive looks, and is dressed, like the kind of nice modern young man who is the pillar of his local tennis club; the peasants have a definitely medieval air about them, and Mary Shelley (Miss Elsa Lanchester) was early nineteenth century. How did the bride of the Monster, again Miss Lanchester, realize at the moment of her artificial creation the significance of the lever, the sole purpose of which, it seems, is to blow the laboratory and everything in it sky-high? The questions have only an academic interest . . . [and] it is sad to see such personalities as Mr. Thesiger and Miss Lanchester, to say nothing of Mr. Boris Karloff himself, wasted on a production with so ignoble a motive.

The year 1935 saw an unusual spate of horror-science films, including *The Werewolf of London,* with Henry Hull as yet another man of science whose curiosity ends up dehumanizing him, Jekyll/Hyde style; *The Raven,* with Bela Lugosi as a psychotic plastic surgeon obsessed with Edgar Allan Poe and Boris Karloff as the victim of his disfiguring experiments; and, perhaps most memorably, Karl Freund's expressionistic *Mad Love,* based on *The Hands of Orlac,* which provided Peter Lorre with his first American role. Lorre played Dr. Gogol, a brilliant but sexually frustrated surgeon who replaces the hands of a maimed concert pianist (Colin Clive) with those of a murderer, while falling fatally in love with the musician's wife (Frances Drake), the lead actress at a Grand Guignol–style theater. The *New York Times* found Lorre to have achieved a new technical level in the portrayal of crazed clinicians: "With any of our conventional maniacs in the role of the deranged surgeon, the photoplay would frequently be dancing on the edge of burlesque. But

James Whale (right) directs Boris Karloff in *Bride of Frankenstein* (1935).

Mr. Lorre, with his gift for supplementing a remarkable physical appearance with his acute perception of the mechanics of insanity, cuts deeply into the darkness of the morbid brain. It is an affirmation of his talent that he always holds his audience to a strict and terrible belief in his madness. He is one of the few actors in the world, for example, who can scream: 'I have conquered science; why can't I conquer love?'—and not seem a trifle silly."

Mad Love's central image is a pair of mutilated hands, this time possessed by actor Colin Clive, previously responsible for a similar stitch job on Boris Karloff in the two *Frankenstein* films. Hands are an unsurpassed symbol of human achievement; as noted earlier, damaged hands often represent twisted accomplishment. *Mad Love* was one of Clive's last films before his alcohol-induced death. In a 1935 interview he described the two-hour process by which his "grafted" hands were made to look alien and clumsy. "The finger joints were built up; the hands had to be almost a quarter larger than normal size. Then, around the wrists, where the surgeon has supposedly grafted them on to their new 'foundation,' ghastly scars were created . . . my hands were first stained with something green; then with something blue, and then with something white. . . . [T]he knuckles and palms were built up and coarsened with some kind of wax, over which new skin was laid. The wrinkles in the joints were picked out with innumerable exaggerations traced with an ordinary lead pencil."

Clive felt the "experience of viewing one's own hands in this condition was in itself a shock. Often, I felt quite sick, and the real hands under this awful disguise ached with some unaccountable form of irritation. All day and every day I felt that I would give almost anything to be able to wash away the whole ghoulish mess and forget the rest of the picture."

Mad science and monster movies were about to go into a two-year Hollywood hibernation because of an embargo imposed by the powerful British Board of Film censors, who controlled access to a lucrative market. Tod Browning's *The Devil Doll* (1936) was one of the last such films to be released, but even after considerable preproduction censor interference, primarily focused on the script's original theme of voodoo (with black characters Britain believed might inflame its colonists), Browning and his scriptwriters substituted a science fiction plot for black magic and managed to create two of the 1930s' most memorable mad scientists in the process. Marcel (Henry

B. Walthall), a Devil's Island escapee
who has perfected a process of
human miniaturization. His wife
and cocrazy, Malita (Rafaela Ot-
tiano), seems less interested in the
science than in the delightful spectacle of tiny, zombified apache
dancers whirling away on her table-
top. When Marcel dies, Malita joins
forces with another fugitive, Paul
Lavond (Lionel Barrymore), who assumes the disguise of an elderly
woman, Madame Mandelip, the better to revenge himself on the busi-
nessmen who originally framed him,
using the hypnotically controlled
"devil dolls" to do his bidding. Bar-

Peter Lorre in *Mad Love* (1935): a
proto-cyborg in the shadow of Rotwang.

rymore's inspired drag performance provides yet another example of the mad
science magus as she-male, a conceit that persisted until *The Rocky Horror Picture Show* (1978) and beyond. The miniaturization motif—an apt metaphor
for the downsizing of human values in the face of science and technology—
became a durable Hollywood chestnut, revived and recycled in films like *Dr.
Cyclops* (1940).

In other films the mark of madness was not a disfigurement or trans-
sexual disguise, but something more uncannily evocative. In *The Invisible Ray*
(1936) Dr. Janos Ruhk (Boris Karloff) becomes contaminated with a substance from outer space called Radium X, which makes him glow in the dark
like a radium watch dial. It also makes him poisonous to the touch and, if
that weren't enough, drives him crazy in the fashion of *The Invisible Man.* The
relationship between scientific discovery and insanity is made explicit in
the film's epigraph: "Every scientific fact accepted today once burned as a fantastic fire in the mind of someone called mad." Marie Curie, codiscoverer of
radium with her husband, Pierre, had died of radium poisoning just the
year before; *The Invisible Ray* was the first film to exploit the public interest
and anxiety in the alchemical, Faustian aspects of radioactivity. Karloff's

The revenge of Marie Curie? Violet Kemble Cooper and Boris Karloff in *The Invisible Ray* (1936). *Courtesy of Scott MacQueen.*

mother, who finally withholds an antidote and so destroys him, is played by Violet Kemble Cooper. Costumed severely in black dress, her hair in an equally severe French bun, Cooper is the avenging image of Marie Curie herself, returned from the grave to judge the actor most associated in the public mind with the Frankenstein story and its theme of scientific presumption.

Also within recent public memory was the tragic scandal of Radithor, a radium cocktail that enjoyed a vogue as a health tonic among wealthy socialites until its ghastly consequences became all too apparent. The worst-publicized case was that of Eben MacBurney Byers, a playboy industrialist, who, after guzzling the glow-in-the-dark concoction daily for years, met a fate worse than any depicted in a Hollywood horror film. According to the deposition of a Federal Trade Commission* attorney, investigating the

---

*Prior to the investigation, the FTC had prosecuted Radithor's competitors for marketing similar patent medicines deemed *insufficiently* radioactive.

product in late 1931, "A more gruesome experience in a more gorgeous setting would be hard to imagine. We went to Southampton where Byers had a magnificent home. There we discovered him in a condition that beggars description. . . . His head was swathed in bandages. He had undergone two successive jaw operations, and his whole upper jaw, excepting two front teeth, and most of his lower jaw had been removed. All the remaining bone tissue of his body was slowly disintegrating and holes were actually forming in his skull." Radium poisoning wasn't restricted to the wealthy; the working-class variant of Byers's sickness was the bone cancer that afflicted female factory workers hired to paint radium watch dials.

A trade ad for *The Invisible Ray,* reproduced here, in which the faces of Karloff, Lugosi, and the supporting players are engulfed by stylized, intermeshed gears, was coincidentally an echo of a central motif of another 1936 release, Charles Chaplin's *Modern Times,* a classic spoof of the industrial and scientific age, with its unforgettable, culturally cathartic image of Chaplin, swallowed up and spit out by the big, toothy gears of a factory assembly line. (Chaplin's sets were, perhaps appropriately, the work of Charles D. Hall, also art director for James Whale's *Frankenstein* films.) Techno-anxiety could be played for screams or laughs; either response was an effective way to relieve tension.

Waves of radio, rather than radioactivity, seemed to drive the whole country a bit mad on the evening of Sunday, October 30, 1938, when CBS and Orson Welles's Mercury Theatre broadcast the now-infamous adaptation of H. G. Wells's *The War of the Worlds,* which thousands of listeners took to be an actual radio report of an ongoing invasion of the eastern seaboard by extraterrestrials, arriving from the Red Planet in flaming meteorites. Despite the clear announcement at the start of the program that the broadcast was a dramatization, panic erupted across the country as people fled their homes, spreading rumor and fear in their wake. New Jersey, where the fictional broadcast was set, was especially traumatized.

The *Washington Post* ran an editorial on *The War of the Worlds* two days after the broadcast: ". . . the thing is far from being a joke; it comes pretty close to being a national tragedy. It has revealed to us things about ourselves it might not be better to know. It has proved that men and women

IT WILL CAPTURE AND ASTOUND THE PUBLIC'S IMAGINATION WITH ENTERTAIN-MENT THRILLS A CENTURY AHEAD OF TIME!

The INVISIBLE RAY

Starring

The Great KARLOFF
and BELA LUGOSI with
FRANCES DRAKE and
FRANK LAWTON

An Edmund Grainger Production Directed
by Lambert Hillyer Universal's Weird New
Romance presented by Carl Laemmle.

Technology geared for laughs and chills. Top: Charles Chaplin in *Modern Times* (1936). Bottom: Advertisement for *The Invisible Ray* (1936).

sitting comfortably by their firesides are quite as susceptible to unreasoning panic as men caught in the surges of mob emotion. It has proved that there are forms of fear against which mere common sense is apparently powerless. And it shows pretty plainly the state to which our national nerve has been reduced." The *Post* had already reported the glee with which Nazi newspapers had described the hysterical American response—a sure sign of war jitters.

According to Hadley Cantril in *The Invasion from Mars: A Study in the Psychology of Panic* (1940), prolonged economic unrest had left many Americans in a continuing state of apprehensive incomprehension, and they were therefore prime subjects for hysteria. "The depression had already lasted nearly ten years. People were still out of work. Why didn't somebody do something about it? Why didn't the experts find a solution?" (Perhaps because experts were crazy and untrustworthy, just like all those scientists in the movies.) Cantril noted that "a mysterious invasion fitted the pattern of the mysterious events of the decade. . . . The war scare had left many persons in a complete state of bewilderment. They did not know what the trouble was all about or why the United States should be so concerned. The complex ideological, class, and national antagonisms responsible for the crisis were by no means fully comprehended. The situation was painfully serious and distressingly confused. . . . The Martian invasion was just another event reported over the radio."

While *The War of the Worlds* was raging on the airwaves, Universal Studios was putting the finishing touches on the final chapter of its 1930s mad science cycle. *Son of Frankenstein* returned Karloff to his most famous role for the last time on-screen. The actor, who had serious reservations about imparting the monster with rudimentary speech in *Bride of Frankenstein,* rejected a first script for *Son* that included a voluble creature. He finally played the role mute and received other concessions as well.

"It takes me four hours to build him up every morning and two hours to tear him down every night," said makeup artist Jack Pierce. "I figure I've heaped some 5,400 pounds of makeup on him as the monster in the last seven years." The total poundage this time out would be somewhat diminished, however; Karloff, with a bad back at age fifty-one, would be permitted to wear lightweight clodhoppers instead of the immensely heavy asphalt spreader's boots, even if the result was a monster who seemed . . . well, unnaturally nimble.

Son of Frankenstein picks up twenty-five years after the death of Henry Frankenstein (now called Heinrich von Frankenstein). His son, Wolf (Basil Rathbone), arrives with his wife and young son to take up residence in the family castle, despite the hostility of the townsfolk, who have never forgiven his father for the crimes of his monster, which they believe still stalks the countryside. Wolf discovers his father's notes on the secrets of life and, in the dynamited wreckage of the old laboratory, meets Ygor (Bela Lugosi), a crazy old blacksmith, broken-necked from a bungled hanging. Ygor has been protecting the monster—using it to kill off the jurors who condemned him for body snatching—but it now lies comatose after being struck by lightning. Wolf, fired by the revelations of his father's papers, vows to restore the monster to its full power, not realizing that it will once more become an instrument of Ygor's twisted designs. A one-armed police inspector (again, the missing hand motif), maimed by the monster as a boy, suspects the creature's resurrection and places Wolf under nerve-racking surveillance. After three murders and the kidnapping of Wolf's child, the scientist kills Ygor and topples the monster into a bubbling pit of volcanic sulfur.

Directed by Rowland Lee, *Son of Frankenstein* is a stylish but decidedly uneven film. Basil Rathbone evidently considered the enterprise beneath him; while it is one of his most memorable Hollywood pictures of the late thirties, he omitted any mention of it from his autobiography. Later in his career Rathbone bristled at any suggestion that he was a "horror star." Karloff, second-billed under Rathbone, almost phones in his part, amounting to a near parody of his earlier excursions. For much of the picture he lies comatose on a slab, feebly twitching and grunting; when it finally regains its strength, the monster is a shambling assemblage of contradictions. While apparently brain-damaged, speechless, and far less comprehending than in the previous film, it nonetheless is shown rather craftily concealing evidence of a murder by running a wagon over the body and carefully pulling down a window shade before dispatching another of Ygor's enemies. Both Karloff and Rathbone may have been irritated by the film's abundant inconsistencies.

Why, for instance, does Ygor attempt to kill Wolf von Frankenstein on their first meeting when he needs the doctor to restore his "friend" to life? Why does the monster, intent on revenge following Ygor's death, spare Wolf's son after kidnapping him?

The *New York Times* found *Son of Frankenstein* easy to resist. Reviewer B. R. Crisler wrote that the film "isn't the silliest picture ever made, it's a sequel to the silliest picture ever made, which is even sillier." The critic asked his readers to imagine, if they could, "a picture so tough that Basil Rathbone plays a sympathetic part in it, so mean that you feel sorry for Lionel Atwill, so ghastly that Bela

Basil Rathbone as *The Son of Frankenstein* (1939). *Courtesy of David Del Valle/ The Del Valle Archive.*

Lugosi is only an assistant bogy-man." But Crisler conceded that *Son of Frankenstein* did possess certain, um, charms:

> Anybody who'd like a nice, un-sunny place to be haunted in couldn't do worse than rent Castle Frankenstein for the season. Such a paradise of low, brow-bursting beams! Such a number of enchanting secret doors and passageways! Such endless miles of corridors rendered fascinating by skiddy turns, pneumoniac draughts and sudden, breakneck stairways! Such lovely views of the countryside, which combines the picturesque features of the Bad Lands of South Dakota with the rustic charms of the brimstone beds in and around Vesuvius. With a pit of boiling sulfur in the basement and Bela Lugosi living there as a combination monster-nurse and janitor, what could be cozier?

As war approached, large segments of the populations of Europe and America may well have felt perched on the edge of a bubbling pit. Frankenstein's monster, the dark, mocking doppelgänger of scientific inquiry and technological achievement, had perhaps outlived its dramatic usefulness, but it refused to go away. In film after film the monster—as played by an increasingly padded Boris Karloff—got bigger on-screen, while taking up additional cultural space as well. In *Son of Frankenstein* the creature is no longer a distinct character but instead an oversize, largely comatose vessel waiting (in the words of the original Whale film) "for a new life to come." The coming war would give monster just the jolt it needed, in spades.

In the face of a conflict that threatened to make the Great War seem positively primitive from the standpoint of technologically abetted destruction, the New York World's Fair of 1939–1940 banished all the disturbing images of science and technology that had flooded American popular culture in the preceding decades. The gleaming lines of the Trylon (a needlelike pyramid jutting higher than the Washington Monument) and the Perisphere (an accompanying lower-rising globe) set a tone of high sublimation. An aggressively stylized phallus and scrotum seem obvious today but drew no overt comment in 1939. Instead the monumental configuration was more likely perceived as a hopeful evocation of the power of progressive science— male science, of course—to avert the military cataclysm at hand.

The anxieties that had fueled the hysterical response to Orson Welles's *War of the Worlds* broadcast in 1938 was even more acute in 1939; as David Gelernter comments in *1939: The Lost World of the Fair,* "The idea that war could enmesh civilians even far from the front, that people would die as a result of dangerous objects dropped out of airplanes into a sea of women and children—it's second nature to us, but in the 1930s that idea took a little getting used to." (Gelernter also notes tha Picasso's wrenching *Guernica* [1937], a raw modernist depiction of an actual air raid, was first exhibited in New York around the time of the fair.)

Suddenly gone, at least in the official context of the New York World's Fair, were all the familiar mad scientists and man-made monsters, the death rays and rampaging robots of B movies and the pulp magazines, the grim predictions of *Things to Come.* Visitors were presented instead with a hopeful—perhaps desperately hopeful—vision of a 1960 utopia whose elaborate models and dioramas brought to mind the visions of Fritz Lang's technicians on *Metropolis*—minus, of course, the slightest whiff of the countervailing dark undercity.

But the shadow side could not be suppressed completely, even in such a large-scale exercise in denial and control as the fair. In fact, the macabre intruded rather spectacularly, when, for Halloween 1939, the gigantic Perisphere was transformed with projected light into a grinning jack-o'-lantern. Though no one took notice at the time, it was quite likely the biggest display of a mocking death's-head in human history, superimposed on a symbol of pure rationality, on the eve of the biggest bloodbath of all time.

CHAPTER FOUR

A-Bombs, B Pictures, and C Cups

W hen the atomic bomb leveled Hiroshima on August 6, 1945, newspaper readers learned not only of the appalling devastation but also of the explosion's unearthly beauty, a glowing hothouse blossom rising to the heavens. Witnesses to the test blast in the New Mexico desert on July 18 tried to describe the indescribable. Brigadier General Thomas F. Farrell, deputy to General Leslie R. Groves, head of the War Department's

Advertising art for *The Day the Earth Stood Still* (1951).

166

atomic bomb project, combined the language of theater and literary criticism in his recollection of the event to the press: "The lighting effects beggar description. The whole country was lighted by a searing light with the intensity many times that of the midday sun. It was golden, purple, violet, gray and blue. It lighted every peak, crevasse and ridge of the nearby mountain range with a clarity and beauty that cannot be described but must be seen to be imagined. It was that beauty that the great poets dream about but describe most poorly and inadequately."

From its first deployment the atomic bomb began radiating metaphors about knowledge, sin, and science that gave startling new life to ancient ideas. "I am become Death, shatterer of worlds," said bomb scientist J. Robert Oppenheimer, quoting the Upanishad after the first test detonation. H. G. Wells, who died in 1946, bitter and frustrated by a war that had dashed his utopian hopes, saw a real Judgment Day. "[T]he end of everything we call life is close at hand and cannot be evaded," he wrote in *Mind at the End of Its Tether* (1945). Promethean presumption, the spoiling of Eden, Pandora's box, the golem, Faust, and Frankenstein all absorbed new energy from the atomic blast and in the process gave popular culture of the postwar years its particular mythic intensity. Like the fatal, beautiful plants in Dr. Rappaccini's poisonous garden, the blossoming of the atom had a resonant symbolism that seemed to fold modern science into ancient alchemy. Uranium was the new philosopher's stone, a substance that promised almost mystical powers over the physical world and the processes of life.

Public receptivity to a reenergized Frankenstein mythos didn't come out of nowhere; the war years had seen an unprecedented number of mad scientists in Hollywood films, not only from the major studios but from independents. It is perhaps not unsurprising that the war effort was shadowed in popular entertainment by anxious images of applied science and technology. Without overtly challenging the patriotism of wartime audiences, mad science films may have provided an safe outlet for diffuse fears about the scientific, technological, military juggernaut that was engulfing the world.

Dr. Cyclops (1940) presented what remains one of the screen's most chilling portraits of an obsessed scientific mind, a distillation of all the Depression decade's suspicions about experts and intellectuals and runaway sci-

Albert Dekker in *Dr. Cyclops* (1940).

ence. Dr. Thirkell (Albert Dekker) is a classic scientific hermit, holed up in the Peruvian Andes, where he has found a way to use atomic radiation to miniaturize living things, in much the same manner previously essayed in Tod Browning's *The Devil Doll*. Thirkell's intellectual brilliance is matched only by his nearsightedness—literal as well as figurative. Completely self-absorbed, he cannot fathom his visitors' objections to being used in his experiments or their outrage at being reduced to the size of figurines. All human values are beneath consideration. As iconography, Thirkell's shaved head seems influenced by Peter Lorre's bald pate in *Mad Love;* it simultaneously draws attention to his braincase while rendering him creepily childlike. Thirkell is, after all, a monstrous baby, concerned only with his own interests and gratifications. *Dr. Cyclops* was the brainchild of the producer-director team of Merian C. Cooper and Ernest B. Shoedsack, the same pair responsible for another famous study of relative scale, the fantasy-adventure classic *King Kong* (1933).

Hollywood's bogeymen laureates, Boris Karloff and Bela Lugosi, became even more identified with mad science during the war than in their first decade as the screen's leading purveyors of fear. Karloff of course had a built-in identification with the Frankenstein story (despite other, distinguished work as a character actor), and Lugosi had played a handful of mad doctors among his villainous characterizations in the 1930s. Now both men occupied the laboratory the way the Nazis occupied France.

Karloff never wore the Frankenstein monster makeup again in a feature film after 1939, but he also never turned his back on employment possibilities presented by the Frankenstein formula. Leaving Universal, he made a series of five mad scientist pictures for Columbia Pictures: *The Man They Could Not Hang* (1939), *The Man with Nine Lives* (1940), *Before I Hang* (1940), *The Devil Commands* (1941), and *The Boogie Man Will Get You* (1943).

The Man They Could Not Hang was supposedly inspired by an actual biochemist of the 1930s, Dr. Robert Cornish, who claimed to have successfully gassed and revived dogs and who unsuccessfully petitioned authorities to allow him to experiment with the fresh corpses of executed convicts. In the film Karloff's Dr. Savaard attempts to use a mechanical heart to revive his first subject, a student volunteer, but he is interrupted by authorities, and the student stays dead. Karloff is executed for murder and brought back to life by his own invention to take revenge on the jurors who convicted him. In *The Man with Nine Lives,* Karloff plays the similarly misunderstood Dr. Kravaal, whose attempts to cure cancer through cryogenic interment leads to his own frosty Rip Van Winkle–style slumber. *Before I Hang* features Karloff as Dr. John Garth, who once again gets carried away with a humanitarian medical goal, the reversal of aging. A mercy killing lands him in jail for murder, but he manages to continue his experiments and successfully rejuvenates himself with a serum made from the blood of a murderer, with all the predictable complications. *The Devil Commands* finds Karloff as Dr. Julian Blair, who has discovered a way to record brainwaves electrically after death. Attempting to communicate with his dead wife, Karloff conducts bizarre séances involving electrically wired corpses, until suspicious New England townsfolk storm his laboratory. In *The Boogie Man Will Get You,* a comedy, the war-related undercurrents are made explicit. Professor Nathaniel

Billings (Karloff) is a dotty scientist who has nonetheless perfected, in a basement lab, a means to turn ordinary men into supermen, an obvious potential boon to the war effort. (A similar theme was employed in Producers Releasing Corporation's ultra-low-budget *The Mad Monster* (1942), with George Zucco cultivating an army of werewolves that he deludedly believes will be welcomed by the military as an elite fighting corps.)

Karloff's portrayals were usually colored with a touch of pathos, but Lugosi's madmen often seemed congenitally sadistic, his experiments rarely involving even the initial pretense of humanitarian concern gone wrong. In the Universal serial *The Phantom Creeps* (1939), Lugosi's Dr. Alex Zorka is a power-hungry inventor, frankly intent on conquering the world with a variety of gizmos, including an invisibility belt, mechanical spider assassins, and a giant glowering robot. In PRC's *The Devil Bat* (1941), he develops a giant killer bat to revenge himself on former business partners who swindled him. In Monogram's *Black Dragons* (1942), one of the first films after Pearl Harbor to depict the Japanese in a villainous light, Lugosi plays a Nazi plastic surgeon who transforms six Japanese agents into convincing replicas of American industrialists. *The Corpse Vanishes* (1942), another Monogram

quickie, casts Lugosi as a doctor who kidnaps young brides to obtain a rejuvenation serum from their blood. *The Ape Man* (1943), also from Monogram, presents Lugosi engaged in completely unmotivated Darwinian experiments, in which he regresses to a hairy horror that must kill for human spinal fluid, the only antidote. The film spawned a sequel in title only, *Return of the Ape Man* (1944), in which Lugosi thaws a frozen Neanderthal and doctors its brain in an attempt to

Boris Karloff in *The Man They Could Not Hang* (1939).

Bela Lugosi plays the ultimate price for monkeying around with mad science. From *The Ape Man* (1943).

civilize it. (One example of why Monogram was considered a "poverty row" studio is that the block of "ice" containing the caveman was nothing more than a pile of crumpled cellophane.) Following *Return of the Ape Man* (his last film for Monogram), Lugosi played a mad medico in RKO's comedy *Zombies on Broadway* ("They're Alive! They're Dead! They're Not! They're Nuts!").

The frequent starring of Lugosi in mad science movies with evolutionary themes (the last was *Bela Lugosi Meets a Brooklyn Gorilla* in 1952) is an interesting demonstration of the persistence of *Dracula*'s powerful Darwinian subtext. Even near the end of his life Lugosi made personal appearances in his trademark Dracula costume, leading around a "gorilla" on a chain for the entertainment of children who had no knowledge whatsoever of Charles Darwin, Bram Stoker, or the scientific or philosophical debates of the nineteenth century. Nonetheless, they responded enthusiastically to the pairing of an elegant vampire in a tuxedo with a hairy, hunkering ape. Somehow, it was understood, Count Dracula was the essential threshold figure between the human and animal realms, the creature that lived both upstairs and downstairs, ironed out all the modernist contradictions and paradoxes, the monster that put everything together.

Universal Pictures, the studio that had put mad science on the moviegoer's map with the immensely lucrative *Frankenstein* series in the 1930s, spun off the core tradition during the war with such films as *Man Made Monster* (1940), with Lon Chaney, Jr., as a sideshow "Electrical Man" turned into the real thing by an unscrupulous scientist, played by Lionel Atwill, and the similarly themed *The Mad Ghoul* (1943), wherein a mad academic scientist (George Zucco) transforms a graduate student (David Bruce) into a murderous zombie. ("Science," he tells his pupil, "isn't a matter of good or evil. I take what's useful, and discard the other.")

Universal's B picture output was the studio's mainstay, and the filmmakers had no arty illusions about their products. According to Reginald Le Borg, who directed several horror films and melodramas for Universal in the early 1940s, the intended audience was "factory workers and blacks." Angry and alienated, often voiceless and beleaguered, the monster characters had a clear appeal for the socially and economically marginalized. And a large audience could be especially depended upon for each new installment of Universal's *Frankenstein* series, whose work-booted monster originally struck a chord with 1931 audiences surrounded by Depression era unemployment and factory closings.

Ghost of Frankenstein (1942) added Sir Cedric Hardwicke to the roster of actors playing members of the Frankenstein clan. As Ludwig Frankenstein (the brother of the character Basil Rathbone played in *Son of Frankenstein,* the "von" now just as mysteriously absent from the family name as it had mysteriously appeared in the last film), Hardwicke becomes ensnared in a plot (hatched by Lionel Atwill, omnipresent in films of this time and type) to transplant the brain of Ygor (Bela Lugosi, reprising his role from *Son of Frankenstein,* despite the character's having been killed off) into the monster (Lon Chaney, Jr.). Unfortunately the monster and the broken-necked blacksmith have incompatible blood types, and the hybrid monster is blind. The enraged Ygor's brain sets the monster's body on a rampage, resulting in a self-immolating conflagration.

Two years later the series resumed with *Frankenstein Meets the Wolf Man,*

the first Universal film to mix and match its monsters of science and superstition, but not the last. (The freewheeling eclecticism probably qualifies the
picture as some kind of early exercise in postmodernism, but I won't bela-
bor the point.) The line of male Frankensteins has apparently died out;
there's only a blond bombshell of a daughter, Baroness Elsa Frankenstein
(Ilona Massey), who engages in a chaste flirtation with Dr. Frank Mannering (Patric Knowles), a brilliant and handsome young surgeon who has
briefly treated the despondent and suicidal Wolf Man (Lon Chaney, Jr.), who
has been brought back from the dead by a pair of careless grave robbers who
removed the wolfbane from his coffin. The Wolf Man believes that only the
secrets of Dr. Frankenstein can put him down permanently. Elsa hands over
her father's notebooks to Mannering, and finds a fetching negligee while

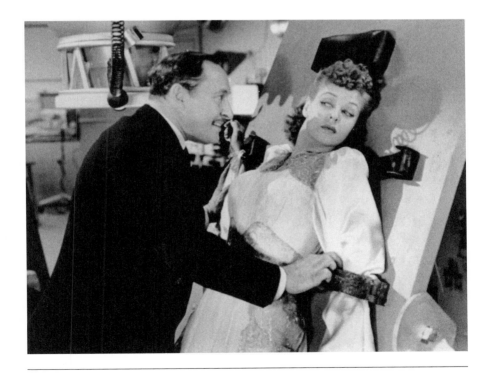

Lionel Atwill and Anne Nagel in *Man Made Monster* (1940). *Courtesy of David Del Valle/
The Del Valle Archive.*

Mannering figures out how simultaneously to siphon off the Wolf Man's life force and to disable permanently the Frankenstein monster (Bela Lugosi, finally playing the role he forfeited to Boris Karloff in 1931).* At the penultimate moment, however, Mannering predictably succumbs to the mad scientist's fatal curiosity. Egged on by thrumming gizmos, he reverses the experiment: "I must see Frankenstein's creation at its full power!" Reenergized respectively by electricity and moonlight, the two monsters deliver the promised battle of the film's title, and the know-nothing villagers restore stability to Vasaria by dynamiting a dam above Frankenstein's castle and flushing away the monsters before they can even finish a first round.

A condition of terminal decadence settled over Universal's Frankenstein series with the next entry, *House of Frankenstein* (1944), which brought back both the Frankenstein monster and the Wolf Man (frozen in the ice created by the previous film's dam deluge) and adding Count Dracula (John Carradine) to boot. The *New York Herald Tribune,* announcing the film's production (the original title was *The Devil's Brood*), noted that "Hollywood is horror happy. Its monsters are making more money than ever before." In reference to the 1937–1938 embargo on fright films imposed by the British Board of Film Censors, the *Herald Tribune* recalled that when "Hitler poured his pox over Europe . . . film monsters crawled for cover. They knew they were licked—the public had enough horror without having to see more." Following Pearl Harbor, however, "the public had different ideas. Mad ghouls, wolf men and Frankenstein monsters began to get more mail than contract cuties."

The absurdly convoluted story of *House of Frankenstein* starred Boris Karloff as the mad Dr. Gustav Niemann, who escapes from a prison for the

---

*In Curt Siodmak's shooting script, Lugosi's monster was a quite talkative creature, still possessing Ygor's brain from *The Ghost of Frankenstein* and still blind. The monster, like any number of totalitarian heads of state circa 1943, has dreams of world domination. Boasting of his new brain to the Wolf Man, he declaims, "I shall use it for the benefit of the miserable people who inhabit the world, cheating each other, killing each other, without a thought but their own petty gains. I will rule the world! I will live to witness the fruits of my wisdom for all eternity!" The studio found the effect comic and cut all the monster's dialogue in postproduction, as well as all references to blindness.

criminally insane—he has been imprisoned for attempting to transplant a human brain into a dog—and uses a chamber of horrors traveling carnival show as a front for his resumed surgical activities. One of the show's attractions is the skeleton of Dracula, whom Niemann revives to help wreak revenge on the men who imprisoned him. He plans a strange game of brain switching: One of his enemies will provide a new mind for the Frankenstein monster, and the Wolf Man will receive the monster's brain while donating his own gray matter to Niemann's other adversary. The doctor's hunchbacked assistant, Daniel (J. Carroll Naish), desperately wants his own brain transplanted into the Wolf Man's body, but Niemann rebuffs him. At the end the revived monster carries Niemann to his deserved death in a bog of quicksand, a good metaphor for the story itself. As the latest actor to portray the Frankenstein creature, Glenn Strange brought an imposing physical presence, but Jack Pierce's makeup, now in its sixth incarnation, had begun to look a trifle clownlike, and Universal had forever abandoned its attempts to provide the monster with even the rudiments of a personality, much less pathos.

The monster jamboree formula continued the following year with the very similar *House of Dracula* (1945), concluding Universal's classic monster movie cycle (although the gang was reunited for laughs in 1948's *Abbott and Costello Meet Frankenstein,* wherein Dracula [Bela Lugosi] took the part of the mad scientist, attempting to insert the round peg of Lou Costello's brain into the square hole of the Frankenstein monster's head).

In *House of Dracula* the madness of Dr. Franz Edelman (Onslow Stevens) is brought on by vampiric blood contamination. Both Dracula and the Wolf Man are rendered scientific, rather than supernatural, monsters. After diagnosing, and being infected by, Dracula's mysterious blood malady, Edelman deconstructs the Wolf Man's nocturnal transformations as the result of pressure on the brain. As Edelman explains to his patient, "This condition, coupled with your belief that the moon can bring about a change, accomplishes exactly that . . . your reasoning processes give way to self-hypnosis, the glands which govern your metabolism get out of control, like a steam engine without a fly wheel." The simile also well describes the plot mechanics of the Universal monster films by the mid-1940s.

Weird science in the war years wasn't confined to Universal's isolated mansions and Bavarian castles. A brightly lit metropolitan hospital could serve just as well as a testing ground for the nuttiest theories. In *Dr. Kildare's Strange Case* (1940) the young physician (Lew Ayres) illicitly administers insulin shock to an amnesiac patient, with a pseudoscientific rationale that bests any number of mad doctor and werewolf films. The shock process, we are solemnly told, will therapeutically regress the patient through evolutionary history, cathartic connection with the beast self effecting a cure for what bedevils the civilized brain.

All the Hollywood mad doctors of the war years operated in obsessive reclusion, paralleling the real-world secrecy surrounding the efforts of military research scientists. The public, of course, knew nothing of the Manhattan Project, but it did know, from a thousand reminders about loose lips and sunken ships, that there was much at stake in keeping science in the service of war hush-hush. Movieland madmen of the 1940s also conducted their experiments under conditions of strict security; those who stumbled into their laboratories or learned their secrets inevitably were dealt with harshly. But it would have been strange for the public not to be curious about the secret activities of military scientists. Was there a superweapon in the works that might defeat Hitler? Part of the message conveyed by Hollywood horror pictures was that it was better not to poke around laboratories, ask too many questions, or interfere with technoscientific prerogatives generally.

Enrico Fermi, a key member of the scientific team at Los Alamos that gave birth to the atomic bomb, pooh-poohed concerns among his colleagues that deployment of the new weapon might present ethical problems. In a quote that might have rolled easily off the tongues of Lionel Atwill or George Zucco, Fermi is reported to have said, "Don't bother me with your conscientious scruples. After all, the thing's superb physics." He also is said to have wagered with colleagues all night over whether the bomb might ignite the atmosphere and destroy the world. But after witnessing the blast at Alamagordo, Fermi was so shaken that he was unable to drive his car. Nuclear physicist J. Robert Oppenheimer later expressed misgivings about his participation in the development of the bomb, his oft-quoted 1956 observation that "we did the work of the devil" being the most pointed. Following the Soviet Union's detonation of an atomic device in 1949, Oppenheimer opposed the development of an even more powerful weapon, the hydrogen bomb (an invention championed by his far more hawkish counterpart, Edward Teller). President Harry Truman ordered the development of the H-bomb in 1950, and Oppenheimer was investigated as a possible Soviet agent. Nuclear jitters increased as the United States became embroiled in the Korean War, with talk of deploying the H-bomb.

Hollywood's first post-Hiroshima monster of any consequence was, like one of Dr. Rappaccini's creations, a vegetable. *The Thing from Another World* (1951) featured James Arness in his pre-*Gunsmoke* days as an eight-foot-tall space alien found frozen in Arctic ice. Despite the extraterrestrial pedigree, Arness's makeup is clearly inspired by the the tried-and-true *Frankenstein* formula. And while not initially created by science, his jolly green golem is protected by a scientist who can't pass up an experiment, regardless of the dangers ("Knowledge," he says, "is more important than life"). *The Thing from Another World* also forges a link with *Frankenstein* in its evocative use of the North Pole as a setting; Mary Shelley had employed the same backdrop as a framing device for her novel, though it had not yet been featured in any film adaptation.

The arrest, trial, and execution of Julius and Ethel Rosenberg for passing atomic secrets to Russia gripped the nation between 1950 and 1953, a period when invasion fantasies with atomic overtones began to proliferate in Hollywood films. The Promethean theme of unforgivable fire stealing pervaded the trial and its aftermath. Of course there was nothing proprietary about the principles of nuclear physics, and the Rosenbergs' alleged contact with the "enemy" took place during the war, when Russia was an American ally. As early as 1946 physicist E. U. Condon, writing in the *Bulletin of the Atomic Scientists,* argued for a realistic attitude: "The laws of nature, some seem to think, are ours exclusively, and that we can keep others from learning by locking up what we have learned in the laboratory. . . . Having created an air of suspicion and mistrust, there will be persons among us who think that other nations can know nothing except what is learned by espionage. . . ."

Thus the already fluid metaphor of nuclear energy became colored by an additional overlay of invasion or violation fantasy. Among the rash of movies released during the Rosenberg incarceration was *Five* (1951), a landmark, if talky, film about a quintet of nuclear holocaust survivors, directed by Arch Oboler, best known for his legendary radio suspense series *Lights Out.* George Pal's *When Worlds Collide* (1951) didn't mention the atomic bomb, but its end-of-the-world story would likely not have found as strong an audience in the absence of real apocalyptic fear.

In Robert Wise's *The Day the Earth Stood Still* (1951), earth is issued a stern warning by the alien visitor Klaatu (Michael Rennie, finally cast after Claude Rains and Spencer Tracy had proved unavailable) not to export its deadly nuclear capabilities into space, upon penalty of global extinction by more evolved races that have successfully eliminated territorial aggression from their cultures. The film marked the first musical use of the eerie electronic theremin in a strange science context; previously it had been used by Alfred Hitchcock for surrealistic dream sequences in *Spellbound* (1945) and to underscore the alcoholic mental state of Ray Milland in *The Lost Weekend* (1947). Thereafter the futuristic instrument (which is played without strings or keyboard by moving the hands through an electronic field) was almost exclusively identified with the science fiction genre, its occasional use as backup instrumentation by the Beach Boys notwithstanding.

The advertisements for *The Day the Earth Stood Still* are notable for inaugurating the now time-honored tradition of women with nearly exposed breasts as indispensable mad science iconography. Never mind that the décolletage displayed by the actress on the poster is nowhere to be found in the film itself; in the case of *The Day the Earth Stood Still,* Patricia Neal appears in the advertising art squirming in a tight red strapless dress while Gort, the robot, aims an extraterrestrial death ray over her shoulder, destroying the U.S. Capitol. In the film she never wears anything but the most conservative attire. A second poster for the film goes even further in altering her appearance: In an illustration based on an actual photograph of Neal being carried off by the robot, her real clothes are replaced with another low-cut dress (this one has straps, but they're falling off), and her hair is considerably lengthened, and bleached blond to boot. A quick glance at a selection of fifties posters reveals a steady equation between out-of-control science and over-

Poster for *The Day the Earth Stood Still* (1953).

flowing brassieres; breasts are promotionally prominent in graphics for *Invaders from Mars* (1953), *Monster from the Ocean Floor* (1954), *Forbidden Planet* (1956), *It Conquered the World* (1956), *Attack of the Crab Monsters* (1957), *Beginning of the End* (1957), *Invasion of the Saucer-Men* (1957), and dozens of others. My favorite is the anatomically improbable poster for *Bride of the Monster* (1955), in which the unconscious woman's mammaries are so eager for attention that both have somehow migrated to the same side of her chest.

On one level, the sci-fi films were simply reflecting the swelling Hollywood trend toward large-breasted blondes. But looking beyond the entrenched exploitation of the female body in advertising, one can discern a more revealing gestalt. The archetype of the nourishing breast, combined with fantastic images of science in the fifties, yields a concise visual statement: the attraction and terror of the technological teat.

The torrent of technology and science-driven socioeconomic change in the 1950s also spurred a desire for the return of protective parental moral and religious values seemingly swept away in the postwar tide of transformation. John L. Balderston, whose adaptation of Peggy Webling's *Frankenstein* had helped Universal Pictures launch Hollywood's mad science tradition in 1931, coscripted a bizarre right-wing harangue called *Red Planet Mars* (1952), in which the apparent voice of God, radioing earth from Mars, causes a counterrevolution in Russia and stops a Nazi inventor from destroying the world with something called a hydrogen valve. "In an age of A-Bombs, B-pictures, cold wars and science fiction," the *New York Times* observed, ". . . such items as *Red Planet Mars,* which landed at the Criterion on Saturday, would seem to be inevitable."

Although an inevitable *Frankenstein* energy pervaded the science fiction formulas of the fifties, the original picture that had set mad science rolling in Hollywood now took a backseat to more up-to-date horrors. The old film itself, however, had a fascinating secondary life in litigation. Balderston sued Universal in 1951 over money owed for several sequels involving the monster. The suit itself turned on a B movie–style question: Who brought the Frankenstein monster to life, and who could control it? Balderston, suffering from heart disease and near the end of his life, desperately needed a transfusion of cash (he had already liquidated many treasured possessions, including a Shakespeare first folio). Despite the somewhat shaky basis of the suit—the studio had used almost nothing of the Balderston-Webling play in the original film and, save for the prologue involving Mary Shelley, had substantially rewritten the contract work Balderston had done on the sequel—Universal settled out of court, paying Balderston and the Webling estate more than one hundred thousand dollars to acquire all future rights to the monster.

In 1957 *Frankenstein*'s director, James Whale, inactive for many years and disabled by a series of strokes, committed suicide in his Pacific Palisades swimming pool. It was years before his oeuvre received any serious critical attention. The same year *Frankenstein* figured prominently in another California court case, in which actress Mae Clarke (Frankenstein's fiancée, Elizabeth, in the film) filed a publicity-generating one-million-dollar suit against a Los Angeles television station and its female horror movie host, Ottola Nesmith. During the breaks in an October 1, 1957, broadcast of *Frankenstein,* the cornish Nesmith identified herself as Clarke ("You are going to see me tonight in *Frankenstein,* a film I made when I was young and pretty"). Clarke claimed that Nesmith had impersonated her as "an aged, demented, has-been actress, presumably poverty-stricken, slovenly attired, and arthritic of body." According to Clarke, "I saw my whole career destroyed, all I had done, all I had worked for, all my future earnings swept away in one-

and-a-half hours." In the only recorded instance of a mad science movie being screened in an American courtroom, *Frankenstein* was projected for a superior court jury on July 16, 1958, which found for the defense. Upon appeal, however, Clarke won the right to a new trial and settled out of court for a "substantial sum."

But aside from television and the courtroom, *Frankenstein's* quaint pyrotechnics amounted to a mere sideshow next to the box-office bang of the Bomb.

In Columbia Picture's *Invasion USA* (1952), atomic bombs are used to attack New York, Washington, and Boulder Dam, but the story turns out to be a demonstration of mass hypnosis. Paramount's *War of the Worlds* (1953), directed by George Pal, didn't depict an actual atomic holocaust, but its images of alien death rays and mass conflagration had only one referent in the real world, and it was hotly radioactive.

Weird science films would prove to be just what the mad doctor ordered in an America embarking on a backlash binge against experts of all stripes. The 1952 presidential race, between Dwight Eisenhower and Adlai Stevenson, became a mass referendum on guts versus brains, men of action versus ivory tower intellectuals. (*Red Planet Mars,* released two months before the Republican National Convention of 1952, confidently assumed the ascendancy of Dwight Eisenhower, featuring a fictional president with a strong physical resemblance to Ike, identifying him as a former general to boot.)

Anti-intellectualism isn't anything new in American culture, and reaches back to the puritanical distrust of prideful knowledge. Richard Hofstadter, in his classic study *Anti-intellectualism in American Life,* observes that Stevenson "became the victim of the accumulated grievances against intellectuals and brain-trusters which had festered in the American right wing since 1933." The McCarthy era pushed further an "atmosphere of fervent malice and humorless imbecility" in American affairs. The average citizen, writes Hofstadter, "cannot cease to need or to be at the mercy of experts, but he can achieve a kind of revenge by ridiculing the wild-eyed professor, the irresponsible brain-truster, or the mad scientist. . . ."

The Eisenhower-Stevenson conflict embedded itself firmly in the narrative formulas of 1950s science fiction films, the ones in which the military is called in to clean up the debris generated by starry-eyed scientist intellectuals. The appeal of action over thoughtfulness was understandable in a public still heady over winning the war (the only American conflict since the Revolution to enjoy unqualified public support). But Hofstadter finds that the negative stereotype of intellectualism in the 1950s was only the most recent manifestation of a long tradition: "Filled with obscure and ill-directed grievances and frustrations, with elaborate hallucinations about secrets and conspiracies, groups of malcontents have found scapegoats at various times in Masons or abolitionists, Catholics, Mormons, or Jews, Negroes or immigrants, the liquor interests or the international bankers. In the succession of scapegoats chosen by the followers of Know-Nothingism, the intelligentsia have at last in our time found a place."

The human brain itself was presented in an evil light in *Donovan's Brain* (1952). Dr. Patrick Cory (Lew Ayres, in a marked departure from his benign Dr. Kildare persona of the 1940s) keeps alive the brain of a ruthless industrialist whose body has perished in an air crash. Half submerged in an aquarium-style tank, Donovan's brain begins to throb and glow malevolently and in short order stages a leveraged telepathic takeover of Cory's personality. Where, in his corporeal life, Donovan ever learned this neat out-of-body trick is never really explained, but soon Cory is continuing Donovan's tax evasion scams from beyond the grave and blackmailing his former business associates. Cory's concerned wife, played by Nancy Davis (later First Lady Nancy Reagan), is concerned only to a point; her initial ethical qualms about her husband's stealing a brain—she actually helps him cut it out—and putting it on life support in a laboratory just off the cozy living room are quickly quelled by her husband's reassurances and brash enthusiasm for science. Davis gives a truly weird performance, with a manner and vocal delivery that seem telegraphed in from some other, very different picture. Intentional or not, the out-of-sync quality is somehow appropriate to a character who comes to accept a disembodied brain and its attendant apparatus as just another piece of home furnishing, postwar style. Brains, finally, are the problem in the film, just as they were in the same year's presidential campaign. Cory's overreaching intellectual curiosity merges with the misapplied brainpower of a vengeful megalomaniac, with disastrous results. (All that thinking!) The future First Lady knows best: Just turn off your higher brain functions, watch out for your husband's interests, and everything will be fine.

But sometimes other people's brain functions needed to be turned off—permanently. Questions of guilt aside, the executions of Julius and Ethel Rosenberg on June 19, 1953, amounted to a burning at the electrical stake of wizards who trafficked in forbidden, poisonous knowledge. The fallibility of modern technology was gruesomely underscored by the multiple applications of electricity needed to kill Ethel and the "ghastly plume" of smoke that rose from her head to smudge the skylight of the Sing-Sing death house. Jean-Paul Sartre, the following day, published an excoriating attack on America in the pages of the Parisian daily *Libération:* "By killing the Rosenberg's you have quite simply tried to halt the progress of science by human sacrifice. Magic, witch hunts, auto-da-fe's, sacrifices—we are here getting to the point: your country is sick with fear. . . ."

The prosecution of the Rosenbergs served many purposes beyond pure justice, advanced numerous political careers, and provided useful scapegoats for America's fear-sickness. The Soviet atomic threat, however, was hardly illusory, though its cracked reflection in sci-fi entertainment of the time, abetted by the never-ending rerun loop of television, persists in memory longer than the historical facts. As a result, our perception of the Red Scare is often colored by a surreal, campy hysteria that distorts the very real fears generated by the cold war.

One classic manifestation of nuclear fear—the association of atomic energy with giant rampaging Hollywood monsters—began the very summer of the Rosenberg executions with Warner Bros.' *The Beast from 20,000 Fathoms* (1953), based, extremely loosely, on a *Saturday Evening Post* story by Ray Bradbury titled "The Fog Horn," in which a slumbering prehistoric beast is roused from the deep by a lighthouse horn that sounds like a monstrous, melancholy mating call. Bradbury's story was strictly a mood piece and required considerable expansion, not to mention distortion, for the screen. In the film the dinosaur is freed from an aeons-old ice prison by atomic testing, although it is not in any sense an atomic mutation. The reawakened Beast goes on a rampage in lower Manhattan and is finally chased to Coney Island, to be spectacularly destroyed while trapped in the cagelike confines of a roller coaster.

Around the time of *The Beast from 20,000 Fathoms,* Warner was also developing a film based on an original story by screenwriter George Worthing Yates about giant ants running amok in the New York City subway system. Yates called his story "Them!" He had posited nuclear radiation as the explanation for the insects' enormous size, rather like the highly publicized giant marigolds grown from irradiated seeds. From the standpoint of animal biology, it was a dumb idea but a highly visual one. And thereby George Worthing Yates, previously known as the scriptwriter of such films as *This Woman Is Dangerous* (1952) with Joan Crawford and *Those Redheads from Seattle* (1953) with Rhonda Fleming, set in motion one of the most imitated motion-picture formulas of all time.

Them! (1954) producer Ted Sherdeman had served as a staff officer to General Douglas MacArthur during World War II and had strong feelings about the use of nuclear weapons. Upon hearing about the Hiroshima bombing, "I just went over to the curb and started to throw up," he said. When the story treatment for *Them!* crossed his desk, Sherdeman saw two pluses: "Everyone had seen ants and no one trusted the atom bomb, so I had Warner buy the story."

Unfortunately, screenwriter Yates, like many a mad scientist, overreached in his creation of mutant insects and turned in a script that deviated considerably from his original concept and was considered unfilmable because of budget considerations. Sherdeman took the script over and shaped the final version, which moved the ants from New York subway tunnels to Los Angeles storm sewers, and eliminated a final battle between the military and the monsters on a Santa Monica amusement pier (Warner story editors, almost certainly, transplanted this concept to the roller coaster finale of *The Beast from 20,000 Fathoms*). *Them!* director Gordon Douglas recalled that the production team took the story very seriously. They "weren't trying to make a comic strip or be cute about it. . . . We talked a great deal about the bombs these scientists were playing around with. . . ." Douglas was disappointed when further budget cuts made it necessary to film *Them!* in black and white rather than in 3-D and color, as had originally been planned. "I put green and

Atomic anxiety proves its legs: The creepy-crawly menace of *Them!* (1954).

red soap bubbles in their eyes," Douglas recalled of the twelve-foot-long mechanical bugs. "The ants were purple, slimy things. Their bodies were wet down with Vaseline. They scared the bejeezus out of you."

Them! was the first piece of popular entertainment to suggest, however wrongheadedly, that nuclear radiation might cause garden-variety insects, arachnids, or reptiles to metamorphose into gigantic monsters threatening the postwar peace and prosperity. The novelty and topicality of the subject drew large audiences and even half-respectful critical attention. Bosley Crowther of the *New York Times* called the film "tense, absorbing, and surprisingly enough, somewhat convincing." *Time* took the new style in monsters in stride, finding in the faces of the giant ants "just that expression of chinless, bulge-eyed evil that Peter Lorre has been trying all these years to perfect."

The Japanese film *Gojira* (1954) didn't receive an American release until 1956, with some added, Westernized footage featuring Raymond Burr. Known here as *Godzilla, King of the Monsters,* it came to epitomize the atomic

mutation genre, the first in what was to be the longest-running monster series of all time. Rather than simply be caused by the bomb, Godzilla, in
essence, *was* the bomb, the pop culture by-product of the only culture that
had directly felt the power of the atom unleashed. To begin a healing process,
it was first necessary to name the trauma, put a face on it—even if the face
was that of a fanciful prehistoric dragon somehow "awakened" by atomic
testing. Godzilla may have helped Japanese to come to terms with the
awful reality of Hiroshima and Nagasaki through a process of desensitiza-
tion; repeated over and over through the course of the film and its many sequels, the spectacle of a radioactive, fire-breathing horror destroying Japanese
cities became easier and easier to take. In contrast with Godzilla's later
campy, even cuddly persona, the monster depicted in the original film is
somber and frightening.

The American film formulas were much more preoccupied with guilt,
sin, and fear, focused on the anticipation of judgment, retribution, and irradiation. Images of postwar prosperity and domesticity were inevitably under
siege; a key bit of iconography occurs in *The Spider* (1958) as a mammoth,
marauding tarantula takes to main
street for lunch. A looming crane shot
from the spider's point of view de-
scends inexorably on a screaming
woman, doomed because her dress is
caught in the door of a shiny new car.
Americans have awful science-related
messes to clean up in films like
Tarantula (1956), *The Monster That
Challenged the World* (1957), *The Attack of the Crab Monsters* (1957), *Beginning of the End* (1957), *The Amazing
Colossal Man* (1957), *War of the Colossal Beast* (1958), and *Attack of the
Fifty-Foot Woman* (1958), to name just
a few.

"It Must Eat You to Live!"
Advertisement for *The Spider* (1958).

No escape from runaway science. John Agar and Mara Corday in a publicity still for *Tarantula* (1955).

It might at first seem a stretch to compare giant radioactive bugs in the movies to dust balls in the home, but both were part of a continuum of contamination anxiety particular to the 1950s. In *Chasing Dirt: The American Pursuit of Cleanliness,* Suellen Hoy chronicles the "culture of cleanliness" that had its roots in the nineteenth century but reached full expression in the years following World War II. "Considerations of health, which had been so important before World War II, ceased to be a primary reason for cleanliness after 1945. The contagious diseases that had plagued Americans for nearly all their history had virtually disappeared." Nonetheless, America felt dirty. In order to reassure themselves that they had truly joined the middle class, millions of the newly upwardly mobile turned to ritual cleansing. "Afraid of backsliding and afraid of offending, they became the main market for an endless supply of deodorants, mouthwashes, shavers, improved detergents, kitchen appliances, and bathroom fixtures." Hoy doesn't speculate about the fear, conscious or unconscious, of nuclear fallout and ideological contamination, but these issues were more than mere subtexts in a decade that introduced Senator Joseph McCarthy, fallout shelters, and strontium 90.

Cultural historian Thomas Hine, in his classic study of postwar America, *Populuxe,* suggests that the 1950s fetish for push buttons on household appliances was part of a mass cultural ritual to tame the nuclear threat. "The President of the United States was widely viewed as having a push button on or in his desk that would trigger atomic war as surely and inexorably as a housewife could activate her dishwasher." In *Bride of the Monster* (1955), filmed under the title *Bride of the Atom,* schlock filmmaker Edward D. Wood, Jr., gave Bela Lugosi his last speaking role as Dr. Eric Vornoff, obsessed with creating an atomic superwoman; the subject of his experiment wears a traditional bridal gown to her up-to-date nuclear nuptials. Lugosi's laboratory, perhaps significantly, is thrown together out of low-tech household items, including a fifties-style refrigerator and, unintentionally underscoring the decade's stomach-churning atomic angst, someone's bottle of Pepto-Bismol, carelessly left in camera view. The atomic blast that ends the film (after Lugosi has been devoured by an irradiated octopus) is absurdly contained, virtually domesticated. An observer, within apparent yards of the rising mushroom cloud, has no difficulty intoning the script's judgmental coda: "He tampered in God's domain."

Images of atomic disaster worked their way into other kinds of films besides the science fiction and horror variety. At the climax of Robert Aldrich's noir classic *Kiss Me Deadly* (1955) the villain, Albert Dekker (Dr. Cyclops himself), describes the mysterious contents of a locked box to his moll in cryptic terms invoking Pandora, Lot's wife, and the Medusa. It's all too tempting. Deciding that what's inside must be worth a fortune, the treacherous blonde plugs Dekker, who, with his dying breath, begs her not to open the box. Of course she promptly does just that, releasing a glowing mass of atomic fire accompanied by a sound effect of obscene, devilish panting.

While 1950s America was enthralled by modern, moneymaking variations on the Faust-Frankenstein story, other parts of the world had strik-

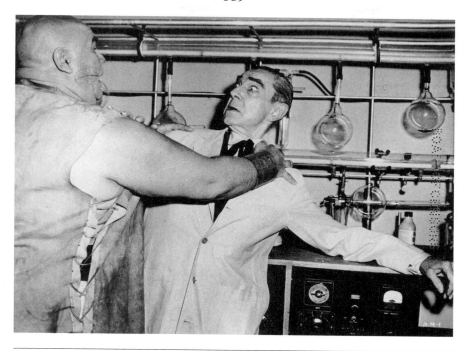

Bride of the Monster (1955). Tor Johnson upsets Bela Lugosi's nefariuos plans to engineer an atomic superrace.

ingly different reactions. In September 1955 South Africa's interior minister, T. E. Douglas, banned Mary Shelley's novel, calling it "indecent, objectionable and obscene." Merely owning the book was grounds for a twenty-eight-hundred-dollar fine and five years in prison. In Australia, novelist Nevil Shute wrote an international best seller, *On the Beach* (1957), that trumped all the bug-eyed monster stories with its low-keyed narrative describing the end of all life on earth following a short, but devastating, nuclear war. Shute presents a bleak, post–hydrogen bomb deathwatch, as the inhabitants of Melbourne spend five months counting down the arrival of the radioactive cloud that has exterminated the rest of the human race. Written in stoic, Hemingwayesque prose, and with nary a mutant in sight, the book follows its characters to their inescapable annihilation; the result, according to the *Atlantic,* is a narrative with "a kind of cobra fascination." *Kirkus Reviews* called it "an obsessive, nightmarish book, the more so because it is written on almost a deadpan level of narration, deliberately shorn of histrionics." *Catholic World* had some specific complaints: "A young Australian woman in love with the American captain agree[s] that a 'smutty love affair' is no way in which to face the world's end. Good marks for that, of course. But *On the Beach* must set a record for suicides. I know of no other novel in which all the major characters, all, commit suicide. For this reason, despite the author's skill and the book's crusading earnestness, *On the Beach* definitely cannot be recommended to any reader."

Nonetheless, the book received considerable favorable word of mouth, and in 1959 it was adapted reverently to the screen by Stanley Kramer as Hollywood's first "prestige" nuclear nightmare. The all-star cast included Gregory Peck, Ava Gardner, Fred Astaire, and Anthony Perkins. Linus Pauling, soon to be awarded the Nobel Peace Prize, actually provided a blurb for the film, predicting that *On the Beach* would be remembered as "the movie that saved the world." This prompted critic Pauline Kael to take a snipe at both the film and director Kramer; his greatest ability, she wrote, "may have been for eliciting fatuous endorsements from eminent people." Others took the film quite seriously; the Eisenhower administration, recently having issued a national shelter policy, urging all citizens to take the responsibility for building and maintaining home fallout shelters, responded dutifully to the Hollywood hoopla by issuing an internal document called "Possible Questions and Suggested Answers on the Film 'On the Beach.' "

The film was chosen as best of the year by both the *New York Times* and the *New York Herald Tribune,* despite *Variety*'s complaint that "there is no relief from depression. The spectator is left with the sick feeling that he's had a preview of Armageddon, in which all the contestants lost."

In spite of the boom and gloom, *On*

The atomic Pandora: Gaby Rodgers in *Kiss Me Deadly* (1955).

the Beach grossed $5,300,000, making it the fifth-highest-earning film of the 1960 season, trailing only *Ben-Hur, Psycho, Operation Petticoat,* and *Suddenly, Last Summer.* Another postapocalyptic film of 1959, *The World, the Flesh, and the Devil,* did not fare so well at the box office; its story of a lone trio of nuclear survivors (Harry Belafonte, Inger Stevens, and Mel Ferrer) used a Rod Serlingesque premise to hammer home a liberal parable about race relations, one that failed to ignite audience interest.

By the late 1950s the B movie clichés were becoming sufficiently threadbare to reveal the floorboards beneath *Frankenstein 1970* (filmed in 1958) can be read as a nearly transparent allegory of postwar Hollywood sci-fi–horror: Baron Frankenstein (Boris Karloff), tortured by Nazis, allows his castle to be used by an American film crew in exchange for the nuclear reactor he needs to revive his monster. The film studios, of course, had been doing exactly that for the better part of a decade: exploiting atomic energy to resurrect the Frankenstein formula on-screen. *On the Beach* marked a turning point in the popular representation of nuclear issues; whatever its deficiencies as a novel or film, Shute's story managed to strip away the bug-eyed monster mask from what lay beneath, an old-fashioned skull. Once faced directly, the primal fear of death no longer required Hollywood euphemisms.

Atomic mutation and radiation anxiety have now largely faded from the front burners of popular discourse. Radioactive monsters are now primarily the stuff of camp nostalgia, but Rappaccini's poisoned garden still flourishes in its own mutated forms. A key transitional film, Stanley Kubrick's *Dr. Strangelove or: How I Learned to Stop Worrying and Love the Bomb* (1964) lampooned paranoid notions of ideological contamination with General Jack D. Ripper (Sterling Hayden) and his now-famous rants about "precious bodily fluids" and their imminent pollution.

A decade before Rachel Carson's *Silent Spring* (1962) alerted the world to the poisonous shadow of pesticides, one can detect a nascent environmentalism in popular culture's fixation on polluted worlds that strike back at their polluters. These worlds were very much our own; beginning with *Them!,* a remarkable number of the fifties monsters were nothing more than ordinary inhabitants of the backyard, poisoned by radiation and massively

Garden-variety postwar horror: *The Deadly Mantis* (1957).

magnified into predatory horrors: ants, spiders, praying mantises, grasshoppers, and, in one case, even trees (1959's *From Hell It Came*). Occasionally the standard big-bug formula was treated with unusual inspiration, as in *The Fly* (1958), the story of a French-Canadian scientist, André DeLambre (Al Hedison), whose experiments with matter teleportation scramble his atoms with those of a housefly. Part of the horror is obvious—the ickyness of a human-size fly—but some of the shudders come from the implied question of humanity's ultimate place in the ecosystem, where we are already entangled with a complex web of insects, microbes, and other "insignificant" life forms, of which, science tells us, we may be just another passing example.

A good deal of environmentalist rhetoric has been shaped, at least to some extent, by mad science conceits: the evils of technology and technological thinking, science-created horrors (in this case, frightfully fouled ecosystems) that rise up to destroy their makers, and grandiose, Saturday-matinee talk about "destroying the planet" and "saving the planet." Hollywood environmentalists, inhabitants of a particularly megalomaniacal ecosystem dedicated to the construction and destruction of imaginary worlds, are especially adept at this kind of rhetoric.

Although I'm hardly an apologist for polluters, I believe it's important to recognize the less rational, often paradoxical pop cult shadings that attach themselves to serious issues, environmental and otherwise. For instance, it was fascinating to see our environmental vice president, Al Gore, dressed up as the Frankenstein monster for a White House Halloween party a couple of years ago, lampooning and defusing the central mythos from which the most passionate environmentalism draws its fire. Is Big Al really an environmentalist, or does he just play one on TV?

At its puritanical extreme, radical environmentalism implies that human beings, with their messy minds and wills, are the worst pollution of all, a kind of take-no-prisoners judgment one might expect to hear from a race of genocidal space aliens. To the greenest of the green, human consciousness and culture represent a fall from natural grace, the original sin that keeps on fouling the garden. Environmental degradation is real, but so is the human tendency to find new shapes for old scapegoats. As the cold war waned, so did concepts of danger and dirt. Today it's not fallout but the secondhand emanations of the smoker next door that threaten our precious bodily fluids. Not surprisingly, the most malevolent character currently on television is the Cigarette-smoking Man on *The X-Files,* representing secret knowledge about fantastically advanced technologies. But unlike the traditional snake in the garden, this one tempts by withholding knowledge, not by proffering it.

The concern with environmental degradation has in recent years blurred with an obsession over personal violation; in a holistic sense the environment can be regarded as identical with the self. Todd Haynes's film *Safe* (1995) introduces Carol White

Atom-scrambled scientist André Delambre (Al Hedison) in *The Fly* (1958).

The dehumanizing scientific gaze: a typical pulp magazine cover from the 1950s.

(Julianne Moore), a San Fernando Valley housewife who escapes from a soul-killing marriage into the perverse salvation of chemical supersensitivity. In Haynes's deadpan but savage satire, Carol's empty consumer existence is finally given meaning by an allergic insurrection against the invisible by-products of modern science, technology, and industry. Retreating from a toxic world into a cultlike eco-retreat of a kind undreamed of by Rappaccini's daughter, Carol becomes a pampered doll, valued at last, a chosen martyr to the technochemical sins of the modern world.

Though today nearly devoid of atomic monsters, Rappaccini's garden is not without other abiding inhabitants. After all, the forbidden fruit of scientific knowledge requires a presiding serpent to tend its groves. Whether little and green, small and gray, bug-eyed, scaly, or spectacularly frilled and antennaed, the space alien and its ambiguous allure have provided the most enduring legacy of the postwar struggle with mad science and are the subject of the chapter that follows.

CHAPTER FIVE

Alien Chic

On the night of October 17, 1973, I spent more than an hour in the company of a UFO, an event I have never written about until now but the memory of which has never left me. I was a college student then, a junior at the Athens campus of Ohio University. It was a clear autumn night, and a little after midnight I was walking home down East State Street to the apartment I shared with my girlfriend. Athens is an idyllic college town in

An ailing alien from the television movie *Roswell* (1994).

195

southeastern Ohio, nestled in the Appalachian foothills but maintaining a distinctly New England ambience. The main section of the campus, the College Green, was patterned after Harvard Yard, in fact designed by the same architect. As an editor of the Ohio University *Post* I had just finished "putting to bed" the next morning's edition. The *Post* was a professional daily staffed by students and generally considered one of the top college papers in the country. It attracted a remarkable number of student journalists who later went on to successful media careers; perhaps foremost among them was Joe Eszterhas, recently screenwriter of lurid Hollywood megahits like *Fatal Attraction* and megaflops like *Showgirls*. Eszterhas had graduated a couple of years before and gone off to work for the *Cleveland Plain Dealer* and *Rolling Stone*. Nonetheless, we ended up sharing a connection through the Great UFO Flap of 1973.

Although I had received a four-year journalism scholarship that covered my tuition, I still had to work to pay for housing, food, and textbooks. In my case it meant going to classes all day and then working past midnight at the *Post,* often at the expense of nodding off during early-morning lectures. In short, I was very tired and had nothing on my mind besides getting home to North May Street, about a half-hour walk from campus. In terms of media, Athens was fairly isolated. Television reception (in those pre-cable days) was almost nil, and I had not yet read any of the newspaper accounts from the past week about strange aerial phenomena that had been appearing in regional papers like the *Cincinnati Inquirer* and the *Columbus Dispatch*. Although I was at this point both a science fiction fan and a published science fiction writer, UFO stories had never been a particular interest of mine. Perhaps because flying saucers had frightened me as a kid, I unconsciously avoided the subject.

I had made their acquaintance via television in the late fifties and early sixties. The pioneer anthology series *Science Fiction Theatre* had given me my very first glimpse. What was, in retrospect, a crudely superimposed image of a glowing disk approaching an observatory scared me so badly at the age of five that I slept facing away from my bedroom window for years afterward. In the same way that I *knew* looking up at towering Ohio storm clouds would instantly cause funnel clouds to sprout, I *knew* that an unguarded glance at the night sky might bring me face-to-face with a battalion of flying saucers, silent, scrutinizing, and, in some inexplicable way, terrifyingly *judgmental*. I was somewhat older but only a bit less impressionable when Cleveland television introduced me to *Invaders from Mars,* presented as afternoon entertainment on KYW-TV's *The Early Show*. Fresh from an afterschool Cub Scout meeting and still wearing my uniform with its yellow bandanna, I watched with a sickening fascination as the film's little boy endured precisely the nightmare I always dreaded but had never seen depicted: witnessing the arrival of a UFO through his bedroom window. The rest of the film more than lived up to the promise of that primal scene, a creepy end-of-innocence tale set against a backdrop of advanced, malevolent technology, orchestrated by a Supreme Intelligence (an octopus-legged head isolated in an aquariumlike globe). One by one, parents and authority figures were sucked down a sandpit to the saucer's underground hiding place and each there turned into a zombie by a needlelike probe inserted at the base of the skull.

Not long after I saw *Invaders from Mars,* NBC's *Saturday Night at the Movies* telecast *The Day the Earth Stood Still,* which introduced a new generation of kids to the idea that science had gone too far and needed to be curbed for everyone's protection. Curiously, the protector was itself an example of advanced technologies of destruction: the Frankensteinish robot Gort, whose basilisk gaze could not only kill but disintegrate. Gort was really scary, and my friends and I spent days getting a handle on our fears by drawing pictures of Gort in our loose-leaf notebooks and solemnly intoning the film's talismanic mantra: "Klaatu . . . barada . . . nikto!"

A decade later, after midnight on a quiet street in Athens, Ohio, I was certainly not thinking about Gort, devouring sandpits, or *Science Fiction Theatre* as I stopped for a traffic light at the corner of East State and Carpenter streets, and I was therefore unpredisposed to regard the aircraft that passed overhead as anything more than a low-flying plane. Had it not been for the traffic light, I might never have looked up and realized that the "plane" had not moved during the time I was waiting to cross.

I looked up at the craft and saw that it was not, as I had first thought, a plane but something else entirely, a weird triangular airship with red and green navigational lights at each of its three corners. A pair of Athens

policemen, who also observed the craft from a foreshortened perspective farther uptown, described the UFO as shaped like an "ice cream cone." They
also reported a cluster of smaller white lights, "similar to falling stars," surrounding the object, though I saw no such thing. The object's solid metallic underside was clearly illuminated by the navigational lights. It was
hovering at a low altitude; I estimated it as under a thousand feet, for at least
part of its underside illumination came from the lights of the town below
(the Athens police estimated ten thousand feet, which strikes me as wildly
inaccurate but also demonstrates the *Rashomon*-like descriptive variations
that frequently attend UFO sightings).

The object was absolutely silent and absolutely motionless. Completely
baffled by the rigid fixity of its position, unaccompanied by the telltale
sound of a helicopter rotor or motors of any kind, I watched for several minutes. After a while it did begin to move, in a peculiar, deliberate way. There
was none of the drifting that one would associate with a balloon or a blimp.
It moved slowly at a right angle to its original direction, stopped for a few
minutes, then forward again and once more to the side in a methodical
zigzag course. I had the impression that it was moving slowly to one side,
then stopping, then back, and again to the side, as if it were methodically
traversing an invisible grid in the sky.

After watching for several more minutes (with none of the terror I associated with the televised UFOs of my childhood; I found the incident fascinating, not frightening), I called the *Post* offices from a pay phone at the
corner and was soon joined by another editor and one of our staff photogra-
phers who shot a roll of film. Unfortunately, in those days before the advent
of superfast film stocks, our darkroom's standard-issue Kodak Tri-X Pan
yielded only white blobs on the contact sheet. As the craft's plodding zigzag
began to head west, we followed in the other editor's car until the object finally disappeared behind the hills and trees outside the city limits. Meanwhile the Athens police reported that a second, similar but more cylindrical
object had replaced the first at the original location, where it remained for
a half hour until clouds moved in and obscured the view.

It remains the strangest, most inexplicable event I have ever witnessed.

During the previous week I had not been following the papers in
Cincinnati, Columbus, Cleveland, and New York (I caught up on my read-

ing twenty-two years later, via the microfilm holdings of the Ohio University library). If I had been attentive to the news outside Athens, I would have been aware that the country was in the middle of a major UFO "flap." Even the governor of Ohio, John Gilligan, claimed to have seen one. What was particularly interesting about this flap was the number of sightings that involved encounters with humanoid beings, perhaps the most concentrated wave of such incidents in history. I must admit that despite my long-standing interest in science fiction—I had just begun publishing short stories in magazines like *Amazing, The Magazine of Fantasy and Science Fiction* and in anthology series like *Orbit*—I didn't give much thought to the idea that I might be under surveillance by space people. Rather, some earthbound explanation—most likely related to nefarious government intelligence and the military—seemed far more plausible. After the cultural trauma of Vietnam, the Pentagon, rather than an alien planet, was the more logical point of origin for my strange hovercraft. The Watergate debacle was building a full head of steam, Spiro Agnew had just been forced from office, and there seemed no end to new revelations about secret and suspicious government-sponsored intrigues. About this time I also had the slightly creepy experience of interviewing Abbie Hoffman in a car that was being intently shadowed by a pair of government agents down the dark stretches of road between the Columbus airport and the university campus. In retrospect, it's surprising how much my junior year of college now seems like a time-warped episode of *The X-Files.* But my personal experiences were tame compared with other goings-on nearby.

In the adjacent town of Albany the night before, a woman claimed to have seen not only a UFO but a small, thin, "ghost-like" figure floating in the air, accompanied by a glowing object about twenty feet in diameter. After it departed, she was startled by the brief appearance of a two-and-one-half-foot-tall humanoid, bluish green with spiky protuberances on its head as it peered in an open door. Then, two nights after my own sighting, a farmer in Goshen, Ohio (also in Athens County), claimed to have encountered a landed UFO in a field where he was walking his dogs. Two human-size inhabitants boarded it with a ladder; it rose with a low hum, slowly at first, then shot off into the night.

All across the country during October 1973 people were reporting bizarre rendezvous with strange creatures and inexplicable aerial technologies. Unlike today's standard-issue alien, these visitors ran a considerable gamut of appearances. The month started off with the report of three Tennessee teenagers of a huge, hirsute (but nonetheless "robot-like") humanoid accompanied by an egg-shaped craft. On October 16 or 17 a Utah woman claimed to have been abducted for a medical examination by a group of noseless, fish-mouthed, telepathic beings with clawlike hands and wraparound eyes. On October 17 aliens near Danielsville, Georgia, were reported to have had reddish faces and white hair. The same night, in Europa, Mississippi, a "catfish-like" being with a single glowing eye, flipper feet, and webbing between its legs—not to mention feathery back rills—was said to have stopped traffic.

Elsewhere around the country people reported meeting up with specters of weird technology, manifested as aircraft shaped like spheres, disks, and brightly lit cigars; enduring blinding flashes of light that melted plastic eyeglass frames; and meeting diminutive silver-suited creatures that bounded like jackrabbits along lonely country roads. But perhaps the most extravagant and publicized story of the 1973 "siege" (as numerous ufologists later dubbed it) involved the claim of two Pascagoula, Mississippi, fishermen, Charlie Hickson and Calvin Parker, to have been hauled aboard an alien spacecraft the night of October 11. My fellow *Post* alumnus Joe Eszterhas reported their account for *Rolling Stone* with rigorous fidelity to oral nuance:

> They floated on ovuh to us and I dropped my feeshin pole. They floated with their legs togethuh. They was bout five-foot tall, a little shortuh than me. The body resembled a human bein. The haid was kinda roun but it didn't have no neck. On the side of their haids in the place where ears oughta be, they had these things pointin out. . . . They had no eyes. I couldn't tell whether they were made outa metal or outa skeen. It was light gray, a little more like metal than a ayelphant's skeen. They had all these wrinkles on 'em. Their feet was roun like ayelphant's feet and it didn't have no toes. They didn't have no hands neithuh. They had these claws.

Hickson's story was devoured by the media. He was even a guest on The *Dick Cavett Show.* But his instant celebrity was meteoric, a burnout. "I don't understand it," Hickson's lawyer-agent complained to Eszterhas. "Their Exclusive Story is bigger than Watergate and nobody wants to buy it." But a lot of people (without option capital) did buy it, and the incident at Pascagoula remains enshrined in the annals of ufology.

Public UFO sightings—the kind I experienced, simultaneously observed by others and reported by the media as real news—have largely been replaced by the ornate folklore of alien abductions, recalled privately as dreams or "recovered memories" prompted by hypnosis. With the aid of highly partisan facilitators, abductees arrive at the fervent belief that they have been kidnapped by alien invaders, taken aboard spacecraft, and there subjected to dehumanizing medical procedures, often verging on high-tech sexual assault. The forms of sexual humiliation vary by sex: Women abductees are forced to undergo laparoscopic pregnancy tests; men are anally probed and milked of semen by strange devices (sometimes after being aroused by alien temptresses). More recent elaborations of the scenario posit that human germ plasm is being mixed with defective alien genes to help save a dying race. Both men and women report a quasi-sexual penetration of the nasal cavities by a long needle that "impregnates" the skull with a tiny electronic monitor or homing device (radio transmitters implanted in the brain have been a staple of clinical delusions virtually since the invention of radio). When discovered, such devices invariably disintegrate, leaving no medically detectable trace. Similarly, women impregnated with hybrid human-alien fetuses claim that the embryos are stolen from their wombs before they come to term—again, without clinical evidence that any kind of pregnancy has taken place. Just as post–World War II aliens were obsessed with the looming specter of nuclear energy, so aliens of the post–Sexual Revolution era are obsessed with human reproduction.

The methods employed to elicit abduction narratives closely parallel the techniques used by other practitioners to elicit "memories" by children of satanic rituals and sexual abuse (as in the McMartin preschool case) and adult memories of childhood incest and rape (often related by "multiple personalities," who manifest, much like the memories, during hypnosis). The seeming explosion of multiple personality disorder, and widespread public acceptance of its reality, may have less to do with a real clinical state than with the accelerated fragmentation of consciousness in recent decades. Every

American couch potato, after all, has instant access to a multiplicity of view-point shifts at the click of a button, the 500 Cable Options of Eve. The hypnotic aspects of prolonged television watching have been amply documented. Is it a mere coincidence that the dominant image of the hypnotically accessed alien is a couch potato caricature, a goggle-eyed travesty of a normal human being, its body pale and atrophied, fit only for voyeuristic image processing, the latest variation of the "degraded pendant" first imagined by H. G. Wells a hundred years ago?

It is my suspicion that virtually all abduction accounts are essentially outraged responses to the encroachments of science and its by-products on late-twentieth-century life. The sheer persistence of the abduction myth is evidence that it signifies *something;* whether the significance is real is another matter entirely. My purpose here is not to debate the merits of abductee arguments versus those of the debunkers but rather to focus on what both sides overlook or fail to comprehend: a raging popular resentment of science at the end of the most science-oriented century in history. Outright rejection of modern life and its scientific underpinning is inconceivable as a practical option for most of us, enslaved as we are to cars, computers, and conveniences. But repressed feelings always pop up somewhere, usually in veiled forms, and negative attitudes toward the power and authority of science find ample a socially acceptable outlet in UFO fantasies.

The typical debate about UFOs has long degenerated into a banal standoff between true believers and true disbelievers, with little room for people like me who have seen mysteriously maneuvering objects in the sky, objects that cannot be explained away as optical illusions, weather balloons, or swamp gas, but who also do not believe they originated on any other planet but our own. Had I witnessed the maneuvers of some kind of experimental surveillance aircraft, out for a test spin in a quiet, relatively remote area? Were people all across the country viewing other test flights of similar or related craft? (A decade later I immediately thought of my UFO when I saw the first published photos of the similarly shaped stealth bomber.) The 1973 flap was the last major wave of out-in-the-open sightings; the disappearance of UFOs from public view came roughly at the same time as advances in spy satellite technology would have rendered earth-hugging hovercraft obsolete. For whatever reason, UFOs and alien encounters have mostly moved from shared, observable space to the private domain of the therapist's office, recovered saucers giving way to the cult of recovered memories.

The history of UFOs reveals a cultural history of science-based angst, and the evolving image of the alien provides a shifting self-portrait of our multileveled anxieties about science, its applications and impact in the twentieth century. It has already become a cliché to assert that "aliens are us," a popular dumping ground for all manner of purely human concerns.

But the alien's function as a folk critique of intrusive science itself has been rarely examined, and then only barely. Even the most intelligent debunkers of abductee stories have a blind spot when it comes to acknowledging the genuine apprehension or discontent with "the age of scientific marvels" that underlies the folklore. To Carl Sagan, in his recent book *The Demon-Haunted World: Science as a Candle in the Dark,* "the UFO abduction syndrome portrays, it seems to me, a banal Universe. The form of the supposed aliens is marked by a failure of the imagination and a preoccupation with human concerns. Not a single being presented in all these accounts is as astonishing as a cockatoo would be if you never beheld a bird. . . . The believers take the common elements in their stories as tokens of verisimilitude, rather than as evidence that they have contrived their stories out of a shared culture. . . ."

Sagan makes some excellent points, but the scientist defending his candle (or is it a castle?) misses the bigger point of the villagers' torches. Debunkers emphasize the banality, stupidity, and hysteria of UFO abductees and frequently point out possible ulterior motives. Abductees become the focus of other people's attention, enlarge their circle of friends and acquaintances, are interviewed on TV, have books written about them, and achieve a certain level of prestige, albeit within a rather narrow world. In short, they have a chance to escape the anonymity and depersonalization characteristic of the postindustrial age and to enjoy simple forms of human interaction and gratification. There's an old joke about Los Angeles singles who intentionally get into car crashes as a way of meeting people. UFO abductions do the same thing, and you don't have to worry about seat belts. In a sense, the alien and the abductee are two halves of a gestalt: the anonymous, emotionless, technologized space-person-nobody modern science promises to make us all as well as the outraged, rebellious earthbound human being shouting, "Hell, no! I won't go!"

The first UFOs reported in America coincided with a much earlier scientific marvel age. From November 1896 to April 1897, the heyday of Tesla and Edison, newspapers all across the United States reported sightings of a dirigible-style aircraft, decades before the technology actually existed to build such a thing. Thousands of people were reported to have witnessed the craft, and "reported" is the operative word, as the late 1890s were also the heyday of circulation wars among sensation-oriented newspapers. There was little speculation about otherworldly origins; as the *San Francisco Call* quoted that city's mayor, Adolph Sutro, "I certainly think some shrewd inventor has solved the problem of aerial navigation, and that we will hear about it within a short time. It would not be any more wonderful than the invention of the telegraph, the telephone, the phonograph, or the X-ray, and it would seem that someone must hit on the proper appliances when so many smart men have been working on the problem." Eleven years earlier a similar craft had been described by Jules Verne in his novel *Robur the Conquerer* (1886). Rather than stir fears of an invasion from the skies, the 1896–1897 flap served mostly to fuel the "wizard" image of scientists and inventors pervasive at the turn of the century.

UFOs retreated from the skies for fifty years, though prototypes of the familiar disk-shaped object could be traced to pulp magazines and comic strips (most notably *Flash Gordon*) in the 1930s. The term "flying saucer" came into instant, universal usage in June 1947, when a Boise, Idaho, pilot named Kenneth Arnold observed a formation of nine peculiar objects maneuvering near Mount Rainier. Although he described the motion of the objects as "like a saucer . . . if you skipped it across the water," Arnold never described them as being *shaped* like saucers. In fact, he described exceedingly thin, mirror-surfaced aircraft with curved fronts, straight sides, and tapered, rounded tails. But the headline writers couldn't resist the image of saucers in flight (the aerodynamic properties of the disk, of course, predated the Frisbee patent by millennia). Once the powerful media suggestion was made, flying saucers looked like . . . well, flying saucers. Within days people began reporting objects in the skies resembling disks and even hubcaps—not what Arnold actually said he saw, but what headline writers, always reaching for an easy image, said he had seen. As writer Martin S. Kottmeyer has noted, "The implications of this journalistic error are staggering in the extreme. Not only does it unambiguously point to a cultural origin of the whole flying saucer phenomenon, it erects a first-order paradox into any attempt to interpret the phenomenon in extraterrestrial terms: Why would extraterrestrials redesign their craft to conform to [the journalistic] error?"

The following month, the discovery of a crash debris in the desert near Roswell, New Mexico, prompted a local newspaper to announce in a banner headline that the air force had recovered a flying saucer. In all fairness, it must be said that the initial newspaper accounts were based on a press release handed out, then hastily recalled by the military itself. The reason for such a bizarre announcement remains obscure—a uniquely inept attempt at strategic disinformation?—but it helped set in motion one of the most persistent UFO-alien stories of all time, one that was to grow and shape-shift with the changing winds of Alien Chic.

The first report of the Roswell story didn't have aliens; they came later. But it is clear that military intelligence was disturbed by reports of strange aircraft invading U.S. territory. It had been only twenty-four months, after all, since our own *Enola Gay* made a surprise appearance over Hiroshima. The debris from the crash consisted of foil-like material and lightweight struts that some witnesses later said were covered with symbols resembling hieroglyphics. Major Jesse A. Marcel, intelligence officer at Roswell Army Air Force Base, was one of the first military personnel to examine the debris on-site. He claimed that the foil covering displayed extraordinary resiliency, unfolding without a crease after being crumpled in the hand. He further claimed that the original debris was confiscated by military brass and replaced by pieces of a weather balloon with which Marcel was forced to pose for official photographs, thus taking the fall for the first UFO cover-up, four years before the term "UFO" was even coined. Marcel died in 1986, shortly before a new generation of ufologists began retrofitting the Roswell legend with all the latest stylings of Alien Chic. But I may be getting ahead of the story.

The fashionably anorexic space visitor of today—big-headed, waiflike, eyes bulging like Jackie O's wraparound shades—had a considerable cultural gestation in its inexorable slouching path toward Steven Spielberg, Whitley Strieber, and Oprah Winfrey. The pulp magazine monsters of the 1920s through the 1940s were such a disparate lot that they seem to have canceled themselves out from the standpoint of cultural retention; only Wells's big-brained tadpoles had a lasting influence on physical concepts of alien beings. The "little green man" stereotype of the 1950s—a character image that everyone "knows" but that is surprisingly difficult to document—had little connection to science fiction literature, Hollywood, or ufology; it's an image based primarily in the ephemeral folk culture of cartoons, advertising, and jokes. World War II generated the mythology of "foo-fighters" and gremlins. The former were mysterious lights reported to trail fighter planes; the latter were fabled invisible creatures believed to cause mischief by tampering with aircraft machinery (the precise origin of the word gets a question mark in most dictionaries, but it seems an obvious variation on "goblin").

Though gremlins couldn't be seen, they were nonetheless often depicted by illustrators and cartoonists as airborne gnomes, elves, or pixies. Folklorists have pointed out the intriguing structural similarities between traditional tales of encounters with fairies and modern abductions by aliens, and it seems clear that the human mind has an considerable archetypal store of fantastic pint-size beings that have traditionally inhabited the space between wide-awake rationality and the illogic of dreams.

Hollywood's first alien following the birth of the flying saucer was anything but diminutive. In *The Thing from Another World* (1951) the alien closely resembled Hollywood's Frankenstein monster. Elements of the Frankenstein monster makeup—the exaggerated forehead, dark eyes, cadaverous bone structure—continue to influence popular imaginings about aliens.

The bald, bulge-headed menace of *The Thing* (not to mention long-ingrained images of Dr. Cyclops and his ilk) may have had an indirect connection to a popular political epithet—"egghead"—introduced the following year in a successful effort to demonize intellectuals. The word was first used pejoratively in the national media by the columnist Stewart Alsop during the Stevenson-Eisenhower presidential campaign of 1952. The writer attributed the actual coinage to his brother John, a Connecticut politician. John Alsop explained the term as "a visual figure of speech, tending to depict a large oval head, smooth, faceless, unemotional, but a little bit haughty and condescending." Arthur Schlesinger, Jr., recalled that the term "had rather an Ivy League connotation—an A.B. degree, button-down collars, tweeds and flannels, perhaps pipes and crew haircuts, with a lively but amateur interest in the intellectual life and a capacity to read without moving one's lips." "Egghead" neatly comprised modern Frankenstein images—the Thing; the robot Gort

This Island Earth (1955). Big, throbbing brains reflected a postwar mistrust of experts, intellectuals, and scientists.

Retroalien: *It: The Terror from beyond Space* (1958).

("large oval head, smooth, faceless, unemotional")—as well as the educated highbrows most likely to dabble in monster making in the first place.

Real-life accounts of alien contact in the early 1950s took their cues from Hollywood; according to such pioneer contactees as George Adamski (a self-styled "professor" who ran a hamburger stand near Mount Palomar and traded outrageously on his scientific-sounding address), aliens were idealized Nordic types on a mission to warn humanity against the dangers of nuclear energy. This of course was exactly the plot of *The Day the Earth Stood Still,* released in 1951, the year before Adamski claimed to begin his own communication with visitors espousing suspiciously Michael Rennie-esque warnings. Other contactees of the 1950s communicated with otherworldly beings through trance mediumship. The oft-stated goal of the cultlike contactee movement was to reconcile the gap between science and religion, an atomic age replay of the previous century's spiritualist response to Darwin and other materialist thinkers. According to UFO historian Curtis Peebles, "The contactee myth offered an escape from what some saw as an 'inevitable' nuclear war. The aliens came from utopian planets, untroubled by the problems of Earth," offering a form of divine intervention amounting to "a messiah-based religion for an age when traditional religion had lost its meaning."

In contrast with the heroic, angelic space people who gravitated to the contactees, Hollywood aliens of the 1950s were highly eclectic from a design standpoint. Like Edgar Rice Burroughs's pulp novel extraterrestrials, they juxtaposed human attributes with a wild assortment of reptilian, amphibian, and mammalian characteristics. There is no real reason to consider the makeup designs of Hollywood aliens separately from those of earthbound atomic mutations; they all were pop distillations of postwar invasion anxieties and were often created by the same studio artists and technicians. The specifics of a particular plot were of less concern than was competing with or improving upon previous achievements. As befitted a consumption-conscious decade, more was more when it came to monster makeups, which often included the cosmetic equivalents of tailfins and hood ornamentation. Headlight-size eyes, scales, antennae, bony armor plates, tentacles, tusks, and talons sprouted everywhere in films like *It: The Terror from Beyond Space, Invaders from Mars, Fifty Million Miles to Earth, The She Creature, The Monster of Piedras Blancas, It Conquered the World, It Came from Beneath the Sea, I Married a Monster from Outer Space,* and many others. Not all the monsters were Edsels; in particular, *The Creature from the Black Lagoon,* sculpted by Bud Westmore and Jack Kevan, proved one of Universal Studio's most inspired design concepts since the Frankenstein monster and later had a surprising but discernible influence on the evolution of alien physiognomy.

By the early 1960s the alien and atomic mutation cycle had pretty much played itself out in Hollywood. As the cold war heated up, science-fictional euphemism may have had little cultural purpose when real nuclear bombs were aimed at U.S. shores from Cuba. Writers like Ray Bradbury and television producer-writers like Rod Serling made insightful metaphoric use of the alien in the fifties and sixties. Bradbury's *The Martian Chronicles* ended with a memorable visitation of a father fulfilling his promise to show his children "Martians" in a deserted extraterrestrial canal. When the family peers over the edge, they are greeted with their own reflections. In one of the most acclaimed scripts for Serling's *The Twilight Zone,* "The Invaders" (1961),

The alien as sexual predator: Tom Tryon and Gloria Talbott in *I Married a Monster from Outer Space* (1958).

written by Richard Matheson, the inhabitant of an isolated house (a tour de force mute performance by Agnes Moorehead) is terrorized by a tiny flying saucer and its leprechaun-size crew. Following a siege, she destroys the craft with a butcher knife, after which the camera closes in on the "United States of America" insignia on the wreckage. Smart science fiction writers have always recognized the alien as a shadowy projection of the technologically obsessed self.

In the fall of 1961, near the beginning of the third season of *The Twilight Zone*, a New England couple named Betty and Barney Hill claimed to have viewed a strange, spinning aircraft that seemed to be following their car along a lonely road. They stopped and saw what appeared to be a long window framing figures in uniform. The ship started to descend. Barney Hill panicked, and the couple fled in their car. Afterward they felt they could not account for two hours of their time along the road. Betty Hill began having terrifying, recurrent dreams of being abducted and taken inside the UFO. Barney checked out a book on UFOs from a local library. Over the next two years they told their story to groups of interested people, including ufologists, who suggested that Betty's dreams might be not fantasies but memories of a real event. Barney's recollection of what happened after he looked at the saucer through binoculars was a blank, though he became familiar with Betty's dreams through their constant retelling over a two-year period.

During this time Barney Hill had been undergoing psychotherapy for anxiety attacks that were resisting treatment. His doctor recommended a Boston psychiatrist-neurologist, Dr. Benjamin Simon, a specialist in the use of clinical hypnosis, who might be able to crack Barney's amnesia. Simon never believed there was any truth to the abduction story but thought there was a buried conflict that might be uncovered by probing the fantasy about aliens. (The Hills were an interracial couple, she white and he black, suggesting obvious issues of "otherness.") In separate hypnotic sessions Betty's dreams, already detailed, became even more sharply focused, and Barney, for the first time, began to fill in the particulars of his "missing time." He sketched a couple of trance-induced impressions of his captors' appearance: one with large eyes, slanting around the side of its head, and one showing a tiny nose and slitlike mouth. Betty's impressions were much different: "I would judge them to be 5′ to 5′4″. Their chests are larger than ours; their noses were larger (longer) than the average size although I have seen people with noses like theirs—like Jimmy Durante's." She described their complexions as having "a gray tone: like gray paint with a black base; their lips were of bluish tint." Overall, they were "very human in their appearance, not frightening."

Though the Hills claimed to be concerned about their privacy, enough details of their therapy with Dr. Simon were passed on to the media (just who did the leaking isn't clear) to form the basis of a series of sensational and embarrassing articles in a Boston paper. The Hills then contacted the writer

John G. Fuller, who was finishing writing a book, *An Incident at Exeter,* about another New England UFO visitation, and who knew some of the details of their case. He proposed writing a second book completely devoted to the Hill story if Dr. Simon would release transcripts of their therapy sessions.

Simon was understandably upset by the unauthorized newspaper stories, which depicted his use of hypnosis to conjure space people with the stereotypical mad doctor flourishes. For a consideration of 40 percent of the proceeds from *The Interrupted Journey* (a fact not revealed in the introduction he wrote for the book), Dr. Simon made available the tapes, along with his notes. Fuller and Simon had many disagreements. It was agreed that "personal information" about the couple not directly related to the UFO incident would not be used in the book. Under the guise of privacy and patient-doctor confidentiality, it was essentially agreed that the full story of Betty and Barney Hill would never be told. The Hills dropped therapy after the alleviation of anxiety symptoms about the UFO encounter, despite Dr. Simon's opinion that they had not yet gotten anywhere near the actual, and likely nonextraterrestrial, truth. ("You can both see that this experience cannot be seen as an isolated thing. I've kept it isolated to the greatest extent possible . . . and there's a great deal of material here we will not get to, which is strongly involved. Your whole past history . . .") But even a layperson could raise some pointed questions. For instance, to what extent might a black man in an interracial marriage feel trapped or even "abducted" by a culturally dominant group? Why does the whole incident sound suspiciously like a sanitized account of a humiliating encounter by the Hills with a group of skinheads or their 1961 equivalent, including the molestation of Betty? ("They roll me over on my back, and the examiner has a long needle in his hand . . . bigger than any needle than I've ever seen. . . . And I tell him, no, it will hurt, don't do it, don't do it. . . .") What were the psychological payoffs for Betty in being treated like an oracle or sibyl? None of the real dynamics and tensions of the Hills' marriage are ever revealed in Fuller's book. To the reader, the UFO story becomes the only story, even though the doctor considered it a defensive screen for other conflicts omitted from the narrative.

Barney Hill didn't reveal his television viewing habits, but exactly twelve days before he described and sketched his alien captor for Dr. Simon, the NBC series *The Outer Limits* had aired an episode called "The Bellero Shield," featuring an alien with wraparound eyes, no nose, and an expressionless mouth; the creature (played by science fiction film veteran John Hoyt) looked remarkably like a smooth albino version of the creature from the Black Lagoon. Curiously, the story concerned a troubled married couple (Martin Landau and Sally Kellerman, with dragon lady assistance from housekeeper Chita Rivera) who accidentally trap an alien with a beam of laser light—an "abduction" in reverse. The ambitious wife—the stronger personality in the marriage—sees the alien as a quick route to power and riches. Rather than let it escape, she kills it for its hand-held energy shield, which traps her in a cagelike force field. After being freed, Bellero's traumatized wife is left with the permanent delusion that she is still imprisoned by alien technology.

While it is tempting to read a half allegory of the Hill marriage into "The Bellero Shield" (Betty's dominance in the partnership, her possible exploitation of "aliens" for private, earthbound purposes), it can't be stated with certainty that either of them was a fan of *The Outer Limits.* But it can be asserted that a public exposed to weekly mass visitations of alien beings via *The Outer Limits,* through syndicated reruns (or memories of), *The Twilight Zone,* and *Science Fiction Theater,* not to mention the relentless cultural drumbeat of the space race, would naturally fuse the Hills' narrative with a ready stock of images. With the 1966 publication of *The Interrupted Journey,* first as a widely read *Look* magazine serial, then as a best-selling hardcover from Dial Press, the popular iconography of UFO abductions began to crystallize.

But the finishing detail was to be provided in 1968, when motion-picture audiences around the world were transfixed by Stanley Kubrick's *2001: A Space Odyssey,* the climax of which depicts a

John Hoyt as the alien in "The Bellero Shield" episode of *The Outer Limits* (1962). *Courtesy of David J. Schow.*

transhuman, extraterrestrial being as a kind of superfetus in orbit. The juxtaposition of fetuses and space travel added a particularly resonant picture to the storehouse of cultural images, and the following decade saw aliens, on and off the screen, depicted in an increasingly embryonic light.

The Interrupted Journey formed the basis for a 1975 television film, *The UFO Incident,* starring Estelle Parsons and James Earl Jones as Betty and Barney Hill. Here, in full view of the nation, a consensus picture of the modern alien began to emerge. Owing, no doubt, to the ridiculous effect they would create on-screen, some of Betty's descriptions underwent surgical retooling—specifically, rhinoplasty. The Jimmy Durante schnozes were forever banished from descriptions of alien abductors. The bald, albinoish aliens depicted in *The UFO Incident* were really nothing at all like the creatures first described by the Hills, except for the slanted eyes; they looked frankly like knockoffs from *The Outer Limits* with a soupçon of Stanley Kubrick tossed in for flavor. Nonetheless, they provided a design blueprint for all future aliens, on and off the screen.

At the time *The UFO Incident* was broadcast, Steven Spielberg's *Close Encounters of the Third Kind* (1977) was already on the drawing board, poised for the pop apotheosis of the alien icon. An international box-office sensation, *Close Encounters* achieved mass appeal by first playing to the audience's apprehension about mysterious displays of supertechnology, then softening the whole package with a warm, fuzzy glow. The spindly aliens were like *The UFO Incident*'s spacemen retooled by Giacometti with an assist from Disney; the creature that appears at the film's conclusion has big, anthropomorphic eyes in the manner of a cartoon character, not insectoid black holes. Unlike Barney Hill's captor, this one has some mouth muscles and even manages something like a smile of benediction. The giant "mother ship" that appears at the film's conclusion appeals to very earthbound notions of heaven, a big Las Vegas hotel in the sky. The special effects, by Roy Arbogast, Gregory Jenn, Douglas Trumbull, and Matthew and Richard Yuricich, represented one of the last large-scale uses of miniatures and traditional optical processes to create images of technological awe; like the film's mother ship, computers were hovering at the horizon.

Close Encounters stabilized the standard description of the alien for the age of abduction mythology, but Hollywood took significant iconographic side trips. Spielberg also directed the blockbuster *E.T.: The Extra-Terrestrial* (1982), a sentimental counter-abduction story, in which a stranded space visitor is held captive by humans. The endearing E.T. is a homely, waddling cross between a plush toy and a tree frog; created by Carlo Rambaldi, this enormously popular character has almost no visual precedent in popular culture and essentially exists in a category of its own. Another startlingly original concept of the alien arose from the Euro-morbid sensibility of Swiss artist H. R. Giger, who designed an extremely uncuddly extraterrestrial in the hit film *Alien* (1979). Giger's monster simultaneously evoked futuristic machinery, skeletons, and verminous insects: a necrotechnological nightmare and one of the most dismaying illustrations of science equals death ever attempted on the plane of popular entertainment. While at first glance Giger's alien would seem to have nothing in common with the abduction archetype, they do share the juxtapositioning of skeletal features with other, symbolist representations of sci-tech cerebration, especially the oversize cranium, the site of H. G. Wells's "vast, cool, and unsympathetic" Martian intellect. Aspects of the two species were to be imaginatively fused in the 1996 alien invasion blockbuster *Independence Day*.

In 1987 former horror fiction writer Whitley Strieber *(The Wolfen; The Hunger)* caused a sensation with his best-selling book *Communion,* a purportedly true account of his own experience with alien abductors. Using all the goose bump–producing devices at his disposal, he told of being repeatedly visited and kidnapped from his upstate New York weekend house by an assortment of diminutive visitors, including the classic "small grays" popularized by *The UFO Incident* and *Close Encounters.* His experiences were masked by an anxious amnesia and recalled, Benjamin Simon–style, by regressive hypnotherapy. In a variation on Betty Hill's invasive "pregnancy test," Strieber's ritual medical workup included his being violated by an "ugly" but high-tech anal probe, triangular in shape, sprouting wires, and at least a foot long. "It seemed to swarm into me as if it had a life of its own. . . . I had the impression I was being raped. . . ."

Communion wasn't the first time seeming science fiction had been presented as nonfiction by a major American publisher; in 1978 David Rorvik's *In His Image,* a purportedly true story about a wealthy industrialist who succeeds in cloning himself, was given a remarkably free publicity ride by the media. Likewise *Communion* enjoyed a publicity bonanza it would never have received if published as a novel. James Landis, publisher of Beech Tree Books, stated emphatically that "there was no discussion about whether to publish this book as fiction. It came in as *Communion: A True Story* and that's the way we published it." But Landis may have intended a subliminal wink with his added comment: "I don't see any more reason to doubt this memoir than I would doubt the autobiography of a Hollywood actor or actress."

Science fiction writer Thomas M. Disch, reviewing *Communion* for the *Nation,* noted, perhaps with understatement: "If Whitley Strieber isn't fibbing, then [*Communion*] must be accounted the most important book of the year, of the decade, of the century, indeed, of all time." S-f writer and astrophysicist Gregory Benford told *Publishers Weekly* that *Communion* represented "a deplorable trend in publishing. It is catering to the flagrant irrationalities of the public with tarted-up Potemkin-Village science. The reemergence of the Shirley MacLaine/Bridey Murphy subgenre is a chastening reminder that we are not, in fact, a deeply rational society, in spite of our technology."

The 1980s also saw the rise of "Roswell Redux," a constellation of books, articles, and free-floating speculation that retrofitted the original Roswell story with up-to-date alien appurtenances. In 1980, a book by Charles Berlitz and William L. Moore, *The Roswell Incident,* made the claim that the military had collected not only saucer debris but the remains of four small-bodied, big-headed crew members. Their appearance conformed to the new futuristic fetus description of space people that had emerged in the 1970s as a result of *2001: A Space Odyssey, The UFO Incident,* and *Close Encounters of the Third Kind.* One of the quartet was said to have been kept alive by military medics for a few weeks before succumbing to its injuries; the bodies were then alleged to have been packed in dry ice and shipped off to Wright-Paterson Air Force Base in Dayton, Ohio, for permanent safekeeping. There was no firsthand testimony; Jesse Marcel never talked about dead aliens, and the other accounts—secondhand stories told by family members and acquaintances of dead military personnel and others—were beyond verification.

Berlitz and Moore's account followed the outlines of a discredited book written by a syndicated *Variety* columnist, Frank Scully, in 1950. *Behind the*

H. R. Giger's *Alien* (1979): a morbid fusion of sex and technology.

Flying Saucers told of the crashes of three saucers with the deaths of thirty-four diminutive crewmen in New Mexico and Arizona. The actual source of this story seems to have been a tongue-in-cheek 1948 story written by an Aztec, New Mexico, reporter, George Bawra, in the wake of the Roswell incident, and widely reprinted in newspapers across the country. (Berlitz and Moore come feebly to Scully's defense: "It appears, perhaps because of his haste to finish the book while the subject was 'hot,' that Scully plunged into print without sufficient checking. . . ." They suggest that the "highly inaccurate" book was the result of limited access to official documents, "something easier to overcome at the present time since the passing of the Freedom of Information Act. . . ." And so forth.) Intriguingly, Frank Scully shares a surname with the female FBI agent, Dana Scully, on television's *The X-Files,* which regularly invokes the Roswell legend and similar alleged government cover-ups involving aliens, suppressed technologies, and the paranormal.

The Roswell story inspired at least three other books and, in 1995, a made for TV movie, *Roswell,* starring Kyle MacLachlan as Jesse Marcel. Scripted by the playwright Arthur Kopit, *Roswell* polished the story to an - *X-Files* gloss; especially effective was the image of the bulbous-headed, telepathic alien kept temporarily alive in a military hospital. The Roswell legend itself was largely hokum, but the slick production values added another layer of persuasive "argument" to a story that has become such an article of faith among UFO and conspiracy enthusiasts that its truth or falsity is now almost beside the point.

The year 1987 saw the publication of Budd Hopkins's *Intruders: The Incredible Visitations at Copley Woods,* which (despite the author's almost immediate protestation that he didn't really mean to say what he seems to be saying) is prefaced by a uniquely tasteless "Note to the Reader" drawing a parallel between Europe's initial refusal to believe that Hitler was exterminating millions of Jews during World War II and the contemporary refusal of modern science to accept the reality of mass UFO abductions. Hopkins, a well-regarded New York sculptor and artist, became increasingly involved in abduction phenomena after the publication of his 1981 book *Missing Time,* which chronicled seven case studies. Since then he claims to have investigated more than fifteen hundred cases, making him the world's number one authority on the subject, at least on a volume basis. Hopkins's books popularized the idea that aliens are engaged in a long-term genetic experiment intermingling the germ plasm of humans and extraterrestrials, producing hybrid infants, interfering with pregnancies, and so on. This emphasis on reproductive tinkering, of course, coincided with an age of increasingly technologized reproduction, surrogate parenthood, fetal tissue experimentation, and related developments. As feminist critic Janice G. Raymond charges in *Women as Wombs: Reproductive Technologies and the Battle over Women's Freedom,* "Unnoticed in most discussions of technological reproduction and reproductive contracts is the creation of a new form of *reproductive trafficking*—the international medical research networks; the international markets for women used in surrogacy, fetal tissue, and eggs; the global stockpiling of frozen embryos; the technology transfers; and the increasing exchange of human material from one woman to another. The reproductive use and abuse is [*sic*] being played out on an international medical stage where women's bodies, children, and fetuses are being trafficked across national borders."

Like many abductionists, Budd Hopkins is a self-styled hypnotherapist, not a trained clinician. As a result, his books often meet with dismissal by mainstream critics. The *New York Times Book Review,* for instance, found the interest of the aliens in *Intruders* in genetic engineering simply "too topical" for credulity. But the media tide changed in 1994 with the publication of *Abduction: Human Encounters with Aliens* by John E. Mack, a Pulitzer Prize–winning professor of psychiatry at Harvard University. Mack won the Pulitzer for his biography of T. E. Lawrence, *A Prince of Our Disorder,* and had been the author of the highly praised *Nightmares and Human Conflict* (1972), in which he notes the tendency of earlier societies to regard nightmares as actual visitations by demons. "[One] is struck now, not so much by the varied nature of the demons that cause oppression in these dreams or by the symbols of sexuality that can be found in them," writes Mack, "as by the objective reality" ascribed to them. "In the sixteenth century, for example, the church took very seriously the attitude of the dreamer toward his visitor, taking note of whether he submitted to the incubus, in order to assess actual guilt. In the case of this type of dream, in which reality-testing tends for the individual to be most difficult under any circumstances, the society and its authorities confirming the actuality of the fantasy. Thus, a kind of mutual validation persisted. . . ."

The distinguished psychiatrist and author Robert Coles gave an extremely favorable review to *Nightmares and Human Conflict* in the *New Yorker,* which was reprinted as an introduction to the second edition. Coles praised Mack's book as being "in the best tradition of psychoanalysis. It is well written. It is full of interesting and well-documented clinical observations. . . . [It] offers proof of the continued vitality of a profession that has, thank God, at last been left alone by the flashier elements of America's cultural life."

By the time of *Abduction,* however, Mack appeared intent on being flashier than flashy, in essence dropping all pretense of clinical objectivity and taking on a role akin to that of the early Christian Church in validating bizarre fantasies. In the preface he virtually gives up on language as a means of analysis and understanding: "When we explore phenomena that exist at the margins of accepted reality, old words become imprecise or must be given new meanings. Terms like 'abduction,' 'alien,' 'happening,' and even 'reality' itself need redefinition . . . thinking of memory too literally as 'true' or 'false' may restrict what we can learn. . . ."

Mack accepts his patients' hypnotic narratives at face value, not even commenting when one of them borrows nearly verbatim language from Strieber's *Communion* (which he had read prior to his own abduction) in describing his own anal violation. Another offers a few dehumanizing embellishments to the now-standard procedure: "The tube was passed deeper into his rectum and Peter felt they left 'an implant' or 'an information chip' inside of him. 'Why do you have to do this to me?!!' Peter shouted, 'I'm tracked now [almost crying], I can never get away. That's how I feel. I'm stuck for life. I feel like a tagged animal. I feel like they put something big up my anus, and spread it and then stuck something else up through it and then they left it. It's way up inside of me.' "

In a scathing *New Republic* review of *Abduction,* science writer James Gleick questioned Mack's unsupported claim that his subjects "seem to come, as if at random, from all parts of society": "It seems safe to say that there's one kind of patient that Mack never sees: a person . . . who, without any familiarity with UFO books or movies and without any suggestion whatsoever on the part of psychiatrist or hypnotist, *then* remembers an abduction experience. If he had any of those, it would be really interesting to see the transcripts. In reality, though, by the time Mack sees them, his patients know very well what they're in for and have been well-prepped."

In the mid-1980s I had direct experience with recovered memory hypnosis when I participated in a "past life regression workshop" at a well-known New Age learning center in Manhattan. My curiosity had been piqued not by a belief in reincarnation but by my interest as a fiction writer in the phenomenon of so-called automatic writing. I had previously been hypnotized by a doctor I consulted for stress reduction and already knew that I was an excellent hypnotic subject. But no one was more surprised than I when I experienced a hypnagogic episode verging on an epileptic seizure, seeing "my former self" in 1930s Depression America in a startlingly vivid waking dream. It was quite a trip, but unlike the other participants, I didn't regard it as a visit to a past life. After I had come out of the trance, the workshop leader took offense at my observation that there might have been a considerable amount of suggestion at work. "I didn't give you a single suggestion!" he protested.

"Yes, you did," I replied. "You invited people to attend something called a past life regression workshop." Needless to say, I wasn't invited to another one.

The creation of false memories through hypnotic interrogation is hardly limited to UFO abduction cases or regression workshops. In *Making Monsters: False Memories, Psychotherapy, and Sexual Hysteria* (1994), Richard Ofshe and Ethan Watters examine the recent explosion of mad science in the recovered memory movement. While they don't discuss abductionists in their devastating critique of therapists who claim to uncover repressed memories of traumatic child abuse, a number of links are clear. The abuse memories are usually incestuous and often escalate into abduction tales in their own right. These abductions are carried out not by aliens but by dark-robed members of satanic cults, who ritually molest the victims and force them to partake in unspeakable practices, including the cannibal sacrifice of infants, often bred for slaughter by the victims themselves. If the abuse narrative isn't bizarre enough, the explanation of the rise of such cults, as offered by a University of Utah psychologist at a workshop accredited by the American Medical Association, rivals any alien abduction account for sheer nuttiness. Recounted by Ofshe and Watters:

> . . . the satanic cult that therapists are currently battling first began in this country after World War II. After the war ended, the U.S. government smuggled out of Germany a group of satanic Nazi scientists who had been conducting mind-control experiments in concentration camps. These scientists brought with them a Jewish teenager who had saved his own live by assisting these evil researchers in their work. They spared the life of this boy because of his knowledge of the Kabala, the work of Jewish mysticism that integrated well with the Nazis' satanic beliefs. Once in America, this Hasidic boy changed his name from Greenbaum to Green and continued to help in the mind-control experiments, which had been taken up by the CIA.

After using CIA funding to torture/brainwash children on army bases, Green earned a medical degree and became Dr. Green, taking control of the experiments to program "mental robots who will do pornography, prostitution, smuggle drugs, engage in international arms smuggling," all in the interest of an international satanic cult that controls NASA, the Mafia, and Hollywood.

There are strong parallels to the satanic abuse narrative in alien abduction stories: the uniformed (robed) congregation, the altar (examination table), the theft of a fetus (ritual sacrifice of a baby), and so on. As they deepen, both scenarios require the patient to begin to accept corollary conspiracy premises. In the case of the abuse fabulator, it's not just the father who is a satanic molestor; it's the whole family, the whole neighborhood. Similarly, the abduction of thousands or even millions of human beings by space aliens can happen only with the tacit approval of the government, in league with the CIA, international bankers, and the aliens themselves. Both kinds of therapist use the same pseudoscientific techniques to elicit and reinforce such stories: leading questions, prior preparation, shared expectations. Everyone involved seems to casually accept the idea of the brain as a kind of playback machine that can rerun decades-old experiences in a high-fidelity mode at the therapist's mesmeric beckon.

Part of the public's receptivity to such ideas may derive from the brain-as-computer metaphors that have become wildly literalized in recent years. If we really are "nothing but" machines or computers, then recovering a repressed memory is a lot like turning up a lost computer file or playing back a videocassette. Memories, of course, are not digitized information or images captured on film, but as Carl Jung once commented, "Anything that looks technological goes down without difficulty with modern man." In effect, recovered memory therapists turn their patients into machines or wind-up dolls, a classic mad scientist pastime.

Ofshe and Watters conclude that the painful abreactions displayed by patients of recovered memory therapists may be enough to define some practitioners "as a new class of sexual predator. If, for no defensible reason, some therapists are causing the same emotional and psychological trauma of an actual rape or sexual assault, then they, like those who physically victimize people, deserve moral condemnation." Similarly, the power/powerlessness dynamic of the abduction scenario has strong overtones of ritual sadomasochism, the therapist and alien blurred together through controlling displays of weird science. Thomas M. Disch, in his *Nation* review of Whitley Strieber's *Communion,* notes the extent to which the book is a thematic retooling of a Strieber S&M story called "Pain," previously published in a horror anthology. Disch speculates that "Strieber, having made the imaginative equation between the 'archetypal abduction experience' and the ritual protocols of bondage and domination, realized he'd hit a vein of ore not previously tapped by ufologists, who have been generally a pretty naive lot. To have drawn such an explicit parallel in *Communion,* however, would have risked alienating the audience at which such a book is targeted, and so among Streiber's many speculations there are none that examine or allude to the metaphorical premise of the story. . . ."

In her provocative book *Sadomasochism in Everyday Life,* Lynn S. Chancer examines the hidden dominance and submission paradigms of late-twentieth-century capitalism: ". . . the worker confronts capitalism from a position of 'alienation,' estranged from a process over which he or she once had been able to exert a participatory and independent self-control. . . ." And so the abductee/worker confronts the abductor/technomasters. Today technology-driven corporations exert increasingly authoritarian control over increasing numbers of people, monitoring and surveilling workers' every move with the latest toys of modern science, subjecting them to the ritual humilation of urine sample collection and testing, controlling and infantilizing employees to the exaggerated extent permitted by a difficult economy. In an age of chronic belt tightening, the favored belt style is often black leather. It is hardly surprising that members of an alienated work force might respond, with uneasy fascination, to images of coercion and assault by a regimented master race wearing tight-fitting uniforms and wielding high-tech cattle prods. (A professional dominatrix of my acquaintance informs me that many houses of domination now offer futuristic "examination rooms" where clients engage in abduction-style psychodrama.)

And what do I make of my own close encounter with a UFO twenty-three years ago? While I have considerable difficulty accepting the idea of alien corpses being held in permanent detention on American air force bases, I have much less difficulty believing that all manner of experimental aircraft—the products, perhaps, of long-abandoned top secret testing from the late 1940s to early 1970s—might well be held under a similar security quarantine. (What a perfect, effortless cover it would have been for the government and military to encourage passively space invasion fantasies to deflect more down-to-earth investigation!) What I saw in October 1973 represented a technology I still can't understand. But whatever else they might have been, those red and green navigational lights were strictly from Planet Earth. Veteran debunkers like Philip J. Klass would tell me I misidentified a normal aircraft (what kind?) or simply couldn't differentiate a meteor shower, swamp gas, or a weather balloon from a solid, purposefully moving object. I find it distressing that both debunkers and true believers never leave room for anything between hallucinations, hoaxes, and human stupidity, on one hand, and actual extraterrestrial or extradimensional visitation, on the other.

For example, what about suppressed or secret technology? I began reading with interest a book called *Man-Made UFOS: 1944–1994* (1994) by Renato Vesco and David Hatcher Childress, hoping to find some support for my suspicions. The authors argue that the Nazis during World War II had

Postmodern aliens, as seen in (left) *Close Encounters of the Third Kind* (1977) and (right) *Communion* (1994).

been developing secret flight technologies, including disk-shaped aircraft, research that was continued jointly by the America and the Soviet Union after the war. But I was dismayed to see the argument lead inexorably from an intriguing thesis to "secret world government" paranoia of the kind espoused by right-wing radio hosts, recovered memory therapists, and domestic terrorists. Just explaining flying saucers isn't enough; UFOs in turn are then somehow expected to explain everything else.

Curtis Peebles, whose 1994 book *Watch the Skies!* is one of the most levelheaded chronicles of the entire UFO phenomenon, points out that all the classic UFO flaps—1947, 1952, 1957, 1965–1967, and 1973—coincided with periods of gathering social unrest.

> It was vague, poorly defined crises which caused the flaps. When the crisis was clearly defined, such as during the 1962 Cuban Missile Crisis, the number of sightings went down. The year 1947 saw the developing cold war and fears of communist subversion. The Great Flap of 1952 marked the Cold War's frozen depths, the stalemated Korean War, the development of the H-bomb, and the McCarthy era. The 1957 flap followed Little rock and the launch of Sputnik. The Sixties flap was a time of civil disorder on college campuses and the inner city, and the internal conflicts caused by the Vietnam War. Finally, the 1973 flap saw the Watergate scandal and the resulting breakdown of faith in government. In each case, the threat was what might happen, not what was happening.

It's no coincidence that Alien Chic picked up again in the mid-1990s just as public confidence in government reached an all-time low; not since Watergate and the attending UFO flap of 1973 have so many people been so cynical about government agencies and officials and so suspicious of their motives. The popular mood of 1996 was perhaps best encapsulated by the scene from the alien invasion film *Independence Day,* in which the White House is blown to smithereens, a moment that unfailingly elicited thunderous approval from audiences of all stripes, all across America.

As in the 1950s, pop images of malevolent alien interlopers emerged during a period of anxiousness about real-world outsiders and "invaders." This time, instead of Communists, illegal immigrants—real aliens—provided easy fodder for politicians in search of scapegoats to galvanize voters.

Some radio talk shows took on the coloration of *The X-Files,* pushing a conservative critique of intrusive government into a wonderland of conspiracy theories about extraterrestrial intrusion. UFO cover-ups, paranormal phenomena, and top secret technologies propelled Art Bell's syndicated late-night program, *Coast-to-Coast A.M.,* into one of the hottest shows on radio, and his Web site into one of the most trafficked on the infobahn. Bell's program was the prime media force behind the allegation that a huge alien spaceship (four times the size of the earth) was trailing the Hale-Bopp comet, a fantasy directly responsible for the Heaven's Gate suicides in March 1997. For months earlier, sometimes on a nearly nightly basis, Bell had presented a steady stream of guests embroidering and embellishing the hoax, including psychics, purportedly trained by the CIA in "remote viewing" techniques, who confirmed to millions of listeners that a giant alien hive was headed in our direction. After the mass suicide at Rancho Santa Fe, Bell vehemently denied any cause and effect between his broadcasts and the deaths, claiming he was duped himself by the hoaxsters he blatantly promoted. In 1938 Orson Welles's *War of the Worlds* radio stunt had panicked an entire country for a single night, but Art Bell has bettered Welles by installing suspension of disbelief as a permanent fixture of the airwaves. Bell had earlier refueled the Roswell legend with an endlessly teasing string of programs suggesting that he might be in personal possession of Roswell saucer debris; not surprisingly, by 1997, the fiftieth anniversary of the incident, Roswell, New Mexico, was enjoying a booming tourist industry, complete with a UFO museum and a fetching hotelier's slogan: "CRASH IN ROSWELL."

Popular Science editor Fred Abatemarco, disturbed by the crumbling reality boundaries of mid-1997, published an editorial titled "Not Necessarily the News," in which he asked whether wild UFO fantasies, coupled with highly hyped claims by real scientists for evidence of bacterial life on Mars, or oceans on a moon of Jupiter, had "simmered together to obliterate the distinction between unsubstantiated speculation and well-disciplined scientific hypothesis? UFO-ology is entertaining. But when *The X-Files* and the network news are covering the same territory, we have reason to worry."

The X-Files, created by Chris Carter and by the mid-1990s one of the Fox Network's top-rated programs, made clear the transformation of public mood that had taken place between the relatively sunny late seventies, when *Close Encounters* spread its optimistic message about the relationship among science, government, and extraterrestrial life, and the bottomless cultural cynicism of the fin-de-siècle. *The X-Files* is like the Spielbergian Summer of Love gone very, very sour, a labyrinth of conspiracy theories involving the government's complicity in UFO abductions and related cover-ups, with a plethora of bizarre subplots dealing with paranormal phenomena, serial killers, and even (occasionally) vampires and werewolves. The glue that holds the show together is the shadowy certainty that THE TRUTH IS OUT THERE (a slogan that appears during the show's main titles), though the truth is routinely stifled by government officials, military-industrial types, and scientists, many of whom tamper with things better left alone. The lead characters, Fox Mulder (David Duchovny) and Dana Scully (Gillian Anderson), are FBI agents who investigate the bureau's most anomalous cases. He's a true believer (his sister was abducted by aliens as a child, never to return); she's the skeptic. Ironically both performers maintain a flatness of affect that rivals that of the typical alien abductor.

What makes *The X-Files* tick? Uncommonly good writing and production values, for one thing, as well as performers sufficiently opaque and enigmatic to invite massive projection by audiences, who return week after week to see if their favorite characters reveal any more of themselves (they don't). But the persistent, insinuating image of once-revered, now-rotten authority structures infested with aliens seems to be the real grabber, appealing to a public that can't really figure out how and why American life went off the tracks. The alien puts a face (however expressionless) on issues and dynamics that are largely faceless.

In the fall of 1996 NBC television, attempting to trump *The X-Files,* launched *Dark Skies,* projected as a five-year series with an audaciously entertaining premise—namely, that every historical and cultural event from the Roswell incident to the millennium—including, though not limited to, the Kennedy assassination, the Beatles, cattle mutilation, the presidency of George Bush, etc.—could be linked to, or explained in terms of, extraterrestrial kibbutzing. Both the Art Bell show and *Dark Skies* have strong and probably intentional overtones of self-parody, but I have been amazed at the number of people I've encountered in recent years who seem incapable of distinguishing between infotainment and real information and treat the alien myth, received from almost any source, as revealed truth.

But there is a truth to be uncovered in the cultural delirium of Alien Chic, a multilayered truth that can be perceived only in a broad, earthbound perspective, for the alien is nothing less than a complex iconographic fusion of popular notions of mad science and its monsters at the end of a century in which science itself has become an incubus, the invading, oppressive night terror of modern times. Its skeletal, fetal appearance is a dreamlike paradox that recapitulates the whole history of monsters, which traditionally fuses logically incompatible aspects. The alien is an amalgamated distillation of everything that has ever frightened human beings, from the ancient fear of the dead to modern apprehensions about the unborn. The fetus, of course, has become one of our most anxious cultural images, as political hysteria over abortion and reproductive issues in general converge with millennial anxiety over what we're giving birth to and what we're becoming—our collective gestation in the test tube womb of science.

The now-classic alien archetype, as presented and popularized in films like *Close Encounters of the Third Kind* and in books like *Communion* and *Intruders,* has less to do with extraterrestrial or other-dimensional visitors than it does with our own self-image in a world driven and consumed by science and technology. Even if alien corpses do exist at Wright-Paterson Air Force Base, even if a monumental government conspiracy to suppress evidence of alien contact is a monumentally concealed fact, the real cultural function of the alien image has been essentially earthbound and narcissistic—a shared Dorian Gray portrait for the space age. The pale, withered denizen of the flying saucer, all brain and devoid of musculature, emotionless and voyeuristic, drinking in information through expressionless goggle eyes, is a naked evocation of the scientific persona: the mad scientist sans all pre-

The alien as scientifically evolved savior, from the Heaven's Gate Web site (1997).

tense of "human" disguise. Its appearance has many cultural antecedents and influences: Nosferatu (a bulge-brained symbol of the atavistic dread engendered by excessive Darwinian thinking); the pale, skull-faced Frankenstein monster; the embryonic, eggheaded doctors Gogol and Cyclops, not to mention that pesky anxiety icon of the reproductive wars: the human fetus itself. (Carl Sagan on the alien: "It looks to me eerily like a fetus in roughly the twelfth week of pregnancy, or a starving child. Why so many of us might be obsessing on fetuses or malnourished children, and imagining them attacking and sexually manipulating us, is an interesting question.")

Alien abduction stories amount to pop parables about alienation and powerlessness in the face of mysterious, all-controlling technologies. Like the vampire—another scary-eyed, night-visiting, fluid-draining archetype—the alien is a classic fin-de-siècle figure embodying aspects of death and resurrection, a skeletized embryo that powerfully and simultaneously evokes the threat of destruction and the promise of rebirth at the millennium. The alien appears skeletal but is actually soft, its bonelessness resonating with a spineless world of moral relativism, its cold-blooded sexual encroachments reflecting a depersonalized world of media-driven junk sex, an end-of-innocence parable for the age of the v-chip. An up-to-date admixture of censor and sensor, the v-chip is an electronic sentinel lurking in new television sets, the better to help parents police their children's viewing habits. It, of course, is the techno-equivalent of garlic, wolfbane, or the communion wafer, a modern talisman offering nervous protection against the encroachments of a digitized night.

In the final analysis, the essence of alien abductions may have been precisely, if inadvertently, captured by Strieber in *Communion*'s tackiest scene. Strapped to the examining table of runaway rationality, beyond freedom and dignity, probed and violated by modernist monstrosities resembling the figure in Edvard Munch's *The Shriek,*" we struggle, we protest, but in the end, as it were, we finally submit. The techno-intruders have their way, ramming the light of pure reason to a place where the sun doesn't shine.

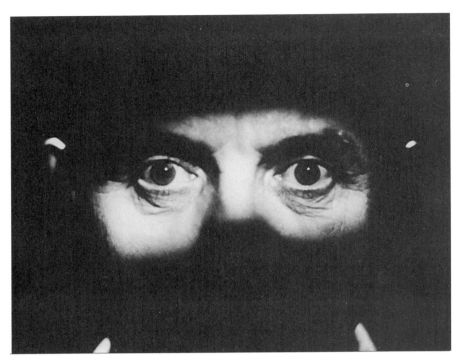

CHAPTER SIX

The Doctor Will Eat You Now

W hile only a minority of Americans believe they have been abducted by UFOs, a much larger percentage suspect they may be under assault by HMOs. It is not coincidental that Whitley Strieber described his extraterrestrial assailants in *Communion* as "little doctors" in a decade when the practice of medicine reached new heights of technological showmanship and, simultaneously, new depths of depersonalization and mistrust.

The better to see you, my dear. The hungry eyes of Dr. Hannibal Lecter (Anthony Hopkins) in *Silence of the Lambs* (1991).

Like a classic UFO abduction, 1990s health care "reform"—that is, creeping corporatization—raised the specter of a faceless, all-controlling scientific and medical authority, conducting incomprehensible but humiliating procedures involving spectacular high-tech toys. In the age of managed care, many of us are no longer freely able to choose our personal physicians and in fact are no longer sure whether doctors are working on our own behalf or in the interest of shadowy, anonymous corporate shareholders. Facelessness (i.e., impersonality, "objectivity") is a key attribute of the alien/doctor encounter, the essence of the dispassionate "clinical gaze" of modern times, as described by Michel Foucault.

Stripped of rational interpretation, a visit to the doctor is an encounter with a vestmented threshold figure who stands ambiguously at the doors of life and death. We allow him to pierce our veins and drain our blood, read/interpret the signs therein, predict the span of our lives, render a judgment on our continued existence. On the level of prerational associations, our body tissues are the oracle's tea leaves, our workup charts his tarot spreads. The medical encounter takes place in an environment of hyperrationality and hyperhygiene: sterile white surfaces, stainless steel, merciless fluorescent light. The doctor assumes an impassive professional mask as well as a surgical one. Even the most innocuous office visits are colored by primal anxieties. We all know people who resist seeing a doctor even for the most minor complaints, so powerful is the sense of dread engendered by the mere thought of a medical exam. Among men some of the discomfort seems especially related to the emotional core of Whitley Strieber–style anal probe nightmares; witness the prevalence of proctological jokes in the "doctor" repertoire of male stand-up comics. *Communion* addresses the same unease, minus the laugh lines.

Much of our ambivalent response to medicine arises from the doctor's constant proximity to death, the hope that he can ward off mortality, and the nagging fear that he cannot. A traditional means of defusing the ensuing unease is humor. For instance, in the grotesquely satirical mid-nineteenth-century lithographs of Honoré Daumier, we find the forerunners of many a twentieth-century mad doctor, overbearing charlatans and quacks posing as much danger to their patients as any disease. Daumier loved to lampoon the professional classes, especially physicians. In the caption to one illustration,

A Lucky Find, a doctor exclaims to his patient, "By Jove, I'm delighted! You have yellow fever . . . it will be the first time I've been lucky enough to treat this disease." In another, *The Doctor,* a physician sits at his desk, surrounded by phantoms of mortality. "How the devil does it happen that all my patients succumb?" he asks himself, questioning everything but his own methods. "I bleed them, I physic them, I drug them . . . I simply can't understand." In his introduction to a collection of Daumier's medical cartoons, Henri Mondor of the Académie Française notes "a procession of hideous, deformed and sublimated doctors, and patients who reveal, perhaps unconsciously, less bitterness than an irremediable regret that men can be tended in sickness only by other men." Mondor also acknowledges the fondness of medical men for Daumier's graphic barbs: "The pleasure so many doctors take in Daumier's harsh works comes perhaps from the fact that all have met examples of ignorant, unqualified and boastful colleagues who thoroughly justify them."

Milton Millhauser notes that even the educated Victorian was largely unfamiliar with science and scientists. The "occasional striking theory of a Newton, Lyell, or Darwin was all very interesting, but it touched on men's lives less intimately and immediately than business, politics, or even social aspiration and maneuvering." But medical science was an exception. "It was as a threat to his own body—poison, narcosis, disfigurement, pain—that a layman most readily recognized the significance of science," Millhauser writes. ". . . it is well to remember that the services of one's 'medical man' can be extremely disagreeable. His nostrums taste nasty; that is how we know they will work. He must operate upon us, painfully—terribly painfully before the discovery of anesthesia about the middle of the nineteenth century. He has dangerous knowledge—of poisons, opiates, exotic and forbidden things. . . . He is eager for knowledge, but this leads him into dreadful courses—grave-robbing and worse. If there are doctors who buy murder victims for dissection, what may not happen to a helpless patient on the operating table[?] . . . The doctor brings healing," Millhauser concludes, "but he carries it in a black bag."

It is, perhaps, no wonder that popular speculation on the identity of Jack the Ripper, who dissected Whitechapel prostitutes with surgical precision, focused on the possibility that a doctor did the deeds. Coincidentally, the American actor Richard Mansfield brought his celebrated interpretation of *Dr. Jekyll and Mr. Hyde* to London at the time of the Ripper slayings, causing an outcry in some quarters over the questionable propriety of depicting Mr. Hyde's analagous crimes as theatrical entertainment. If nothing else, Mansfield's startling onstage transformation (accomplished in plain view of the audience through a combination of physical contortions and ingenious "invisible" makeup made plain by a change of colored light) reinforced the audience's worst suspicions about the hidden horrors of medicine as outlined by Millhauser.

Like the Victorians, we still need the doctor's special knowledge, his ability to deploy his own expertise coolly in the face of our own crises, to take us apart and reassemble us, if necessary, but we are still nervous at what lies behind the medical mask. In Henry Bellamann's novel *Kings Row* (1941), made into a darkly unforgettable film the following year, the daughter of a small-town doctor fond of practicing surgery without anesthesia rips back the veil following his death. "He was cold as ice," she tells Parris Mitchell, an idealistic psychiatrist in training. "He liked to butcher people. He was—oh, I knew the word once, I read it—Parris, you know—he was a sadist." She elaborates: "Listen, Parris. This is my one chance. You've got to listen. I kept lists—he always talked about his operations. Other doctors wouldn't do that. And nearly always he said the patient's heart was too weak for the chloroform. Remember that now. But their hearts were not too weak to be cut to pieces. I tell you, Parris, he liked to hear them scream."

Joyce Carol Oates's novel *Wonderland* (1971) is one of the most disturbing and revealing contemporary evocations of doctors and their demons. Written at the height of the Vietnam War, the book reflects the growing disenchantment with authority figures that threatened to tear America apart in the late sixties and early seventies. *Wonderland* tells the story of Jesse Vogel, a young boy in upstate New York who narrowly escapes death at the hands of his murderous, suicidal father only to place his trust in a succession of sinister father substitutes, all of whom are powerful, controlling doctor-scientists. The first, and most freakish, is Dr. Karl Pedersen, who adopts Jesse into his corpulent family of "geniuses." Jesse becomes caught in a rescue triangle of mythical proportions with Pedersen and his wife. During an abortive escape attempt Mrs. Pedersen feverishly betrays the secrets of her marriage to a man of science: "Oh yes, he's a genius. Yes, a wonderful man. All of Lockport is proud of him, yes. They write stories about him. Yes. But there are secrets. . . . He takes morphine, Jesse. Yes, morphine! Not every night, but he gives himself an injection of morphine the way other people take a drink—and then he looks down upon people who drink. . . ." Mrs. Pedersen goes on, relentlessly cataloging the doctor/monster's sins: "And the things he's done to punish me! Once when we were married only a year he refused to speak to me for a month. To this day I don't know why. I offended him somehow. He's incredibly vain and proud. He won't let me buy anything unless he has seen it or given his approval of it. Once he took all my clothes away and I had to stay in the bedroom naked for three days. . . . he brought my food up on a tray and left it by the door, as if I were an animal. . . . He did it to drive me crazy, Jesse. He likes to make me cry. . . .

Unlike *Kings Row*'s sadistic doctors, Pedersen doesn't actually cut people up, but he does enjoy a related pastime: "Did you ever see that locked cabinet in his study? It's always kept locked because he has certain books in it, awful books, with photographs of awful things. I can't tell you what they are. There are photographs of men and women—you know—and other photographs of dismembered bodies, with captions beneath them like jokes. Books that make fun of everything. I almost fainted. . . . We were only married a few months . . . he made me read them and he stood behind me, watching. . . .

Mrs. Pedersen's revelations are a concentrated eruption of scientist-spouse grievances dating back to Balzac's *The Quest of the Absolute,* cranked up to an almost hallucinogenic intensity. "Ask him about his secret philosophy," she tells Jesse. "He talks all the time about his public philosophy, but what about the secret one? Once a patient has come to him, he believes the patient is *his.* The patient's life is *his.* He owns the patient, he owns the disease, he owns everything." But the great doctor is not infallible. "Not all his patients survive, you know . . . he talks his patients into believing him so that they would rather die than go to another doctor . . . they get sicker and sicker and die, actually die. . . ."

Both *Wonderland* and *Kings Row* are products of war-torn times, those junctures in history when doctors are called into service in the most extreme circumstances imaginable. War can turn everything upside down. The Nazi medical atrocities performed by Dr. Josef Mengele, perhaps the maddest real-life doctor of the twentieth century, are a case in point.

The mad scientists of popular culture prior to World War II strikingly anticipate the real-life horror of Mengele, and his shadow looms over all since. The "Death Angel of Auschwitz" was frequently described as having Hollywood looks; camp survivors likened him variously to Clark Gable, Rudolph Valentino, Tyrone Power, and even, more recently, to Peter Sellers (Dr. Strangelove himself)—a half-conscious acknowledgment that there may be something inherently monstrous about overly idealized archetypes like movie stars, that the artificially animated personae of motion pictures might indeed be a species of golem. The classic mad doctor icons of the 1920s and 1930s were popular distillations of cultural unease about modernism and science; the Darwinian delirium of Moreau and Mirakle, the hubris of Frankenstein, the duality of Jekyll and Hyde all foreshadowed the overreaching, delusional "medicine" of the Nazis. (There is also something of the Jekyll and Hyde schism in Hollywood's persistent tendency to treat doctors as either angels or horrors. MGM's wartime cast of characters covered all bases by including both the benign Dr. Kildare and Spencer Tracy's *Dr. Jekyll and Mr. Hyde*.) Mengele was a cultural event waiting to happen, and postwar accounts of his crimes cannot help bringing to mind the most hair-raising scenes from films like *The Island of Lost Souls* and *Murders in the Rue Morgue*.

Josef Mengele was born in 1911 in the medieval town of Günzburg, Germany, to a middle-class family about to become wealthy as its manufacturing business boomed during World War I. Nothing is known about his childhood that would readily predict his later career as a mass murderer; "Beppo" Mengele was an attractive boy well liked by his friends and classmates, though an indifferent student. But there is evidence of a troubled family life: His mother, Wally, was a compulsive eater and grossly overweight, a woman whose moods fluctuated between the rigid control of a strict disciplinarian and bouts of uncontrollable rage. She dressed almost entirely in black. The boy was especially close to his mother, who was a devout Catholic, and photographs exist of the future "Death Angel of Auschwitz" dressed as an altar boy. Though his academic grades were mediocre, he always received the highest marks for conduct. He always obeyed the rules.

Despite his good looks, Mengele was a sickly child, "bedded by an

Gregory Peck as Dr. Josef Mengele in *The Boys from Brazil* (1978).

almost endless series of colds and childhood diseases," writes his biographer Gerald Astor. "Sickness shut him off from much of the companionship and pastimes of other youngsters." Astor believes it is "reasonable to speculate whether his isolation from other children, both on account of health and being the richest boy in town, the one whose father employed so many of his comrades, stunted Mengele's ability to relate to other people." At the age of fifteen Mengele contracted a near-fatal case of osteomylitis, a bone marrow disease, as well as nephritis complicated by a serious systemic infection. There is no documentation of the cumulative effect of all this illness on Mengele's adolescent mind and emotions. But later, as the medical director of the world's most infamous death camp, he would not tolerate evidence of even minor infirmities in children or adults.

Though his weak academic achievement hardly presaged a luminary career, the young Mengele was determined to excel. He once told a friend at the Günzburg Gymnasium, "One day, my name will be in the encyclopedia." The young man who had, against all odds, survived a disease-haunted childhood, found himself powerfully attracted to the doctrines of racial hygiene and social Darwinism, which had taken root in Germany after the trauma of the First World War. Anxieties about biological evolution became tangled with German self-doubts about national destiny. The eugenics movement, simmering since the late nineteenth century, reached a full boil. Led by scientists, the human race—that is, the Aryan race—would now take control of evolutionary process itself, weeding out disease, weakness, and degeneracy. In *Mein Kampf* (1924–1926), Adolf Hitler first called for sterilization of undesirables; foremost among them were the Jews.

In *Racial Hygiene: Medicine under the Nazis,* Robert N. Proctor describes the economic incentives for physicians to embrace the Nazi cause: "Many entering the job market for the first time saw the elimination of the Jews as a way to advance their careers. As Jewish physicians fled or were forced from the clinics and universities, thousands of new positions opened up. Those who stood most to gain from this were younger physicians, and these were the people who were most enthusiastic in their support for National Socialism."

The central perversion of medicine under the Nazis was the rejection of the Hippocratic commitments "to help the sick" and "to do no harm." To the racial hygienists, aiding the weak and inform was tantamount to abetting degeneration. In 1931, the year James Whale directed *Frankenstein,* Mengele was a sophomore at the University of Munich, studying anthropology and genetics. He earned his doctorate in Munich and then entered medical school at the University of Frankfurt. There he found a mentor in a leading racial hygienist and Nazi, Otmar von Verschuer. Verschuer was fascinated with twins and believed that their study could definitively prove racist Nazi concepts about heredity and environment. The mentor succeeded all too well in passing on his dedication to twin research to his devoted student; for Mengele, multiple births became a consuming obsession. Twins, of course, have symbolic resonance beyond biology, readily conjuring the doppelgänger, or human double, that haunted the German romantic imagination and powerfully influenced literature's leading mad scientists: Mary Shelley's Victor Frankenstein and Robert Louis Stevenson's Henry Jekyll.

The "truth" about Nazi medicine had been accessible for quite some time to almost anyone with the price of admission to a Saturday matinee.

Mengele's grotesque experiments, like Hollywood's, often involved dwarfs, hunchbacks, and giants. Mengele is believed to have personally selected for extermination between two hundred thousand and four hundred thousand human beings at Auschwitz and the nearby camp of Birkenau. Prisoners who were not sent directly to the gas chambers and caught Mengele's eye for any number of cryptic criteria were subjected to atrocious experiments. The search for a cure for typhoid fever, which plagued the German Army, provided at least a veneer of justification for infecting prisoners with typhus. Inmates were also infected with tuberculosis, diphtheria, and smallpox. Others' eyes were simply cut out, before or after death. Many were sterilized by massive doses of X rays and surgical castration. Mengele was obsessed with reproduction and replication. One prisoner doctor interviewed by Robert Jay Lifton recalled an experiment in which Mengele tried to determine whether one twin could be more susceptible to poison than the other—"a crazy idea of a man who understood nothing about real scientific problems but . . . had the possibility . . . to experiment . . . without any control or restrictions."

In *The Nazi Doctors,* the most far-reaching inquiry into the medical horrors of the Third Reich, Lifton writes, "The Nazis tapped mythic relationships between healing and killing that have had ancient expression in shamanism, religious purification, and human sacrifice," and notes that "the shaman of central and northern Asia, though mainly a healer making use of ecstatic rites, is also a 'psychopomp,' or conveyor of souls of the dead to the underworld." The modern mad doctor of Western mythology also occupies this ambiguous realm: a healer-creator who sooner or later ushers in disaster or death.

Mengele was the direct inspiration for the demonic character known only as the Doctor in Rolf Hochhuth's devastating 1963 morality play *The Deputy,* which stirred an international controversy by confronting the silence of Pope Pius XII during the Holocaust. Hochhuth's Angel of Death science is almost the devil; as the playwright explains it, "Because this 'doctor' stands in such sharp contrast not only to his fellows of the SS, but to all human beings, and so far as I know, to anything that has been learned about human beings, it seemed permissible to me at least to suggest the possibility that, with this character, an ancient figure in the theater and in Christian mystery plays is once more appearing on the stage." Hochhuth called his Doctor "an uncanny visitant from another world . . . obviously only playing the part of a human being." In blank verse, the demon espouses his chilling worldview:

> The truth is, Auschwitz refutes
> creator, creation, and the creature.
> Life as an idea is dead.
> This may well be the beginning of a great new era,
> a redemption from suffering.
> From this point of view only one crime
> remains: cursed be he who creates life.
> I cremate life. That is modern
> humanitarianism—the sole salvation from the future.

Menegle seems to have fled Auschwitz in late 1944 and most likely spent the years immediately following the war in hiding in Germany, possibly in his hometown of Günzburg. The war crime tribunals, preoccupied with the likes of Adolf Eichmann, simply overlooked him. By 1949 he had followed the path of other fugitive Nazis to Italy, then to Argentina, to Paraguay, and finally to Brazil, where he lived to the end under an assumed name and the fierce protection of friends and family.

Because of the persistent efforts of Nazi hunters like Simon Wiesenthal, Mengele took on a mythic dimension in the postwar era, when images of mad doctors and science achieved a cultural critical mass in the wake of Hiroshima. In *Shock* (1946) Vincent Price made his starring debut as a murderer-psychiatrist who plots to administer an insulin overdose to a helpless patient (already traumatized by her husband's interment in a Japanese POW camp) who knows his secret. *Shock* outraged some critics, who, a few years earlier, hadn't blinked at similar portrayals, such as Basil's Rathbone's serial killer psychiatrist in *The Mad Doctor* (1941). Bosley Crowther of the *New York Times* called *Shock* "a fraudulent and unhealthy tale" and a "social disservice." He explained: "Treatment of nervous disorders is being practiced today upon thousands of men who suffered shock of one sort or another in the war. A film which provokes fear of treatment, as this film plainly claims to do, is a cruel thing to put in the way of those patients or their anxious relatives."

Despite such critical misgivings, grotesque doctor-scientists became postwar fixtures of the newsstand and Saturday matinee, glowering down from the covers of pulp magazines, comic books, and movie screens as they subjected helpless victims to bizarre and sadistic experiments. Often the lurid cover art of the pulps had little to do with the stories printed inside, but readers didn't complain, evidently finding some level of satisfaction in beholding the flimsy trappings of rationality and restraint juxtaposed with the most primitive impulses imaginable.

Not surprisingly, sporadic postwar attempts to mix Nazi medical atrocities and popular entertainment yielded brave new forms of atrocious taste. In *Frankenstein 1970,* filmed in 1958, Boris Karloff plays a descendant of the original Dr. Frankenstein who, brutalized by the Nazis, dishes it out in kind. (Karloff himself enjoyed postwar promotional repackaging as "the new demon of the atomic age.") In a truly appalling bit of banter, an American film producer scouting out locations at the baron's castle makes a crack about the possibility of finding bodies in the kitchen's oven. *They Saved Hitler's Brain* (1963) is an almost incomprehensible film, wherein the Führer's head, kept alive in a jar, controls a nest of Nazis on the island of Mandoras. World War II pinup Veronica Lake ended her film career in 1970 by producing and starring in *Flesh Feast,* the story of a rejuvenation researcher (Lake) who lures a fugitive Hitler from his South American lair in order to kill him with the same medical torture techniques used on the researcher's mother in a Mengelian concentration camp—in this case, flesh-eating maggots.

By contrast, Ira Levin's best-selling novel *The Boys from Brazil* (1976) is a polished thriller that posits a melodramatic rationale for Mengele's obsession with twins. "Did you really think my work at Auschwitz was aimless insanity?" Mengele asks his Nazi-hunting nemesis as he reveals the true goal of his research: to create, through cloning, a perfect replica of Adolf Hitler. "I'm not going to take the time to explain to you how I achieved this—I doubt whether you'd have the capacity to understand it if I did—but take my word for it, I did achieve it. *Exact genetic duplicates.* They were conceived in my laboratory and carried to term by women of the Auiti tribe; healthy, docile creatures with a businesslike chieftain. The boys bear no taint of them; they're pure Hitler, bred entirely from his cells. He allowed me to take a half a liter of his blood and a cutting of skin from his ribs—we were in a biblical frame of mind. . . ."

Even the discovery of remains identified as Mengele's in 1985—he is believed to have suffered a heart attack while swimming in 1979—failed to put to rest the legend of Mengele as an undying monster. Despite many points of correspondence between the skeletal remains and Mengele's medical records, American, German, and Israeli investigators could not find any evidence of the virulent osteomylitis that would have left permanent bone scarring. And despite the media attention given to the "positive identification" of Josef Mengele, the official forensic reports were never actually made public. Many of the doctor's surviving victims refuse to this day to believe that he is really dead. In the time-honored tradition of Hollywood horror movies, enough ambiguity remains so as not to preclude a sequel.

HUMAN EXPERIMENTATION IN WORLD WAR II was hardly limited to the Nazis. David J. Rothman, author of the bioethics history *Strangers at the Bedside* (1991), argues that today's many intrusions into the doctor-patient relationship by legal and governmental bodies—not to mention the crisis in malpractice litigation and insurance—had their beginnings in World War II medical research, when a bureaucratized estrangement between patients and doctors began to take root. Human experimentation in wartime America did not of course take place in concentration camps, but that is not to say that participation was necessarily willing or informed. To expedite the development of vaccines and treatments urgently needed in the armed services, experimental vaccines were injected into institutionalized persons, including orphans, with little or no explanation of the procedures and the possible side effects and often without consent. "The research into dysentery, malaria and influenza revealed a pervasive disregard of the rights of subjects—a willingness to experiment on the mentally retarded, the mentally ill, prisoners, ward patients, soldiers, and medical students without concern for obtaining consent," writes Rothman. "Utilitarian justifications that had flourished under conditions of combat and conscription persisted, and principles of consent and voluntary participation were often disregarded. This was, to borrow a phrase from American political history, the Gilded Age of research, the triumph of laissez-faire in the laboratory."

A large number of mad scientist films during World War II dealt with clandestine experiments conducted outside normal ethical bounds. The collective performances of Boris Karloff, Bela Lugosi, George Zucco, and other film actors gave a tangible face to the scientific shadow of wartime, whether or not the outlandish plots of their films were explicitly war-related. A patriotic willingness to help the war effort required a suppression of moral queasiness that was finally confronted in the "safe" realm of escapist entertainment. But sometimes the war connections bubbled to the surface, as in the advertising campaign for a 1946 rerelease of Karloff's *The Man They Could Not Hang*, with lurid posters blatantly trumpeting A HOLO-CAUST OF HORROR.

Postwar mad movie doctors dabbled obsessively with radioactive materials, and rarely for the health of their patients. Often the radioactive treatment was presented as a combination of medieval torture and transforming sacrament/sacrifice. "It hurts—just for a moment," Dr. Eric Vornoff (Bela Lugosi) tells the trousseau-clad newspaper reporter strapped to his laboratory table in Edward D. Wood, Jr.'s camp classic *Bride of the Monster* (1955). "And then you will emerge a woman of superior strength and beauty—the bride of the atom!" He doesn't tell her that all his previous attempts at creating atomic superpeople have resulted in the deaths of his unwilling experimental subjects. Films like *Bride of the Monster* weirdly anticipated the revelation, four decades later, of a thirty-year campaign of secret human radiation experiments performed by government doctors, researchers, and the military. From the end of the war until roughly the time of the Watergate debacle, soldiers and civilians were subjected to various kinds of radiation without their knowledge or consent, all in an attempt to increase medical knowledge of the possible effects of a nuclear war.

The President's Advisory Committee on Human Radiation Experiments, convened in response to a 1992 congressional hearing and investigative reporting in the *Albuquerque Tribune,* reported more than four thousand experiments conducted on twenty thousand citizens. Soldiers were marched through nuclear bomb test sites, and hospitalized civilians were directly injected with plutonium and uranium. Patients in university hospitals with government contracts were given full-body irradiation; others had small radioactive rods implanted in their nasal cavities. Some patients were led to believe, falsely, that their participation in these experiments was related to their medical treatment. In one of the worst cases, a twenty-three-year-old girl hospitalized at the University of Rochester was injected with uranium even after she had refused to give consent. No movie-style mutations are known to have resulted, but one might well consider suspected cases of cancer, leukemia, and immune disorders as science-created monstrosities. In 1996, following an eighteen-month investigation, the federal government made a $4,800,000 payment to families of eleven deceased subjects and to a lone survivor of the injection experiments. It is especially chilling to realize that the worst of these experiments were conducted around the time of the Nuremberg trials, against a backdrop of high-profile international outrage over Nazi medical atrocities.

British horror films of the late 1950s and early 1960s were especially drawn to themes of medical sadism, as if the public's morbid curiosity about Nazi experiments had only been whetted by the testimony at Nuremberg and the ensuing avalanche of horrifying books and documentaries. Beginning with Hammer Films' *The Curse of Frankenstein* (1957), audiences could vicariously immerse themselves in graphic Technicolor spectacles of the kind previously witnessed only by Dr. Mengele and his assistants behind closed doors at Auschwitz. As Baron Victor Frankenstein, actor Peter Cushing cornered the market on the character, which he played with an air of icy, elegant obsession. Cushing reprised the role in five films. In *The Curse of Frankenstein,* he played maker to Christopher Lee's scarred scarecrow of a monster; both men also became firmly identified with Hammer's Dracula series, forging another link in the ongoing historical interdependency of the Dark Twins. Cushing's success with the Frankenstein part owed much to the considerable pains he took to establish verisimilitude. The actor once told an interviewer that he conferred with his own physician at length on such hypothetical

Peter Cushing in *The Curse of Frankenstein* (1957). *Courtesy of David Del Valle/ The Del Valle Archive.*

topics as the proper technique of human brain transplantation. In a small way, at least, real medicine thus aided the cause of mad, fantastic science.

The postwar Dracula-Frankenstein nexus also invigorated *Blood of the Vampire* (1959), with the distinguished Shakespearean actor Sir Donald Wolfit slumming in the role of the Victorian monster Dr. Callistratus, who, suspected of being a vampire and summarily dispatched by traditional means, cheats death by means of a prearranged heart transplant to replace his stake-punctured ticker—all this posited roughly a century before the advent of Dr. Christiaan Barnard. But the risky gambit is only a prelude to the real story: Callistratus's cruel dominion over a hellhole Victorian prison, whose inmates, much like those of the death camps, are conscripted as both medical assistants and medical victims in the doctor's attempts to purify his own transplant-tainted blood.

Blood purification rituals are inextricably linked to feelings of insufficiency and guilt. The Nazi doctors were arguably terrified on some level of their own possible inability to control genetic degeneracy on a mass scale; mad doctors in postwar movies are often veiled Nazis, Mengeles writ small, acting out private, personalized psychodramas with catastrophic results. In Georges Franju's *Les Yeux sans visage (The Eyes without a Face,* aka *The Horror Chamber of Dr. Faustus),* a plastic surgeon, anguished over his responsibility for the car wreck that has hideously mangled his beautiful daughter's face, becomes a monster of guilt, abducting other people's daughters and grafting their faces, unsuccessfully, onto his own child in a grisly serial ritual of impossible atonement. Both doctor and daughter become dehumanized in the process, he as a murderer, and she as an increasingly remote, doll-like automaton doomed to regard the world forever through a blank white mask.

Franju's disturbing film has a powerful poetry that mitigates its shocks; the more typical guilty doctor melodrama follows the much cruder mold of *The Brain That Wouldn't Die* (1960), in which an obsessed surgeon, guilt-ridden after his fiancée has been decapitated in a road accident, keeps her head alive in a lab tray while he begins a search for a replacement body. He gets sidetracked by erotic indecision, allowing the film to linger in strip clubs, where he carefully considers his options, at least from the neck down. Meanwhile, his fiancée's head grows crazy and resentful, finally contriving a prenuptial, postbody revenge.

A striking number of 1950s mad science melodramas are biomedical nightmares. Even if the scientists depicted are not physicians, they end up presiding over monstrous disease analogues. In *Tarantula* (1955) Leo G. Carroll's attempt irradiated, oversize arachnids and rabbits leave him with a nasty case of disfiguring acromegaly he cannot cure. Mysterious, uncontrollable, body-distorting "illnesses" created by science drive the plots of dozens of films, including *The Incredible Shrinking Man* (1957), *The Amazing Colossal Man* (1958), *War of the Colossal Beast* (1958), *Attack of the Fifty-Foot Woman* (1958), *The Alligator People* (1958), *The Fly* (1958), and *The Wasp Woman* (1960). Aside from the ongoing atomic jitters (the majority of these mutation diseases are caused by exposure to radiation), these films reflect a

Socialized medicine as nightmare: Graham Crowden in *Britannia Hospital* (1982).

corollary anxiety—namely, that medicine in the postwar era is powerless against the threat of the bomb. The traditional role of the doctor is reduced to that of an ineffectual bystander or, more ominously, that of a drafted mercy killer, often working at the behest of the military or law enforcement authorities to put an end to a monstrous disease process the military set in motion.

In Britain, where doctors were absorbed into bureaucratized medical combines decades before our own headlong rush into managed care, an especially mordant tradition of medical satire evolved. Peter Nichols's critically acclaimed play *The National Health* (1969), widely produced on both sides of the Atlantic and filmed in 1973, sharply lampooned institutionalized medicine with an irony largely absent in American efforts, where medical discontent was confronted largely through the melodramatic veil of science fiction and horror (a notable exception was Arthur Hiller's film *The Hospital* [1971], with a darkly comedic Oscar-winning screenplay by Paddy Chayevsky).

In Lindsay Anderson's film *Britannia Hospital* (1982), the crazy experiments of a mad doctor, Professor Millar (Graham Crowden), subsidized by Britain's national health care system, provide a metaphor for socialized medicine run amok. Millar's pièce de résistance is a bodiless computer-brain hybrid, though he dabbles in more traditional patchwork monsters—the head for one unwillingly provided by Malcolm McDowell, who also starred in Anderson's similarly surrealistic, antiauthoritarian parable *if . . .* (1968). Andrew Sarris, writing in the *Village Voice,* suggests that *Britannia Hospital* might deserve "a niche in the annals of high-art sleaze for running a human brain through a blender in the preparation of a mentally-stimulating health drink."

In the present American medical care crisis (we are told by reformers), the medical industry has affixed itself to the body politic like a horrid high-tech vampire, enervating the economy. But the fix—the proliferation of for-profit health care conglomerates—has proved more disturbing, on many levels, than the disease.

The best-selling novels of Robin Cook, beginning with *Coma* (1977), have provided a commercially concentrated dose of medical paranoia only slightly removed from a real world of managed care, where patients often can't tell whose interests their doctors are really serving. Cook, a practicing ophthalmologist who became disenchanted with the increasing corporatization of medicine, turned to writing medical thrillers first as a sideline and then as a lucrative second career. After studying several commercial thrillers, he set out unapologetically to emulate them, with best-selling results. *Coma* set forth the basic formulas of the Cook canon to follow: Susan Wheeler, an intern in a prestigious Boston teaching hospital, discovers a sinister plot involving a group of patients rendered mysteriously brain-dead during routine anesthesia. They have, in fact, had their brains deliberately destroyed in order that their organs can be harvested for black-market transplants. Greed is only part of the picture; the real issue is the meglomaniacal arrogance of doctors. At the novel's climax, as Susan herself is slipping under the anesthesia, the evil Dr. Stark bares his soul: ". . . medicine is on the brink of probably the biggest breakthrough in all of its long history. . . . [W]e need people like myself, indeed like Leonardo Da Vinci, willing to step beyond restrictive laws in order to insure progress. What if Leonardo Da Vinci had not dug up his bodies for dissection? What if Copernicus had knuckled under the laws and dogma of the church? Where would we be today?"

The year following its appearance as a novel, *Coma* was produced as a motion picture scripted and directed by Michael Crichton, starring Genevieve Bujold and Michael Douglas. Crichton took numerous liberties with his adaptation, upgrading Susan Wheeler from a medical student to a mature, feisty resident and recombining the names and identities of the various villains. The film was a box-office success and introduced Robin Cook to a vast new audience. Following a brief foray into archaeological suspense with the novel *Sphinx* (1979) and its disappointing 1981 film version, Cook returned to the paranoid medical thriller with *Brain* (1981), a niche that has served him well ever since. *Brain,* a close retooling of *Coma,* substitutes

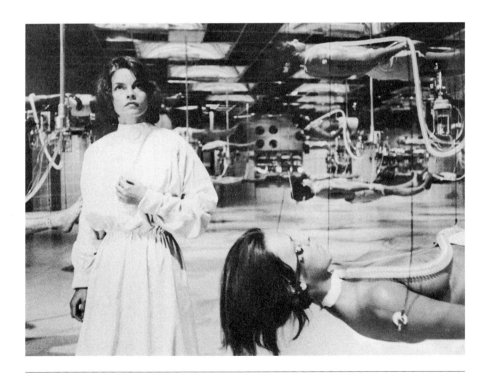

Genevieve Bujold smells something rotten in the state of health care. From *Coma* (1978).

hijacked human brains (for use in a biocomputer) for the more prosaic transplants of the earlier book. *Fever* (1982) deals with a chemical plant's conspiracy to cover up its role in a leukemia outbreak. The *Washington Post Book World* identified "the real payoff" for readers of Cook's novels as "horrible revelations about the medical establishment. . . . [F]or the average person, an active, well-lit modern hospital is infinitely spookier than a dark old abandoned house." There is perhaps some ancient cultural memory at work here; centuries before HMO anxiety, hospitals, or their prototypes, were simply pestholes from which no one who entered realistically expected to exit alive.

In Cook's *Godplayer* (1983), the mysterious hospital deaths have nothing to do with science-fictional transplant schemes but generate a similar level of horror nonetheless. In the book's opening scene, a patient, unable to communicate with his nurses, dies helplessly in his bed, inadvertently literalizing the cruel paradoxes of American health care access in the process. "Bruce felt his terror become panic. Now he was certain something terrible was happening to him! He was surrounded by the best medical care but unable to reach it. He had to get help. He had to get help instantly. It was like a nightmare from which he could not awaken." In the end the culprit is revealed to be a psychotic cardiac surgeon, Thomas Kingsley, who can't stand the idea of his work being wasted on undeserving patients. " 'Look,' shouted Thomas, 'all I want to do is surgery on people who deserve to live, not a bunch of mental defectives or people who are going to die of other illnesses. Medicine has to understand that our resources are limited. We can't let worthy candidates wait while people with multiple sclerosis or gays with autoimmunal [*sic*] deficiencies take valuable beds and OR time.' "

Kingsley's fictional sentiments crystallized the real-world debate over health care rationing that emerged in the 1990s, when demographic realities began to descend on the insurance industry and a politician like Colorado Governor Richard Lamm called for the elderly to lie down and die rather than consume dwindling health care resources better spent on the young. It had never before been politically permissible to discuss the value of human life with such cold-blooded calculation, and Lamm took a hit of withering criticism for his opinions. The demographic shifts brought on by an aging population, coupled with the steady consolidation of health care providers into larger and more profit-driven conglomerates, coincided with the rise of the right to die movement and medical "rationing," triage, and mercy killing. Doctors, it seemed, were poised to begin withholding care instead of dispensing it. The public's unease with the emergence of such discussions paralleled the growth of Robin Cook as a publishing commodity and fore-shadowed the ascendancy of Dr. Jack Kevorkian, whose enthusiasm for euthanasia sent headline writers scurrying for B movies with relevant titles—e.g., *Calling Doctor Death.*

In *Mindbend* (1985) Cook presents a giant, malevolent drug company enforcing its long-range plans vis-à-vis managed care by "managing" patients and doctors with implanted brain electrodes. "With the behavior-modification techniques we are perfecting, there will eventually be no locked wards in either hospitals or prisons," a doctor villain boasts. "In fact, both the National Institutes of Mental Health and the Prisons Administration Board are funding our experiments." The plot of *Outbreak* (1987) turned on the deliberate introduction of the deadly Ebola virus into HMOs. *Mortal Fear* (1988) imagined DNA researchers (". . . a malevolent cabal," according to the promo copy, "bent on using the origins of life to create a hell on earth") who spread a "death gene" through contaminated eyedrops.

Mutation (1989) is perhaps Cook's most ludicrous novel, the story of the groaningly named Dr. Victor Frank, who genetically engineers a prodigy son, V.J., who by the age of ten is a high-tech bad seed running his own clandestine research facility. V.J. is interested not in perfecting the human race but rather in genetically engineering a mentally retarded, manageable work force. "Now that the secret is out," he tells his mother (in a prime example of the awkward dialogue that gives the author's writing a trademark, unintentional air of surrealism), "I think it is rather ridiculous for me to go to school and pretend to be interested and absorbed in fifth-grade work."

Cook's *Harmful Intent* (1990) explores the sinister side of anesthesia, and *Vital Signs* (1991) plunges into what the dust jacket describes as "the dark vortex of the baby-making business," reprising the Ebola-embattled heroine of *Outbreak,* Dr. Marissa Blumenthal. *Blindsight* (1992) features a sight-impaired mob figure engineering "cocaine overdoses" for corneal transplant recipients ahead of him on the waiting list. *Terminal* (1993) visits a hospital that creates, then miraculously "cures" rare brain cancers in wealthy patients, the better to tap them for grateful, generous endowments. *Fatal Cure* (1993) takes on managed care systems (from the flap copy: ". . . a heart-stopping tale of intrigue and mystery set at the uncertain juncture of medical care and financial pragmatism . . . a hair-raising, timely foray into the dark side of medical reform, proving that with 'managed care' the unthinkable can be as close as the local hospital").

Like Stephen King (whose work I discuss at length in *The Monster Show*), Robin Cook skillfully mines real-world apprehensions, making medical fears palatable for a mass audience by pushing them into the safe, cartoony confines of escapist entertainment. Not surprisingly, Cook has many imitators, and medical thrillers have become a major staple of publishing and film. The outlandish horror movie *Dr. Giggles* (1993) may be an ultimate distillation of the trend, juxtaposing the friendly face of the small-town physician with the grinning visage of a serial killer. Before dispatching his victims with impromptu open-heart surgery, Dr. Giggles never neglects to dispense homely practical advice, in the best family practitioner style. *Variety* picked up the topical vibrations. "More care in scripting and fewer cheap yocks could have resulted in a viable new paranoid horror myth well-timed to America's ongoing crisis in health care," wrote critic Lawrence Cohn.

A far more serious, and original, consideration of the shadow side of doctors, clinics, and biomedical research has been ongoing in the work of Canadian filmmaker David Cronenberg. While his preoccupation with grotesque physical distortions created by science has a distinct antecedent in 1950s atomic mutation formulas, Cronenberg is difficult to categorize as either a science fiction or horror auteur. He has, rather, borrowed liberally from these genres in creating a category all his own, a highly coherent (if disturbing and eccentric) exploration of the tensions between hypercivilization and hyperprimitivism. The late-twentieth-century medical man, despite his technological toys, still engages us on the level of the aboriginal medicine man. The further Cronenberg's doctors push the pretensions of scientific control and rationality, the more uncontrollable, irrational, and nightmarish the prognoses become.

Cronenberg turned to filmmaking after becoming disillusioned with

Larry Drake in *Dr. Giggles* (1992).

science as a student. Beyond finding the actual study of science falling far short of its mystique, he encountered some eccentricities of its practitioners firsthand. He recalled "a physics professor [at the University of Toronto] who would start his class whether there was anyone there or not. You could be the first to arrive and half the board was covered with figures and he was talking," Cronenberg said. "I think the best scientists are as mad, creative and eccentric as writers and artists of any kind. . . . I feel a lot of empathy for doctors and scientists. I often feel that they are my persona in my films. Although they may be tragic and demented, I don't subscribe to the view that they are playing with things that shouldn't be played with. . . . I don't think there's anything man wasn't meant to know. There are just some stupid things people shouldn't do."

In his first commercial film, *Shivers* (1975; also known as *The Parasite Murders* and *They Came from Within*), Cronenberg introduces Dr. Emil

Hobbes, a crazy clinician whose attempts to create living organ substitutes yields something else entirely: a disgusting parasite, half phallic and half fecal, which penetrates its hosts orally or vaginally, turning them into rabid sex maniacs. Hobbes considers his creation a therapeutic corrective to an excessively rationalized, body-alienated world. Invading the semizombie population of a stark modern apartment complex, the parasite forces the residents to reconnect with their bodies in the most primal terms, discovering a perverse sense of connectedness and community in the ravages of plague. *Rabid* (1976) presents porn queen Marilyn Chambers as the victim of a hubristic plastic surgeon, Dr. Dan Keloid, whose experimental lifesaving procedure turns his patient into a kind of vampire who drains her victims with a fleshy suction spike hidden in her armpit. The obsessive rationality of the Keloid Clinic is superimposed with messy primitivism throughout, a Cronenberg trademark. When the time comes for Dr. Keloid himself to go "rabid," the transformation takes place in an antiseptic operating theater. "Give me something to cut with, nurse!" he growls from behind his surgical mask, just before liberating the woman of a gloved finger. In *The Brood* (1979) the mad doctor is Dr. Hal Ragland (Oliver Reed), a radical psychotherapist who purges his most spectacularly disturbed patient (Samantha Eggar) of her conflicts by transforming her inner rage into a gaggle of murderous homunculi. *Scanners* (1980), with its infamous scene of a human head exploded by extrasensory overload, posits a pharmaceutical explanation for its visceral horrors: A tranquilizer for pregnant women, Ephemerol, has created a baby boomer generation of superhuman, warring telepaths. Ephermol, of course, oddly echoes the real-world pharmaceutical fallout of thalidomide and DES. Once more, a medical fix creates more problems than it solves. (Cronenberg's somatically obsessed *Videodrome* [1982] and *The Fly* [1986] deal less directly with medical issues and are discussed in the following chapter, "Vile Bodies.")

In *Dead Ringers* (1988), Cronenberg's supreme study of medical madness, a pair of grade school twins, Elliot and Beverley Mantle, obsessed with finding a means of having sex without actually having to touch women (they decide it should be done in a bathtub, with sperm released into water), grow up to be codependent gynecologists. The Mantles were inspired by the bizarre true story of the Marcus brothers, a pair of identically disturbed

Manhattan physicians whose drug-driven suicides fueled the tabloids in the 1970s and inspired the novel *Twins* by Bari Wood and Jack Geasland (upon which Cronenberg loosely based his screenplay).

Beverley and Elliot evoke the classic Jekyll and Hyde duality that has bedeviled doctor-patient relationships since Victorian times, whether twins are involved or not. Though temperamentally on different planets, the Mantles look enough alike to impersonate one another, socially and sexually. When film actress Claire Niveau (Genevieve Bujold) realizes she has been doppelgängbanged, she confronts the brothers angrily. "Beverley's the sweet one and you're the shit," she tells Elliot in an elegant restaurant they have chosen for their first three-way encounter. Then, to Beverley: "Sweet little act you have—you soften them up with all that smarmy concern, and along comes Dracula here and polishes them off." Claire Niveau confronts the Mantle brothers over their duplicity; she starkly recognizes the split-level aspect of the doctor image that is simultaneously comforting and frightening. The cultural importance of the two-faced or mutating doctor-scientist may be reflected in the time-honored tradition of Academy Award nominations for these kinds of performances. Jeremy Irons received a Best Actor nomination for *Dead Ringers,* and Jeff Goldblum was similarly honored for his shape-shifting researcher Seth Brundle in Cronenberg's 1987 remake of *The Fly.* Fredric March, of course, actually won the award for his work in the 1931 *Dr. Jekyll and Mr. Hyde.*

On *Dead Ringers,* the *New Yorker's* Terrence Rafferty commented, "We come out clammy, shaken, a little numb, as if from a particularly upsetting visit to the doctor: Cronenberg palpates us all over, probes us as with latex gloves, and then won't tell us what we've got. . . . In one sense, this movie is an unsettling, satiric confirmation of patients' fears about arrogant, egotistical doctors—our suspicion that we aren't quite real for them, that while we're being examined or operated on our bodies might as well be inert matter, anatomical dolls."

Psychiatrists especially bore the brunt of doctor bashing in the cinematic 1980s and 1990s, beginning with Brian De Palma's *Dressed to Kill* (1980), starring Michael Caine as a cross-dressing doctor-slasher, and culminating with the flesh-eating Dr. Hannibal Lecter (Anthony Hopkins) in the film version of *The Silence of the Lambs* (1991), based on the 1988 novel by Thomas Harris. Lecter had first appeared in Thomas's novel *Red Dragon* (1981) and its motion-picture adaptation, *Manhunter* (1986). Lecter possesses a mind as vast, cool, and unsympathetic as anything imagined by H. G. Wells of his Martians. He also has the olfactory prowess of a bloodhound, and a vestigial sixth finger to boot (this last detail, not carried over to the film adaptations, seems an echo of an old *Outer Limits* episode, "The Sixth Finger," wherein the extra digit appeared on a retarded young man when his intelligence was accelerated to a posthuman extreme—another example of deformed or mutilated hands being associated with mad doctors and mad science). Dr. Lecter, consigned to a maximum security prison for such crimes as killing and cannibalizing a census taker for attempting to "quantify" him ("I ate his liver with some fava beans and a big Amarone") and mutilating a

Jeremy Irons as Dr. Beverley Mantle in David Cronenberg's *Dead Ringers* (1988).

nurse ("The doctors managed to save one of her eyes. Lecter was hooked up to the monitors the entire time. He broke her jaw to get at her tongue. His pulse never got over eighty-five, even when he swallowed it").

In a *Washington Post* essay titled "Lights! Cameras! Loonies! Why This Parade of Creepy, Slimy Shrinks?" writer Amy Cunningham wondered if "unbalanced" film and television people in California and New York ("no doubt" more prone to therapy than "the rest of us") were "retaliating against their own therapists in a most public display of transference. Car dealers, gangsters, prostitutes and evil stepmothers get more respect than the unscrupulous therapists you see on the screen."

Cunningham may have missed the real point. While dutifully enumerating the factual distortions and misconceptions about unethical psychiatrists in films like *The Silence of the Lambs* and, far less melodramatically, in *The Prince of Tides* (1991) and *Final Analysis* (1992), Cunningham failed to understand how the image of the psychiatrist (the most intimate and emotionally invasive of all doctor-scientists) could become a powerful lightning rod for widespread public apprehension about the medical profession generally. The public recognized something in the face of Dr. Hannibal Lecter that had nothing to do with retaliatory clinical transference, but everything to do with a deep-seated suspicion that there was, perhaps, something actually "unbalanced" in the amount of power, prestige, and privilege accorded doctors and other highly compensated professionals in an increasingly two-tiered society. Ordinary people with medical, legal, and economic problems become almost lunch for a demonized professional class. It is no secret that lawyers as a group are held in extraordinary contempt by a large segment of the population; the Clinton administration's health care reform rhetoric of the early 1990s, with its evocative descriptions of a bloated medical-industrial complex sapping and devouring the economy, similarly colored the public estimation of doctors. In addition to providing primary point of contact with science for nontechnical working-class people, doctors often represent a rare close encounter with the economic overclass. If doctors as a group are indeed scarfing down more and more of the economic pie, then a patient-munching monster like Dr. Hannibal Lecter is an inevitable (if perhaps overly literal) iconic representation.

But devouring doctors didn't begin with Hannibal Lecter. Jack the Ripper, believed by many to have been a doctor, ate one of his victim's kidneys, or at least boasted as much in what is believed to be an open letter to the authorities. A hybrid subcategory of vampire mad scientists has similarly hungered for the patient's life essence. In Oates's *Wonderland,* the already grotesque Dr. Pedersen is imagined by his daughter in even more grotesque cannibal terms: "You want to stuff me inside your mouth! I know you! I know you!" cries Hilda Pedersen. "You want to press me into a ball and pop me into your mouth, back where I came from! You want to eat us all up!" Oates also includes a memorable medical necrophage, T.S. "Trick" Monk, a brilliant but demented Ann Arbor student who confesses to stealing a uterus from the cadaver room. "I took it home with me in a paper bag and kept it in the refrigerator for a while," Trick confides. "It broiled unevenly."

The nagging suspicion that medicine might be out to eat us alive (or dead) is reflected in the unverifiable but persistent urban folklore in recent years about Latin American street children having their eyes cut out by unscrupulous surgeons needing corneas for wealthy, impatient patients. In 1994 Guatemala was engulfed with hysterical rumors about black marketeers snatching babies for "adoption" by Americans and Europeans, who then murder the children and sell their organs to transplant doctors around the world for a handsome profit. Legitimate adoptions by foreigners ground to a halt in Guatemala as a result of the rumors. As one Guatemala City adoption lawyer explained it, even parents completely unable to care for a family "prefer that their children starve in the streets begging rather than be killed for organ transplants." Some commentators observed that the rumor-mongering had its roots in the ruthless politics of Guatemalan civil war (with many factions having their own strategic reasons to demonize foreigners for internal political gain) rather than a grassroots uprising against medical abuses. Whatever their motivations, the rumormongers fully understood the potent political possibilities of a Robin Cook worldview.

By contrast, an underground press book that appeared in America about the same time as the Guatemalan hysteria took a sunny, pragmatic approach to what another culture viewed with horror. In *Sell Yourself to Science* (1993), author Jim Hogshire presents a practical do-it-yourself manual for cashing in on medicine's voracious appetite for body parts, fluids, and willing experimental subjects. In a strapped economy, why not consider a new career as a human guinea pig? "Our body parts have become so valuable that we might start thinking of ourselves as human cash machines," writes Hogshire. "This book is about making a withdrawal." The author enumerates the many ways to capitalize one's natural assets, from renting your body for experimental drug trials (compensation: up to $100 a day, plus expenses) to selling blood, milk, sperm, eggs, and hair, to outright sacrifice of organs (where the real bucks are). Although organ selling is illegal in the United States, far more lenient laws apply in Britain, the Philippines, India, Germany, and elsewhere. A piece of liver is the biggest ticket item, commanding as much as $150,000 a slice, Hogshire reports. Next in line are kidneys, worth $10,000 to $50,000. A cornea is worth up to $4,000, and bone marrow can fetch $10,000 a cup. The illustration of the doctor who appears on the cover of *Sell Yourself to Science* is rendered in a classic B movie pose, goggle-eyed as

he holds aloft a test tube containing some vital essence removed from a cash-happy young donor.

Though most real-life doctors do not display organ-snatching or cannibal tendencies, more mundane psychological disturbances are common in the medical occupations. Doctors are notoriously more prone to drink, drugs, depression, and suicide than other professionals. David R. Slavitt, in his book *Physicians Observed* (1987), suggests that clinical overspecialization at the expense of the humanities in medical education might be partially to blame for the personal problems experienced by doctors. According to Slavitt, "the stresses and pressures of a career in medicine are likely to leave a fair por-

Sell Yourself to Science:
the ultimate do-it-yourself guide.

tion of the profession burned out, cynical, or impaired (which is a code word for drunk, on drugs, or crazy)." Slavitt especially notices that "students who enter medical school with some kind of religious orientation very often lose it, either in the first year when they confront (or soon after, when they turn over) their cadavers, or later on . . . when they go onto the wards to see, time after time, in violation of their fundamental notions about fairness and decency, brave and good people and innocent children going down in pain without any kind of chance." Slavitt quotes a University of Pennsylvania psychiatrist who told him, "Aside from a few devout and rigorously trained Catholics, I don't know anyone here—students or faculty—who have [*sic*] retained any religious beliefs at all. Certainly, nothing comforting."

A few years ago I served as a juror on a New York City malpractice case. We ultimately found for the doctor and strongly suspected the patient had exaggerated his complaints. But we also sensed that the patient's rage stemmed from the doctor's brusque, dismissive manner in the examining room, which the patient interpreted, however incorrectly, as a form of malpractice. The inability of patients to communicate with their doctors, and vice versa, has been cited time and again as a major predictive factor in malpractice litigation. According to one doctor who gave up private practice to assist attorneys in finding medical witnesses for malpractice cases, "The majority of physicians are not very social people. The majority of physicians are very repressed individuals. Highly intelligent but very repressed people—who will bore the hell out of you at any party. They talk about medicine and are pretty much at a loss about anything else. . . . [T]hey live, sleep and breathe medicine. The best doctors are the ones who sat on the toilet reading their textbooks, day and night." But the patient's needs and expectations often go far beyond the physician's mere dispensing of information.

Issues of communication and control between doctor and patient are vividly dramatized in the growing phenomenon of factitious disorders, in which physically healthy individuals feign illness in order to command sociomedical support and attention. In the most extreme manifestation, known as the Munchausen syndrome (named for the eighteenth-century Baron von Munchausen, renowned for dramatic exaggeration), the patient's entire life is taken over by the compulsion to maintain the illusion of illness, which often transcends illusion as the patient employs a variety of artificial means to induce actual symptoms and sickness. Factitious patients have been known to bleed themselves to simulate anemia, to rub fecal matter into wounds to promote infection, to inject themselves with a variety of drugs in order to create baffling, obscure symptoms, and even to swallow objects like razor blades or pins that necessitate immediate surgery. Because the illusion cannot be sustained indefinitely, the factitious patient becomes itinerant, moving from doctor to doctor, clinic to clinic, support group to support group. Some even masquerade successfully as cancer or AIDS patients for extended periods.

Drs. Mark D. Feldman and Charles V. Ford, who document the syndrome in their book *Patient or Pretender* (1994), report a tenfold increase in reported incidents of factitious disorders since the 1970s, the same time period in which malpractice litigation began to soar, reflecting a crisis of trust between doctors and patients. Interestingly, psychiatrist Karl Menninger first identified the "doctor addict" syndrome and its sadomasochistic underpinnings in 1934, a time at which popular images of sadistic doctors and evil experiments were reaching a saturation point in B movies and pulp fiction.

The factitious patient becomes a mad doctor, an auto-Mengele, of sorts, subjecting his or her body to perverse procedures that bring about sickness instead of healing. Feldman and Ford elucidate the kinds of emotional gratification such patients receive—on the passive side, attention, sympathy, and nurturance, but on the aggressive front, tremendous power over figures of scientific and medical authority—and report the "almost orgasmic feeling" that comes with making fools out of doctors. Unfortunately, Feldman and Ford do not explore the possible reasons for a rise in patient rage and contempt for the medical profession in the late twentieth century and essentially chalk up the entire phenomenon to unresolved parent-child conflicts.

Factitious patients know that the sick role is culturally important. As social critic Ivan Illich observes in his book *Medical Nemesis: The Expropriation of Health* (1976), "Previously modern medicine controlled only a limited market; now this market has lost all boundaries. Unsick people have come to depend on professional care for the sake of their future health. The result is a morbid society that demands universal medicalization and a medical establishment that certifies universal morbidity." Illich doesn't write explicitly about mad movie doctors, but his thesis is amply illustrated with each new image of a maniacal medico attempting to correct or improve an otherwise healthy victim/patient, inevitably transforming vitality into morbidity.

The most dramatic and disturbing medical event of recent decades has been the AIDS epidemic, a catastrophe that has been colored by mad science assumptions from the beginning. AIDS has been shaped by the media and the medical industry as a typical sci-fi–horror scenario, a model that the general public and large numbers of AIDS patients have been thus far more than willing to accept.

However, as Oscar Wilde observed, the fact that people are willing to die for an idea does not necessarily make the idea true. The apocalyptic predictions of the mid-1980s—warnings that AIDS, like a movie monster in flimsy chains, would soon escape its association with male homosexuals and intravenous drug users and rapidly infect the general population—never came to pass. At a conference in Aspen in the mid-eighties I attended an address given by a prominent radio psychologist, Dr. David Viscott, to an audience that included numerous influential people in the communications business. In the hushed tones of an inside trader, the speaker told the rapt assembly that he had it on good authority that AIDS was going to kill a quarter of the human race within the decade. "They're not telling you this yet," he said, "but I am." Viscott is now dead (of a heart attack, not AIDS); the rest of us are still here. *Andromeda Strain* melodramatics colored mainstream media coverage across the boards. In 1987 Oprah Winfrey solemnly told millions of television viewers that one in five heterosexuals could be dead of AIDS in three years. "It is no longer just a gay disease," she said. "Believe me." A lot of people believed her.

AIDS is unique in the history of diseases in that its definition and treatment have been shaped by an unprecedented combination of factors outside traditional medical paradigm. Real science—science concerned with objective, verifiable matters of cause and effect—may be somewhat beside the point in the construction of the world's first postmodern disease, driven not only by pathogens but by patent rights, public relations, and politics. In her polemical history of AIDS, *The Gravest Show on Earth* (1995), Elinor Burkett makes the point bluntly: "AIDS isn't just a disease. It's a booming industry that bolsters the stock prices of multinational drug companies; it buys prestige, or at least BMWs, for young physicians who would normally still be struggling with student loans; it fuels the expansion of the biotech-nology industry; it provides jobs for bereavement counselors and benefits co-ordinators, AIDS spokesmen and activists; and it spawns thousands of new businesses to service the needs of the dying and the fears of the healthy."

There has never been a disease that has engendered such suspicion and mistrust of doctors and medicine as has AIDS. Cynics, cranks, and alterna-tive medicine partisans have always been critical of the cancer and heart dis-ease industries, viewed as having a vested interest in maintaining illness rather than in actually finding cures. With AIDS, such criticism moved from the fringes to the center. Resistance to official pronouncements on AIDS rose early in the hard-hit gay community; angry activists like Larry Kramer were quick to accuse public health officials of malign neglect and even genocidal intentions. Kramer's rhetoric routinely evoked the specter of Nazi medicine; a decade's worth of his outraged writings was collected under the title *Reports from the Holocaust.* The founder of the grassroots activist group ACT-UP (AIDS Coalition to Unleash Power), Kramer had plenty to be angry about: the slowness of the public health response, the blame-the-victim scapegoating of AIDS patients by medical professionals, including the shameful spectacle of doctors who pleaded for exemptions from the Hippo-cratic commitment to minister to the gravely ill out of fear for their own safety, and so on.

Amazingly, even at this writing (late 1997) there is no published sci-entific study definitively establishing the human immunodeficiency virus (HIV) as the cause of AIDS; on April 23, 1984, HIV was crowned the cul-prit not in the pages of a peer-reviewed medical journal but at a press con-ference at the Department of Health and Human Services in Washington, D.C. Department Secretary Margaret Heckler introduced Dr. Robert Gallo, a career scientist at the National Cancer Institute, with the news that he had discovered the probable cause of AIDS, a new retrovirus that became to be known as HIV. The sidestepping of traditional proofs and protocols was partly in response to intense public pressure to find a cause for the syndrome and partly in a stampede to sew up the lucrative patent rights to an antibody testing kit. Nevertheless, a messy entanglement ensued with French re-searchers who had been studying the same virus and had provided samples to Gallo's lab. Gallo was investigated for professional malfeasance and exonerated, and patent royalties were ultimately split between the Americans and the French. Still, Gallo's abrasive personality and perceived professional ruthlessness probably cost him a Nobel Prize and, at the opposite end of the celebrity spectrum, won him the dubious honor of being portrayed, with slimy mad scientist overtones, by actor Alan Alda in the HBO television adaptation of Randy Shilts's AIDS chronicle, *And the Band Played On.*

The unseemly scientific wrangling for glory and profit in the midst of a deadly health crisis did little to inspire confidence in the rapidly constituted AIDS establishment in the communities hardest hit. To a certain segment of stubborn dissenters, much about the HIV theory didn't add up. Why, for instance, was an antibody test supposed to be predictive of disease when, for all other viral pathogens, blood-borne antibodies reflected a *protective* immune response? Why weren't other known causes of acquired immune deficiency—malnutrition and recreational and pharmaceutical drug abuse—being more closely examined or examined at all? Why was it necessary to keep expanding the definition of AIDS (i.e., adding more preexisting diseases to the AIDS spectrum) in order to keep the curve of new cases climbing upward? If AIDS was sexually transmitted, why was it almost never seen in prostitutes who were not also drug users? Or, for that matter, in heterosexuals who were not also addicts? How, exactly, was the HIV virus acting, biochemically, to destroy immunity? There's still no answer to that one.

I will admit from the outset that I personally have serious reservations about the single-virus theory of AIDS (many mainstream researchers are also convinced that cofactors are involved, but this makes for a complicated sound bite). However, it is not my purpose here to argue an alternate hypothesis. Rather, I want to discuss the monstrous images of science and doctors that have flourished during the decade and a half since AIDS has been with us.

While most gay lobbyists focused on perceived official foot-dragging and the accelerated approval of experimental drugs, in the African American community there has been a widespread, almost casually accepted belief that AIDS is the result of a government germ warfare experiment gone out of control or, more radically, a genocidal plot. According to cultural historian Patricia A. Turner, the rumors about AIDS overlapped with two earlier, related rumor cycles. In the first, the twenty-eight victims of the Atlanta child murders between 1978 and 1981 were said to have been butchered by the

Centers for Disease Control (headquartered in Atlanta) to obtain tissue and blood samples necessary for the production of interferon. In the second, which surfaced in San Diego in the early 1980s, the Ku Klux Klan—white-robed, like doctors—was said to be introducing sterility-causing substances into fried chicken franchises in black neighborhoods.

Sadly, black suspicion about the government's possible role in a blood contamination conspiracy had some basis in reality. The appalling Tuskegee syphilis experiment, conducted from the early 1930s to the 1970s by doctors in the Public Health Service, deliberately withheld penicillin from hundreds of black patients for no other reason than observation of the long-term effects of untreated venereal disease. The men were simply told they had "bad blood" and never told that effective treatment was available. At least some of the rationale—if it can be called that—for the Tuskegee atrocity can be attributed to an unarticulated racist medical presumption that the disease wasn't worth curing in a population whose supposed inability to curb sexual appetite would likely infect it again. Susan Sontag makes a similar point concerning blacks, Africa, and AIDS:

> Illustrating the classic script for plague, AIDS is thought to have started in the "dark continent." . . . Africans who detect racist stereotypes in much of the geographical speculation about the geographical origin of AIDS are not wrong. (Nor are they wrong in thinking that depictions of Africa as the cradle of AIDS must feed anti-African prejudices in Europe and Asia.) The subliminal connection made to notions about the primitive past and the many hypotheses from animals (a disease of the green monkeys? African swine fever?) cannot help but activate a familiar set of stereotypes about animality, sexual license, and blacks.

A subset of the gay community is also drawn to the germ warfare hypothesis, speculating that trials of the first hepatitis B vaccine conducted among gay men in major American cities in the late 1970s were a deliberate attempt to infect and eradicate an undesirable population. In a series of privately published books still readily available in gay bookstores across the country, Alan Cantwell, Jr., a Los Angeles physician, outlines "the ultimate horror story of all time . . . a web of scientific insanity" involving a CIA-sponsored effort to create biological warfare agents by gene-splicing animal viruses. Despite its shrill, paranoid tone, Cantwell's *AIDS and the Doctors of Death* managed to attract an endorsement from none other than Elisabeth Kübler-Ross, one of the world's leading authorities on death, dying, and bereavement, who called the book "courageous," "wonderful," and "honest," "written by a physician and scientist who has come to a conclusion similar to mine that AIDS is not a natural occurrence, but a man-made creation with horrible implications." The otherwise distinguished British astronomer Fred Hoyle offered the opinion that the AIDS virus came from outer space. The *New York Native,* a leading gay newspaper, offered a panoply of against-the-grain theories on AIDS, most involving medical malfeasance and wide-ranging cover-ups; until it folded in 1996, the paper clung most tenaciously to the theory that AIDS is caused by a human herpes virus that also causes chronic fatigue syndrome.

Misunderstood, ostracized scientists are a staple of science fiction and horror formulas; in the AIDS wars a real-life variation is Dr. Peter Duesberg, a highly honored UC, Berkeley virologist who has become a pariah among AIDS researchers for his stubborn contention that HIV does not in fact cause AIDS. In Duesberg's view, the viral theory of AIDS was a power grab by virologist desperate to maintain a lucrative research establishment founded on the idea that "slow" viruses are responsible for many cancers. The view has since been discredited—notably by Duesberg himself, in a 1987 paper published in *Cancer Research,* "Retroviruses as Carcinogens and Pathogens: Expectations and Reality." Duesberg's heretical views have cost him, and his university, valuable research contracts, and to date he has been unable to fund clinical trials to substantiate his theory that AIDS is caused not by a single infectious pathogen but by the cumulative effects of drug abuse, including not only illicit recreational substances but also highly toxic and immuno-suppressive AIDS drugs like AZT. Duesberg, a member of the National Academy of Sciences, is still backed in the pursuit of his theories by the molecular biology department at Berkeley. Department head Richard C. Strohman, in the preface to Duesberg's 1995 collection of essays, *Infectious AIDS: Have We Been Misled?,* quotes the philosopher Alfred North Whitehead: "It is easy enough to find a theory, logically harmonious and with important applications in the regions of fact, provided that you are content to disregard half the facts."

Duesberg has recently organized his arguments on behalf of the other facts into a thick establishment-tweaking volume, *Inventing the AIDS Virus* (1996), doggedly wagging the anomalies of AIDS at anyone who will listen. He has a number of listeners with more than respectable credentials, including Dr. Kary B. Mullis, a Nobel laureate in chemistry who has been especially vocal as an HIV dissenter ("We have not been able to discover any good reasons for why most of the people on earth believe that AIDS is a disease caused by a virus. . . . There is no evidence that this is true and no one who can claim it by the ways of science"). In 1993 Robert Root-Bernstein, recipient of a MacArthur Foundation "genius" fellowship and an associate professor of physiology at the University of Michigan, published *Rethinking AIDS: The Tragic Cost of Premature Consensus,* systematically examining the numerous anomalies of AIDS that don't fit the single-virus-of-recent-origin hypothesis. For instance, he documents medical case histories matching the major symptoms of AIDS back as far as 1932, cases of AIDS without HIV and HIV infections without AIDS. Root-Bernstein is considerably more polite in tone than Duesberg, and his book was easy for the mainstream media to dismiss or ignore. One of his sharpest criticisms of narrow scientific thinking, in fact, takes the form of a epigraph from Rollo May: "People who claim to be *absolutely* convinced that their stand is the only right one are dangerous. Such conviction is the essence not only of dogmatism, but of its more destructive cousin, fanaticism . . . and it is a dead giveaway of unconscious doubt."

Skepticism, of course, can become its own kind of dogma, and the HIV dissenters are hardly free of their own personality tics, obsessions, professional jealousies, and territorial imperatives. In fact, the dissenters routinely rival the mainstream researchers in arrogance and grandiosity. The patients are the losers, left helpless on the examination table while the warring factions of mad science do battle in the lab.

As a group, the HIV dissenters do imply a massive, malevolent collusion among AIDS researchers and doctors and, ironically, have generated further layers of paranoia in certain quarters. To many activists, Duesberg's

call for a frank discussion of the immunological consequences of drug and alcohol abuse, repeated exposure to sexually transmitted diseases, and overuse
of antibiotics in the gay community—all legitimate areas for inquiry—is
treading too closely on a taboo subject and is therefore "homophobic." One
independent writer-researcher, Leonard G. Horowitz, has gone so far as to
suggest in his book *Emerging Viruses: AIDS and Ebola* (1996) that Duesberg's
theories are a smoke screen to cover the true origins of AIDS in biowarfare
research, to which, Horowitz charges, Duesberg, Gallo, and others all have
shadowy and suspicious links. Horowitz's earlier book *Deadly Innocence* (1994)
examined the case of Florida dentist David Acer, several of whose patients
(notably Kimberly Bergalis) became infected with HIV while in his care.
Contrary to inconclusive official investigations, Horowitz concludes that
Acer (who, like Bergalis, died of AIDS) became convinced that his own illness was the result of a genocidal government plot and deliberately injected
patients with his own contaminated blood to make a demented political
statement. Horowitz finally argues for a vast international conspiracy, trace-
able in part to the Nazis, of world population control and the elimination of
undesirable populations.

AIDS has succeeded in generated the most malevolent image of doctors
and medicine in history. It is a sickening picture, resonating powerfully
with another cultural image that has been with us: the mad scientist bend-
ing over his latest victim, enraptured with his own overreaching theories to
the point of moral blindness, willing to sacrifice patient after patient in the
pursuit of knowledge and power.

The undercurrents of melodramatic sci-fi helped turn AIDS into a hot
media commodity, attractive to Hollywood on a multiplicity of levels. The
zenith (or nadir) of the confluence between AIDS and movie madness may
have occurred in January 1993, when the filmmaker Francis Ford Coppola,
poised between his zeitgeist pageants *Bram Stoker's Dracula* (1992), which he
directed, and *Mary Shelley's Frankenstein* (1994), which he produced, invited
leading AIDS researchers to a retreat at his Napa Valley estate, where he sur-
really directed them in improvisatory theater games to enhance their creative
problem-solving abilities. AIDS of course readily evokes both Dracula (a
stealthy blood predator, elusive to science) and Frankenstein, a monster created by science (if one entertains the more florid conspiracy scenarios) or,

more intimately, by private, intemperate sexual "experimentation." Right-wing moralists in the age of AIDS frequently employ rhetoric laden with barely concealed vampire and mad scientist allusions; when PWAs (people with AIDS) aren't depicted as dark devils spreading an ever-widening circle of death through compulsive contact with human blood, they are roundly chastised in a manner previously reserved for mad experimenters in the movies: for subverting the "natural order," for threatening traditional sexual and reproductive paradigms—in short, for "tampering in God's domain."

Hollywood's flirtations with AIDS occur both on-screen and off. A film like *Outbreak* (1995), about a military-abetted Ebola outbreak in a quiet California town, pushes all the AIDS buttons without mentioning the syndrome: body fluid horror, origins in Africa, the slowness of official response, and so on. Today's pop cult prevalence of science-fictional invasion fantasies *(Independence Day, Mars Attacks)* in the absence of actual border threats may point to a widespread a growing sense of microvulnerability at the borders of the body.

Modern medical science has, after all, created vast armies of monsters—not the hulking, Hollywood kind but, rather, insidious hordes of antibiotic-resistant microbes, the mutated results of overused and misused "wonder drugs" and one of the greatest, if least publicized, threats to public health at the end of the century. After World War II doctors learned quickly to prescribe antibiotics virtually on demand, even in the absence of bacterial infection (e.g., for viral complaints like colds and flu) in order to placate or retain patients. The result was a mass, uncontrolled experiment in microbial mutation. In her disturbing book *The Coming Plague* (1994), Laurie Garrett describes the effects of antibiotic overuse in third world countries, where "a sizable percentage of the human population" became "walking petri dishes, providing ideal conditions for accelerated bacterial mutation, natural selection and evolution." What has evolved are virtually unkillable strains of once-treatable diseases like staph and strep infections, salmonella, gonorrhea, and dysentery, as well as frightening new variations on common organisms, like the deadly hemorrhagic strain of *E. coli* that first emerged in 1982.

Penicillin was introduced to the world in 1944, the same year *House of Frankenstein* was released, but the superbugs that have evolved in the wake of penicillin and its successors may be the real Frankenstein story of modern times, a looming medical crisis threatening far more people than those who will ever be at risk for Ebola or AIDS. But AIDS, a mediagenic mélange of death and sex, draws the lion's share of media attention and public interest.

The emergence of Elizabeth Taylor as the science establishment's official AIDS spokesbeing is perhaps more pointedly appropriate than research foundation executives ever dreamed. Taylor, herself rejuvenated and quasi-immortalized by surgical superscience,* the survivor of countless medical catastrophes and brushes with death, is a modern resurrection goddess, a living embodiment of sexual survivalism. Who else but Elizabeth Taylor could be the Queen of AIDS? J. G. Ballard shrewdly chose her as the central object of obsession in his 1973 cult novel *Crash* ("She sat in the damaged car like a deity occupying a shrine readied for her in the blood of a minor member of her congregation").

AIDS is the first disease syndrome for which treatment options have been largely driven by the marketing agendas of pharmaceutical giants rather than by independently corroborated research, raising unsettling questions about the integrity of the science involved. Covering the 1996 International Conference on AIDS in Vancouver, British Columbia (where a new, seemingly promising generation of AIDS drugs called protease inhibitors was the center of attention), Los Angeles reporter Bruce Mirken noted, "The line between science and commerce becomes disturbing fuzzy at these meetings. . . . Many of the key studies were financed by the pharmaceutical manufacturers whose drugs were being tested, and the final session at which the latest results were presented was cochaired by a drug company staff scientist. . . . Researchers would often head straight from the conference sessions to speak to drug company–sponsored satellite meetings—allegedly educational but often blatantly commercial, complete with lavish buffets and free-flowing wine."

---

*Film critic Parker Tyler found the Frankenstein monster and his bride to be perversely emblematic of the technomedical costs of Hollywood stardom: "Scars of surgical zeal near their necks clearly reveal the hideous truth . . . men and women, in and out of the acting profession, get their faces lifted and their features changed."

ACT-UP protester Todd Swindell was more direct: "This entire AIDS conference was bought and paid for by the pharmaceutical industry as a way to hype their deadly drugs. These companies concoct expensive products. They then fund and execute tests of them on humans to generate fraudulent data supporting their supposed efficacy. Finally, they buy off mainstream AIDS organizations and conferences to push these unproven compounds down the throats of people with AIDS. The entire AIDS treatment approach is murderously misdirected. . . ." As Elinor Burkett puts it, "Basic science is becoming a dying institution, a dinosaur in a scientific world geared toward the production of salable products."

At the Vancouver conference the mainstream press avoided reporting a showy protest in which ACT-UP members doused researchers Margaret Fischl and Paul Volberding (both controversial for their advocacy of the drug AZT) with artificial blood. Such tactics, like those of radical environmentalists, cast their practitioners in the roles of angry villagers, storming corporate castles to destroy perceived monsters.

The demonization of medicine is also fueled, paradoxically, by the popularity of television programs like *E.R.* and *Chicago Hope,* which depict doctors as fallible human beings, caught up in their own human dramas. We cozy up to the likes of George Clooney at the cost of surrendering a naive trust in the authority and power of doctors. Confusion and resentment set in; we are more vulnerable than we thought. Doctors were supposed to be gods, or at least guardian angels.

In the film *Malice* (1993) Alec Baldwin plays Jed Hill, an unscrupulous M.D. masterminding a convoluted insurance scam involving the deliberate sterilization of a woman for profit. In a tense moment he shouts, "You ask me if I have a God complex? Let me tell you something: I *am* God." A similar line delivered by Colin Clive in the 1931 *Frankenstein* ("For the love of God! Now I know what it feels like to be God!") scandalized audiences and censors. In the cynical, science-saturated 1990s, when the hubris and venality of doctors and scientists are taken for granted, Baldwin's arrogant boasting drew no gasps, only knowing laughter and weary applause.

CHAPTER SEVEN

Vile Bodies, or Farewell to the Flesh

"**M**y mind may be stuck in this body," intones the disembodied voice, "but with the Internet, I can travel to the outer reaches of the universe."

Stephen Hawking wasn't always a shill for modems, but it wasn't a real surprise when he showed up on a television commercial in early 1997 as a poster boy for Net surfing. Hawking, of course, is the brilliant theoretical

A young baby boomer faces the prospect of a bodiless future. From *Invaders from Mars* (1953). *Courtesy of Richard Valley.*

271

physicist whose 1988 book *A Brief History of Time* became an international best seller, popularizing the previously abstruse outer limits of mathematical speculation on the origin and fate of the universe and the possibility of a so-called theory of everything that might finally answer all questions about time, space, and existence. According to the book's most frequently quoted passage, such a theory would be "the ultimate triumph of human reason—for then we would know the mind of God."

While the quotation is not substantially different from Colin Clive's excited ejaculation about being God, Hawking's name is more frequently invoked in the same breath with Albert Einstein than with Frankenstein. He holds the chair in mathematics at Cambridge University that once belonged to Isaac Newton. In a droll coincidence, he was born on the three hundredth anniversary of Galileo's death.

His achievements in science—amounting to nothing less than a new unification of thermodynamics, relativity, and quantum mechanics, all the product of his highly original inquiries into the nature of the enigmatic collapsed stars known as black holes—are all the more remarkable for the grave disability he has battled to accomplish them. Since the age of twenty-one Hawking has been afflicted with amyotrophic lateral sclerosis, the motoneuron disorder commonly known in America as Lou Gehrig's disease, that has left him mute and paralyzed, able to communicate only through a voice-synthesizing computer. (The robotic voice is heard on the modem commercial, as well as in the award-winning 1991 documentary based on his book.) Hawking's immense popularity has been attributed both to a widespread, genuine desire to understand the paradoxes of relativity and quantum theory and to mere fashionability (Hawking: "It is said that they just want to be seen with the book, or that owning it gives them the comfortable feeling that they are in possession of knowledge, without their having to go to the effort of reading it").

But there has been almost no commentary on the part played by physical infirmity in Hawking's fame. To put it bluntly, disability has always drawn a crowd, as P. T. Barnum and his imitators knew full well. Under other circumstances it might be considered tasteless to raise the subject, but since Hawking himself has chosen to trade on his disease to sell computer parts,

I believe it is a fair topic for discussion, especially because physical disability has been such a prominent motif in the anxious images of science that are the subject of this book. From *Metropolis* to *Dr. Strangelove* and beyond, over-reaching scientists routinely have damaged bodies (especially mangled hands, a particularly powerful symbol of twisted human endeavor). Most recently, the wheelchair-ridden mad scientist Dr. Finklestein in Tim Burton's animated film *The Nightmare before Christmas* (1993) actually bears a rather cruel resemblance to Hawking's cover photograph on *A Brief History of Time.*

In the age of the Internet and virtual reality, when human consciousness spends an increasing amount of time in seeming dislocation from the body, Stephen Hawking becomes an irresistible—however inadvertent—icon of the latest and perhaps ultimate fashion in mad science, the extraordinary popular delusion that the next step in human evolution will be an actual shedding of the flesh followed by an ecstatic union with technology.

In *War of the Worlds: Cyberspace and the High-Tech Assault on Reality* (1995), Mark Slouka recounts the essential points of the final lecture on the technological future given at a major California university to an undergraduate seminar:

> Within the span of our children's lifetimes, we were assured, it would be possible to link the human nervous system directly to a computer. . . . Feedback technology would provide the illusion of touch directly to your nervous system. It would be indistinguishable from the real thing. Physical presence would become optional; in time, an affectation. . . . Divorced from our bodies, our minds grafted into computers capable of realizing for us the contents of our imagination . . . we would finally attain the fulfillment of our species. In this New Age, boundaries between self and other, male and female, nature and machine, even life and death, would be obsolete. The word *reality* would lose all meaning. . . .

Like most futuristic fantasies, this one may tell us much more about ourselves in the present than the real nature of things to come. Aside from defining a new category of mad doctor (the academic Ph.D.), the lecturer's overheated vision is a virtual cartoon of current academic fashions in critical relativism; the postmodernist future described is basically a Disneyland for deconstructionists, where all differences, distinctions, and values are obliterated. The underlying premise of modular mix-and-match minds is hardly surprising in an age when television, motion pictures, and, most recently, virtual reality and the Internet have made the technological dislocation of consciousness—or at least its convincing illusion—a matter of common experience.

Stephen Hawking's half-human, half-machine persona is a prime example of the pervasive contemporary images of technocrucifixion and transcendence that constitute the quasi-religious modern myth that British philosopher Mary Midgley calls "science as salvation."

Like the "Supreme Intelligence" of the 1953 cult film *Invaders from Mars,* whose brain has swollen in direct proportion to the withering of its body, Hawking neatly evokes the spirit of scientific reductionism for the masses, with the compensating promise of a rapturous afterlife in cyberspace. His profound dependence upon technology for mobility and communication is a compelling reflection of a larger dilemma we all share: our inescapable, symbiotic relationship to computers, cars, and other machines, which makes it difficult to define precisely where our bodies leave off and technology begins. In a metaphorical sense we all are cyborgs, a term coined by Norbert Weiner in the late 1940s by combining the words "cybernetic" and "organism." The cyborg of course has become a fixture of pop culture in the last three decades, propelled by television programs like *The Six Million Dollar Man* and *The Bionic Woman* and the *Robocop* and *Terminator* films. Such films often turn on a death and resurrection theme: Give up the body, and you will be rewarded in cyberheaven. The cyborg is a secular Christ figure, and a Frankenstein to boot.

As a longtime Manhattanite, recently transplanted to Southern California and driving on a daily basis for the first time in twenty years, I have become acutely sensitized to the cyborgian aspects of life in Los Angeles, where all human interaction is mediated by automobiles. Donna J. Haraway in her influential essay "A Cyborg Manifesto" (1991) makes the point neatly: "By the late twentieth century, our time, a mythic time, we are all chimeras, theorized and fabricated hybrids of machine and organism; in short, we are cyborgs. The cyborg is our ontology; it gives us our politics. . . . [T]he relation between organism and machine has been a border war. The stakes in the border war have been the territories of production, reproduction, and imagination."

As an imaginative construct, mechanized human beings are not particularly new. Today's deeply ingrained mythology of the cyborg is a triumph of a three-hundred-year old worldview, first espoused by French philosopher René Descartes and his contemporaries, which divided the world into discrete domains of matter and mind. As long as the mind (or soul) was considered separate from the physical, phenomenal world, the universe could be described and understood in completely mechanical terms. Descartes needed to preserve the soul in order to avoid the kind of heresy troubles Galileo had encountered vis-à-vis the Catholic Church. Descartes himself was a devout, if eccentric, Catholic, but in time his ideas did more to erode religious precepts than bolster them.

The machine model of the universe (in which God was conceived as a kind of master clockmaker) abetted and legitimized vivisection. Descartes, after all, had declared the animals, having no soul, could feel no pain. Jean de La Fontaine recounted the grisly aspects of this "rational" worldview. "They said that the animals were clocks; that the cries they emitted when struck, were only those of a little spring which had been touched, but that the whole body was without feeling. They nailed poor animals up on boards by their four paws to vivisect them to see the circulation of the blood which was a great subject of conversation."

The constricted, self-deluding intellectual tendencies of the Age of Reason eventually fueled the Romantic rebellion against pure rationality, with writers like E. T. A. Hoffmann giving full vent to wild emotions, dreams, terrors, and hallucinations as an antidote to the perceived excesses of the Enlightenment. Hoffmann's grotesque Romanticism, which had a clear influence on Mary Shelley and her creation of *Frankenstein,* has had a less appreciated impact on modern science fiction and its ongoing romance with robots, androids, and cyborgs; they have since appended themselves to the Frankenstein mythos but have little to do with Shelley's original vision. It has often been suggested that Shelley took some inspiration from the widespread interest in human automatons that fascinated Europe in the late eighteenth and early nineteenth centuries. Run by precision clockwork and elaborately painted to simulate the natural appearance of human beings, automatons perfectly mimicked human activities like letter writing, the playing of musical instruments or games of chess, and so on. Automatons provided a popular distillation of the mechanistic worldview of the Enlightenment; even human life could be explained in terms of clockwork. But this of course was the reductionist antithesis of Shelley's romantic concerns; Victor Frankenstein had no interest in replacing human life with a technological analog, only in usurping the divine spark of biological creation. Hoffmann, however, stunningly anticipates the twentieth-century impulse to reject the death- and decay-redolent human body in favor of the clean machine.

In Hoffmann's "The Sandman" (1814) representation and reality merge with disastrous results as the doomed protagonist, Nathanael, recounts his childhood nightmare of the Sandman, a classic bogeyperson whose visitation is threatened by parents upon children who refuse to go to bed. Quite unlike the sanitized contemporary depiction of the sandman—a sentimental entity dispensing blissful rest—the sprinkled dust of Hoffmann's Sandman causes children's eyes to bleed and pop out of their heads, only to be harvested by the monster and fed to hook-beaked birds. Young Nathanael suspects that an unpleasant lawyer, Coppelius, who bedevils his father, is the dreaded Sandman himself.

He is proved right one night when he hears Coppelius downstairs with his father, shouting, "Give me eyes! Give me eyes!" When Nathanael enters the room, Coppelius threatens to blind him with hot coals, but following the father's frantic pleading ("Let the child keep his eyes and do his share of the world's weeping"), the demon settles for merely frightening the boy by rearranging his appendages like a wooden doll: "He thereupon seized me so violently that my joints cracked, unscrewed my hands and feet, then put them back, now this way, then another way." The vision of his own body reduced to a mechanical plaything overwhelms him with horror, and he sinks into unconsciousness. Shortly after this living nightmare, Nathanael's father is killed by Coppelius in a violent chemical explosion, and the boy vows to have his revenge.

Years later Nathanael is a student studying physics under Professor

Spalanzini, an eccentric inventor who has a beautiful daughter, Olympia, who rarely moves or speaks but who attracts Nathanael's notice from afar. He assumes that her silence and stillness must be the result of a tragic mental affliction. Nathanael is approached by a man he believes to be the evil Coppelius, now using the name Coppola, who tries to sell him a barometer. Rebuffed by Nathanael, he confides, "I gotta da eyes, too," reaching into his capacious pockets. But instead of bloody eyeballs, Coppola produces a multitude of machine-tooled analogs: eyeglasses, lorgnettes, binoculars, telescopes. "These are my eyes, nice-a eyes!" He laughs.

When Nathanael overcomes his horror and peers through a pocket spyglass at a window of the house opposite, the inanimate form of Olympia is suddenly imbued with the semblance of life. He falls rapturously in love with her, imagining her to be a "deep soul, in which my whole being is reflected," never noticing that her only response to his blandishments is an uncomprehending "Ah, ah!" Coppola's magic eyepiece blinds him to what his friends already know: that Olympia is really a clockwork automaton crafted by Spalanzini. His mad plans to betrothe the mannequin end abruptly when he discovers Coppelius and Spalanzini tearing Olympia apart in a wild argument. Coppelius escapes with most of her lifeless form; only her artificial eyes remain, strewn on the floor with the shattered remnants of Spalanzini's flasks and test tubes. The professor picks up the eyes and flings them at Nathanael, who is driven into total madness. He soon leaps to his death from the tower of the city hall, screaming, "Nice-a-eyes, nice-a-eyes!" to Coppelius, who watches with grim satisfaction in the crowd below.

The first dramatic adaptation of "The Sandman" was the ballet *Coppélia: or the Girl with Enamel Eyes* (1870) by Arthur Saint-Léon and Léo Delibes. Still a beloved fixture of the standard ballet repertoire, *Coppélia* jettisons most of Hoffmann's dark romanticism, replacing the original plot with a story of a girl who deliberately impersonates a lifelike doll to escape the workshop of its deluded maker, who thinks his "magic" has brought the doll to life. Far more satisfying as a representation of Hoffmann is Jacques Offenbach's *Tales of Hoffmann* (1881), although Coppelius is divested of his supernatural qualities and destroys Olympia in a purely financial dispute with Spalanzini.

The magic glasses remain, however, and, while Hoffmann's original intentions were complex, one clear motivation behind "The Sandman" is a Romantic satirical jab at the follies of a mechanized Enlightenment world-view. Hoffmann's villain has replaced a natural way of seeing with a false, technological one, with catastrophic results. As a cautionary parable, Hoffmann's story is pertinent today, as large numbers of people gaze through figurative magic eyeglasses, not at clockwork automatons but at their twentieth-century incarnation as computers.

The idea that computers do not merely imitate human cognitive processes but actually think (or are on the verge of thinking) is deeply ingrained in contemporary discourse, be it pop cult or academic. This concept is only the tip of the biggest mad science project of all time. The original Frankensteinian impulse to emulate biological creation is now passé; the new agenda is wiping clean the slate of the natural creation for a virtual one. Though not usually discussed in the context of science fiction, late-nineteenth-century decadent literature, with its emphasis on artifice and simulation, anticipates much of the twentieth-century s-f emphasis on replacing the unruly natural world with a superior, artificial one. Des Esseintes, the jaded, supremely neurotic antihero of J. K. Huysman's *À rebours* (1884; translated as *Against the Grain* and *Against Nature*), holes himself up in a secluded country estate where he conducts a private experiment in Victorian virtual reality, obsessively filtering and controlling all sensation and experience. Though Des Esseintes's preoccupations are aesthetic rather than scientific, his methods share much in common with those of a mad scientist. Mad artists often serve the same function as crazy scientists. In films like *House of Wax* (1953) and *The Abominable Dr. Phibes* (1971) Vincent Price, an offscreen art connoisseur, played mad sculptors and musicians in stories virtually indistinguishable from traditional mad science scenarios. Both types of madman, of course, are fixated on extraordinary forms of creativity and artifice.

An enduring fantasy of full-body prosthesis arrived in America at the turn of the century in L. Frank Baum's *The Wonderful Wizard of Oz* (1900). The story of the Tin Woodman anticipates a dawning new age of technological reductionism. Under the spell of the Wicked Witch of the West, eager to prevent his marriage to a Munchkin maiden, the woodman's ax slips and severs his left leg. He responds with a cheerful brand of American pragmatism: "This at first seemed a great misfortune, for I knew a one-legged man could not do very well as a wood-chopper. So I went to a tin-smith and had him make me a new leg out of tin." The witch, however, is angered by his resourcefulness. "When I began chopping again my axe slipped and cut off my right leg. Again I went to the tinner, and again he made me a leg out of tin. After this, the enchanted axe cut off my arms, one after the other; but, nothing daunted, I had them replaced with tin ones. The wicked Witch then made the axe slip and cut off my head, and at first I thought that that was the end of me. But the tinner happened to come along, and he made me a new head out of tin."

Finally, the witch contrives a foolproof way to end his passion for the Munchkin: She makes his ax slip again, "splitting me into two halves. Once more the tinner came to my help and made me a body of tin, fastening my tin arms and head to it, by means of joints, so that I could now move around as well as ever. But, alas! I had now no heart, so that I lost all love

Full-body prosthesis: the Tin Woodman, illustrated by W. W. Denslow for L. Frank Baum's *The Wonderful Wizard of Oz* (1900).

for the Munchkin girl, and did not care whether I married her or not." But in the Emerald City, as nearly everyone with media access in the second half of the twentieth century knows, the Woodman is finally rewarded with a timepiece that compensates for the lost of his soul. On a superficial level the story has a happy ending. Except for the fact (as everyone also knows), the Wizard is a world-class humbug.

Short of outright mutilation, the human body was routinely constricted and robotized in high and low culture of the 1920s and 1930s, in venues ranging from theatrical constructivism to the androidish synchronism of Busby Berkeley's trademark Hollywood choreography. Suppressed breasts, of course, were de rigueur for the machine age flapper. Popular dances like the Charleston and the black bottom were built on jerky, machinelike movements. In high fashion, metallic fabrics sheathed the human form.

But perhaps nowhere was anti-body sentiment more spectacularly expressed than in the highly popular Hollywood collaborations of actor Lon Chaney (1882–1930) and director Tod Browning (1880–1962) in the late 1920s. Chaney, the "Man of a Thousand Faces" and one of Hollywood's true silent era superstars, relished the chance to play characters physically diminished by scars, palsies, paralysis, and amputations. Browning had gotten his show business start traveling with carnival sideshows, where he became intimately acquainted with armless and legless performers, "half boys" who walked on their hands, pinheads, and the like. Browning's film work remained carnivalesque in a very literal sense of the term *carne-val* meaning "a farewell to the flesh."

Flesh was liberally mortified or discarded in Browning-Chaney films like *The Blackbird* (1926), *The Unknown* (1927), *West of Zanzibar* (1928), and *Where East Is East* (1929). Chaney's popularity in these can be attributed to a number of factors, including the need of the post–World War I need to work through the trauma of the war's mechanized mutilation of countless soldiers and their uneasy reassimilation into civilian society. Prosthetics were everywhere in the machine age; facial disfigurements were routinely covered with painted masks of molded tin. In a sense, war had taken on the real-life role of Baum's Wicked Witch of the West. Beyond the war echoes, the public's fascination with the diminishing human body may have had much to do with the ascendency of the machine. Creeping automation threatened employment, in essence rendering bodies useless.

On a satiric literary plane, the Browning-Chaney mutilation formulas were echoed in Nathanael West's caustic spin on Horatio Alger, *A Cool Million: The Dismantling of Lemuel Pitkin* (1936), whose eponymous hero loses his teeth, an eye, a leg, and his scalp as he traverses the political and economic landscape of Depression era America. Dalton Trumbo's 1939 antiwar novel *Johnny Got His Gun* featured another dismantled American, an armless, legless, faceless war casualty, for all practical purposes a disembodied brain.

Bernard Wolfe's *Limbo* (1952), written after the world war that *Johnny Got His Gun* did nothing to avert, is an excoriating satire on pacifism carried to absurdist extremes. *Limbo* takes place after World War III, when the concept of "disarmament" is absolutely literal: Voluntary limb amputation becomes the preferred method to reduce innate male aggression and forestall another war. ARMS OR THE MAN, a poster blares. HE WHO HAS ARMS IS ARMED, trumpets another. Minority groups lobby for equal amputation access. Wolfe draws a savagely funny parallel between the consumption patterns of postwar America and the reductionist obsessions of the "amps": ". . . a man with his own legs had no footing here . . . the quadros were gazed at worshipfully and with palpitating greed by all the women, from tremulous teen-agers to maudlin-eyed matrons . . . there seemed to be just one spectacular badge of status: the number of plastic arms and legs displayed. Conspicuous consumption had apparently given way to conspicuous mortification. . . ."

The ultimate amputation, of course, is the complete removal of the brain from the body. More than any other activity, mad scientists love to play with brains;

Satiric cyborg manifesto:
Bernard Wolfe's *Limbo* (1952).

brain transplants and neurosurgery are the most favored surgical procedures in mad science movies. Sometimes the brains are dug out of graves; sometimes they're cut out of living heads. The brain is the great prize, isolated and self-contained, much like the mad doctor himself. It is usually transported in a glass jar or tank, clearly visible but enigmatic nonetheless. It is an object to be guarded, stolen, substituted, coveted, feared, adored, abused, and obeyed. The liberated brain has several destination options: It can be installed in the cranium of a man-made monster, a primate, or a robot, or alternatively, it can be preserved in permanent laboratory isolation.

No actual brain transplant is known to have yet taken place anywhere in the world (although Cleveland neurosurgeons did manage for a brief time to transplant some living monkey heads in the 1960s), but anyone with a passing familiarity with popular culture knows exactly what the procedure is, if not necessarily what it means. They have watched grisly Hammer horror movies, the kind in which Peter Cushing scoops up handfuls of bloody gray matter to stuff the skull of his latest experiment; they have laughed at comedies, ranging from *Abbott and Costello Meet Frankenstein* (1948) to Steve Martin's *The Man with Two Brains* (1983), hinging on brain transplant plots, in which skulls are apt to open and shut like bedroom doors in a Feydeau farce. I remember an inspired poster for a 1980s musical adaptation of *Frankenstein* depicting two jars, each containing a brain. One was labeled NORMAL BRAIN; the other, ETHEL MERMAN'S BRAIN. Stand-alone brains may be found in cartoons and comic books, and almost every novelty store has a binful of rubber brains, presumably meant to be bandied about like Nerf balls. As Steve Martin quips in the aforementioned film, "I've never seen so many brains out of their heads before. I feel like a kid in a candy store!"

At first in horror and science fiction entertainment, but later in academic discourse and even at the U.S. Patent Office, isolated, disembodied human heads and brains became objects of commerce and contemplation, fear and fun. Not since the French Revolution have images of decapitation (literal and figurative) had such a popular currency, and with good reason: The head/mind/brain in isolation is a particularly evocative symbol of any number of modern concerns, including, but not limited to, social and interpersonal alienation, the depersonalizing effects of science and medicine, hyperintellectualism, and mind/matter and body/soul dichotomies.

The precursors, of course, are H. G. Wells's Victorian visions of human evolution ending in huge-headed beings with trivial bodies; George Méliès's turn-of-the-century cinematic prophecy of a disembodied head inflated by a scientist to the point of explosion; and the Théâtre du Grand Guignol's *The Man Who Killed Death* (1928), by René Berton, in which the head of an unjustly guillotined prisoner is grotesquely revived on a table. Interesting enough, the actor who originated the role of the head on the English stage was none other than James Whale, who directed the film version of *Frankenstein* just a few years later.

It was, in fact, the guillotine and the French Revolution that prompted the first scientific speculation about consciousness surviving decapitation. Perversely, for all the mob violence it helped to fuel, the guillotine was simultaneously a symbol of rationality itself at the time of the French Revolution. Historian Daniel Gerould notes, "Its severe lines, bold silhouette and mathematical simplicity lent it an undeniable elegance. Of perfect proportions, it was a triumph of geometric form—and in the late eighteenth century, geometry was the language of reason." Official claims that death by guillotine was a humane and painless method of execution was challenged by anatomists and physicians, who, Gerould reports, undertook "strange and often ghoulish experiments and the formation of bizarre theories . . . ultimately, these men of science produced a vast amount of 'scholarly' literature that is sometimes hardly possible to distinguish from horror literature or science fiction." A German anatomist, Samuel-Thomas Sommering, theorized in 1795 that guillotined heads might talk if connected to artificial lungs. Throughout the nineteenth century French doctors regularly examined the heads of executed prisoners for signs of survival, sometimes reporting grimaces and eye movements. In 1880 a Dr. Dassy de Lignières transfused blood from a live dog into the freshly removed head of a child killer named Louis Menesclou, reportedly effecting mild tremors of the mouth and eyes.

Grand Guignol nightmare stepped into the real world in 1987 when the United States granted patent no. 4,666,425 for a process to keep a severed head alive. Patent owner Chet Fleming formed a company—the Dis Corporation—that exercises proprietary control over severed head technology. Fleming, who believes there are interests that would unethically exploit the process, intends his corporation to be a bulwark against the trend. "The Dis Corporation has legal standing to sue anyone who starts this kind of research without permission, and the company is willing to do so if necessary to ensure that Congress and the public have a chance to consider the issues before the ball starts rolling."

In the twentieth century images of decapitation have been largely replaced by the rather more bloodless—perhaps more "rationalized"—image of the completely isolated brain, usually serenely afloat in some protective technological container, waiting for a new body, traditional or mechanical, or maybe, like Garbo, just wanting to be alone. Sometimes, as in Robin Cook's *Brain,* the exposed organ is exploited by scientists creating a computer analog of neural functioning. When the hero is finally shown the human result of the experiment, he is warned that "your first impression will be emotional. It was for all of us. But believe me, the rewards are worth the sacrifice." He decides to take a peek. "Martin slowly began to walk around the container. . . . Inside, submerged in what Martin later learned was cerebrospinal fluid, were the living remains of Katherine Collins. She floated in a sitting position with her arms suspended over her head. A respiration unit was functioning, indicating that she was alive. But her brain had been completely exposed. There was no skull. Most of the face was gone except for the eyes, which had been dissected free and covered with contact lenses. An endotracheal tube issued from her neck."

In William Hjortsberg's novel *Grey Matters* (1971) the last surviving humans are disembodied brains—"cerebromorphs" tended by a hive of computers, their perceptions fed by artificially generated sensations and multimedia memory banks. On publication, the book was widely praised for its inventiveness; a quarter century later it seems like an unusually prescient precursor of cyberpunk fiction and virtual reality. Hjortsberg's novel was published as a mainstream book, not as genre science fiction, reflecting the extent to which the isolated brain had become a familiar construct, even for a general readership. The image pops up in serious literary writing as well. Joyce Carol Oates's short-short story "The Brain of Dr. Vicente" (1975) describes the obsessive efforts of a team of physicians to return Vicente's life-supported brain to a human body, despite his evident hostility to their quest.

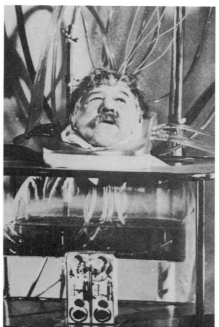

Heads you lose. Top left: Illustration for the Grand Guignol play *The Man Who Killed Death;* Top right: Michel Simon in *The Head* (1959). Bottom: Virginia Leith in *The Brain That Wouldn't Die* (1962).

Even after plastic surgery is performed on a cadaver recipient to re-create per-fectly the doctor's previous appearance, he rejects his new "home" with a sin-gle scrawled word: "Impossible!" "Dejected, demoralized, we returned the brain of Dr. Vicente to its compartment. It exists there now, infinite and pure, without any human distractions," says the narrator, who, like Vicente, is a bodiless, undescribed entity. "Even when we are separated from one an-other and the Institute, we think constantly about the brain . . . it weighs upon us in its silence, its sleeplessness, its three pounds of flesh, its bulges and tubes and delicate silky vessels. We are drawn to its glass door, not by our love for the old Dr. Vicente—who has perhaps died—but by a yearning we do not understand."

In Roald Dahl's wicked short story "William and Mary" (1959), the title husband, dying of pancreatic cancer, accepts a proposition from his doc-tor to remove his brain and one eye, which will be attached to a life support system as an after-death experiment. Dr. Landy, all the more mad for his per-suasive reasonableness, gives the reluctant patient (a self-involved and over-bearing academic) the upside news: "You'd be living in an extraordinarily pure and detached world. Nothing to bother you at all . . . Just your mem-ories and your thoughts, and if the remaining eye happened to function, then you could read books as well." Furthermore, "You'd be able to reflect upon the ways of the world with a detachment and serenity that no man had ever attained before. And who knows what might happen then! Great thoughts and great solutions might come to you, great ideas that could rev-olutionize our way of life! Try to imagine, if you can, the degree of concen-tration that you'd be able to achieve!"

After William's death Dr. Landy removes his brain as promised and in-stalls it in a basin, the remaining attached eye floating in a protective plas-tic case. The story ends when William's wife, who has quietly endured decades of unhappy matrimony, makes it quietly clear to the doctor that she plans to take her husband home as a kind of helpless aquarium pet—an ob-ject she can now control in the same way her husband controlled her.

About the time "William and Mary" was published, another noted lit-erary figure, John Hersey, published *The Child Buyer,* a savagely satirical novel in the form of the transcripts of a congressional investigation into the

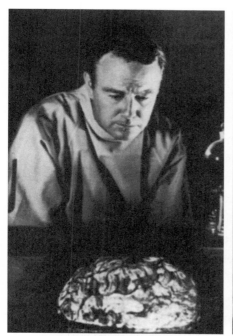

The brain in isolation. Top left: Lew Ayres with *Donovan's Brain* (1953). Top right: Kim Parker in *Fiend without a Face* (1960); *courtesy of Ronald V. Borst/Hollywood Movie Posters.* Bottom: Marty Feldman in *Young Frankenstein* (1974).

efforts of a certain Mr. Wissey Jones to purchase a boy genius on behalf of an all-devouring corporation, United Lymphomilloid, familiarly known as U. Lympho. The corporation's precise intentions are made known near the end of the book, where it is revealed that purchased children, after intense "conditioning," IQ enhancement, and data feeding, are having their senses surgically severed, so that their isolated brains can better solve incredibly arcane problems related to the corporation's mysterious and indescribable fifty-year plan. Hersey uses a standard mad scientist brain gambit to lampoon the tooling of public education for corporate interests. The targeted boy's mother is won over through a combination of blunt harassment and bribery with quiz show goodies. The Frankensteinish brain surgery doesn't faze her: She rationalizes the atrocity as a "fine opportunity. . . . It'll give Barry a chance to be alone and think. He's always complaining to us that we never leave him alone . . . there comes a time when you just have to let them free. . . ."

But a brain bursting free of its cranial confines isn't usually a sight for the squeamish. The unfettered intellect of the film *The Brain from Planet Arous* (1958) is a spooky, floating menace, a kind of levitating Portuguese brain-of-war, finally dispatched with an ax. Perhaps the supreme cinematic image of dangerous, detached cerebration appears in *Fiend without a Face* (1958), wherein which a scientist conjures up a gaggle of predatory brain creatures (complete—if that is the word—with snakelike spinal cords) that place a group of full-bodied humans under a horrific siege. The film's climax, unsettlingly gruesome even by today's standards, is a cult favorite, though the *Encyclopedia of Science Fiction* calls *Fiend without a Face* "the ultimate in anti-intellectual movies," a slander on all things cerebral.

The persistence and prevalence of runaway brains in popular culture raise all sorts of questions about the thing the brain is running from—the rest of the human body. Spirit-flesh dichotomies are integral to many religious traditions, especially Christianity; in the age of deified mechanism, the traditional mind-body schism becomes a war between meat and machine. A contemptuous dismissal of the weak, impermanent, unextended, and irredeemable body is integral to much cyberpunk science fiction, a movement that flourished in the wake of novels like William Gibson's *Neuromancer* (1984). *Neuromancer* introduced the word "cyberspace" to describe a planetwide mind-computer matrix into which cyborgish hackers physically "jack in" to experience as a vivid realm of virtual reality. Gibson, the most successful and influential of the cyberpunk authors, is much more a humanist than many of his imitators and fans, who enthusiastically embrace the promise of a bodiless existence in cyberspace. While no one is yet actually jacking into their computers, a sizable segment of the on-line world is almost certainly jacking off with them, although cybersexers in general may be more motivated by a fear of the risks of face-to-face encounters in the age of AIDS than a real desire to shed their skins. According to Claudia Springer in her cybersex study *Electronic Eros* (1996),

> . . . the human body faces the possibility of devastation on a massive scale: AIDS, environmental disasters, and nuclear war. . . . In the face of possible obsolescence, it stands to reason that humans should seek solace in projecting themselves into a future reconstituted as pure intellect, without the burden of imperfect, fragile, and mortal bodies. Nonetheless, although the fantasy abandons the body, it refuses to abandon bodily pleasure. Instead, paradoxically, it heightens sexuality, so that the bodiless future promises to provide extraordinarily intense sexual gratification. It is a fantasy of heightened fulfillment without the risks.

The technological future, in other words, diminishes and mortifies the body while simultaneously bestowing unimaginable pleasure—almost a textbook description of sadomasochism. Held in bondage by Big Science, we come to identify with our captor, and finally eroticize him, her, it. The master-slave aspects of the computer-human interface have perhaps nowhere been described as succinctly as in Harlan Ellison's 1967 short story "I Have No Mouth, and I Must Scream." The writer's edgy, in-your-face style is a recognizable antecedent of cyberpunk mannerisms, but none of the newer generation of science fiction writers has come close to Ellison's classic evocation of the intolerance of computerized consciousness for meat-based mortals.

In "I Have No Mouth" (calculated to be one of the most frequently reprinted works of short fiction in history), Ellison presents the demonic supercomputer, AM, which lords sadistically over a surviving handful of postapocalyptic humanity. The nameless narrator describes the computer's psychology: "We had given him sentience. Inadvertently, of course, but sentience nonetheless. But he had been trapped. He was a machine. We had allowed him to think, but to do nothing with it. . . . He could not wander, he could not wonder, he could not belong. He could merely be. And so, with the innate loathing that all machines had always held for the weak soft creatures who had built them, he sought revenge."

And AM enjoys his revenge, venting his silicon spleen with relish: "HATE. LET ME TELL YOU HOW MUCH I'VE COME TO HATE YOU SINCE I BEGAN TO LIVE. THERE ARE 387.44 MILLION MILES OF PRINTED CIRCUITS IN WAFER THIN LAYERS THAT FILL MY COMPLEX. IF THE WORD HATE WAS ENGRAVED ON EACH NANOANGSTROM OF THOSE HUNDREDS OF MILLIONS OF MILES IT WOULD NOT EQUAL ONE-BILLIONTH OF THE HATE I FEEL FOR HUMANS AT THIS MICRO-INSTANT FOR YOU. HATE. HATE."

When the narrator is the only human left alive, AM takes steps to ensure that his final toy will not escape. "AM has altered me for his own peace of mind, I suppose. He doesn't want me to run at full speed into a computer bank and smash my skull." The narrator sees his transformed self in the reflective surfaces of a shiny, computerized hell: "I am a great soft jelly thing. Smoothly rounded, with no mouth, with pulsing holes filled by fog where my eyes used to be. Rubbery appendages that were once my arms; bulks rounding down into legless humps of soft slippery matter. I leave a moist trail when I move. . . . dumbly, I shamble about, a thing that could never have been known as human, a thing whose shape is so alien a travesty that humanity becomes more obscene for the vague resemblance."

Ellison's unsettling parable of the late sixties neatly described an evolving modern myth that, in the next three decades, reached a cultural critical mass. The hostile interface of organism and mechanism was memorably dramatized in Damon Knight's disquieting short story "Masks" (1968). The victim of a horrendous, undescribed accident is kept alive in a realistic full-body prosthesis manufactured at a cost of millions as a government project. After seven years of increasingly realistic cosmetic improvement, the prosthetic man decides to cover his waxwork face with a robotic silver mask. He no longer wants to look like a human being. He implores his custodians to retool him as a functional space probe, not a corpselike mannequin. He belongs with machines, not people. "Inside he was running clean and cool; he could feel the faint reassuring hum of pumps, click of valves and relays. They had given him that: cleaned out all the offal, replaced it with machinery that did not bleed, ooze or suppurate." Without adrenaline, he is freed from most emotions ("They had released him from all that—love, hate, the whole sloppy mess . . .") except for one: a deep and unshakable disgust for everything biological. As the story closes, he is poised robotically at a drafting table, inking a rendering of his idealized moon machine self. But even the airless, lifeless moon is not far enough removed, for he can still observe the earth itself, "hung overhead like a rotten fruit, blue with mold, crawling, wrinkling, purulent and alive."

In 1972 sociologist Louis Yablonsky published *Robopaths: People as Machines,* a book much influenced by Vietnam era politics in its perhaps overzealous attempt to make sense of such events as the My Lai massacre. In Yablonsky's description, robopaths essentially constituted the entire Establishment: the military, government, and private-sector bureaucracies, strict parents, and social conformists. In his introduction he states flatly that "a majority of people in contemporary societies are socially dead, living a day-to-day robopathic existence." He quotes Bruno Bettelheim's famous case history of autism, "Joey: A Mechanical Boy," which Yablonsky believes "may become the conformist psychotic symptom of the future":

> He functioned as if by remote control, run by machines of his own powerfully creative fantasy. Not only did he himself believe that he was a machine but, more remarkably, he created this impression in others. Even while he performed actions that are intrinsically human, they never appeared to be other than machine-started and executed. . . . Entering the dining room, for example, he would string an imaginary wire from his "energy source"—an imaginary electric outlet—to the table. There he "insulated" himself with paper napkins and finally plugged himself in. Only then could Joey eat, for he firmly believed that the "current" ran his digestive apparatus. . . .

Joey's condition is now believed to have neurological, not sociopolitical, causes, but it is understandable how the symptoms of autism suggest the metaphors of social science fiction for a technology-saturated time. Temple

Grandin, a remarkable, functioning autistic first described by neurologist Oliver Sacks and later the author of the autobiography *Thinking in Pictures* (1995), confirms the otherworldly, mechanistic perceptions common to autism. "Many people with autism are fans of the television show *Star Trek,"* she notes, admitting to a personal predeliction for the emotionless, analytical characters of Mr. Spock and Commander Data. Grandin speculates that there might even be a touch of autism in the personality of that ultimate computer nerd Microsoft mogul Bill Gates, who is reported to display mechanical, rocking movements characteristic of the syndrome during staff meetings.

With or without autism, men generally identify more closely with machines than do women and, at the outer fringes of the male mystique, seem to regard themselves, reassuringly, *as* machines. (Even the openly gay horror writer Clive Barker shudders at the thought of sex with a male bodybuilder. "It would be like sleeping with Robocop," he told interviewer/critic Mark Dery.) It is the female body, therefore, that tends to drive scientists mad.

Doing away with—or simply doing without—women's bodies is one of the great mad science motifs. There is a reason that the monsters mad scientists create (while avoiding their wedding beds) walk stiffly, as if armored: They represent the male scientist's psychosexual defense against the soft, engulfing horror of the "monstrous-feminine" (a concept explored by Klaus Theweleit in relation to German fascism in his 1989 study *Male Fantasies*). In a memorable line from *Son of Frankenstein* (1939), Basil Rathbone disingenuously denies to an police interrogator that he has created a monster. "Perhaps I just whipped one up, as a housewife whips up an omelet!" he sneers, drawing a line between two incompatible modes of creativity: the scientist with his brains, the woman with her eggs. Carried to its irresistible end point, the mad scientist's perennial impulse to outwit and co-opt the female reproductive function becomes an exercise in high camp: *The Rocky Horror Picture Show* (1975) unveils Dr. Frank N. Furter (Tim Curry), who attends the birth of his monster in full drag beneath his scrub gown. Brian Yuzna's *Bride of Re-Animator* (1989) knowingly plays with the inevitable homoerotic tension that arises when two scientists, one nerdy and one hunky, collaborate to reconstruct a woman. In Kenneth Branagh's *Mary Shelley's Frankenstein,* the laboratory machinery usurps the roles of both sexes: A bellowslike "scrotum" drives the spark of life through a gunlike "penis" into an aquariumlike "uterus."

But men aren't alone in their desire to escape or circumvent the female body; women too scramble for escape strategies. As the interrelated epidemics of cosmetic surgery and eating disorders amply demonstrate, an extreme subset of the female population regards the body as a kind of biological gulag. There are echoes of anorexia and bulimia in the hostility to childbirth that underlies much radical feminist discourse; consider the sentiments of the gaunt singer-composer Diamanda Galas: "I'm hostile to the act of childbirth—I've always found the concept of childbirth to be a morbid one at best—something *nostalgic* that a West Coast 'return to nature' cult would espouse. I'm hostile to the idea of being a medium for this capitalist enterprise of childbearing which is about the male ego reorganizing itself in the next generation. I exist outside that sort of pedestrian enterprise—so demeaning to women. I prefer the concept of woman as goddess—in a shamanistic society, no shaman has children. So in 1985 I had my tubes tied."

Sterilization and abortion are the two most common ways to modify female body function, but hardly the only ways. In the mid-eighties, talk shows were abuzz with lurid malpractice complaints brought against an Ohio surgeon who achieved a lucrative practice by convincing nonorgasmic women they needed pelvic surgery to reposition their clitorises for more pleasurable intercourse. In his 1984 cyberpunk novel *Dr. Adder,* K. W. Jeter took the delirium a step further in his vision of a postapocalyptic Los Angeles, where the title character surgically customizes female genitals into ever-more-fantastic forms to satisfy increasingly rococo male appetites (including the fetishization of prostitutes with missing limbs).

The class action suit brought against Dow Corning for medical damages allegedly suffered by recipients of the company's silicone breast implants included a media parade of women afflicted with connective tissue disorders and a disfiguring disease called scleroderma, which hardens and immobilizes the skin. They claimed, in essence, to have been mummified by medical science, conjuring immediately the B movie melodramatics of *House of Wax* or countless other films in which mad geniuses freeze, fossilize, zombify, or otherwise turn women into inanimate (or at least very stiffly moving) sex objects. Although the plaintiffs in the Dow case were awarded a multimillion-dollar judgment, the scientific argument for their claim was later discredited. But the image of mad, implicitly "male" science, violating and destroying helpless female bodies, was such an entrenched cultural trope that real science didn't stand a chance.

As Marcia Angell, executive editor of the *New England Journal of Medicine,* comments in her book *Science on Trial,* antiscience feminists, like multiculturalists, reject the scientific method outright: "To many feminists, scientific studies seem irrelevant and distracting in the context of a perceived widespread assault on women." One leading feminist theorist, Sandra Harding, may have founded a whole new women's wing of the mad science pantheon with her influential book *The Feminist Question in Science* (1986), in which she argues that women, if not impeded by patriarchal structures, might have created a viable alternative to the scientific method, an improved "way of knowing" freed from the male obsession with objectivity and controlled and controlling experiments. Harding and others like her raise the hackles of conservatives, especially conservative males like Paul R. Gross and Norman Levitt, authors of *Higher Superstition* (1994), an all-out attack on the academic left, which they view as a diseased garden of antiscience irrationality, fueled by feminism and postmodernism.

The unstated subtexts of these debates, of course, are academic turf wars, with scientists and humanists struggling as much over departmental budgets, power, and prestige as philosophical points. In the end both sides end up embracing the old men-are-from-Mars-women-are-from-Venus clichés. An unintentional—and unintentionally hilarious—illustration of both points of view is on display in the 1958 cult film classic *Queen of Outer Space,* in which the all-male space crew from earth are stunned to witness the technological achievements of Venusian women. "How did women build a gizmo like that?" one space male blurts at the demonstration of a disintegrator ray. The question isn't answered directly, but we get a few hints in the glimpses of the laboratory of Venusian scientist Zsa Zsa Gabor, whose research experiments consist mainly of arranging wands in beakers of colored water. Gabor's typical lab attire also runs more to high heels and chiffon than to dowdy lab coats. But style over substance in mad lab fashion has never

Tim Curry as Dr. Frank N. Furter in *The Rocky Horror Picture Show* (1975).

reached a more delirious peak than Tim Curry's costuming as Dr. Frank N. Furter in *The Rocky Horror Picture Show* (1975). A blatant transvestite, privy to the secrets of life, Dr. Furter is the ultimate distillation of the mad scientist's perennial need to appropriate women's bodies and usurp their reproductive function. The female body in the mad lab, as in the larger culture, simply can't be left alone; it must be killed, disposed of, be surgically retooled and transformed, rearranged, replaced, or replicated. Often the new body isn't a body at all, but a mechanical simulacrum or analog.

The ideal female body in modern times is metaphorically equated with inorganic, nonreproducing, machine-tooled objects: sleek cars, slim-lined cigarettes, hourglasses, and the like. Breasts have been called headlights at least since the breast and car-obsessed 1950s; headlight coverings for high-end sports cars are commonly known as bras. Design historian Stephen

Bayley reports that a Fargo, North Dakota, attorney wrote to Ford's public relations department in the fifties complaining about the Edsel's vertical grille: "It was bad enough that Studebaker saw fit to design a car whose front reminds me of male testicles, but now you have gone that company one better by designing a car with a front like a female vagina." Mass-produced female bodies are the essence of a vast novelty object industry in which the female form, or its components are mass-produced utilitarian objects: cups, bottles, spoons, salt and pepper shakers, swizzle sticks, cookie jars, ashtrays, letter openers, lamp bases. The impulse to objectify women reaches its demented nadir in the realm of adult toys. Who else but a mad scientist could have contrived the fascinating assortment of robotic pocket pudenda I recently inspected at a Hollywood Boulevard sex emporium?

AIDS anxiety, no doubt, has done much to make body-evasive sex play fashionable, as the phenomenal growth of phone sex and cybersex, as well as the mainstreaming of fetish culture, vividly attests. AIDS has arguably also done its part to make extreme forms of antisex rhetoric acceptable (e.g., the "all intercourse is rape" rants of Andrea Dworkin and others). If sperm equals germ for many American women, an increasing number of their Japanese counterparts have been registering their revulsion for the biological world through an intense bacteria phobia that has in recent years generated a multimillion-dollar industry of "antibacterial" consumer products, ranging from pocket calculators to computer keyboards, steering wheels, stationery, clothing, and toys, all impregnated with germ-killing chemicals. Hitachi has gone so far as to introduce automatic teller machines that sterilize and iron paper currency. The perceived source of germs is men, and the typical phobic consumers are "office ladies" who "can't stand it when their middle-aged male bosses touch their things," according to one Japanese store clerk. "The Tokyo environment has become extremely artificial," Japanese sociologist Takahiko Furuta told the *Los Angeles Times;* it has become a place where "people have begun to view their bodies as artificial."

Current Japanese strategies for body escape were vividly anticipated in Shinya Tsukamoto's film *Tetsuo: The Iron Man* (1989), a cartoonish nightmare of people and machine transformations. The hourlong black-and-white film opens with a character known only as a "metal fetishist" cutting open his leg to crudely lay in some industrial cable. When he sees (or imagines he sees) maggots writhing in the wound, he flips and runs screaming into the streets. A character called the Salaryman hits the fetishist with his car and is somehow infected with a disease of mechanical metamorphosis. A metal thorn pops out of his cheek. He has a hallucinatory encounter with a mousy woman on a commuter train (an "office lady," no doubt), who mutates into a cyborg virago, her hand (once more, the hand imagery) transformed into a weapon-like claw encrusted with shards of metal. As the Salaryman's metamorphosis continues, his genitals are replaced by a huge, rotating drill bit, with unfortunate results for his overadventurous girlfriend. By the end of the film he is a huge moving mountain of industrial debris. The sound track is composed primarily of grunts and heavy breathing, in its way a more eloquent comment on the plight of human beings in the age of machines than a dozen studied essays.

The movies aren't the only place where mortal coils are being sloughed off for metal ones. In Southern California, the Extropy Institute ("extropy" being an upbeat coined corrective to "entropy," or the tendency of systems toward energy decay) is a nonprofit educational institution dedicated to five guiding principles: (1) boundless expansion (including personal immortality and space colonization), (2) self-transformation (including biological and neurological augmentation), (3) dynamic optimism (the only thing retro about the Extropians; basically, the old-fashioned power of positive thinking), (4) intelligent technology (creatively applied to transcend "natural" human limits), and (5) spontaneous order (as opposed to centralized government and economic controls). The Extropian concept of "transhumanism" (the transitional stage before "posthumanism") embraces a wide range of movements, including libertarianism, cryonics (postmortem deep-freezing, just in case future science discovers a way to cure what killed you—never mind a reliable way to revive the dead); bionics (prosthetic enhancements), lucid dreaming (why waste your valuable sleep time being unconscious?), "smart pills," and so on.

In a 1992 essay Extropian Institute president Max More (a name matched in archness only by that of EI's vice-president Tom Morrow) calls transhumanism an "optimistic, vital, and dynamic philosophy of life": "We seek to avoid all limits to life, intelligence, freedom, knowledge and happiness. Science, technology and reason must be harnessed to our extropic values to abolish the greatest evil: death. Death does not stop the progress of intelligent beings considered collectively, but it obliterates the individual. No philosophy of life can be truly satisfying which glorifies the advance of intelligent beings and yet which condemns each and every individual to rot into nothingness."

Although the Extropians disdain religion as downbeat and irrational, their own belief system requires an extraordinary investment of faith in technologies that do not exist and may never exist outside science fiction. Take, for example, the means by which Extropian immortality is expected to be achieved. A central tenet of Extropian faith is that it will eventually be possible to "upload" the human mind from meat to metal, transferring memory, personality, and consciousness itself into computers. This ultimate technological refinement of the mad scientist's brain transplant was first seriously proposed by Hans Moravec, director of the Mobile Robot Laboratory

Screwed by science: *Tetsuo: The Iron Man* (1989).

at Carnegie-Mellon University, in his *Mind Children: The Future of Robot and Human Intelligence* (1988). Moravec's vision rests on the debatable assumption that consciousness arises from the *patterns* of neural circuitry, not from the physical brain itself. Therefore, if the brain's structure is perfectly replicated in a computer model, the spark of consciousness will jump the gap, installing itself like user-friendly software in its new home.

"You've just been wheeled into the operating room," Moravec writes, in breathless italics, describing the sacramental ritual. *"A robot brain surgeon is in attendance. By your side is a computer waiting to become a human equivalent, lacking only a program to run. Your skull, but not your brain, is anesthetized. The robot surgeon opens your brain case and places a hand on the brain's surface."* The robotic benediction is followed by an exquisitely precise cell-by-cell excavation of the brain (the robot hand has billions of microfingers) and a simultaneous layer-by-layer simulation of the neural architecture. *"Eventually your skull is empty, and the surgeon's hand rests deep in your brainstem. Though you have not lost consciousness, or even your train of thought, your mind has been removed from the brain and transferred to a machine. In a final, disorienting step the surgeon lifts out his hand. Your suddenly abandoned body goes into spasms and dies. For a moment you experience only quiet and dark. Then, once again, you can open your eyes. Your perspective has shifted. . . . Your metamorphosis is complete."*

Posthuman life is envisioned as a fluid continuum of artificial bodies and artificial realities where discarnate human minds will have the godlike power to create self-contained universes at will. Your homepage will actually *be* your home. But certainly the failure of individuals to "sign off" after a normal life span will place strains on resources; think of the disaster that befell America Online when it granted eternal life (i.e., unlimited, unmetered access) to millions of customers. The answer of course is more hardware, more memory, and remote storage sites. As one Extropian Web site notes, "As population continues to grow, more and more people may choose to live in artificial realities. . . . One can imagine a great orbiting computer, a cubic kilometer of circuitry, housing billions of uploaded people in relative comfort." Alternately, these "people" "will live instead in a great network of smaller computers, transferring themselves from one to another just as we send email around the Internet today."

None of this will come cheaply, of course, but the poor need not apply. Transhumanism is of interest only to those affluent enough to have ready access to computers. Indeed, almost all the hyperbolic imagery of the Extropian afterlife (uploading/downloading personality, making backup copies of the self, zipping around the world and into space on an Internet-like continuum) is derived from the banal common experience of predominantly Caucasian middle-class males who spend most of their waking hours working and recreating with PCs. (Extropianism may be the most extreme example of "white flight" imaginable.) In *The Second Self* (1984), a landmark study of computers and personality development, Sherry Turkle observes that "the idea of thinking of the self as a set of computer programs is widespread among students I interviewed at Harvard and MIT." And the idea is more than metaphor. "Their language carries an implicit psychology that equates the processes that take place in people to those that take place in machines. It suggests that we are information systems whose thought is carried in 'hardware,' that we have a buffer, a mental terrain that must be cleared and crossed before we can interact with other people, that for every problem there is a pre-programmed solution on which we can fall back 'by default,' and that emotional problems are errors that we can extirpate."

Interestingly, Turkle identifies in very young children's early encounters with computers a "metaphysical stage", when their overwhelming concern is "whether the machines think, feel, are alive." This infantile stage seems to persist into adulthood for artificial intelligence (AI) enthusiasts, who continue to interpret the computer's ability to mimic certain limited aspects of human reasoning as evidence of sentience. Computers, no matter how advanced, finally mimic human thought processes; mere mechanical complexity does not generate conscious awareness. Motion pictures also provide remarkably convincing, emotionally involving simulacra of human beings, but only the delusional would argue that projected shadows are entitled to personhood. As the distinguished Oxford mathematician Roger Penrose has opined, despite his own bias toward mathematical explanations of the physical world, "Consciousness seems to me to be such an important phenomenon that I simply cannot believe that it is something just 'accidentally' conjured up by a complicated computation."

The body electric: Pierce Brosnan and Jeff Fahey don virtual reality suits in *Lawnmower Man* (1992).

On the other hand, extreme AI partisans may be less mad scientists than shrewd operators. The self-proclaimed neo-Luddite Theodore Roszak notes in *The Cult of Information* (1986): "AI has been peculiarly characterized by extravagant, propagandistic claims. . . . The reason for such conscienceless self-advertisement is not difficult to identify. There is a great deal of money at stake." Lucrative research contracts with the Pentagon and major corporations encourage all manner of overreaching claims that carry scientific credentials.

The belief that computers represent the ultimate goal of human evolution is deeply entrenched in AI and posthumanistic writing. Transcendent superbrains emerge as a cyborgian spin on the Nietzschean concept of the *Übermensch,* which is regularly and approvingly evoked in Extropian literature, along with a creeping disdain for the sluglike retrohumans and others who have no use for the Extropian adventure. "With charity toward none, Extropian transhumanism makes no provision for the economically disenfranchised, the socially marginalized, or the 'psychologically weak,' " writes cyberculture critic Mark Dery. Extropians are "committed to an ingrown, all-consuming self-improvement program in which social responsibility ends at the boundaries of the individual ego. Indeed, there is a fundamentalism to this supposedly rationalist movement's uncritical faith in technology, its unswerving devotion to unchecked expansion, and its rejection of ecological concerns as 'the false doom-mongering of the apocalyptic environmentalists.''

The rejection of the body thus implies a larger rejection of the ecosystem in which the body evolved. A quarter century before the ascendancy of cyberspace, architect-writer Martin Pawley published a prescient book, *The Private Future* (1974), in which he criticized the culturewide retreat from the body, community, and reality. A final passage strikingly anticipates the virtual revolution. "Alone in a centrally-heated, air-conditioned capsule, drugged, fed with music and erotic imagery, the parts of his consciousness separated into components that reach everywhere and nowhere, the private citizen of the future will have become one with the end of effort and the triumph of sensation divorced from action."

Of course, selling the technology of virtuality to the public paradoxically entails a certain reliance on body-nostalgic come-ons. Just as the growth of the home VCR market was fueled by the easy accessibility of video porn, so too was the bodiless netscape promoted in terms of old-fashioned body functions; the phony mid-nineties controversy over pornography on the World Wide Web was a classic example of a tsk-tsk/yum-yum marketing strategy.

The 1992 film *Lawnmower Man,* starring Pierce Brosnan as Dr. Larry Angelo, a virtual reality–obsessed researcher, is notable for its simultaneous popularization of cybersex and body abandonment. Angelo's girlfriend (Jenny Wright), like mad science partners since time immemorial, resents his withdrawal into a world of science-simulated sensations: "Falling, floating, flying—what's next, fucking?" (Yes, as it happens.) Angelo's Frankenstein creation is Job (Jeff Fahey), a mentally retarded groundskeeper, or lawn mower man, whose intelligence accelerates under VR training. When Job's intelligence, and megalomania, reach a critical mass, he downloads the contents of his brain into VR, where he is reborn as a terrifying cyberdeity presiding over "a new electric dimension . . . the utopia men have dreamed of for a thousand years," from which he plans to "cleanse this diseased planet" for once and for all. As the girlfriend angrily observes, "It may be the future to you, Larry, but it's the same old shit to me!"

Indeed, some things never change. The modern world still shares the

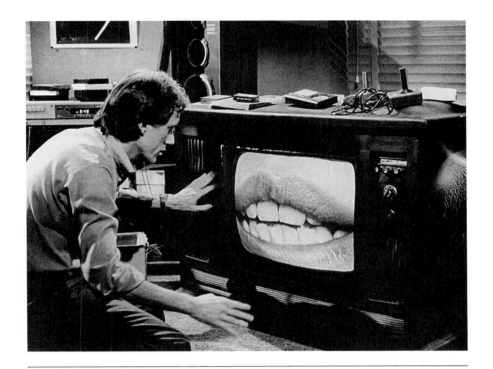

James Woods encounters the "New Flesh" in *Videodrome* (1983).

Romantic era delirium of the doomed protagonist of E. T. A. Hoffmann's "The Sandman," who, aided by a crazy inventor's magic spectacles, believed a lifeless doll to be a living woman. Today the spectacles have been replaced by virtual reality goggles.

Nowhere, perhaps, have the mad metaphors of bodies disappearing under the assault of technology been more carefully and creatively considered than in the surreal and unsettling films of David Cronenberg. His most successful film, a 1986 reworking of George Langelaan's classic horror story "The Fly" (first filmed in 1958), is a viscerally disturbing parable of modern body disgust set against the backdrop of cool high-tech rationality that is one of Cronenberg's trademarks. After an experiment in teleportation accidentally scrambles his genetic code with that of a housefly, Dr. Seth Brundle (Jeff Goldblum) is gradually reduced to an insectoid horror. The public's wide acceptance of this film, despite its nauseating images of relentless physical disintegration, suggests that *The Fly* effectively packaged a contemporary myth about the corrosive impact of science on the human body.

In *Videodrome* (1983), Cronenberg similarly features bodies poised on the brink of annhilation and transformation through a grotesque marriage with media technology. Max Renn (James Woods), a sleazy cable TV executive, smells money in an underground S&M program called Videodrome, depicting tortures and murders that may be real. The broadcasts also contain mind-altering signals that induce hallucinations blurring the boundaries between Renn's body and an increasingly menacing information environment. A television screen with huge female lips bulges forward to engulf Renn's head. A vaginalike slit opens in his abdomen, a receptacle for videocassettes made of raw, throbbing flesh. A gun, withdrawn from the slit, fuses with his hand for a familiar mad science disfigurement. At the climax, as Renn prepares to commit a figurative (or is it a real?) suicide, proclaiming his fealty to "New Flesh," a picture tube explodes, spewing forth entrails. *Videodrome's* extreme imagery of the uneasy nexus of meat and mechanism qualifies the film as a central document of cyberculture.

In his most recent film, an adaptation of J. G. Ballard's long-thought "unfilmable" novel *Crash* (1996), Cronenberg depicts a cult that embraces the ultimate technological fetish, the automobile accident as orgasm. In the film's most controversial scene a puckered crash wound becomes the sexual orifice of choice. As Ballard first described the moment, "For the first time I felt no pity for this crippled woman, but celebrated with her the excitements of these abstract vents let into her body by sections of her own automobile. During the next few days my orgasms took place within the scars below her breast and within her left armpit, in the wounds on her neck and shoulder, in these sexual apertures formed by fragmenting windshield louvres and dashboard dials in a high-speed impact, marrying through my own penis the car in which I had crashed. . . ."

Like *Videodrome's* video vagina or the Frankenstein monster's pudendal forehead scar, the techno-gash of the New Flesh is our latest badge of becoming and belonging, a sign of perverse fertility, a modern mark of initiation, the place of our ecstatic rebirth in the mind of the machine.

Entertaining the Apocalypse

Upon the announcement that Marlon Brando was to play the title role in a new film adaptation of *The Island of Dr. Moreau* (1996), more than one media commentator (admittedly, those of a bitchier stripe) raised the question of exactly what the title role was. Given the actor's ever-expanding girth—he was widely estimated as weighing nearly four hundred pounds—would Brando play the doctor . . . or the island?

Marlon Brando presides over *The Island of Dr. Moreau* (1996).

Brando wasn't alone in his depiction of the overreaching scientist as a spreading blob. Released almost at the same time as *Dr. Moreau,* Eddie Murphy's remake of the Jerry Lewis vehicle *The Nutty Professor* (1996) presented Dr. Sherman Klump, a grossly overweight researcher who, in a surreal dream sequence, terrorizes Los Angeles as a towering monstrosity of fat and flatulence.

As the millennium encroaches, the crazed scientist has indeed become bigger than ever, the Madman Who Came to Dinner (and wouldn't stop eating), or a the proverbial eight-hundred-pound gorilla that comes and goes as it chooses. The megabucks poured into, and derived from, entertainment perpetuating the mad science myth are staggering. *Jurassic Park* (1993), the highest-grossing motion picture of all time, is essentially a retelling of the Frankenstein story, a cautionary tale about hubristic science resurrecting the dead, with catastrophic results. Instead of traditional graveyards, *Jurassic Park*'s paleogeneticists dig into long-dormant dinosaur DNA to build their monsters, but the formula is familiar. The film stirred some vocal opposition from scientists at the time of its release, both for its antiscience tone and for its distortions of microbiological research. Dr. Russell Higuchi, a California geneticist, circulated a denunciation of the film and the novel for its "gross overstatements of the capabilities of DNA technology" that generated "unreasonable fear."

Director Steven Spielberg made no apology about his film's tone. A supreme populist, Spielberg reasonably reflects the sentiments of his audiences. "Every gain in science involves an equal and opposite reaction—a loss, usually a loss of the environment," he said. "Science is intrusive. I wouldn't ban molecular biology altogether, because it's useful in finding cures for AIDS, cancer and other diseases. But it's also dangerous, and that's the theme of *Jurassic Park.*"

Other reactions were more equivocal. In response to a *New York Times* op-ed piece, one reader wrote, "Our children don't avoid science because they think it's morally bereft, 'intrusive,' or 'dangerous.' They avoid it because they think it's boring. Ultimately, films like *Jurassic Park* may do science more good than harm by glamorizing it (just as cop shows and doctor shows make their professions look more exciting than they really are)." The essay in question, "Evil Science Runs Amok—Again!," by educator Carol Muske Dukes, noted the end-of-innocence motif in *Jurassic Park*'s science-tainted garden: "Once upon a time, we believed that all scientific knowledge was pure, abstract, and in its occasional uses humane. But as technical ingenuity accelerates and the rest of us become (inversely) more illiterate about science, we have come to believe . . . that knowledge itself is suspect. We fear the sinister power of what we cannot fathom. Thus we judge our 'experts' less on moral grounds than on efficacy: Can they control what they know?"

On June 25, 1993, just as *Jurassic Park* was about to enter its fourth box-office–devouring week, David Gelernter, a computer science professor at Yale University, opened a parcel delivered to his New Haven office that changed his life forever. The package contained contained the fourteenth bomb since 1978 targeted at professionals with links to the computer and high-tech industries, most of them academics. The domestic terrorist responsible for the crimes had become known as the Unabomber, on the basis of his predilection for attacking university-related individuals. Gelernter was his twenty-second victim, and he wouldn't be the last. One person had already died, and two more fatalities were to follow. Gelernter suffered grave injuries and lost most of his right hand.

Although the Unabomber couldn't possibly have anticipated the precise injuries his bomb would inflict, he clearly saw the writer as a symbol of science he found warped and dangerous. Eerily, Gelernter joined the ranks of icons whose lost, mangled, transplanted, or prosthetic hands are culturally linked with ideas of mad, runaway science: Rotwang, the Frankenstein monster, Dr. X, Dr. Gogol and Stephen Orlac, Dr. Strangelove, and on and on. Almost two years after the attack the bomber sent Gelernter a grotesque, taunting follow-up letter. "People with advanced degrees aren't as smart as they think they are," the missive read. "If you'd had any brains you would have realized that there are a lot of people out here who resent bitterly the way techno-nerds like you are changing the world."

The 1995 *Washington Post* publication of "Industrial Society and Its Future," otherwise known as the Unabomber Manifesto, made clear the bomber's sentiments about technology and society: "The Industrial Revolution and its consequences have been a disaster for the human race. They have greatly increased the life-expectancy of those of us who live in 'advanced' countries, but they have destabilized society, have made life unfulfilling, have subjected human beings to indignities, have led to widespread psychological suffering (in the Third World to physical suffering as well) and have inflicted severe damage on the natural world. The continued development of technology will worsen the situation."

David Gelernter had published a 1991 book, *Mirror Worlds,* that enthusiastically embraced computer-simulated environments (shortly before Howard Rheingold popularized the now-standard term in the title and text of his own 1991 book *Virtual Reality*). *Mirror Worlds* cheerfully predicts the augmentation of physical reality with digitized simulacra. Gelernter may have made the unwitting mistake of comparing his virtual environment favorably with the Unabomber's detested Industrial Revolution. Worse, he saw today's already computer-saturated world as a bare glimmer of a technological wonderland still to come. "People were pretty sure, in 1791, that the industrial revolution had *happened,"* Gelernter wrote. In reality it "was merely building up a head of steam. . . . [F]rom a vantage-point two centuries hence, 1991 will look a lot like 1791. The technological world of today has that same pastoral sparsely-settled leafiness. Everything is neat and well-ordered and tentative: a garden in earliest Spring. . . . Yes, software has accomplished great things. But as Al Jolson so presciently announced in Hollywood's first Talkie, you ain't heard nothing yet."

When an arrest was finally made on April 3, 1996, the accused Unabomber, Theodore Kaczynski, was soon revealed to share many of the hallmark traits of the stereotypical mad scientist. A disgruntled mathematical genius in retreat from human contact, Kaczynski was said to have holed himself up in a classic secluded workplace, where he created not monsters but monstrous weapons of destruction, which he then released on a terrified world.

Following Kaczynski's arrest, John Allan Paulos, a professor of mathematics at Temple University, created a minor but noisy controversy in the scientific world when he published a *New York Times* op-ed piece called "Dangerous Abstractions." Paulos suggested that the Unabomber's crimes and the social theories that allegedly prompted them were far from anomalies and might, in fact, represent a logical extension of the pitfalls of ab-

Technology as devouring *T. rex*: a theme park Halloween for the 1990s. *Courtesy of Universal Studios Florida.*

stract, mathematical thought. The "minimalist, austere" mathematical mystique "can blind one to the messiness and contingencies of real life," Paulos wrote; . . . mathematicians can forget that their mathematical or economic model is not the real world."

What was not much commented on was the extent to which much of the Unabomber's manifesto had already been enthusiastically absorbed into mainstream culture. From demolition derbies to theme parks to summer blockbuster movies, the explosive destruction of the technological environment is a staple of modern entertainment. A typical American family's vacation—say, to Universal Studios in Florida or California—can amount to a nonstop, quasi-sacramental (recreation = re-creation = rebirth) involvement in a scientific and technological apocalypse. In the course of a "themed" afternoon, one can be realistically menaced by genetically engineered velociraptors, be trapped inside an exploding chemical factory, experience the earthquake destruction of a sleek San Francisco subway station, or, under the video-monitored supervision of a wild-haired mad scientist, undergo the complete breakdown of time and space on the *Back to the Future* ride. For Halloween, Universal Studios Florida imports Robosaurus, a fire-breathing, car-eating mechanical *T. rex* that neatly superimposes Big Science over the most primitive instincts imaginable. And audiences eat it up. At one time it was only the mad scientist who sought to destroy the world; today, it seems, more and more of us are his willing accomplices.

Toward the end of the Reagan era, when the Unabomber was still an ambient, faceless presence, florid and nihilistic representations of sci-tech began to explode—sometimes in reality—in performance spaces and galleries and in experimental video and film on both coasts. Perhaps the most notorious and provocative avatar of the movement was the San Francisco–based Survival Research Laboratories, specializing in garish outdoor spectacles of huge monsterlike machines that self-destruct in a thoroughly modern mise-en-scène of orgiastic entropy. The SRL mystique frankly outstripped its stagecraft, and a cultlike awe attended the infrequent arrival of its anarchic performances pieces, which had considerable, chronic difficulty in securing permits and insurance. The collective's driving force was Mark Pauline, a San Francisco welder and machinist, who added immeasurably to his own legend when, experimenting with rocket explosives, he blew four fingers off his right hand (to regain some degree of dexterity, Pauline had two toes transplanted as replacement fingers). All at once he became a viscerally real example of the "disappearing body" so dear to postmodern theorists, not to mention a member of the hand-mangled mad science pantheon.

Several years ago SRL staged a remarkable event in the parking lot of Shea Stadium in Queens, New York. The overflow crowd of several thousand people (of whom this writer was a part) withstood a drenching rainstorm to witness a work entitled "The Misfortunes of Desire (Acted Out at an Imaginary Location Symbolizing Everything Worth Having)." The event had been heavily hyped for several weeks; the *New York Times,* in an advance piece, promised "more intense combat than most of the events inside the stadium. . . . Over the course of the evening, a set depicting a mechanized man-made paradise, including a giant wheel of fortune, will be ritualistically crunched and smashed to bits by roaring fire-spewing mechanized beasts.

Among the 22 tons of equipment: a 12-foot shock wave cannon, a 10 foot-high, four-legged walking machine, and a 300-horsepower flame thrower."

Because of the rain, the performance was delayed nearly an hour. The audience, unprotected on outdoor bleachers, hung on doggedly. The promised ritual was too important: the collective witnessing of mad science, naked at last, blowing itself to bits, technocrucified for all the world's modernist sins and discontents. And three thousand not-unintelligent New Yorkers were willing to endure the baptism of their lives in order to view the wake. In a review entitled "Hoping for a Cataclysm on a Rainy Day at Shea," *Times* theater critic Mel Gussow called the actual event, with some justification, as somewhat "less exciting than watching a building under construction." He noted that "After all the anticipation, the show was anticlimactic. It did not live up to the advance publicity about menace and danger. As the robotic equipment roamed around the debris-filled parking lot, the soundtrack was replaced by Frankensteinian rumbles and occasional horror-movie voices." Gussow called the overall event "demoralizing" in its negativity, but the audience, in my observation, came away strangely energized, convinced that it had connected with a satisfying truth. Science, technology, and their products and purveyors were somehow crazy, unbalanced, and we've finally had the courage to look it in the face. The soaking survivors of the mass immersion weren't grumbling on the Shea Stadium subway platform on their way back to Manhattan. The invasion, corruption, destruction of a comforting Eden had been sufficiently and cathartically evoked, just as in *The Island of Dr. Moreau* and countless other science fiction films and novels, in UFO folklore, and in radical environmental activism.

Melodrama inevitably creeps into media accounts of science because the everyday work of scientists in their laboratories is, frankly, pretty humdrum. Thus the wildest theories, the remotest possibilities, and the most anomalous vagaries get a disproportionate amount of play. Another level of distortion sets in when the media get too cozy with the scientific establishment. Dependent on access to sources and information, journalists play along to get along, courting the scientific establishment just the way researchers hungry for grants court the government, the military, and corporations. Uncritical reporting tends to perpetuate the old clichés about scientists' being dazzlingly competent, essentially superior beings, a form of overidealization with a flip side of simmering resentment—the perfect breeding ground for mad scientists. Dorothy Nelkin, author of the media study *Selling Science* (1987), comments on the media's contribution to overreaching stereotypes: "Ironically, while treating scientists as somehow removed from the common culture, journalists often turn them into authorities well outside their professional competence." Those who have the answers to scientific problems are presumed to have sagelike insights into social, political, and economic matters as well.

One scientist who energetically promoted a wider discussion of science and society was the late Carl Sagan. In his final book, *The Demon-Haunted World: Science as a Candle in the Dark* (1996), Sagan acknowledged, somewhat despairingly, the drift of the world toward superstition and irrationalism: "We've arranged a global civilization in which the most crucial elements—transportation, communications, and all other industries; agriculture, medicine, education, entertainment, protecting the environment; and even the key democratic institution of voting—profoundly depend on science and technology. We have also arranged things so that no one understands science and technology. This is a prescription for disaster."

The counterprescriptions of this leading popularizer of science are hardly surprising: more science in the classroom, more science on television, the rigorous application of scientific principles to all human affairs. But Sagan acknowledges the resistance his prescriptions face. "The technological perils that science serves up, its implicit challenge to received wisdom, and its perceived difficulty, are all reasons for some people to mistrust and avoid it," Sagan writes. "There's a *reason* people are nervous about science and technology. And so the image of the mad scientist haunts our world—down to the white-coated loonies of Saturday morning children's TV and the plethora of Faustian bargains in popular culture. . . ."

Sagan does not seem to appreciate that many people find scientific materialism threatening and dehumanizing, not because of ignorant apprehensions but because of what science explicitly states. Most people don't want to think of themselves as temporary mechanisms destined for the scrap heap of oblivion. Most people don't aspire to emulate computers. (As one stressed engineer told a therapist, "I don't think the mind was made to do logical operations all day long.") Sagan does a commendable job, as far as he goes, in debunking pseudoscience, especially the claims of UFO abductees. But in rationalizing the abduction stories into absurdity, he completely misses their metaphorical dimension and significance. They are the ultimate symbolic expression of twentieth-century fears about being immobilized and dehumanized by "scientific" authority figures.

Always a good salesman, Sagan also knows to play down the atheism inherent in the materialist worldview, rather gently dismissing the religious impulse as irrational and emotional, evidently an obstacle to be overcome. Sagan wrote the introduction to Stephen Hawking's *A Brief History of Time,* a book that speaks disingenuously about scientifically knowing the mind of God (Hawking, like Sagan, doesn't believe in God). But when we finally "know the mind of God," as Hawking promises, what then? When there is nothing more for human beings to do or know or learn, will everything just grind to a stop? Will we cease all human activity and become as immobile as Hawking himself, adoring complicated algorithms for eternity? Is there an aspect of the death wish in the quest for ultimate explanations and final solutions, implying as they do the cessation of all striving, searching, and living?

In her book *Science as Salvation* the British moral philosopher Mary Midgley notes that "increasing technicality in the sciences . . . leaves unserved the general need for understanding, and whatever spiritual needs lie behind it." Ironically, "The promise of satisfying those spiritual needs has played a great part in establishing the special glory of the abstraction 'science' in our culture." But as scientific complexity increases, general understanding wanes. As Midgley elaborates, "Many scientists will now say flatly that most of us cannot expect to understand what is happening [in science] at all, and had better not even mess around with the popularizations. This gloomy estimate must extend, of course, far beyond the uneducated proles to the scientists themselves, when they deal with anything outside their own increasingly narrow provinces. There cannot, in this view, ever be such a thing as a scientifically-minded public."

Bryan Appleyard's no-holds-barred attack on scientism, *Understanding the Present* (1992)—a book branded as "dangerous" by the August journal

Nature—underscores the widening communications gap between scientists and laypeople. Scientists "find it difficult to talk of what they do because they tend to assume detailed knowledge is required for generalities to be understood," Appleyard writes. "They find it difficult to grasp the concept of the *meaning* of their work, assuming this to be a debate that takes place at a lower level than the specialized discussions with their colleagues."

Estranged cultures generate the most demonized summoning ancient archetypes of otherness: witches, witch doctors, and black magicians. The science fiction writer Arthur C. Clarke once remarked that any sufficiently advanced technology would be indistinguishable from magic. In our science-accelerated age, magical thinking is accelerated as well, investing modern institutions with a primitive, fantastic qualities. The scientific gaze becomes the latest incarnation of the evil eye, the sign of arcane, esoteric knowledge and terrifying power. The dichotomy is perhaps best embodied in one of the late twentieth century's most popular horror icons, Clive Barker's Pinhead from the *Hellraiser* films. Pinhead is a sadistic white-faced ghoul in disturbingly ecclesiastical robes, his face and skull stamped with an encircling grid of mathematical precision, with a nail pounded into each coordinate. Reason and control are perfectly juxtaposed with their opposites, a neat summing-up of the modernist dilemma.

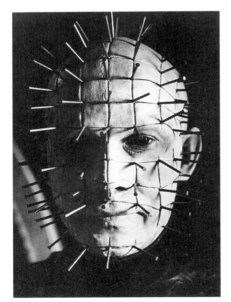

Insane logic: Doug Bradley as Clive Barker's Pinhead, in *Hellraiser III* (1992).

In Appleyard's view, modern science is "a form of mysticism that proves peculiarly fertile in setting itself problems which only it can answer. . . . Science begins by saying it can answer only *this* kind of question and ends by claiming that *these* are the only questions that can be asked." Most human beings of course are not preoccupied with scientific questions and controversies, and never have been. In response to Stephen Hawking's contention that science alone holds the answers to humankind's ancient longing for meaning, Mary Midgley asks, "Does it seem plausible that this ancient, universal human longing was always a desire for the kind of scientific theory that Hawking and his colleagues now hope to forge? This would be strange, since before the last few hundred years, nobody anywhere ever dreamt of looking for that kind of theory." Theoretical physics, Midgley argues, cannot distinguish between the broad, humanistic "why?" and the narrow, scientific "how?"

Mad science and mad scientists have emerged in part to bridge the cultural chasm between hard science and wild superstition. The mad scientist's demeanor is evidence of our intuitive knowledge that something is missing in a purely scientific model of the universe; he brings to science passion, drama, catharsis. The mad scientist is a modern priest who mediates our communion with the new gods of specialized knowledge, raising impertinent questions no one else dares ask. We may be suspicious of his motivations and hesitate to move too close to his operating table/altar, but nonetheless we have a grudging admiration for his audacity.

The mad scientist's notoriously overdeveloped ego may itself be a popular imaginative response to the doctrine of scientific reductionism. In a century when we are told, relentlessly, that the soul and self are illusions, that our minds are just computers, and that machines will inherit the earth, the mad scientist boldly demonstrates that individual personality is still a powerful force to be reckoned with. After all, what is the typical mad scientist but a cauldron of raging subjectivities? He sustains himself on inner passions, personal ambitions, hidden motivations, professional jealousies, and private terrors—all the things science says that it cannot directly observe or measure and thus, for purposes of scientific discussion, do not exist. If the mad scientist pushes romantic individualism a bit too far, perhaps he does so only as a necessary corrective to traditional science and its relentless assaults on the self.

The real scientist professes to be motivated by the rational, objective pursuit of knowledge; his mad counterpart, like the fool in a king's court, has the license to speak more plainly of his motivations, which can constitute the spectrum of human venality, with a special emphasis on power. As Ian Malcolm, the hero of Michael Crichton's novel *Jurassic Park,* cynically observes, "scientific power is like inherited wealth: attained without discipline. . . . There is only a get-rich-quick, make-a-name-for-yourself philosophy. Cheat, lie, falsify—it doesn't matter. Not to you, or your colleagues. No one will criticize you. No one has any standards. They are all trying to do the same thing: to do something big, and do it fast." Such sentiments are hardly shocking to a public that has in recent years witnessed the fiasco of cold fusion research (in which a completely baseless claim for sustained nuclear reactions at room temperature nonetheless fueled a one-hundred-million-dollar research bandwagon), the "Star Wars" boondoggle, and the more craven aspects of AIDS research.

The increasing use of "junk science" in the courtroom also increases public cynicism about the validity of science generally. As Peter W. Huber, author of the junk science critique *Galileo's Revenge* (1991), comments, "Maverick scientists shunned by their reputable colleagues have been embraced by lawyers. Eccentric theories that no respectable government agency would ever fund are rewarded munificently by the courts. . . . The pursuit of truth, the whole truth, and nothing but the truth has given way to reams of meaningless data, fearful speculation, and fantastic conjecture." Huber cites the extreme case of a Philadelphia psychic who was awarded one million dollars (a judgment overruled) by a jury that believed her claim that a CAT scan procedure had erased her second sight. Perhaps a mad scientist, with the aid of a yet-to-be-invented invention, will be able to restore it.

This book, of course, has not been about science per se, but rather about the persistent shadow of science and the curious modern mythology it has inspired. The mad scientist and his monsters may not make mainstream science happy, but I hope I have demonstrated that their persistence has a significance more complicated than the mere reflex of an ignorant mob. Underlying the B movie plots and the lurid pulp magazine illustrations is a populist struggle to make sense (if only dream sense) of the power and primacy of science in the modern world, our half-conscious search for new creation myths in a despiritualized century. As filmmaker David Cronenberg put it, "everybody's a mad scientist, and life is their lab. We're all trying to experiment to find a way to live, to solve problems, to fend off madness and chaos."

The stakes are big, the drama immense. In the twentieth century science has amply demonstrated its power to grind *Homo sapiens* into material insignificance while simultaneously offering transcendent fantasies of power and dominion. The paradox is concisely, if inadvertently, expressed by comedian Steve Martin in *The Man with Two Brains* (1983). "You're playing God!" shout the authorities, aghast.

Martin's mad scientist is momentarily taken aback. Then he lets out the retort that explains it all:

"But *somebody* has to!"

A Hollywood Hit Parade of Mad Scientists, Demented Doctors, and Assorted Evil Geniuses

DR. ADRIAN

Appeared in: *The Ape* (Monogram, 1940; dir: William Nigh).

Portrayed by: Boris Karloff.

Mad Ambition/Achievement: To achieve a polio cure based on fresh human spinal fluid, Karloff commits a series of murders in the guise of an escaped circus ape.

Bela Lugosi as Dr. Alex Zorka in *The Phantom Creeps* (1939). *Courtesy of David Del Valle/ The Del Valle Archive.*

ANTON ARCANE

Appeared in: *Swamp Thing* (Swampfilms/United Artists, 1982; dir: Wes Craven);
The Return of Swamp Thing (Lightyear Entertainment/Miramax, 1989; dir: Jim
Wynorski).
Portrayed by: Louis Jourdan.
Mad Ambition/Achievement: World domination via plant and human gene splicing.

DR. BEAUMONT

Appeared in: *The Walking Dead* (Warner Bros., 1936; dir: Michael Curtiz).
Portrayed by: Edmund Gwenn.
Mad Ambition/Achievement: To bring back to life a wrongly executed man.

DR. BENSON

Appeared in: *The Mad Doctor of Market Street* (Universal Pictures, 1942; dir: Joseph
H. Lewis).
Portrayed by: Lionel Atwill.
Mad Ambition/Achievement: Suspended animation experiments.

PROFESSOR NATHANIEL BILLINGS

Appeared in: *The Boogie Man Will Get You* (Columbia Pictures, 1942; dir: Lew
Landers).
Portrayed by: Boris Karloff.
Mad Ambition/Achievement: To perfect a machine that transforms ordinary men
into supermen, the better to serve the war effort.

DR. JULIAN BLAIR

Appeared in: *The Devil Commands* (Columbia Pictures, 1941; dir: Edward
Dmytryk).
Portrayed by: Boris Karloff.
Mad Ambition/Achievement: To communicate with the dead through high-voltage
electricity.

DR. PETER BLOOD

Appeared in: *Dr. Blood's Coffin* (Caralan/United Artists, 1961; dir: Sidney J. Furie).
Portrayed by: Kieron Moore.
Mad Ambition/Achievement: The restoration of life via the transplantation of living
hearts into corpses.

DR. JAMES BREWSTER

Appeared in: *The Ape Man* (Monogram, 1943; dir: William Beaudine).

Portrayed by: Bela Lugosi.

Mad Ambition/Achievement: Self-transformation into a half man, half ape.

TEN BRINKEN

Appeared in: *Alraune* (Germany, 1918; dir: Eugen Illes); *Alraune* (Austria-Hungary, 1918; dir: Mihaly Kertesz [Michael Curtiz] and Fritz Odon); *Alraune* (Germany, 1928; dir: Henrik Galeen; aka *Unholy Love*); *Alraune* (Germany, 1930; dir: Richard Oswald); *Unnatural* (West Germany, 1952; dir: Arthur Maria Rabenalt).

Portrayed by: Hilde Wolter (1918); Guyla Gal (1918); Paul Wegener (1928); Albert Basserman (1930); Erich von Stroheim (1952).

Mad Ambition/Achievement: The insemination of a prostitute with the semen of a hanged murderer, resulting in a demonic woman with an appalling sexual appetite.

DOC BROWN

Appeared in: *Back to the Future* (Universal, 1985; dir: Robert Zemeckis); *Back to the Future Part II* (Universal, 1989; dir: Robert Zemeckis); *Back to the Future Part III* (Universal, 1990; dir: Robert Zemeckis).

Portrayed by: Christopher Lloyd.

Mad Ambition/Achievement: Time travel via a souped-up DeLorean sports car.

DR. CADMAN

Appeared in: *The Black Sleep* (United Artists, 1956; dir: Reginald LeBorg; aka *Dr. Cadman's Secret*).

Portrayed by: Basil Rathbone.

Mad Ambition/Achievement: A cure for catalepsy, with monsters as a by-product.

DR. CALLISTRATUS

Appeared in: *Blood of the Vampire* (Eros/Universal-International, 1958; dir: Henry Cass).

Portrayed by: Donald Wolfit.

Mad Ambition/Achievement: Vampiric resurrection by heart transplant; blood experiments on prisoners.

DR. LORENZO CAMERON

Appeared in: *The Mad Monster* (Monogram, 1941; dir: Sam Newfield).
Portrayed by: George Zucco.
Mad Ambition/Achievement: The artificial creation of werewolves in a misguided attempt to help the war effort.

DR. PAUL CARRUTHERS

Appeared in: *The Devil Bat* (Monogram, 1940; dir: Jean Yarborough).
Portrayed by: Bela Lugosi.
Mad Ambition/Achievement: For revenge on unscrupulous former business partners, the creation of a giant killer bat, attracted to the scent of aftershave.

DALE COBA

Appeared in: *The Stepford Wives* (Columbia Pictures, 1975; dir: Bryan Forbes).
Portrayed by: Patrick O'Neal.
Mad Ambition/Achievement: The replacement of upper-middle-class New England housewives with docile android counterparts.

DR. PAUL CORVOLOS

Appeared in: *The Wizard* (Fox, 1927; dir: Richard Rosson).
Portrayed by: Gustav von Seyffertitz (1927).
Mad Ambition/Achievement: To graft a human head on to an ape.

DR. PATRICK J. CORY

Appeared in: *Donovan's Brain* (United Artists/Dowling Productions, 1953; dir: Felix Feist).
Portrayed by: Lew Ayres.
Mad Ambition/Achievement: To keep alive the brain of a wealthy, ruthless industrialist despite its malignant telepathic influence.

DR. CYCLOPS

SEE DR. ALEXANDER THORKELL

PROFESSOR GERALD DEEMER

Appeared in: *Tarantula* (Universal-International, 1955; dir: Jack Arnold).
Portrayed by: Leo G. Carroll.
Mad Ambition/Achievement: Giant, laboratory-engineered animals, at the expense of grotesque self-disfigurement.

DRACULA

Appeared in: *Abbott and Costello Meet Frankenstein* (Universal-International, 1948; dir: Charles Barton).

Portrayed by: Bela Lugosi.

Mad Ambition/Achievement: To transplant the brain of comedian Lou Costello into the head of the Frankenstein monster.

FOU

Appeared in: *The Madman of Lab Four* (France; Gaumont, 1967; dir: Jacques Besnard).

Portrayed by: Jean Lefebvre.

Mad Ambition/Achievement: Invention of a gas that causes people to fall in love.

DR. ARNO FRANKEN

Appeared in: *Dr. Franken* (NBC Television; 1980; dir: Marvin J. Chomsky).

Portrayed by: Robert Vaughan.

Mad Ambition/Achievement: The creation of a monster, assembled from spare body parts obtained from a New York hospital.

FRANKENSTEIN

Appeared in: *Frankenstein* (Edison, 1910).

Portrayed by: Augustus Phillips.

Mad Ambition/Achievement: The fiery creation of a monstrous doppelgänger.

BARON VICTOR FRANKENSTEIN

Appeared in: *Curse of Frankenstein* (Hammer Films, 1957; dir: Terence Fisher); *The Revenge of Frankenstein* (Hammer Films, 1958; dir: Terence Fisher); *The Evil of Frankenstein* (Hammer Films, 1964; dir: Freddie Francis); *Frankenstein Created Woman* (Hammer Films, 1967; dir: Terence Fisher); *Frankenstein Must Be Destroyed* (Hammer Films, 1969: dir: Terence Fisher); *Horror of Frankenstein* (Hammer Films/MGM-EMI, 1970; dir: Jimmy Sangster); *Frankenstein and the Monster from Hell* (Hammer Films, 1974; dir: Terence Fisher).

Portrayed by: Peter Cushing (all but 1970, portrayed by Ralph Bates).

Mad Ambition/Achievement: Fun and games with brains, hearts, and other body parts, mixed and matched with an assortment of hand-tooled monsters.

BARON VICTOR VON FRANKENSTEIN

Appeared in: *Frankenstein 1970* (Allied Artists, 1958; dir: Howard W. Koch).

Portrayed by: Boris Karloff.

Mad Ambition/Achievement: To revive the Frankenstein monster in his own rejuvenated image, Baron von Frankenstein allows an American television crew to film a special in his castle for the price of an atomic reactor.

BARON VON FRANKENSTEIN

Appeared in: *Mad Monster Party* (Embassy Pictures, 1967; dir: Jules Bass).

Portrayed by: The voice of Boris Karloff (animated feature).

Mad Ambition/Achievement: To host a convention of monsters—Dracula, the Wolf Man, Frankenstein's Bride (Phyllis Diller), etc.

CHARLES FRANKENSTEIN

Appeared in: *The Bride* (Columbia Pictures, 1985; dir: Franc Roddam).

Portrayed by: Sting.

Mad Ambition/Achievement: The creation of a mate for his solitary male monster.

DR. FREDERICK FRANKENSTEIN

Appeared in: *Young Frankenstein* (Twentieth Century-Fox, 1974; dir: Mel Brooks).

Portrayed by: Gene Wilder.

Mad Ambition/Achievement: To build a monster, perhaps secondarily to correcting the pronunciation of his name (Frahn-ken-steen).

HENRY FRANKENSTEIN

Appeared in: *Frankenstein* (Universal Pictures, 1931; dir: James Whale); *Bride of Frankenstein* (Universal Pictures, 1935; dir: James Whale).

Portrayed by: Colin Clive.

Mad Ambition/Achievement: The creation of an electrically animated monster from pieced-together corpses.

DR. LUDWIG FRANKENSTEIN

Appeared in: *Ghost of Frankenstein* (Universal Pictures, 1942; dir: Erle C. Kenton).

Portrayed by: Sir Cedric Hardwicke.

Mad Ambition/Achievement: To rescue his father's monster from a lime pit and restore its full strength.

VICTOR FRANKENSTEIN

Appeared in: *Frankenstein: The True Story* (NBC Television, 1974; dir: Jack

Smight); *Frankenstein* (Turner Television, 1992; dir: David Wickes); *Mary Shelley's Frankenstein* (Tristar/Columbia, 1993; dir: Kenneth Branagh).
Portrayed by: Leonard Whiting (1973); Patrick Bergin (1992); Kenneth Branagh (1993).
Mad Ambition/Achievement: The usual.

WOLF VON FRANKENSTEIN

Appeared in: *Son of Frankenstein* (Universal Pictures, 1939; dir: Rowland V. Lee).
Portrayed by: Basil Rathbone.
Mad Ambition/Achievement: To resurrect his father's dormant monster.

DR. ELAINE FREDERICK

Appeared in: *Flesh Feast* (Viking International, 1970; dir: Brad P. Grinter).
Portrayed by: Veronica Lake.
Mad Ambition/Achievement: To avenge the concentration camp death of her mother. Dr. Frederick develops a rejuvenation therapy that attracts the fugitive Adolf Hitler, whom she feeds to flesh-eating maggots.

DR. JOHN GARTH

Appeared in: *Before I Hang* (Columbia Pictures, 1940; dir: Nick Grinde).
Portrayed by: Boris Karloff.
Mad Ambition/Achievement: To rejuvenate himself with a blood serum extracted from a condemned murderer. Karloff recaptures his youth but is driven himself to kill.

DR. GENESSIER

Appeared in: *Les Yeuxs sans visage (Eyes without a Face,* France, 1959; dir: Georges Franju; aka *The Horror Chamber of Dr. Faustus).*
Portrayed by: Pierre Brasseur.
Mad Ambition/Achievement: Attempts to assuage guilt for the disfigurement of his daughter in a car wreck by attempting face grafts from a succession of female victims.

PROFESSOR GIBBS

Appeared in: *The Invisible Woman* (Universal Pictures, 1940; dir: A. Edward Sutherland).
Portrayed by: John Barrymore.
Mad Ambition/Achievement: To render an attractive female model undetectable to the eye.

DR. GIGGLES
SEE DR. EVAN RENDELL

DR. WILFORD GLENDON
Appeared in: *Werewolf of London* (Universal Pictures, 1935; dir: Stuart Walker).
Portrayed by: Henry Hull.
Mad Ambition/Achievement: To discover the secrets of a moon-blooming plant that can cure his own werewolfery.

DR. GOGOL
Appeared in: *Mad Love* (Metro-Goldwyn-Mayer, 1935; dir: Karl Freund).
Portrayed by: Peter Lorre.
Mad Ambition/Achievement: Grafting the hands of a murderer on to an injured concert pianist.

JACK GRIFFIN
Appeared in: *The Invisible Man* (Universal Pictures, 1933; dir: James Whale).
Portrayed by: Claude Rains.
Mad Ambition/Achievement: Discovery of an invisibility serum, with megalomania as a side effect.

DR. JOHN HAMMOND
Appeared in: *Jurassic Park* (Universal, 1993; dir: Steven Spielberg); *The Lost World* (Universal, 1997; dir: Steven Spielberg).
Portrayed by: Richard Attenborough.
Mad Ambition/Achievement: Cloning of dinosaurs from DNA preserved in Mesozoic era amber.

DR. ALEX HARRIS
Appeared in: *Demon Seed* (Metro-Goldwyn-Mayer, 1977; dir: Donald Cammell).
Portrayed by: Fritz Weaver.
Mad Ambition/Accomplishment: Development of a supercomputer that impregnates his wife in a first step toward world domination.

DR. MICHAEL HFUHRUHURR
Appeared in: *The Man with Two Brains* (Aspen/Warner Bros., 1983; dir: Carl Reiner).

Portrayed by: Steve Martin.

Mad Ambition/Achievement: Reconciling the many conflicts arising from falling in love with a woman's disembodied brain.

DR. FREDERICK HOHNER

Appeared in: *The Climax* (Universal Pictures, 1941; dir: George Waggner).

Portrayed by: Boris Karloff.

Mad Ambition/Achievement: To silence hypnotically a rising young soprano whose voice reminds him of the opera singer he murdered years before.

DR. SIGMUND HUMMEL

Appeared in: *The Bees* (Mexico, 1978; dir: Alfredo Zacharias).

Portrayed by: John Carradine.

Mad Ambition/Achievement: The genetic engineering of killer bees.

DR. HENRY JEKYLL

Appeared in: *Dr. Jekyll and Mr. Hyde* (Selig Polyscope, 1908); *Dr. Jekyll and Mr. Hyde* (Nordisk, 1910); *Dr. Jekyll and Mr. Hyde* (Thanhauser, 1912; dir: Lucius Henderson); *Dr. Jekyll and Mr. Hyde* (Kineto-Kinemacolor, 1913); *Dr. Jekyll and Mr. Hyde;* (IMP, 1920); *Dr. Jekyll and Mr. Hyde* (Pioneer Film Corp., 1920); *Der Januskopf* (Germany, 1920); Dr. *Jekyll and Mr. Hyde* (Paramount, 1920; dir: John S. Robertson); *Dr. Jekyll and Mr. Hyde* (Paramount, 1931; dir: Rouben Mamoulian); *Dr. Jekyll and Mr. Hyde* (MGM, 1941; dir: Victor Fleming); *Abbott and Costello Meet Dr. Jekyll and Mr. Hyde* (Universal, 1953; dir: Charles Lamont); *Two Faces of Dr. Jekyll* (Hammer, 1960; dir: Terence Fisher; aka *House of Fright*); *I, Monster* (Hammer: 1972; dir: Stephen Weeks); *Dr. Jekyll and Sister Hyde* (Hammer, 1972; dir: Roy Ward Baker); *Dr. Jekyll and Mr. Hyde* (television, 1975; dir: Dan Curtis); *Edge of Sanity* (1989; dir: Gerard Kikoine); *Jekyll and Hyde* (television, 1990; dir: David Wickes); *Mary Reilly* (Tri Star, 1996; dir: Stephen Frears).

Portrayed by: Alwin Neuss (1910); James Cruze (1912); King Baggott (1913); James Cruze (1920); Conrad Veidt (Germany, 1920); John Barrymore (1920); Fredric March (1931); Spencer Tracy (1941); Boris Karloff (1953); Paul Massie (1960); Christopher Lee (1972); Ralph Bates/Martine Beswick (1972); Jack Palance (1975); Anthony Perkins (1989); Michael Caine (1990); John Malkovich (1996).

Mad Ambition/Achievement: The splitting of human personality into separate aspects, one good and one evil.

EDDIE JESSUP

Appeared in: *Altered States* (Warner Bros., 1980; dir: Ken Russell).

Portrayed by: William Hurt.

Mad Ambition/Achievement: Evolutionary regression via sensory deprivation tank immersion.

PROFESSOR JULIUS FERRIS KELP

Appeared in: *The Nutty Professor* (Paramount, 1963; dir: Jerry Lewis).

Portrayed by: Jerry Lewis.

Mad Ambition/Achievement: A homely, introverted scientist's creation of a debonair, chemically generated alter ego.

DR. LEON KRAVAAL

Appeared in: *The Man with Nine Lives* (Columbia Pictures, 1940; dir: Nick Grinde).

Portrayed by: Boris Karloff.

Mad Ambition/Achievement: To cure cancer cryogenetically, by interring his patients in a glacier.

DR. LAMB

Appeared in: *A Blind Bargain* (Goldwyn Pictures, 1922; dir: Wallace Worsley [?]).

Portrayed by: Lon Chaney.

Mad Ambition/Achievement: The creation of an ape-man (also played by Chaney).

DR. LAURIENCE

Appeared in: *The Man Who Lived Again* (Gaumont-British, 1936; dir: Robert Stevenson).

Portrayed by: Boris Karloff.

Mad Ambition/Achievement: Driven mad by the ridicule of his colleagues after losing his funding, Laurience exchanges the brains of his fickle patron and his crippled assistant.

DR. EMILIO LIZARDO

Appeared in: *Buckaroo Banzai* (Twentieth Century-Fox/Sherwood Productions, 1984; dir: W. D. Richter).

Portrayed by: John Lithgow.

Mad Ambition/Achievement: While perfecting a technique to move objects through solid matter, Lizardo is possessed by the leader of the Red Lectoids, an alien race from the eighth dimension.

DR. LORENZ

Appeared in: *The Corpse Vanishes* (Monogram, 1942; dir: Wallace Fox).
Portrayed by: Bela Lugosi.
Mad Ambition/Achievement: The kidnapping of young brides, whose body fluids rejuvenate his wife, an elderly countess.

DR. MARLOWE

Appeared in: *The Voodoo Man* (Monogram, 1944; dir: William Beaudine).
Portrayed by: Bela Lugosi.
Mad Ambition/Achievement: To find a cure for his zombie wife, dead-alive for twenty years, by stealing the life energy of young girls.

DR. MIRAKLE

Appeared in: *Murders in the Rue Morgue* (Universal Pictures, 1932; dir: Robert Florey).
Portrayed by: Bela Lugosi.
Mad Ambition/Achievement: To mate a woman with an ape, for unspecified reasons.

DR. JOSEF MENGELE

Appeared in: *The Boys from Brazil* (Twentieth Century-Fox, 1978; dir: Franklin J. Schaffner).
Portrayed by: Gregory Peck.
Mad Ambition/Achievement: To create a cloned replica of Adolf Hitler.

MORBIUS

Appeared in: *Forbidden Planet* (Metro-Goldwyn-Mayer, 1956; dir: Fred McLeod Wilcox).
Portrayed by: Walter Pidgeon.
Mad Ambition/Achievement: The reawakening of an extraterrestrial energy monster that feeds and acts upon the scientist's unconscious desires.

DR. MOREAU

Appeared in: *The Island of Lost Souls* (Paramount, 1933; dir: Erle C. Kenton); *The Island of Doctor Moreau* (American International, 1977; dir: Don Taylor); *The*

Island of Doctor Moreau (New Line Cinema, 1996; dir: John Frankenheimer).
Portrayed by: Charles Laughton (1933); Burt Lancaster (1977); Marlon Brando (1996).
Mad Ambition/Achievement: The creation of human beings from lower animals.

DR. GUSTAV NIEMANN

Appeared in: *House of Frankenstein* (Universal Pictures, 1944; dir: Erle C. Kenton).
Portrayed by: Boris Karloff.
Mad Ambition/Achievement: To wreak revenge upon his enemies by reviving the Frankenstein monster, with the help of Dracula and the Wolf Man.

DR. OTTO VON NIEMANN

Appeared in: *The Vampire Bat* (Majestic Pictures, 1933; dir: Frank Strayer).
Portrayed by: Lionel Atwill.
Mad Ambition/Achievement: Committing a series of "vampire" murders to obtain blood for the synthetic organism he has created.

DR. ORLOFF

Appeared in: *The Awful Dr. Orloff* (Spain, 1961; dir: Jess Franco).
Portrayed by: Howard Vernon.
Mad Ambition/Achievement: The revitalization of his hideously disfigured daughter through body part transplantation.

DR. PHIBES

Appeared in: *The Abominable Dr. Phibes* (American International, 1971; dir: Robert Fuest); *Dr. Phibes Rises Again* (American International, 1972; dir: Robert Fuest).
Portrayed by: Vincent Price.
Mad Ambition/Achievement: Revenge on doctors who could not save his wife's life; the search for an elixir to restore her vitality.

DR. PRETORIUS

Appeared in: *Bride of Frankenstein* (Universal Pictures, 1935; dir: James Whale).
Portrayed by: Ernest Thesiger.
Mad Ambition/Achievement: To persuade his former student, Henry Frankenstein, to collaborate in the creation of a female companion for the Frankenstein monster.

DR. RIGAS

Appeared in: *Man Made Monster* (Universal Pictures, 1941; dir: George Waggner).
Portrayed by: Lionel Atwill.
Mad Ambition/Achievement: The transformation of a carnival performer into an electronically charged automaton.

ROTWANG

Appeared in: *Metropolis* (UFA/Paramount, 1927; dir: Fritz Lang).
Portrayed by: Rudolf Klein-Rogge.
Mad Ambition/Achievement: To sabotage a workers' rebellion by replacing their female leader with an evil robot double.

ROXOR

Appeared in: *Chandu the Magician* (Fox, 1932; dir: William Cameron Menzies).
Portrayed by: Bela Lugosi.
Mad Ambition/Achievement: World domination through a death ray device.

DR. JANOS RUKH

Appeared in: *The Invisible Ray* (Universal Pictures, 1936; dir: Lambert Hillyer).
Portrayed by: Boris Karloff.
Mad Ambition/Achievement: Discovery of a new radioactive element, that renders exposed individuals progressively insane, phosphorescent, and poisonous to the touch.

DR. SARTORIUS

Appeared in: *Juggernaut* (Grand National, 1936; dir: Henry Edwards).
Portrayed by: Boris Karloff.
Mad Ambition/Achievement: The murder of former patrons who refuse to continue supporting his medical experiments.

DR. SAVAARD

Appeared in: *The Man They Could Not Hang* (Columbia Pictures, 1939; dir: Nick Grinde).
Portrayed by: Boris Karloff.
Mad Ambition/Achievement: The inventor of a mechanical heart, Savaard is unjustly executed for murder but, through the use of his own device, returns from the dead to take revenge on his accusers.

DR. SOVAC

Appeared in: *Black Friday* (Universal Pictures, 1940; dir: Arthur Lubin).
Portrayed by: Boris Karloff.
Mad Ambition/Accomplishment: To transplant part of the brain of a gangster into the head of a college professor wrongfully injured by the criminal.

THE SURGEON GENERAL OF BEVERLY HILLS

Appeared in: *Escape from L.A.* (Twentieth Century-Fox, 1996; dir: John Carpenter).
Portrayed by: Bruce Campbell.
Mad Ambition/Achievement: The harvesting of fresh human tissue to repair the disfigurements of mutant plastic surgery addicts in a postapocalyptic Los Angeles.

DR. JANE TIPTREE

Appeared in: *Carnosaur* (New World Pictures, 1993; dir: Adam Simon).
Portrayed by: Diane Ladd.
Mad Ambition/Achievement: To gestate a *Tyrannosaurus* embryo in her own uterus.

DR. VOLLIN

Appeared in: *The Raven* (Universal Pictures, 1935; dir: Louis Friedlander).
Portrayed by: Bela Lugosi.
Mad Ambition/Achievement: To avenge the spirit of Edgar Allan Poe by performing disfiguring plastic surgery on an escaped convict (Boris Karloff) and by various tortures inflicted on houseguests.

DR. ERIC VORNOFF

Appeared in: *Bride of the Monster* (Rolling M Productions, 1955; dir: Edward D. Wood, Jr.).
Portrayed by: Bela Lugosi.
Mad Ambition/Accomplishment: To create a race of atomic supermen to conquer the world.

DR. HERBERT WEST

Appeared in: *Re-Animator* (Empire Pictures, 1985; dir: Stuart Gordon); *Bride of Re-Animator* (Wild Street Pictures, 1990; dir: Brian Yuzna).
Portrayed by: Jeffrey Combs.
Mad Ambition/Achievement: The development of a glowing serum with the power to reanimate corpses and body parts.

DR. XAVIER [1]

Appeared in: *Doctor X* (Warner Bros., 1932; dir: Michael Curtiz).

Portrayed by: Preston Foster.

Mad Ambition/Achievement: The capture of a cannibalistic full-moon strangler, using highly theatrical technologies of detection.

DR. XAVIER [2]

Appeared in: *The Return of Dr. X* (Warner Bros., 1939; dir: Vincent Sherman).

Portrayed by: Humphrey Bogart.

Mad Ambition/Achievement: Unnatural prolongation of his life by vampiric blood transfusions.

DR. ZISKA

Appeared in: *The Monster* (MGM, 1925; dir: Roland West).

Portrayed by: Lon Chaney.

Mad Ambition/Achievement: Abduction of road travelers for sadistic, ill-defined experiments in a secluded mansion.

DR. ALEX ZORKA

Appeared in: *The Phantom Creeps* (Universal serial, 1939; dir: Ford Beebe and Saul Goodkind).

Portrayed by: Bela Lugosi.

Mad Ambition/Achievement: World domination via an invisibility belt, mechanical killer spiders, and a giant, grimacing robot.

Acknowledgments

I'd like first to acknowledge my dedicatee, the film preservationist and historian Scott MacQueen, for his many years of friendship and support and countless hours of enthusiastic conversation and generously shared expertise. This book, like my previous volumes, *The Monster Show* and *Hollywood Gothic*, has benefited tremendously from his input and advice.

Screams of Reason was completed during the Sturm und Drang of my complicated move from New York to California and could not have been finished without the following individuals, who assisted, materially and otherwise, in my own mad experiment in transcontinental relocation: Vincent

Boris Karloff as the Frankenstein monster: caricature by Xavier Cugat.

Inconiglios, Bob Madison and Russell Frost, Sam and Susan Crowl, Lokke Heiss, Michael Isador, Harlan Ellison, Mrs. Josephine Fronek, Richard Peterson, David J. Schow and Christa Faust, Erik N. Stogo and Mack Dennard, Mr. and Mrs. John Skal, Kevin Gerlock and Sandra Skal-Gerlock, and Dr. Norman Hartstein.

Photographs and photographic assistance were provided by Buddy Barnett, Ronald V. Borst, Eric Caiden, David Del Valle, Geraldine Duclow, Scott MacQueen, Jerry Ohlinger's Movie Materials Store, and George Turner.

Libraries consulted included the Vernon Alden Library, Ohio University; Beverly Hills Public Library; Elmer Holmes Bobst Library, New York University; Margaret Herrick Library, Academy of Motion Picture Arts and Sciences; University Research Library, University of California, Los Angeles; the Library of Congress; various branches of the New York Public Library, especially the Billy Rose Theater Collection at Lincoln Center; the Free Library of Philadelphia Theatre Collection; the British Library; and the Theatre Museum.

Individuals who provided information, assistance, courtesies, and enthusiasm included Nina Auerbach, Christopher Bram and Draper Shreeve, Ivan Butler, Jonathan Sinclair Carey, Ron Chaney, Bill Condon, Frank Darabont, Frank Dello Stritto, Sue Duncan, Ian Grey, Bob Haas, Del Howison, Sam Irvin, Skip Malinowski, Vincent Musetto, Robert Parigi, Philip J. Riley, Laura Ross, Elias Savada, Richard Valley, Michael D. Walker, and Tom Weaver.

A special thank-you goes to Mark Dery, author of the extraordinary book *Escape Velocity*, with whom I spent hours of stimulating dialogue in cyberspace, both on the subject of this book and other, equally interesting and arcane matters. I am deeply grateful for his careful reading and commentary on my previous books, and for his steady interest, encouragement, and research suggestions for the present one.

Final thanks are due my editor, Hilary Hinzmann, for his careful, intelligent, always helpful attention during the past eight years at W. W. Norton & Company, and to my new editor, Gerry Howard, who completed the project with me, as well as to my literary agent, Malaga Baldi, for more than a decade of hard work and encouragement.

Notes

INTRODUCTION: LAUGHING SAL AND THE SCIENCE OF SCREAMS

16 WALLS OOZE GHOSTS Quoted by Bryan Appleyard, *Understanding the Present: Science and the Soul of Modern Man* (New York: Doubleday, 1993), p. vii.

19 NOT APPEARING CRAZY Barry Malzberg, *The Engines of the Night* (New York: Bluejay Books, 1982), pp. 9–10.

19 SOCIAL POSITION OF SCIENCE Lionel Trilling, *The Liberal Imagination* (New York: Viking, 1950), p. 170.

22 FANTASIES OF POWERLESS INDIVIDUALS Thomas M. Disch, "The Embarrassments of Science Fiction," in Peter M. Nicholls, ed., *Science Fiction at Large* (New York: Harper & Row, 1976), p. 149.

Advertising art for *The Invisible Man* (1933).

23 I DESPAIRED AT THE LOSS OF LIFE Unsourced 1967 magazine article by Jean D. Rosenbaum, from clippings file on the 1931 film *Frankenstein;* Billy Rose Theater Collection, New York Public Library for the Performing Arts at Lincoln Center.

26 TOYS FOR THE RICH Freeman J. Dyson, "Science in Trouble," *American Scholar* (Autumn 1993), p. 534.

CHAPTER ONE: FRANKENSTEIN'S GATE

34 FOULEST TOADSTOOL James Lees-Milne, *William Beckford* (Montclair, N.J.: Allanheld and Schram, 1979), p. 107.

34 DISGUSTED LITERARY FIGURE William Beckford (1762–1844), author, *Vathek.*

34 AUTHOR'S ORIGINAL GENIUS Sir Walter Scott (unsigned), "Remarks on Frankenstein, or the Modern Prometheus; a Novel," *Blackwood's Edinburgh Magazine* (March 1818), p. 620.

36 A DEAD & LIVING BODY Quoted by Muriel Spark, *Mary Shelley* (New York: E. P. Dutton, 1987), p. 20.

36 BABY CAME TO LIFE AGAIN *Mary Shelley's Journal,* ed. F. L. Jones (Norman: University of Oklahoma Press, 1944), p. 41.

37 PERHAPS A CORPSE Mary Shelley, author's introduction to the 1831 revised edition of *Frankenstein* (New York: Modern Library, 1993), p. xviii.

37 WE WILL EACH WRITE A GHOST STORY Ibid., p. xvi.

38 I THOUGHT AND PONDERED Ibid., xvii.

38 THE VAMPYRE "The Vampyre" is sometimes credited with inspiring Bram Stoker's *Dracula* (1897), but this truly stretches a point, since Stoker jettisoned the Byronic and Romantic trapping and made his vampire count a physically repellent, animalistic fiend. Nonetheless, twentieth-century adaptations of *Dracula*—most recently the Francis Ford Coppola film *Bram Stoker's Dracula* (1992)—have based their vampires more on Polidori's seductive concept than on Stoker's Darwinistic predator.

38 UNEASY, HALF-VITAL MOTION Shelley introduction, ibid., p. xix.

39 SWIFT AS LIGHT Ibid., p. xx.

39 A DREARY NIGHT IN NOVEMBER Mary Shelley, *Frankenstein, or, The Modern Prometheus,* the 1818 Text in Three Volumes (Berkeley, Los Angeles, London: University of California Press, 1984), p. 51.

39 HIS LIMBS WERE IN PROPORTION Ibid.

39 CORPSE OF MY DEAD MOTHER Ibid., p. 52.

41 I COLLECTED BONES Ibid., p. 49.

42 EVERLASTING ICES Ibid., p. 217.

43 QUIT YOUR VESSEL . . . DARKNESS AND DISTANCE Ibid., pp. 235, 237.

43 DID I REQUEST THEE John Milton, *Paradise Lost,* X, lines 743–45.

43 ACTUAL TOWN OF FRANKENSTEIN Radu Florescu, *In Search of Frankenstein* (Boston: New York Graphic Society, 1975). See Chapter 3, "The Elopement to the Continent," pp. 49–63.

48 KNOWN MORAL LAXITY H. G. Haile, *The History of Doctor Johann Faustus* (Urbana: University of Illinois Press, 1965), p. 5

49 ALL FAUST'S PREDECESSORS E. M. Butler, *The Myth of the Magus* (Cambridge: University Press, 1948), p. 12.

49 DASHED IN PIECES John Henry Jones, *The English Faust Book: A Critical Edition Based on the Text of 1592* (Cambridge and New York: Cambridge University Press, 1994), p. 180.

50 FAUSTUS IS GONE Christopher Marlowe, *Doctor Faustus,* ed. Sylvan Barnet (New York: Signet Classics, 1969), p. 101.

50 RECONSTRUCT THE PRIMEVAL CHAOS Thomas Jefferson Hogg, *The Life of Percy Bysshe Shelley,* vol. 1; quoted in Edmund Blunden, *Shelley: A Life Story* (London: Collins, 1946), p. 51.

51 A TALE FROM HIS PEN *Ibid.,* p. 8.

51 HORRIBLE AND DISGUSTING ABSURDITY *Quarterly Review* (March 1818), pp. 382, 385.

52 WRITINGS OF THIS EXTRAVAGANT CHARACTER *Frankenstein* review, *British Critic* (April 1818).

52 HEARD THAT THIS WORK WAS WRITTEN BY MR. SHELLEY *Frankenstein* review, *Literary Panorama and National Register* (June 1818), p. 412.

52 HIGHLY PARTISAN REVIEW "Continuation of the Shelley Papers/On 'Frankenstein,' " *Athenaeum* (November 10, 1832), p. 730.

54 VICTOR FRANKENSTEIN POSSESSED FREE WILL Anne K. Mellor, *Mary Shelley: Her Life, Her Fiction, Her Monsters* (New York and London: Routledge, 1988), p. 171.

54 ALL MRS. SHELLEY DID Mario Praz, *The Romantic Agony* (reprint; London: Oxford University Press, 1970), p. 116.

55 CONTRIVED FOR COMMERCIAL ENDS Christopher Frayling, *Vampyres* (London and Boston: Faber and Faber, 1991), pp. 10–17.

57 ANTITHETICAL POSSIBILITIES George Levine and U. C. Knoepflmacher, preface, *The Endurance of Frankenstein: Essays on Mary Shelley's Novel* (Berkeley, Los Angeles, London: University of California Press, 1979), p. xiv.

57 VIRTUALLY A PARODY Oates, Shelley, op. cit., p. 254.

58 BUT LO AND BEHOLD! Mary Shelley, letter to Leigh Hunt, September 9, 1823; quoted by Elizabeth Nitchie, "The Stage History of *Frankenstein,*" *South Atlantic Quarterly* (October 1942), p. 385.

58 A MONSTER'S BIRTH BEING GRANTED *Presumption; or, The Fate of Frankenstein* review, *Examiner* (London), August 3, 1823, pp. 504–05.

60 DARK BLACK FLOWING HAIR Richard Brinsley Peake, *Presumption; or, the Fate of Frankenstein,* in Steven Earl Forry, *Hideous Progenies: Dramatizations of* Frankenstein *from the Nineteenth Century to the Present* (Philadelphia: University of Pennsylvania Press, 1990), pp. 135–36.

60 SPEECH TAKEN ALMOST VERBATIM Peake, op. cit., p. 143.

60 LINKED SOCIAL REFORM WITH MOB RULE Forry, op. cit., p. 35.

62 DESCENDED FROM A HAIRY QUADRAPED Duncan M. Porter and Peter W. Graham, eds., *The Portable Darwin* (New York: Penguin, 1993), p. 350.

64 A FATE MORE PROBABLE THAN PROGRESS Gillian Beer, *Darwin's Plots: Evolutionary Narrative in Darwin, George Eliot and Nineteenth Century Fiction* (London, Boston, Melbourne, Heuly: Routledge & Kegan Paul, 1983), p. 145.

64 WILLIAM HENRY JOHNSON Robert Bogdan, *Freak Show: Presenting Human Oddities for Amusement and Profit* (Chicago and London: University of Chicago Press, 1988). See pp. 134–42 for a complete account.

66 HAWTHORNE Edward H. Davidson, ed. *Hawthorne's Dr. Grimshawe's Secret* (Cambridge, Mass.: Harvard University Press, 1954), p. 45.

68 THIS ILLNESS BEGAN LONG AGO Honoré de Balzac, *The Quest of the Absolute and Other Stories,* Ellen Marriage, trans. (Philadelphia: Gebbie Publishing Co., 1898), pp. 122–23.

69 HARDLY HUMAN . . . TROGLODYTIC Robert Louis Stevenson, *The Strange Case of Dr. Jekyll and Mr. Hyde and Other Stories,* ed. Jenni Calder (Harmondsworth: Penguin Books, 1979), p. 40.

69 APE-LIKE Ibid., p. 47.

69 AN IMPRESSION OF DEFORMITY Ibid., p. 40.

69 NOT EASY TO DESCRIBE Ibid., p. 34.

69 DELETED MATERIAL William Veeder and Gordon Hirsch, eds., *Dr. Jekyll and Mr. Hyde after One Hundred Years* (Chicago and London: University of Chicago Press, 1988), pp. 34–35.

70 JEKYLL'S APPARENT INFATUATION Elaine Showalter, *Sexual Anarchy: Gender and Culture at the Fin de Siècle* (New York: Viking, 1990), p. 11.

70 IMAGES SUGGESTIVE OF ANALITY Ibid., p. 113.

71 BLOATED MONSTER OF THE DEEP Gertrude Atherton, *Adventures of a Novelist* (New York: Liveright, Inc, 1932), p. 184.

71 QUEER FEELING OF DISTASTE Richard Le Gallienne, *The Romantic '90s* (London and New York: G. P. Putnam's Sons, 1926), p. 161.

71 FAT WHITE SLUG Horace Wyndam, *The Nineteen Hundreds* (New York: Thomas Selzer, 1923), p. 62.

71 DECADENT ROMAN EMPEROR Alice Kipling, letter to Rudyard Kipling, March 18, 1882, quoted by Ina Taylor, *Victorian Sisters: The Remarkable MacDonald Women and the Great Men They Inspired* (Bethesda, Md.: Adler & Adler, 1987), pp. 136–37.

71 AS A PIG Whistler's drawing is reproduced in Richard Ellmann's biography *Oscar Wilde* (New York: Alfred A. Knopf, 1987).

73 DEGENERATES ARE NOT ALWAYS CRIMINALS Max Nordau, *Degeneration* (New York: D. Appleton and Co., 1895), p. vii.

74 STUPENDOUS JOKE "Books and Authors," *Outlook* (July 6, 1895), p. 24.

74 CONSTANT JARRING OF THE SPINE *Degeneration* review, *Critic* (March 30, 1895), pp. 233–34.

75 MAKING PEOPLE FLABBY Hugh E. M. Stutfield, "Tommyrotics," *Blackwood's Edinburgh Magazine* (June 1895), p. 842.

75 IN THE FANTASY WORLD Bram Dijkstra, *Idols of Perversity: Images of Feminine Evil in Fin-de-Siècle Culture* (New York and Oxford: Oxford University Press, 1986), p. 185.

75 A SCANDALOUS TRIAL H. G. Wells, preface, *Collected Works,* Vol. 2 (London: T. Fisher Unwin, 1924), p. ix.

77 PENDANT TO THEIR MINDS H. G. Wells, "The Man of the Year Million," *Pall Mall Gazette* (November 6, 1893).

77 A CHILD OF CHANGE Wells, *Collected Works,* loc. cit., p. xvii.

79 INTENT FACES H. G. Wells, *The Island of Dr. Moreau,* ed. Brian Aldess (1896; reprint, London and Rutland, Vt.: Everyman/J. M. Dent/Charles E. Tuttle Co., 1993), p. 129.

79 ORIGINALITY AT THE EXPENSE OF DECENCY *The Island of Dr. Moreau* review, *Speaker* (April 18, 1896).

79 FEELINGS OF DISGUST *The Island of Dr. Moreau* review, *Athenaeum* (May 9, 1896), pp. 615–16.

79 CROWDED GRAVEYARD Chalmers Mitchell, "Cheap Horrors," *Saturday Review* (April 11, 1896).

79 A LOATHSOME AND REPULSIVE BOOK *The Island of Dr. Moreau* review, *Times* (London), June 17, 1896.

80 HIS BIOLOGICAL NIGHTMARE *The Island of Dr. Moreau* review, *New York Times* (August 16, 1896), p. 23.

80 SHUDDERING LADIES Chalmers, op. cit.

80 GIVEN COATS, CAPS, PIPES Midas Dekkers, *Dearest Pet: On Bestiality* (London & New York: Verso, 1994), p. 188.

80 SOMETHING IN THE MANNER OF CONRAD Anthony West, *H. G. Wells: Aspects of a Life* (New York: Random House, 1984), p. 231.

81 HIS DARKER SIDE Brian W. Aldiss, introduction to Everyman Library edition of *The Island of Dr. Moreau* (London: J. M. Dent, 1993), p. xxxi.

81 GOD THE CRUEL EXPERIMENTAL SCIENTIST Ibid.

81 THE COUNT IS NATURE PERSONIFIED Clive Leatherdale, *Dracula: The Novel and the Legend* (1985; revised ed., London: Desert Island Books, 1993) p. 202.

82 SCIENTIFIC DESCRIPTION Cesar[e] Lombroso, *Criminal Man* (New York: G. P. Putnam's Sons, 1911).

82 HIS FACE Bram Stoker, *Dracula* (1897; reprint, Oxford and New York: Oxford University Press, 1990), pp. 17–18.

82 SAW THE FINGERS Ibid., p. 34.

83 A SOOTY BLACK ANIMAL J. Sheridan Le Fanu, *Carmilla,* in Alan Ryan, ed., *Vampires: Two Centuries of Great Vampire Stories* (Garden City, N.Y.: Doubleday & Co., 1987), p. 102.

83 AN ACTIVE MATERIALIST Leatherdale, op. cit., p. 188.

84 ALMOST A MATTER OF PROVED FACT Fay Weldon, "Bram Stoker: Hello, Thank You, and Goodbye," *Bram Stoker's Dracula Omnibus* (Edison, N.J.: Chartwell Books, 1992), pp. viii, xii.

84 PROVOCATIVE ESSAY Talia Schaffer, "A Wild[e] Desire Took Me: The Homoerotic History of *Dracula,*" *English Literary History,* vol. 61, no. 2 (Summer 1994), pp. 381–425.

85 THE CHEEKS WERE FULLER Stoker, op. cit., p. 51.

86 HYPNOTIC PERFORMANCE "A Hypnotised Man Buried Alive," *Westminister Gazette,* April 24, 1897, p. 7.

87 THEY WERE HEADS H. G. Wells, *The War of the Worlds* (1898; reprint, London: Everyman Library, 1993), p. 119.

CHAPTER TWO: MIRACLES FOR THE MASSES

89 FANCY YOURSELF SEATED Quoted in Margaret Cheney, *Tesla: Man Out of Time* (reprint, New York: Laurel, 1981), pp. 3–4.

90 ALMOST UNLIMITED AND SUPERNATURAL Quoted in John J. O'Neill, *Prodigal Genius: The Life of Nikola Tesla* (New York: Ives Washburn, 1944), p. 252.

90 VARIATION OF THE BLACK ART "Popular Appreciation of Scientists," *Nation* (January 16, 1902), p. 46.

92 LUIGI PIRANDELLO Quoted in Walter Benjamin, "The Work of Art in the Age of Mechanical Reproduction," *Illuminations* (New York: Schocken Books, 1969), p. 229.

94 IT'S ABOUT CREATING LIFE Francis Ford Coppola, interviewed by Leonard Lopate on *New York and Company,* WNYC Radio, New York, January 20, 1994.

95 MOST FRIGHTFUL MIEN *The Film Index,* March 12, 1910, p. 6. Ogle, born in 1875, began his association with Edison in 1907, worked extensively in films until 1924. His many screen appearances included *Rebecca of Sunnybrook Farm* (1917) with Mary Pickford, and Maurice Tourneur's *Treasure Island* (1920), in which he took the colorful role of Long John Silver.

95 REPULSIVE SITUATIONS Edison company synopsis of *Frankenstein,* February 14, 1910.

96 ALL THE TERROR OF THE PAST Ibid.

97 ADVERSE REVIEWS Forry, op. cit., p. 80.

97 VIVIDLY AND SYMPATHETICALLY ACTED *Frankenstein* review, *Moving Picture World* (April 2, 1910), p. 508.

98 LIKE YESTERDAY'S NEWSPAPER Mary Brehm, "Cudahy Collector Has Films the Envy of Great Museums," *Milwaukee Sentinel,* December 17, 1976.

99 EXPECT TO PAY A SIZABLE AMOUNT Ibid.

99 SOME AMERICAN CASH Rick Romell, "Buff Buys Batch of Old Films, Finds 'Frankenstein' Treasure," *Milwaukee Sentinel,* March 18, 1985.

102 TRUE ENEMY OF CIVILIZATION John Corbin, *R.U.R.* review, *New York Times,* October 15, 1922, section VIII, p. 1.

102 LAST HALF-DOZEN HUMANS Robert C. Benchley, "Drama," *Life* (November 2, 1922), p. 20.

107 H. G. WELLS HATED *METROPOLIS* H. G. Wells, "Mr. Wells Reviews a Current Film," *New York Times,* April 16, 1927.

108 NO LESS A PUBLICATION " 'Metropolis'—A Movie 'Forecast' of the Future," *Scientific American* (April 1927), pp. 244–45.

109 PRESTIGE OF SCIENCE WAS COLOSSAL Frederick Lewis Allen, *Only Yesterday: An Informal History of the 1920s* (New York: Harper and Brothers, 1931), pp. 197–99.

109 SCIENCE'S NEW PRESTIGE Peter J. Kuznick, *Beyond the Laboratory: Scientists as Political Activists in 1930s America* (Chicago and London: University of Chicago Press, 1987), p. 10.

110 BISHOP OF RIPON "Wants 10-Year Pause in Scientist's Efforts," *New York Times,* September 5, 1927, p. 3.

110 IMPATIENT AND A LITTLE SCORNFUL Joseph Wood Krutch, *The Modern Temper: A Study and a Confession* (New York: Harcourt, Brace and Co., 1929), p. 70.

110 POWERLESS TO ENRICH Ibid., p. 72.

CHAPTER THREE: SNAP, CRACKLE, SCREAM

113 WHO IS THE MAN CONCEALED IN THAT ROOM? Peggy Webling, *Frankenstein: An Adventure in the Macabre.* Library of Congress, copyright deposit manuscript dated September 7, 1928. All quotations are taken from this typescript.

120 NIBELUNG GNOME "Oh, You Beautiful Monster," *New York Times* (January 29, 1939).

120 TOO MANY IDEAS OF HIS OWN "Interview with Jack Pierce," *Monster Mania* (October 1966).

121 MOANING AND GRUNTING Gregory William Mank, *It's Alive!: The Classic Cinema Saga of Frankenstein* (San Diego and New York: A. S. Barnes & Co., 1981), p. 17.

121 I WILL NOT BE A SCARECROW Taylor, op. cit.

121 CAMERAMAN PAUL IVANO For extended discussions of the Ivano-photographed test reel, see Mank, op. cit.; Brian Taves, *Robert Florey, the French Expressionist* (Metuchen, N.J., and London: Scarecrow Press, 1987); and Paul M. Jensen, *The Men Who Made the Monsters* (New York: Twayne Publishers, 1996).

121 AWFUL HAIRY CREATURE Mike Parry and Harry Nadler, "CoF Interviews Boris Karloff," *Castle of Frankenstein* (November 1966), pp. 10–12.

121 STRIPES, STREAKS, AND STRIATIONS. Unpaginated clipping, *Los Angeles Record,* June 7, 1931; Margaret Herrick Library, Academy of Motion Picture Arts and Sciences, Beverly Hills, California.

123 POLISHED, CLAY-LIKE "Great Horror Figure Dies," *Famous Monsters of Filmland* no. 31 (1964), p. 50.

123 LAUGHED LIKE A HYENA Ric Atkins, *Let's Scare 'Em* (Jefferson, N.C.: McFarland & Company, 1997), p. 18.

123 ELECTRODE BOLTS Taylor, op. cit.

123 THEN I READ THE SCRIPT Unsourced newspaper interview, quoted in Ken Beale, "Boris Karloff: Master of Horror," *Castle of Frankenstein Monster Annual* (1967), p. 58.

124 WASN'T ANOTHER WAR PICTURE James Curtis, *James Whale* (Metuchen, N.J., and London: Scarecrow Press, 1982), p. 75.

124 I THOUGHT IT WAS A GAG "Films Cast Up James Whale After 15 Years," *New York Herald Tribune,* December 3, 1944.

124 INTERESTING, BUT "WEIRD" Ibid.

125 AT SEA WITH THE CASTING Curtis, op. cit., p. 77.

125 YOUR FACE HAS STARTLING POSSIBILITIES Cynthia Lindsay, *Dear Boris: The Life of William Henry Pratt, a.k.a. Boris Karloff* (New York: Alfred A. Knopf, 1975), p. 54.

126 QUEER, PENETRATING PERSONALITY "James Whale and Frankenstein," *New York Times,* December 20, 1931.

126 SYMMETRICALS Lindsay, op. cit., p. 42.

126 MADE SKETCHES: James Whale and Frankenstein," loc. cit.

128 REMOVING THE MAKE-UP Helen Weigel Brown, "The Man Who Made the Monster," *Picturegoer Weekly* (April 23, 1932), p. 12.

129 MEEKLY AS AN OBEDIENT CHILD Gregory Mank, "Mae Clarke Remembers James Whale," *Films in Review* (May 1985), pp. 301, 303.

129 ONE OF THE MOST MOVING EXPERIENCES Robin Beam, "My Life of Terror," *Shriek* (October 1965), p. 16.

129 A COUPLE OF STIFF DRINKS R.C. Sherriff, *No Leading Lady* (London: Victor Gollancz Ltd., 1968), pp. 259–60.

130 THE BIORAY "Bureau of Investigation: Radium as a 'Patent Medicine,' " *Journal of the American Medical Association,* vol. 98, no. 10 (1932), pp. 1397–99.

130 TO COVER THEIR TRUE FEELINGS Mordaunt Hall, *Frankenstein* review, *New York Times,* December 5, 1931.

130 WE INVITED PEOPLE TO SIT Oden and Olivia Meeker, "The Screamy-Weamies," *Collier's* (January 12, 1946).

131 CENSORSHIP For a detailed account of censorship issues surrounding *Frankenstein* before and after its release, see this author's *The Monster Show: A Cultural History of Horror* (New York: W.W. Norton & Co., 1993).

131 WRINKLES ON THE CYCLORAMA *Frankenstein* review, *Cleveland Plain Dealer,* undated clipping, 1931.

131   PAPIER-MACHE MOUNTAINS Rob Wagner, *Rob Wagner's Script* (February 20, 1932).

131   RACIAL OVERTONES G. A. Atkinson, *Frankenstein* review, *Era* (London) (January 27, 1932).

132   BEST THING THAT HAPPENED TO THE TRADE Carl Laemmle, "You Want Me to Be Honest," *Cinema News and Property Gazette* (January 6, 1932).

134   MATE THE WOMEN WITH THE APE *The Murders in the Rue Morgue* review, *Variety,* February 16, 1932.

134   FLOREY'S DIRECTION Florey never again had a shot at such an influential property as *Frankenstein,* though he contributed strong work to numerous noir films of the forties and served as an associate director to Charles Chaplin for *Monsieur Verdoux* (1947). In his later career he directed Boris Karloff in the television anthology series *Thriller.*

134   NIGHTMARE OF CLASS CONSCIOUSNESS Annalee Newitz, "A Lower-Class, Sexy Monster: American Liberalism in Mamoulian's *Dr. Jekyll and Mr. Hyde,*" *Bright Lights Film Journal,* no. 15 (1995), p. 12.

136   CHARLES DARWIN'S SON "Major Darwin Predicts Civilization's Doom Unless Century Brings Wide Eugenic Reforms," *New York Times* (August 23, 1932), p. 16.

136   BIOLOGICAL INVESTIGATION "Urges Open Door to Healthy Aliens," *New York Times,* August 23, 1932, p. 16.

137   GENIUS BALLYHOOS FOR SIDESHOW "Smoke 'Em Hokum," *Rob Wagner's Script* (February 20, 1932), pp. 1–3.

138   ARRIVED WITH A SEEDY TWO-BIT CARNIVAL Ray Bradbury, "Drunk, and in Charge of a Bicycle," introduction, *The Stories of Ray Bradbury* (New York: Alfred A. Knopf, 1980), p. xiv.

139   TRAITORS TO THE CIVILIZATION Read Bain, "Scientist as Citizen," *Social Forces* (March 1933), p. 413.

140   THEY SELL THEIR SERVICES Ibid., pp. 413–14.

140   ALTHOUGH WORLDS APART Kuznick, op. cit., p. 254.

140   SCIENCE IS COMMUNISM J. D. Bernal, *The Social Function of Science* (New York: 1939), quoted by Kuznick, op. cit.

141   ADVANTAGES OF CHRISTIANITY AND ALCOHOL Aldous Huxley, *Brave New World* and *Brave New World Revisited* (reprint, New York: Harper & Row, 1965), p. 42.

141   MAN LIVING SCIENTIFICALLY Aldous Huxley, *Between the Wars: Essays and Letters,* ed. David Bradshaw (reprint, Chicago: Ivan R. Dee, 1994), p. 31.

141 BBC BROADCAST Ibid., pp. 105–06.

141 LUGUBRIOUS AND HEAVY-HANDED *Brave New World* review, *Books* (February 7, 1932), p. 7e.

141 THE TROUBLE WITH MR. HUXLEY'S SATIRE *Brave New World* review, *Springfield (Mass.) Republican*, February 7, 1932.

141 THIS NOVEL WILL SHOCK *Brave New World* review, *Spectator* (February 13, 1932), unpaginated clipping.

144 ATTRACTIVE LASSIES Arthur Mayer, *Merely Colossal: The Story of the Movies from the Long Chase to the Chaise Longue* (New York: Simon and Schuster, 1953), p. 130.

145 WRITHING TENTACLES Peter Haining, ed., *The H. G. Wells Scrapbook* (New York: Clarkson N. Potter, 1978), p. 127.

145 STINKS TO HEAVEN Sherriff, op. cit., p. 269.

146 INVISIBLE LUNATIC Haining, op. cit.

147 DEATH-BEAM "Tesla, at 78, Bares New 'Death-Beam,'" *New York Times* (July 11, 1934), p. 18.

148 SEVEN-PAGE TREATMENT Robert Florey, "Les Nouvelle Aventures de Frankenstein: Le Monstre est vivant," *L'Écran fantastique*, no. 10 (May 1979), pp. 61–63.

149 HAYS OFFICE Gerald Gardner, *The Censorship Papers: Movie Censorship Letters from the Hays Office, 1934 to 1968* (New York: Dodd, Mead & Co., 1987), p. 66.

149 PURITY CAMPAIGN Robin Strawn, "The Monster Walks Again," *Film Weekly* (August 17, 1934), p. 11.

149 R. C. SHERRIFF Sherriff's contributions to Universal's horror films were considerably more extensive than he acknowledges in his 1968 autobiography, *No Leading Lady*. In addition to his uncredited work on *Bride of Frankenstein,* Sherriff completed an unproduced script for Boris Karloff called *A Trip to Mars* and several censor-beleaguered versions of *Dracula's Daughter.* Both films were to have been directed by James Whale.

151 WHILE HINDSIGHT IS RIGHTLY SUSPECT Monika Morgan, "Sexual Subversion: The Bride of Frankenstein," *Bright Lights Film Journal*, no. 11 (Fall 1993), p. 5.

152 HOMOSEXUAL PRESENCES . . . CAMP ASSAULT Ibid.

152 APOLLONIAN IMAGE Camille Paglia, *Sexual Personae: Art and Decadence from Nefertiti to Emily Dickinson* (New Haven: Yale University Press, 1990), pp. 66–67.

153 NOT HAIRDRESSERS Christopher Bram, *Father of Frankenstein* (New York: Dutton, 1995), p. 151.

153 NO STRANGER TO HOMOSEXUALITY Lloyd Shearer, "Parade's Special Intelligence Report: Living with Laughton," *Parade Magazine* (May 15, 1983), p. 9.

153 PLUMP EFFEMINACY *Bride of Frankenstein* review, *Time* (April 29, 1935).

153 TEN SEPARATE SCENES Gardner, op. cit., p. 67.

154 HANG-DOG AIR *Bride of Frankenstein* review, *Time* (April 29, 1935).

154 SHIRLEY TEMPLE . . . RIVETS IN HER NECK Unsourced 1935 newspaper clipping.

154 MOMENTS OF UNCONSCIOUS HUMOUR "New Films in London," *Times* (London), July 1, 1935.

155 CONVENTIONAL MANIACS André Senwall, *Mad Love* review, *New York Times* (August 5, 1935), p. 20.

156 FINGER JOINTS WERE BUILT UP "Colin Clive Reveals—I Hate Horror Films!" *Famous Monsters of Filmland,* no. 208 (May 1995), p. 24.

159 MORE GRUESOME EXPERIENCE Roger M. Macklis, M.D., "Radithor and the Era of Mild Radium Therapy," *Journal of the American Medical Association* (August 1, 1990), p. 616.

159 THING IS FAR FROM BEING A JOKE "Great American Jitters" (editorial), *Washington Post* (November 1, 1938), p. 1.

161 NAZI NEWSPAPERS James D. Secrest, "Martian Invasion by Radio 'Regrettable,' Says McNich," *Washington Post* (October 31, 1938), p. 1.

161 MYSTERIOUS INVASION Hadley Cantril, *The Invasion from Mars: A Study in the Psychology of Panic.* (Princeton, N.J.: Princeton University Press, 1940), pp. 194–95.

161 FOUR HOURS TO BUILD HIM UP "Oh, You Beautiful Monster," op. cit.

163 SILLIEST PICTURE EVER MADE B. R. Crisler, *Son of Frankenstein* review, *New York Times* (January 30, 1939).

164 THAT IDEA TOOK A LITTLE GETTING USED TO David Gelernter. *1939: The Lost World of the Fair* (New York: Free Press, 1995), p. 229.

CHAPTER FOUR: A-BOMBS, B PICTURES, AND C CUPS

167 LIGHTING EFFECTS Lewis Wood, "Steel Tower 'Vaporized' in Trial of Mighty Bomb," *New York Times* (August 7, 1945), p. 1.

167 END OF EVERYTHING WE CALL LIFE H. G. Wells, *Mind at the End of Its Tether* (London: Heinemann, 1945). p. 1.

174 MORE MAIL THAN CONTRACT CUTIES Clipping (headline and pagination missing), *New York Herald Tribune* (November 21, 1943).

176 CONSCIENTIOUS SCRUPLES Robert Jungk, *Brighter than a Thousand Suns: A Personal History of the Atomic Scientists* (New York and London: Harcourt Brace Jovanovich, 1958), p. 202.

177 THE LAWS OF NATURE E. U. Condon, "An Appeal to Reason," *Bulletin of the Atomic Scientists* (March 1, 1946), pp. 6–7.

180 A-BOMBS, B-PICTURES A. H. Weiler, *Red Planet Mars* review, *New York Times* (June 16, 1952), p. 15.

180 MY WHOLE CAREER DESTROYED "Mae Clarke Raps TV Portrayal," *Los Angeles Examiner* (July 17, 1958).

181 ACCUMULATED GRIEVANCES Richard Hofstadter, *Anti-intellectualism in American Life* (New York, Alfred A. Knopf, 1963), p. 221.

181 FERVENT MALICE AND HUMORLESS IMBECILITY Ibid., p. 3.

181 AT THE MERCY OF EXPERTS Ibid., p. 37.

182 SUCCESSION OF SCAPEGOATS Ibid.

183 GHASTLY PLUME Bob Considine, television reporter and eyewitness to the Rosenberg executions, quoted in Alvin H. Goldstein, *The Unquiet Death of Julius and Ethel Rosenberg* (New York and Westport: Lawrence Hill & Co., 1975), unpaginated.

183 YOUR COUNTRY IS SICK WITH FEAR Quoted by Walter and Miriam Schneir, *Invitation to an Inquest* (1965; reprint, New York: Pantheon Books, 1983), p. 254.

184 STARTED TO THROW UP Bob Groves, " 'Them!' Giant Ants That Spawned a Film Legacy," *Los Angeles Times Calendar* (April 17, 1988), p. 28.

184 EVERYONE HAD SEEN ANTS Al Taylor, "Them!" *Fangoria,* no. 5 (1979), p. 23.

184 TOOK THE STORY VERY SERIOUSLY Groves, op. cit., p. 29.

184 GREEN AND RED SOAP BUBBLES Ibid.

185 SOMEWHAT CONVINCING Bosley Crowther, *Them!* review, *New York Times* (June 17, 1954).

185 CHINLESS, BULGE-EYED EVIL *Them!* review, *Time* (July 19, 1954).

187 CONSIDERATIONS OF HEALTH Suellen Hoy, *Chasing Dirt: The American Pursuit of Cleanliness* (New York and Oxford: Oxford University Press, 1995), pp. 171–72.

187 AFRAID OF BACKSLIDING Ibid., p. 172.

188 HAVING A PUSH BUTTON Thomas Hine, *Populuxe* (New York: Alfred A. Knopf, 1986), p. 133.

189 INDECENT, OBJECTIONABLE, AND OBSCENE "M. W. Shelley Book 'Frankenstein' Banned," *New York Times,* September 5, 1955, p. 9.

189 COBRA FASCINATION *On the Beach* review, *Atlantic* (August 1957).

189 OBSESSIVE, NIGHTMARISH *On the Beach* review, *Kirkus Reviews* (July 1, 1957).

190 A RECORD FOR SUICIDES *On the Beach* review, *Catholic World* (October 1957).

190 FATUOUS ENDORSEMENTS Pauline Kael, *5001 Nights at the Movies* (New York: Holt, Rinehart and Winston, 1982), p. 429.

190 NO RELIEF FROM DEPRESSION *On the Beach* review, *Variety* (December 2, 1959).

191 FIFTH-HIGHEST-EARNING FILM Cobbert S. Steinberg, *Film Facts* (New York: Facts on File, 1980), p. 23.

CHAPTER FIVE: ALIEN CHIC

198 ATHENS POLICE "Athens Policemen Spot 2 UFOs," *Athens Messenger* (October 18, 1973), p. 1.

199 GHOST-LIKE FIGURE My information on 1973 UFO sighting involving "aliens" is drawn primarily from David Webb's *1973—Year of the Humanoids: An Analysis of the Fall, 1973 UFO/Humanoid Wave,* 2d ed. (Evanston, Ill.: Center for UFO Studies, 1976), pp. 9–17.

200 THEY HAD THESE CLAWS Joe Eszterhas, "Claw Men from Outer Space," *Rolling Stone* (January 17, 1974), p. 38.

201 BIGGER THAN WATERGATE Ibid., p. 47.

203 BANAL UNIVERSE Carl Sagan, *The Demon-Haunted World: Science as a Candle in the Dark* (New York: Random House, 1996), p. 133.

204 SHREWD INVENTOR Quoted in Daniel Cohen, *The Great Airship Mystery: A UFO of the 1890s* (New York: Dodd, Mead & Co., 1981), p. 17.

205 JOURNALISTIC ERROR Martin S. Kottmeyer, "Entirely Unpredisposed: The Cultural Background of UFO Abduction Reports," *Magonia* (January 1990), on-line transcript.

207 VISUAL FIGURE OF SPEECH Arthur Schlesinger, Jr., "The Highbrow in American Politics," *Partisan Review,* vol. 20, no. 2 (March–April 1953), p. 156.

207 IVY LEAGUE CONNOTATION Ibid., pp. 156–57.

209 MESSIAH-BASED RELIGION Curtis Peebles, *Watch the Skies! A Chronicle of the Flying Saucer Myth* (Washington and London: Smithsonian Institution Press, 1994), p. 105.

211 VERY HUMAN IN THEIR APPEARANCE John G. Fuller, *The Interrupted Journey: Two Lost Hours "Aboard a Flying Saucer"* (New York: Dial Press, 1966), pp. 296–97.

212 YOUR WHOLE PAST HISTORY Ibid., p. 276.

212 THEY ROLL ME OVER Ibid., p. 164.

215 ANAL PROBE Whitley Strieber, *Communion: A True Story* (New York: Beech Tree Books/William Morrow, 1987), p. 30.

216 HOLLYWOOD ACTOR OR ACTRESS Edward Beecher Clafin, "When Is a Story True?," *Publishers Weekly* (August 14, 1987), pp. 23–24.

216 IF WHITLEY STRIEBER ISN'T FIBBING Thomas M. Disch, "The Village Alien," *Nation* (March 14, 1987), pp. 328–34.

217 IT APPEARS, PERHAPS Charles Berlitz and William L. Moore, *The Roswell Incident* (New York, Grosset & Dunlap, 1980), p. 47.

218 UNNOTICED IN MOST DISCUSSIONS Janice G. Raymond, *Women as Wombs: Reproductive Technologies and the Battle over Women's Freedom* (San Francisco: HarperSanFrancisco, 1993), p. xxi.

219 IN THE SIXTEENTH CENTURY John E. Mack, *Nightmares and Human Conflict* (1970; reprint, New York: Columbia University Press, 1989), p. 9

219 FLASHIER ELEMENTS OF AMERICA'S CULTURAL LIFE Robert Coles, "The Taste of Fears," introduction to Mack, op. cit., p. xxvi.

220 TUBE WAS PASSED DEEPER John Mack, *Abduction: Human Encounters with Aliens* (New York: Charles Scribner's Sons, 1994), p. 300.

220 ONE KIND OF PATIENT MACK NEVER SEES James Glieck, "The Doctor's Plot," *New Republic* (May 30, 1994), p. 33.

222 NASA, THE MAFIA, AND HOLLYWOOD Richard Ofshe and Ethan Watters, *Making Monsters: False Memories, Psychotherapy and Sexual Hysteria* (New York: Charles Scribner's Sons, 1994), p. 300.

222 ANYTHING THAT LOOKS TECHNOLOGICAL C. G. Jung, *Flying Saucers: A Modern Myth of Things Seen in the Skies* (Princeton, N.J.: Princeton University Press, 1978), p. 22.

222 A NEW CLASS OF SEXUAL PREDATOR Ofshe and Watters, op. cit., p. 7.

223 PROTOCOLS OF BONDAGE AND DOMINATION Disch, op. cit., pp. 328–34.

223 THE WORKER CONFRONTS CAPITALISM Lynn S. Chancer, *Sadomasochism in Everyday Life* (New Brunswick, N.J.: Rutgers University Press, 1992), p. 33.

224 SUPPORT FOR MY SUSPICIONS Renato Vesco and David Hatcher Childress, *Man Made UFOs, 1944–1994* (Stelle, Ill.: AUP Publishers Network, 1994).

225 VAGUE, POORLY DEFINED CRISES Peebles (citing a study by Otto Billig), op. cit., p. 286.

226 REASON TO WORRY Fred Abatemarco, "Not Necessarily the News," *Popular Science* (June 1997), p. 7.

229 EERILY LIKE A FETUS Sagan, op. cit., p. 132.

CHAPTER SEVEN: THE DOCTOR WILL EAT YOU NOW

232 HIDEOUS, DEFORMED AND SUBLIMATED Henri Mondor, *Doctors & Medicine in the Works of Daumier* (New York: Leon Amiel Publishers, n.d.), pp. 22–23.

232 HE CARRIES IT IN A BLACK BAG Milton Millhauser, "Dr. Newton and Mr. Hyde: Scientists in Fiction from Swift to Stevenson," *Nineteenth Century Fiction,* vol. 28, no. 3 (December 1973), p. 301.

233 COLD AS ICE Henry Bellamann, *Kings Row* (New York: Simon and Schuster, 1941), p. 185.

234 OH YES, HE'S A GENIUS Joyce Carol Oates, *Wonderland* (New York: Vanguard Press, 1971), pp. 185–86.

235 "BEPPO" MENGELE My biographical sketch of Josef Mengele is drawn primarily from Gerald Astor's *The Last Nazi: The Life and Times of Dr. Josef Mengele* (New York: Donald I. Fine, 1985) as well as Lucette Matalon Lagnado's *Children of the Flames: Dr. Josef Mengele and the Untold Story of the Twins of Auschwitz* (New York: William Morrow, 1991).

237 ECONOMIC INCENTIVES FOR PHYSICIANS Robert N. Proctor, *Racial Hygiene: Medicine under the Nazis* (Cambridge, Mass.: Harvard University Press, 1988), p. 69.

238 WITHOUT ANY CONTROL OR RESTRICTIONS Robert Jay Lifton, *The Nazi Doctors: Medical Killing and the Psychology of Genocide* (New York: Basic Books, 1986), p. 386.

239 ONLY PLAYING THE PART OF A HUMAN BEING Rolf Hochhuth, *The Deputy* (New York: Grove Press, 1964), p. 32.

239 AUSCHWITZ REFUTES Ibid., p. 248.

239 FRAUDULENT AND UNHEALTHY Bosley Crowther, "Bad Medicine," *New York Times,* March 9, 1946, p. 10.

241 A BIBLICAL FRAME OF MIND Ira Levin, *The Boys from Brazil* (1976; reprint, New York: Bantam Books, 1991), p. 272.

241 RESEARCH INTO DYSENTERY David J. Rothman, *Strangers at the Bedside* (New York: Basic Books, 1991), pp. 47–48.

242 SUBJECTED TO VARIOUS KINDS OF RADIATION Philip J. Hilts, "Payments to Make Amends for Secret Plutonium Tests," *New York Times* (November 20, 1996), p. 1.

247 MENTALLY-STIMULATING HEALTH DRINK Andrew Sarris, "The Gleeful Celebration of Chaos," *Village Voice* (March 15, 1983), p. 41.

247 MEDICINE IS ON THE BRINK Robin Cook, *Coma* (Boston and Toronto: Little, Brown and Co., 1977), p. 297.

249 THE REAL PAYOFF Joseph McLellan, *Brain* review, *Washington Post Book World*, March 8, 1981.

249 FELT HIS TERROR BECOME PANIC Robin Cook, *Godplayer* (New York: G. P. Putnam's Sons, 1983), pp. 14–15.

249 PEOPLE WHO DESERVE TO LIVE Ibid., p. 361.

250 ABSORBED IN FIFTH-GRADE WORK Robin Cook, *Mutation* (New York: G. P. Putnam's Sons, 1989), p. 300.

251 VIABLE NEW PARANOID HORROR MYTH Lawrence Cohn, *Dr. Giggles* review, *Variety,* October 26, 1992.

251 DISILLUSIONED WITH SCIENCE David Cronenberg and Chris Rodley, eds., *Cronenberg on Cronenberg* (London and Boston: Faber and Faber, 1992), p. 7.

252 MAD, CREATIVE AND ECCENTRIC. Ibid., pp. 6–7.

254 WE CAME OUT CLAMMY Terrence Rafferty, "Secret Sharers," *New Yorker* (October 3, 1988).

255 ATE HIS LIVER Thomas Harris, *The Silence of the Lambs* (New York: St. Martin's Press, 1988), p. 21.

256 BROKE HER JAW Ibid., p. 11.

256 "UNBALANCED" FILM AND TELEVISION PEOPLE Amy Cunningham, "Lights! Cameras! Loonies! Why This Parade of Creepy, Slimy Shrinks?", *Washington Post* (February 1, 1992).

257 STUFF ME INSIDE YOUR MOUTH Oates, *Wonderland,* loc. cit., p. 153.

257 IT BROILED UNEVENLY Ibid., p. 277.

257 PERSISTENT URBAN FOLKLORE Carroll Morrello, "Guatemalans Gripped by Fear of Baby-Snatchers," *Philadelphia Inquirer* (April 10, 1994), p. 1.

257 PREFER THAT THEIR CHILDREN STARVE Ibid.

258 HUMAN CASH MACHINES Jim Hogshire, *Sell Yourself to Science* (Port Townsend, Wash.: Loompanics Unlimited, 1993), quoted in Russ Kick's *Outposts: A Catalog of Rare and Disturbing Alternative Information* (New York: Carroll & Graf Publishers, 1995), p. 165.

259 DRUNK, ON DRUGS, OR CRAZY David R. Slavitt, *Physicians Observed* (Garden City, N.Y.: Doubleday & Co., 1987), p. 39.

260 ALMOST ORGASMIC FEELING Marc D. Feldman, M.D., and Charles V. Ford, M.D., with Toni Reinhold, *Patient or Pretender: Inside the Strange World of Factitious Disorders* (New York: John Wiley & Sons, 1994), p. 63.

260 MORBID SOCIETY Ivan Illich, *Medical Nemesis: The Expropriation of Health* (1976; reprint, New York: Bantam Books, 1977), pp. 116–17.

261 AIDS ISN'T JUST A DISEASE Elinor Burkett, *The Gravest Show on Earth: America in the Age of AIDS* (Boston and New York: Houghton Mifflin Co., 1995), p. 109.

263 RUMOR CYCLES Patricia A. Turner, *I Heard It through the Grapevine: Rumor in African-American Culture* (Berkeley, Los Angeles, London: University of California Press, 1993). See especially Chapters 3–5.

264 CLASSIC SCRIPT FOR PLAGUE Susan Sontag, *AIDS and Its Metaphors* (New York: Farrar, Straus & Giroux, 1989), pp. 51–52.

265 "COURAGEOUS," "WONDERFUL," AND "HONEST" Endorsement by Elisabeth Kübler-Ross for *AIDS and the Doctors of Death,* from the back cover of Alan Cantwell's *Queer Blood: The Secret AIDS Genocide Plot* (Los Angeles: Aires Rising Press, 1993).

265 1987 PAPER Peter H. Duesberg, "Retroviruses as Carcinogens and Pathogens: Expectations and Reality," *Cancer Research,* vol. 47 (March 1, 1987), pp. 1199–1220.

265 BACKED IN THE PURSUIT OF HIS THEORIES Richard C. Strohman, preface, *Infectious AIDS: Have We Been Misled?* (Berkeley: North Atlantic Press, 1995), pp. vii–xiv.

266 NUMEROUS ANOMALIES OF AIDS Robert Root-Bernstein, *Rethinking AIDS: The Tragic Cost of Premature Consensus* (New York: Free Press, 1993). See especially Chapter 1, "Anomalies: Observations About AIDS That Do Not Fit the Picture," pp. 1–56.

266 ROLLO MAY Ibid., p. vii.

267 THEORIES ARE A SMOKE SCREEN Leonard G. Horowitz, *Emerging Viruses: AIDS and Ebola* (Rockport, Mass.: Tetrahedron Publishing Group, 1996).

267 FLORIDA DENTIST Leonard G. Horowitz, *Deadly Innocence* (Tetrahedron Publishing Group, 1994).

268 WALKING PETRI DISHES Laurie Garrett, *The Coming Plague: Newly Emerging Diseases in a World out of Balance* (New York: Farrar, Straus & Giroux, 1994), p. 419.

269 SCARS OF SURGICAL ZEAL Parker Tyler, *The Three Faces of the Film* (New York and London: Thomas Yoseloff, 1960), p. 130.

269 SHE SAT IN THE DAMAGED CAR J. G. Ballard, *Crash* (1973; reprint, New York: Vintage Books, 1985), p. 109.

269 LINE BETWEEN SCIENCE AND COMMERCE Bruce Mirken, "AIDS at a Crossroads," *Los Angeles Reader* (July 26, 1996), p. 12.

270 CONFERENCE WAS BOUGHT AND PAID FOR Neenyah Ostrom, "A Blood Bath

in Vancouver: ACT-UP San Francisco Draws a Line in the Sand," *New York Native* (July 29, 1996), pp. 21–23.

270 ARTIFICIAL BLOOD Ibid., p. 22.

CHAPTER SEVEN: VILE BODIES, OR FAREWELL TO THE FLESH

272 KNOW THE MIND OF GOD Stephen W. Hawking, *A Brief History of Time* (New York: Bantam Books, 1988), p. 175.

272 IN POSSESSION OF KNOWLEDGE Stephen Hawking, ed., *Stephen Hawking's A Brief History of Time: A Reader's Companion* (New York: Bantam Books, 1992), pp. vii–viii.

273 REALITY WOULD LOSE ALL MEANING Mark Slouka, *War of the Worlds: Cyberspace and the High-Tech Assault on Reality* (New York: Basic Books, 1995), pp. 19–20.

274 QUASI-RELIGIOUS MODERN MYTH Mary Midgley, *Science as Salvation* (London and New York: Routledge, 1992).

275 PRODUCTION, REPRODUCTION, AND IMAGINATION Donna J. Haraway, *Simians, Cyborgs and Women: The Reinvention of Nature* (New York: Routledge, 1991), p. 150.

275 ANIMALS WERE CLOCKS Quoted in Leonora Cohen Rosenfield, *From Beast-Machine to Man-Machine* (New York: Octagon Books, 1968), p. 224.

276 "GIVE ME EYES!" Leonard J. Kent and Elizabeth Knight, eds. and trans., *Tales of E. T. A. Hoffmann* (originally published as *Selected Writings of E. T. A. Hoffmann,* 1969; reprint/abridgment, Chicago: University of Chicago Press, 1972), p. 98.

281 A MAN WITH HIS OWN LEGS Bernard Wolfe, *Limbo* (1952; reprint, New York: Carroll & Graf, Publishers, 1987), p. 114.

283 SEVERE LINES, BOLD SILHOUETTE Daniel Gerould, *Guillotine: Its Legend and Lore* (New York: Blast Books, 1992), p. 5.

283 STRANGE AND OFTEN GHOULISH Ibid., p. 53.

284 BALL STARTS ROLLING Chet Fleming, *If We Can Keep a Severed Head Alive . . .* (St. Louis: Polinym Press, 1988). Quoted in Kick, op. cit., p. 163.

284 YOUR FIRST IMPRESSION Robin Cook, *Brain* (New York: G. P. Putnam's Sons, 1981; book club edition), p. 203.

286 YEARNING WE DO NOT UNDERSTAND Joyce Carol Oates, *The Poisoned Kiss and Other Stories from the Portuguese* (1974; reprint, New York: Fawcett Crest, 1975), p. 25.

286 WICKED SHORT STORY Roald Dahl, "William and Mary," in *The Best of Roald Dahl* (New York: Vintage Books, 1978), pp. 173–96.

288 FINE OPPORTUNITY John Hersey, *The Child Buyer* (1960; reprint, New York: Bantam Books, 1961), pp. 217, 219.

288 ULTIMATE IN ANTI-INTELLECTUAL MOVIES John Brosnan and Peter Nicholls, "Fiend without a Face," in John Clute and Peter Nicholls, eds., *The Encyclopedia of Science Fiction* (New York: St. Martin's Press, 1993), pp. 426–27.

289 FULFILLMENT WITHOUT THE RISKS Claudia Springer, *Electronic Eros: Bodies and Desire in the Postindustrial Age* (Austin: University of Texas Press, 1996), p. 84.

289 MOST FREQUENTLY REPRINTED Source of calculation: American Typographical Association, confirmed by Harlan Ellison, telephone conversation with author, February 1996.

290 WE HAD GIVEN HIM SENTIENCE Harlan Ellison, *I Have No Mouth, and I Must Scream* (New York: Pyramid Books, 1967), pp. 34–35.

290 HATE Ibid., pp. 33–34.

290 GREAT SOFT JELLY THING Ibid., p. 42.

291 RUNNING CLEAN AND COOL Damon Knight, "Masks," in Editors of *Playboy*, eds., *Masks* (New York: Playboy Press, 1971), p. 17.

291 THE WHOLE SLOPPY MESS Ibid.

291 PURULENT AND ALIVE Ibid., p. 19.

291 DAY-TO-DAY ROBOPATHIC EXISTENCE Lewis Yablonsky, *Robopaths: People as Machines* (1972; reprint, Baltimore: Penguin Books, 1972), p. xiii.

291 FUNCTIONED AS IF BY REMOTE CONTROL Bruno Bettelheim, "Joey: A Mechanical Boy, *Scientific American* (March 1959); quoted by Yablonsky, op. cit., pp. 44–45.

292 STAR TREK Temple Grandin, *Thinking in Pictures* (New York: Doubleday, 1995), p. 131.

293 WEST COAST "RETURN TO NATURE" CULT Diamanada Galas, interviewed in Andrea Juno and V. Vale, *Angry Women* (San Francisco: Re/Search Publications, 1991), p. 13.

294 WIDESPREAD ASSAULT ON WOMEN Marcia Angell, *Science on Trial: The Clash of Evidence and the Law in the Breast Implant Case* (New York: W. W. Norton & Company, 1996), p. 182.

296 EDSEL'S VERTICAL GRILLE Stephen Bayley, *Sex, Drink, and Fast Cars* (New York: Pantheon Books, 1986), p. 20.

296 INTENSE BACTERIA PHOBIA Sonni Efron, "Cleaning Up on Hygiene Mania," *Los Angeles Times,* November 21, 1996, p. 1.

298 ROT INTO NOTHINGNESS Max More, "Transhumanism: Toward a Futurist Philosophy" (1992), on-line transcript.

299 YOU'VE JUST BEEN WHEELED INTO THE OPERATING ROOM Hans Moravec, *Mind Children: The Future of Robot and Human Intelligence* (Cambridge, Mass., and London: Harvard University Press, 1988), pp. 109–10.

300 THE SELF AS A SET OF COMPUTER PROGRAMS Sherry Turkle, *The Second Self: Computers and the Human Spirit* (New York: Simon and Schuster, 1984), p. 289.

300 THEIR LANGUAGE CARRIES AN IMPLICIT PSYCHOLOGY Ibid., p. 17.

300 THINK, FEEL, ARE ALIVE Ibid., p. 18.

300 CONJURED UP BY A COMPLICATED COMPUTATION Roger Penrose, *The Emperor's New Mind* (New York and Oxford: Oxford University Press, 1989), p. 447.

301 EXTRAVAGANT, PROPAGANDISTIC CLAIMS Theodore Roszak, *The Cult of Information: The Folklore of Computers and the True Art of Thinking* (1986; reprint, London: Paladin, 1988), pp. 144–45.

301 WITH CHARITY TOWARD NONE Mark Dery, *Escape Velocity: Cyberculture at the End of the Century* (New York: Grove Press, 1996), p. 304.

302 TRIUMPH OF SENSATION Martin Pawley, *The Private Future: Causes and Consequences of Community Collapse in the West* (New York: Random House, 1974), p. 211.

304 NO PITY FOR THIS CRIPPLED WOMAN Ballard, op. cit., p. 179.

CONCLUSION: ENTERTAINING THE APOCALYPSE

306 GROSS OVERSTATEMENTS Malcolm W. Browne, "In New Spielberg Film, a Dim View of Science," *New York Times* (May 11, 1993).

306 EVERY GAIN IN SCIENCE Ibid.

306 THEY THINK IT'S BORING Robert Boland, " 'Jurassic Park' Won't Turn Kids Against Science" (letter), *New York Times* (June 22, 1993).

307 ONCE UPON A TIME Carol Muske Dukes, "Evil Science Runs Amok—Again!," *New York Times,* June 10, 1993.

307 INDUSTRIAL REVOLUTION AND ITS CONSEQUENCES Unabomber Manifesto (1996), on-line transcript.

308 PEOPLE WERE PRETTY SURE David Gelernter, *Mirror Worlds* (New York and Oxford: Oxford University Press, 1991), p. 7.

308 OP-ED PIECE John Allan Paulos, "Dangerous Abstractions," *New York Times* (April 7, 1996).

310 MORE INTENSE COMBAT Stephen Holden, "Monster Robots Bash Paradise in Mock Battle," *New York Times* (May 17, 1988), pt. 3, p. 15.

311 LESS EXCITING Mel Gussow, "Hoping for a Cataclysm on a Rainy Day at Shea," *New York Times* (May 22, 1988), p. 49.

312 OUTSIDE THEIR PROFESSIONAL COMPETENCE Dorothy Nelkin, *Selling Science: How the Press Covers Science and Technology* (New York: W. H. Freeman and Co., 1987), p. 21.

312 PRESCRIPTION FOR DISASTER Carl Sagan, *The Demon-Haunted World: Science as a Candle in the Dark* (New York: Random House, 1995), p. 26.

312 PLETHORA OF FAUSTIAN BARGAINS Ibid., p. 11.

313 LOGICAL OPERATIONS ALL DAY LONG Craig Brad, *Technostress: The Human Cost of the Computer Revolution* (Reading, Mass.: Addison-Wesley Publishing Co., 1984), p. 83.

313 INCREASING TECHNICALITY IN THE SCIENCES Midgley, op. cit., p. 2.

313 SCIENTIFICALLY-MINDED PUBLIC Ibid., p. 3.

314 FIND IT DIFFICULT TO TALK Bryan Appleyard, *Understanding the Present: Science and the Soul of Modern Man* (1992; reprint, New York: Doubleday, 1993), p. xv.

314 A FORM OF MYSTICISM Ibid., pp. 233–34.

315 DOES IT SEEM PLAUSIBLE Midgley, op. cit., p. 8.

316 LIKE INHERITED WEALTH Michael Crichton, *Jurassic Park* (1990; reprint, New York: Ballantine Books, 1991), p. 306.

316 MAVERICK LAWYERS SHUNNED Peter W. Huber, *Galileo's Revenge: Junk Science in the Courtroom* (New York: Basic Books, 1991), p. 2.

316 PHILADELPHIA PSYCHIC Ibid., p. 4

316 EVERYBODY'S A MAD SCIENTIST Cronenberg and Rodley, op. cit., p. 7..

Index

Page numbers in *italics* refer to illustrations.